Accelerated Accounting

Accelerated Accounting

A Managerial Approach

A. Tom Nelson
University of Utah

GOODYEAR PUBLISHING COMPANY, INC.
Pacific Palisades, California

© 1971 by Goodyear Publishing Company, Inc.
Pacific Palisades, California

Current printing (last digit):
10 9 8 7 6 5 4 3 2 1

ISBN: 0-87620-061-7

Library of Congress Catalog Card Number: 79-131418

Y0617-4

Printed in the United States of America

To my princess Nadine

Contents

Preface

This book was written to give the student a basic introduction to financial and managerial accounting through a minimum of mechanics.

The idea that managerial accounting can be taught without any knowledge of financial accounting sounds very appealing, although rational thinking dictates that the business student must be introduced to some fundamental concepts of financial accounting if he is expected to understand how to make intelligent use of accounting information.

The goal of this book is to give the student the knowledge of accounting he needs in order to effectively communicate in the business world. Sufficient financial accounting is presented to enable the student to understand a simple, double entry system, without becoming bogged down in bookkeeping techniques.

The text is divided between financial and managerial topics. The first eleven chapters deal primarily with financial accounting but some managerial topics are introduced where appropriate. Chapters 12 through 21 are significantly management oriented. Chapter 21 presents a summary of generally accepted accounting concepts together with some current accounting problems.

The text may be used in a variety of courses, depending on the extent to which individual topics are explored and the supplementary materials used by the instructor. The material has been used in preliminary form in the MBA program at the University of Utah for students who had no previous experience with accounting. This book should be equally successful at the undergraduate level because it is written in terms easily understandable by a person receiving his first exposure to accounting.

Appreciation is expressed to all who have made contributions to this work through encouragement and criticism. The MBA students who served as guinea pigs have been especially helpful in making the presentation more relevant. A special note of appreciation is extended to my co-workers, the administration, and the secretarial staff at the University of Utah for their valuable assistance. Finally, the encouragement and patience of my wife and children are gratefully recognized.

Accelerated Accounting

1

Introduction
to
Accounting

Accounting is the means by which managers, owners, creditors, governments, and other interested parties are able to appraise the progress and financial health of business units. Through accounting data these parties are able to make pertinent decisions regarding the activities of the business. Investments are made, managers are hired or fired, goods are manufactured and sold, taxes are calculated and paid, operations are expanded or contracted—all based upon the interpretation of accounting data.

DEFINITION OF ACCOUNTING

Accounting has been defined as

> ... the art of recording, classifying, and summarizing in a significant manner and in terms of money, transactions and events which are in

part at least, of a financial character, and interpreting the results thereof.[1]

The word "art" in this definition seems particularly significant. Note that accounting is not termed a "science" but, rather, an "art." This may come as a surprise to the student taking his first course in accounting. He may have thought of accounting as being nearly synonymous with exactness. When a student is asked to picture the accountant, it is not uncommon to hear him describe an old, bald-headed gentleman seated atop a stool, green shield over his spectacled eyes, quill pen in hand, bright light overhead. A huge ledger, meticulously kept by hand, is opened wide; and, of course, the poor old gent will remain at work far into the night until every page balances out to the penny, for such is the lot of the accountant. The student is impressed by the fact that the accountant can report income right down to the very last cent. For example, Walt Disney Studios recently reported to its stockholders a net income of $6,574,321, or $3.81 per share.

The exactness of this report might impress the reader of the financial statement unless he is made aware that the figure reported is a mere estimate. There appears in the same Walt Disney Studios' report an item of $6,100,000 for "estimated federal income taxes." The income taxes must of necessity be estimated, and the reader should note that the amount is not estimated precisely, but is rounded to $6.1 million. If such a major component of income must be estimated so roughly, then it seems difficult to believe that the exact income was $6,574,321. It is quite likely that no two accountants, given all the facts concerning Walt Disney Studios' operations, would independently arrive at this same figure. It is probable that they would be able to agree only that the company earned about $6.5 million; it is almost certain they would not agree right down to the last digit, or even to the second or the third digit.

Accounting is not based upon an exact set of principles that when applied always give the same result. Under the proper circumstances, two atoms of hydrogen combine with one atom of oxygen to produce water. This is a scientific fact. Accounting, however, is not bound by such laws. Good oil painters will utilize accepted principles of art such as perspective and harmony, but they are not bound by these principles, and no two artists will make exactly the same application. Similarly, there are some general rules of conduct, some guidelines upon which accountants generally agree.

The guidelines within which the accountant works are sometimes referred to as principles, or concepts, of accounting. These principles are

---

[1]*Accounting Research and Terminology Bulletins*, final ed. (New York: American Institute of Certified Public Accountants, 1961), p. 9.

introduced throughout the course and are summarized in chapter 21. The student should keep in mind at all times the general nature of these rules and note the many estimates and judgments that must be made in their application.

FIELDS OF ACCOUNTING

There are three major fields of accounting: governmental, private, and public accounting. In simple terms this means that an accountant may be employed by a unit of government, by a private business enterprise, or by himself or a firm selling accounting services to the public.

Governmental units at all levels employ accountants to maintain and check the accounting records. A list of important federal agencies that utilize the services of accountants might include the Internal Revenue Service, the General Accounting Office, the Defense Contract Audit Agency, the Army Audit Agency, and the Air Force Auditor General, among others. States, counties, and municipalities have similar needs for skilled accountants. As the government sector in our economy has grown, this area has become a more significant employer of accountants.

Private accounting includes those accountants who are employed by private business enterprises. These range from the junior accountant maintaining detailed accounting records up to the controller, or chief financial officer. Accountants in industry are required to maintain and interpret all sorts of financial records, including those pertaining to payrolls, receivables, payables, operating costs and revenues, and cash. Generally, these accountants work the same regular hours as other white collar workers. They are paid directly by the party they serve.

Public accountants practice either as individuals or as employees of accounting firms. They are kept busy in much the same manner as attorneys or medical doctors by serving their own independent clients. Public accountants have no single employer as such, but instead make their services available to the public at large. The services rendered include auditing, tax services, and special management consultation.

Public accounting does have at least one unique feature. Unlike most other professional persons, the public accountant is often faced with conflicting loyalties. His first and paramount responsibility is to protect the interests of the public at large; yet he must look to his client for his fee. What may be in the public's interest may not be in the client's interest. This situation creates a triangle that sometimes poses difficulties for the public accountant.

THE ACCOUNTING PROFESSION

The field of accounting includes persons of varying training and competencies. One might ask where in this array of "accountants" do we find the "accounting profession"? Some would argue that accounting is a mere trade, or vocation, and that there is no accounting "profession." Admittedly, many persons practicing some form of accounting could not be classified as professionals—most notably, bookkeepers. The presence of tradesmen, however, does not exclude the presence of the professional. Medicine, law, and religion, the traditional professions, also employ many technical personnel who would not be included as members of the respective professions.

If accounting is to be considered a profession, one might ask who the professional accountant is and how he can be recognized. Most knowledgeable persons would agree that the certified public accountant (CPA) is the professional in this field. Investors, creditors, managers, government agencies, and many others in the business world look to him for professional counsel and advice. Respect for the CPA and recognition of his professional status have increased markedly over the past few decades. An independent marketing and public opinion analyst recently completed a study of some six hundred top executives of large manufacturing enterprises. The results disclosed that the CPA ranks at the top of the list when compared with other outside consultants. The study reported in part:

> The evaluation they gave us [the CPA] was very high. Compared with other outside consultants, such as lawyers, advertising agencies, labor relations or personnel consultants, management consultants, and public relations consultants, it was the accountant that these executives most enjoyed working with. Eighty-six per cent of them said they would give their accounting firm an enthusiastic recommendation. Seventy-two per cent thought of their accountant as making "a real contribution to the profitability of their business," as compared with only 22 per cent who wrote him off as "a necessary evil."
>
> What comes through most markedly is the high professional respect in which most accountants are held. You are unquestionably considered, by most people who use your services, to be people of ability and integrity who are an essential part of any business operation.[2]

WHAT IS A CPA?

The requirements for certification vary from state to state; however, there is a marked trend toward more stringent requirements and more

---

[2]Elmo Roper, "As Others See You," *The Journal of Accountancy* (Jan. 1964), pp. 32–33.

uniformity among the states. All states now offer, and require as a condition for certification, the uniform CPA examination. This rigorous, written examination, prepared by the American Institute of Certified Public Accountants, requires two and a half days to complete. It is given biannually in all states on the same dates during May and November. Each examination is different from preceding ones, but each covers the same general areas: accounting practice, accounting theory, auditing, and commercial law. Other requirements in the various states include education (often college graduation with a major in accounting), practice in public accounting (from one to five years, generally under the direction of a CPA), a high moral character, and residency in the state.

Many CPAs are members of professional associations. The national organization of CPAs is the American Institute of Certified Public Accountants (AICPA), headquartered in New York City. All states also have state societies that work closely with the national organization. The AICPA publishes *The Journal of Accountancy*, as well as numerous books, pamphlets, and periodicals. Another outstanding service offered by the AICPA is professional development courses instituted to increase the knowledge and skill of the CPA beyond that initially demonstrated on the CPA examination.

It is interesting to note that the CPA, like other professionals, subscribes to a stringent code of ethics, formulated to upgrade the profession. For example, the AICPA places the following restriction upon its members in regard to advertising:

> A member or associate shall not advertise his professional attainments or services.
>
> Publication in a newspaper, magazine, or similar medium, of an announcement, or what is technically known as a card, is prohibited.
>
> A listing in a directory is restricted to the name, title, address, and telephone number of the person or firm, and it shall not appear in a box, or other form of display, or in a type which differentiates it from other listings in the same directory. Listing of the same name in more than one place in a classified directory is prohibited.[3]

The requirements necessary for certification and the code of ethics imposed on those who are so certified serve to protect the public interests. These factors create a standard reasonably assuring the public of the quality of the CPA's services.

Many states allow persons other than CPAs to practice accounting. Often there is little, if any, restriction on such individuals and, accord-

---

[3]American Institute of Certified Public Accountants, *Code of Professional Ethics*, art. 3.01, as amended Mar. 4, 1965.

ingly, no protection to the public. Under these circumstances it is very possible for persons with little or no accounting training to advertise "expert tax service" or "complete tax service $5 and up." When the law does not properly regulate who may and who may not practice, the public should carefully appraise the quality of these services. To assure receiving quality services, one should rely on those offered by the CPA.

FUNCTIONS OF ACCOUNTING

Returning to our definition of accounting, we note four major functions: recording, classifying, summarizing, and interpreting. *Bookkeeping* deals primarily with the first two of these. Books are normally set up and maintained in a manner that will assure the orderly classification and recording of business transactions. *Accounting* includes the art of bookkeeping, but goes far beyond it. Since bookkeeping has become greatly mechanized in recent years, there has been some decrease in the demand for the routine bookkeeper. To the accountant, however, mechanization comes as a welcome relief. It has freed him to a large degree from the routine, time-consuming recording function, permitting him to devote more time to the important area of interpretation. It is this last function, interpreting the results of financial activities, that best distinguishes accounting from bookkeeping. Extensive training in accounting, as well as considerable knowledge of other areas of business including management, marketing, economics, and finance, are essential to this phase of accounting. As business enterprises become increasingly complex and move to the routine of machines, the gap between accounting and bookkeeping widens. Bookkeepers are constantly being replaced by machines, whereas the demand for professional accountants continues to soar.

The actual accumulation and interpretation of data may be classified into three areas: *financial accounting, managerial accounting,* and *cost accounting*. These areas are not mutually exclusive but represent major areas of concentration within the overall accounting system. In addition to these three "operating" areas of accounting, we find accountants performing audits, rendering all sorts of tax services, preparing and implementing budgets, designing and installing accounting systems, providing countless management advisory services, and making special investigations of all sorts.

Financial Accounting

Financial accounting deals with the systems, records, and reports developed within a business enterprise primarily for the purpose of accountability. The management of a firm must account in varying degrees to a number of groups, including the owners, the creditors, the workers, the prospective investors, and numerous governmental agencies. This accountability is reflected by the firm's financial accounting system. Records are compiled and reports prepared to reflect the company's financial position at given times and to present the results of its operations for specified periods. The accounting for assets, liabilities, revenues, expenses, and owners' equity discussed in this text is concerned primarily with financial accounting.

Managerial Accounting

Managerial accounting deals with the *use* of accounting data for management purposes. Much of the information used by management in making critical decisions is, of course, developed from the company's financial accounting records. In other cases, however, special systems must be set up specifically to accumulate the necessary data. Analysis of financial statements, funds-flow, standard cost systems, and special cost concepts for decision making are a few managerial accounting topics discussed in this text.

Cost Accounting

Cost accounting systems are generally an integral part of the financial accounting system set up to provide cost data for a variety of purposes. Of paramount importance is the determination of the *cost of goods produced*, although cost accounting does have many uses beyond the production function. It may be used, for example, to determine the least-cost method of distributing the firm's product, or to evaluate the effectiveness of a particular operation. Emphasis in cost accounting systems is generally placed on unit cost. Some of the techniques of cost accounting are discussed in chapters 7, 17, and 18.

Auditing

Auditing is the process of testing and examining accounting systems, records, and reports to determine the efficiency of the enterprise and to assure that the reports are presented in accordance with generally accepted accounting principles. Audits performed by a company's own employees, who then report their findings to management, are called *internal audits*. Audits may also be performed by independent public accountants; these are termed *independent audits*. Although these latter reports are normally addressed to the board of directors and the stockholders, they are really aimed at the public.

After a CPA has audited the financial statements, he will insert ahead of his signature a statement such as the following, called the "short form" report:

> We have examined the balance sheet of X Company as of June 30, 19...., and the related statement(s) of income and retained earnings for the year then ended. Our examination was made in accordance with generally accepted auditing standards, and accordingly included such tests of the accounting records and such other auditing procedures as we considered necessary in the circumstances.
>
> In our opinion, the accompanying balance sheet and statement(s) of income and retained earnings present fairly the financial position of X Company at June 30, 19...., and the results of its operations for the year then ended, in conformity with generally accepted accounting principles applied on a basis consistent with that of the preceding year.[4]

Taxation

The increased complexity of the tax laws, particularly in the area of income taxation, has greatly increased the demand for professional tax service. This increased demand has been felt in both the government and private sectors. The Internal Revenue Service alone employs over 60,000 persons, including some CPAs.[5] Individual and corporate taxpayers likewise seek professional help in solving their numerous and complex tax problems. The filing of returns is only a small part of the total tax workload of most professional accountants, inasmuch as business enterprises are faced with a continual stream of decisions that have serious tax implications. Many of these decisions can be made only after extensive research and consultation with the company's CPA firm. The Tax Court and the Internal Revenue Service will permit either a CPA or an attorney to represent taxpayers in proceedings of this court.

Budgeting

Budgets are financial plans that provide guidance and control over operations. They include skilled forecasts of almost all of the enterprise's

---

[4]Committee on Auditing Procedure of the American Institute of Certified Public Accountants, *Auditing Standards and Procedures, Statement on Auditing Procedure No. 33*, p. 57.

[5]Internal Revenue Service, *Commissioner's Annual Report*, fiscal year 1965, p. 66.

activities, including expected purchases, employment, production, and sales. If properly prepared and implemented, the budget can be a most useful management tool. Budgets cannot be compiled from historical data alone; they require many skilled judgments ranging from forecasts of general economic activity down to detailed expenditures of a particular department. Budgeting is an area of accounting which requires special skill and training, and one to which many accountants devote full time.

Systems

Systems accountants devote their attention to planning, implementing, and "ironing out the bugs" in accounting systems. This service is available not only to newly established concerns that obviously have such a need, but also to long established businesses. Because of technological change and rapid economic growth, many business enterprises outgrow their accounting systems, which become obsolete and ineffective. In this event, a skilled accountant should be called in to carefully lay out a new system. System work includes planning the organizational structure, designing documents and document flow (such as purchase orders, receiving reports, sales slips, etc.), selecting appropriate machines and equipment, and acquainting operating personnel with the system.

Management Advisory Service

Management advisory service is a relatively new area of accounting service offered primarily by CPAs. Some CPA firms have a separate division for management services staffed by personnel with special aptitudes and training in this area. Management services provide a wide array of possible services covering almost any area where management needs special counsel. Should a company borrow funds or seek additional capital from stockholders? Should it lease or buy? How much capital will be required? Should the machines be replaced now or later? Will it be more economical to make or to buy a component part? These are just a few of the questions to which management is seeking answers and which may well be answered, at least partially, by the accountant.

The American Institute of Certified Public Accountants has recognized the increasing interest in management consulting and has recently started publishing a magazine called *Management Services*. To become better acquainted with this growing field of accounting, it might be worthwhile for the student to visit the library and examine an issue of this new publication.

Special Investigations

Accountants are often asked to assist in various special investigations such as establishing the dollar loss in a fire or theft. In such instances, the accountant normally has to recreate, or estimate from incomplete records, certain components of the financial statements. The accountant's role in these investigations is normally confined to appraising the financial implications, and, therefore, he works with experts in other areas to complete the investigation.

SUMMARY

Accounting is not an exact science, but an art requiring the exercise of many skilled judgments. It is concerned with the recording, classifying, summarizing, and interpreting of financial data. Accountants may be employed in the government, private, or public sector. Those who pass a rigorous written examination and meet other special requirements are designated as certified public accountants, or CPAs. This latter group is generally regarded as constituting the accounting profession. Accountants render a number of important services to the business world, including financial accounting, managerial accounting, cost accounting, auditing, tax services, budgeting, systems analysis, management advisory services, and special investigations.

QUESTIONS

1. Why is accounting considered an art rather than a science? In what way is accounting an art? In what ways does accounting resemble a science?
2. List the requirements for becoming a CPA. In what way do these requirements protect the public?
3. What is meant by the accounting "profession"? What does this profession have in common with the "traditional" professions such as medicine and law?
4. What is auditing? What is the nature of the CPA's "short form" report? Does it constitute a guarantee?
5. Does the introduction of electronic data processing equipment pose a threat to the security of the CPA? Why?
6. What is the national organization of CPAs? What purposes are served by organizations of this type?
7. List the four parts of the uniform CPA examination.
8. What relationship do you see between accounting and management? Economics? Finance? Marketing?
9. List some of the services that a businessman might expect to receive from his CPA. Do you see any conflict between any of these services?

10. What are the three major fields of accounting? Would you expect to find CPAs employed in all three fields? Name some companies or other organizations that might fit within each of these fields.
11. Why do professional organizations place advertising and similar restrictions on CPAs? Whom are these rules designed to protect?
12. Distinguish between financial and managerial accounting.

PROBLEMS

Problem 1-1

Many presidents and top executives of large corporations have reached their positions by working up through the financial sector of the corporation as accountants, controllers, financial vice presidents, etc. Explain why you think this is so. Why is an understanding of accounting basic and essential to the functions of top management?

Problem 1-2

Procure an annual report of a large corporation from a library or local brokerage firm. Referring to the income statement, list all items that you think are estimates. To what degree (digit) of accuracy are they reported? Compare this accuracy with that of the reported income figure. What can you conclude from this? Note also estimates in the balance sheet, "reserve" and "appropriated" amounts, and read the footnotes. What conclusions can you draw from this experience?

Problem 1-3

From what you have read and from your own general impressions, distinguish carefully between the bookkeeper and the accountant. What are the major functions of each?

Problem 1-4

Several areas in which an accountant may serve are considered in this chapter. Select one of these and discuss fully its importance and implications in top management functions.

Problem 1-5

Go to the library and make a list of the accounting periodicals available. Examine an issue of each periodical, listing the publisher, frequency of publication, and the audience to whom it is addressed. From any of these periodicals read one article that seems of special interest to you; report briefly on your findings.

Problem 1-6

Comment on the following quote from an article appearing in *The Wall Street Journal*, September 6, 1966:

The $4,868,913 of profit that Westec Corporation reported to its stockholders for 1965 would have shrunk drastically, probably close to the vanishing point, had the company employed more conservative accounting methods.

2

The Accounting Equation

In chapter 1 it was noted that accounting is an art not subject to a lot of irrevocable rules. There are, however, some fundamental concepts or principles upon which accounting is based. In this and several succeeding chapters the student will be introduced to some of these basic concepts through the study of a simple accounting system. It is hoped that he will not become bogged down with the mechanics of the material discussed here. Rather, the student should sufficiently familiarize himself with accounting terms and techniques so that he can intelligently use accounting in his own area of interest.

FORMS OF BUSINESS

In discussing accounting techniques in this course we will consider only private business enterprises which are operated for a profit. There are three principal forms of organization for such a business: *sole pro-*

prietorship (single owner), *partnership* (two or more owners), and *corporation* (also two or more owners). The major difference between these latter two forms of business is that a corporation is treated legally as if it were a person separate from its owners (an artificial being created by law), whereas a partnership is not. By virtue of this legal status, corporations can

1. enter into contracts
2. sue and be subject to suit
3. protect owners against liability (generally limited to the amount invested)
4. raise large sums of capital
5. permit quick and easy transfer of ownership
6. enjoy perpetual life.

In exchange for these privileges they are subject to taxation; they are artificial beings and, therefore, taxpayers. While partnerships enjoy none of the listed advantages, neither are they subject to taxation. The individual partners are, of course, subject to tax on their portion of the firm's earnings, just as stockholders must pay tax on the dividends they receive from the corporation. In the case of the corporation, however, the distributed earnings are really taxed twice.

THE ECONOMIC ENTITY CONCEPT

Accountants are not overly concerned with the legal differences between the three forms of business. They are concerned primarily with the economic fact that each business is a separate *economic* entity, regardless of its legal form. Accordingly, the owner's personal transactions and his business transactions are kept separate. When he performs an act in behalf of the business, this is recorded in the company books. When he performs a personal act not considered as pertaining to the business, this is recorded only in his personal records. Each business unit is thereby treated as a separate entity, distinct from its owners, regardless of the legal form.

By the same token, accountants may overlook some legal entities in preparing financial statements of economically interrelated companies. General Motors, for example, consists of many legal entities, but these assets are agglomerated as if they were one economic entity. For purposes of reporting to the public, the accountant does not prepare a separate set of financial statements for each legal entity, but instead eliminates any intercompany transactions and prepares one consolidated set of statements. This supports the statement that accountants are primarily concerned with accounting for economic, rather than legal, entities. This concept, known as the *entity concept,* is one of the important accounting principles under which we operate.

THE ACCOUNTING EQUATION

For centuries accounting has been based upon a system known as *double entry bookkeeping.* This system finds its roots in what is known as the accounting equation. This equation may be expressed in its most simple terms as follows:

$$\text{ASSETS} = \text{EQUITIES}$$

Assets are owned things of value. They may be tangible, such as buildings or equipment, or may be intangible, such as patents or copyrights. Regardless of their form, however, they must have economic value to the firm.

Equities are the claims against those assets; anything that has economic value is claimed by someone. Because the law ranks claims and in effect disregards any which exceed value, legal claims cannot exceed value. Therefore, the total claims against assets *must* equal the value of the assets themselves. Equities may be broken down into two major categories: claims of the owners (insiders), known as *owners' equity,* and claims of the creditors (outsiders), known as *liabilities.* The student is undoubtedly familiar with the practice of buying an automobile on time. At the time of purchase, the value of the asset (probably best measured by its cost) is exactly equal to the equity of the bank (the amount of the loan) plus the equity of the owner (the amount of the down payment). As time progresses the value of the asset changes, and so do the equities of the respective parties. Written in more common form, the accounting equation is

$$\text{ASSETS} = \text{LIABILITIES} + \text{OWNERS' EQUITY}$$

Transactions are economic events that give rise to changes in the accounting equation; such changes may bring about either increases or decreases in various components of the accounting equation. As mentioned previously, the accounting equation must remain in balance at all times. A change in one part of the equation is always accompanied by an equal change somewhere else. This is where we get the term "double entry" accounting: each transaction consists of two parts.

Because there are three types of accounts (assets, liabilities, and owners' equity), any one of which may either increase or decrease, there are six possible kinds of transactions. These may be summarized as follows:

+A (asset increase) accompanied by

$\left\{\begin{array}{l} -\text{A (asset decrease)} \\ \text{or} \\ +\text{L (liabilty increase)} \\ \text{or} \\ +\text{OE (owners' equity increase)} \end{array}\right.$

−A (asset decrease) accompanied by

$\left\{\begin{array}{l} +\text{A (asset increase)} \\ \text{or} \\ -\text{L (liability decrease)} \\ \text{or} \\ -\text{OE (owners' equity decrease)} \end{array}\right.$

+L (liability increase) accompanied by

$\left\{\begin{array}{l} +\text{A (asset increase)} \\ \text{or} \\ -\text{L (liability decrease)} \\ \text{or} \\ -\text{OE (owner's equity decrease)} \end{array}\right.$

−L (liability decrease) accompanied by

$\left\{\begin{array}{l} -\text{A (asset decrease)} \\ \text{or} \\ +\text{L (liability increase)} \\ \text{or} \\ +\text{OE (owners' equity increase)} \end{array}\right.$

+OE (owners' equity increase) accompanied by

$\left\{\begin{array}{l} +\text{A (asset increase)} \\ \text{or} \\ -\text{L (liability decrease)} \\ \text{or} \\ -\text{OE (owners' equity decrease)} \end{array}\right.$

−OE (owners' equity decrease) accompanied by

$\left\{\begin{array}{l} -\text{A (asset decrease)} \\ \text{or} \\ +\text{L (liablility increase)} \\ \text{or} \\ +\text{OE (owners' equity increase)} \end{array}\right.$

DEBIT AND CREDIT

Changes in the accounting equation are recorded on a device known as an *account*. An account is merely a sheet of paper ruled so that changes in a particular item may be recorded in an orderly manner. The simplest form of account is known as a *T-account* and is nothing more than a piece of paper divided in half, one side to record increases and the other side to record decreases. A separate account is used for each type of asset, liability, and owners' equity. The number of accounts used, of course, is determined by the amount of detail desired by management. A formal account is illustrated in chapter 3 where accounts are discussed in more detail. Note that the formal account also appears as a large T.

The left side of an account has been arbitrarily designated as the "debit" side and the right side as the "credit" side. This is always true, *regardless of the type of account.* As we use the terms "debit" and "credit" in accounting, they mean nothing more than left or right. Because the terms come from Latin words which have other meanings, most students have preconceived notions about them. They think of "credits" as being "bad" because they must be related to "creditors." Then they think that "debits" must also be "bad" because they they are related to "debts." And so the student often becomes confused trying to relate his concepts of these words to his accounting problems. It would save much confusion if the student would forget all previous notions about these terms and think of "debit" as meaning "left" and "credit" as meaning "right." This may not sound very sophisticated, but it is helpful.

It has been stated that the accounting equation must remain in perfect balance at all times. For this reason, we arrange the signs in the accounts so that the balance will be maintained if we always have debits equaling credits. We let the debit (left side) of an asset account always represent an increase, thus:

$$A \quad = \quad L \quad + \quad OE$$

ASSET

+	−

As we move to the right side of the equation, we change the signs so that for liability and owners' equity accounts a "debit" represents a decrease and a "credit" represents an increase (just the opposite of an asset account since liabilities and owners' equity are on the opposite side of the accounting equation). This is seen in the illustration below:

$$A \quad = \quad L \quad + \quad OE$$

ASSET		LIABILITIES		OWNERS' EQUITY	
+	−	−	+	−	+

A double entry accounting system will always be in balance so long as debits equal credits in each transaction. Refer again to the various types of transactions discussed on the previous page and observe this fact.

Debits record	whereas	Credits record
+A (asset increases)		−A (asset decreases)
−L (liability decreases)		+L (liability increases)
−OE (owners' equity decreases)		+OE (owners' equity increases)

Each transaction must involve a debit (which may record an increase to an asset, a decrease to a liability, or a decrease to owners' equity) and an offsetting credit (which will record a decrease to an asset, an increase to a liability, or an increase to owners' equity). Transactions which involve only one debit and one credit are known as *simple* entries. Those which involve at least three accounts in a single transaction are known as *compound* entries. Note that compound entries must also balance, i.e., the sum of the debits must equal the sum of the credits in every transaction.

THE COST CONCEPT

Accounting transactions are normally recorded at cost, that is, at the price agreed upon between buyer and seller in an arm's length transaction.[1] At the time the exchange in goods or services actually takes place, cost is probably the best indication of value that the accountant has. Because value from that moment on is a very subjective matter, the accountant continues to account on a cost basis, paying little attention to market values. This idea, that transactions should be recorded at cost rather than at a subjective or arbitrary value, is known as the *cost concept.*

To illustrate the cost concept, we shall assume that Speedy Service purchases a new delivery truck having a "window" or list price as follows:

Deluxe pick-up	$2,209.00
Custom cab	182.50
Freight charges	139.89
Automatic transmission	172.00
Whitewall tires	32.00
Deluxe wheel covers	17.95
Radio	65.00
Total list price	$2,818.34

The manager of Speedy Service checks the wholesale blue book price and notes that similar trucks have sold recently for $2,295. He has also obtained a written bid of $2,487.80 (plus tax) from another dealer for an identical truck. The state lists the appraised value of this type of vehicle for tax purposes as $2,000. After considerable negotiation the dealer agrees to sell the truck to Speedy Service for $2,352 plus 4 percent sales tax. It is this transaction price of $2,446.08 ($2,352.00 + $94.08 sales tax) that is recorded by both buyer and seller.

Note that all costs incurred in readying the asset for use are a part of that asset's cost. In the previous example, the prices paid for accessories,

---

[1] A common business term meaning "no strings attached."

freight, sales tax, etc., were all considered a part of the truck cost. If the truck were modified in some manner (such as the fabrication of a heavy-duty steel bumper), the modification would also be regarded as a part of the truck's cost.

CHANGES IN THE EQUATION

The use of the account and the operation of the accounting equation may be seen in the following simple illustration. I. M. Painless graduated from dental school and decided to set up his own practice. He took his entire inheritance from Aunt Jezzabell's estate, $55,333, and placed it in a business checking account. This investment would appear in his books as follows:

ASSETS   =   LIABILITIES + OWNERS' EQUITY

CASH		I.M. PAINLESS, CAPITAL	
(1) 55,333			(1) 55,333

For $23,000 Doctor Painless purchased an old home in the business district which he planned to remodel for an office building. He paid $10,000 cash and signed a mortgage for the balance. Following the recording of this transaction, his books would appear as follows:

ASSETS   =   LIABILITIES + OWNERS' EQUITY

CASH		MORTGAGE PAYABLE	I.M. PAINLESS, CAPITAL	
(1) 55,333	(2) 10,000	(2) 13,000		(1) 55,333
	+			

BUILDING	
(2) 23,000	

The old home was remodeled at a contract cost of $5,000 cash, bringing about the following changes in the accounts:

ASSETS   =   LIABILITIES + OWNERS' EQUITY

CASH		MORTGAGE PAYABLE	I.M. PAINLESS, CAPITAL	
(1) 55,333	(2) 10,000	(2) 13,000		(1) 55,333
	(3) 5,000			
	+			

BUILDING	
(2) 23,000	
(3) 5,000	

Dental equipment was purchased for $6,666 with a down payment of $666 in cash and the balance in three equal monthly installments. Again the accounts change, but the equation remains in balance.

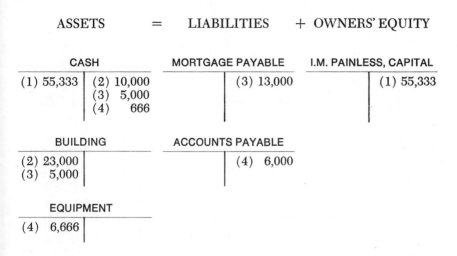

ASSETS   =   LIABILITIES   + OWNERS' EQUITY

CASH		MORTGAGE PAYABLE	I.M. PAINLESS, CAPITAL
(1) 55,333	(2) 10,000	(3) 13,000	(1) 55,333
	(3) 5,000		
	(4) 666		

BUILDING		ACCOUNTS PAYABLE
(2) 23,000		(4) 6,000
(3) 5,000		

EQUIPMENT	
(4) 6,666	

Doctor Painless withdrew $772 from the business to purchase his fiancée an engagement ring. This transaction reduced his equity in the business and left the accounts as follows:

ASSETS   =   LIABILITIES   + OWNERS' EQUITY

CASH		MORTGAGE PAYABLE	I.M. PAINLESS, CAPITAL	
(1) 55,333	(2) 10,000	(3) 13,000	(5) 772	(1) 55,333
	(3) 5,000			
	(4) 666			
	(5) 772			

BUILDING		ACCOUNTS PAYABLE
(2) 23,000		(4) 6,000
(3) 5,000		

EQUIPMENT	
(4) 6,666	

The first installment of $2,000 on the dental equipment contract was paid, leaving the accounts as follows:

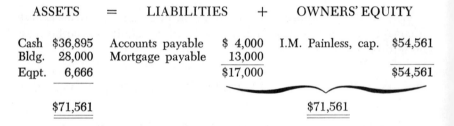

ASSETS   =   LIABILITIES   + OWNERS' EQUITY

CASH		MORTGAGE PAYABLE	I.M. PAINLESS, CAPITAL	
(1) 55,333	(2) 10,000	(3) 13,000	(5) 772	(1) 55,333
	(3) 5,000			
	(4) 666			
	(5) 772			
	(6) 2,000			

BUILDING	ACCOUNTS PAYABLE	
(2) 23,000	(6) 2,000	(4) 6,000
(3) 5,000		

EQUIPMENT
(4) 6,666

Utilization of the debit and credit rules given earlier has kept the acounting equation in balance during the recording of these simple transactions. The equation may be summarized at this point as follows:

ASSETS   =   LIABILITIES   +   OWNERS' EQUITY

Cash	$36,895	Accounts payable	$ 4,000	I.M. Painless, cap.	$54,561
Bldg.	28,000	Mortgage payable	13,000		
Eqpt.	6,666		$17,000		$54,561
	$71,561				$71,561

SUMMARY

There are three principal forms of business enterprises: the sole proprietorship, the partnership, and the corporation. The proprietorship has a single owner, whereas the partnership and corporation each have two or more owners. The distinction between these latter two is primarily a legal distinction: the corporation is recognized as an artificial being created by law, while the partnership is not. The accountant, however, is not overly concerned with this legal distinction. He is concerned primarily with accounting for the economic entities, regardless of the legal form that such organizations may take. In each case, the business is regarded as a specific accounting unit, separate and apart from its owners.

Cost is the basis on which most events are recorded. This means that accountants generally are not overly concerned with values except to the extent that these values are reflected in actual transactions involving the exchange of goods or services. The total cost of an asset includes all costs incurred in getting it in place and ready to use.

All business enterprises normally record transactions by what is known as double-entry accounting. This system is based upon a fundamental equation which reflects that assets must at all times equal the sum of the liabilities plus the owners' equity. The equation is kept in balance by assuring that the debits and the credits are equal in each separate transaction. These principles are the basis of most modern accounting systems.

QUESTIONS

1. List the major types of business organizations. What characteristics distinguish one from another?
2. What is the accounting equation? Define assets, equities, liabilities, and owners' equity.
3. Explain how the terms *debit* and *credit* are used in accounting. What relationship is there between these terms and others that "sound" related?
4. What is economic entity? Are economic entities and legal entities always the same?
5. What is the effect of a debit on an asset account? On a liability account? On an owners' equity account?
6. Explain what is meant by the term *double entry* bookkeeping. Is this expression related to the terms *debit* and *credit*?
7. What is a simple entry? What is a compound entry? What do both types of entries have in common?
8. Summarize the various types of accounting transactions. Express each type of transaction in terms of debits and credits.
9. What effect would the purchasing of office supplies on credit have on the accounting equation?
10. What effect would the purchasing of machinery for cash have upon the equity of the owner? Why?
11. How would the purchase of a delivery truck for a business be recorded in T-accounts if the $3,825 list price were paid in cash? How would the transaction be recorded if an $825 down payment were made, with the balance payable in six monthly installments?

PROBLEMS

Problem 2-1
Required:
    a. Write the accounting equation and explain why it must always be in balance.

b. Use the accounting equation to determine the amounts that belong in the (numbered) blanks below:

ASSETS	LIABILITIES	OWNERS' EQUITY
$ 72,000	(1)	$ 45,000
(2)	$ 20,300	$ 41,700
$ 96,500	$ 38,300	(3)
(4)	$ 46,100	$ 62,600
$ 85,000	(5)	$ 57,600
(6)	$ 89,300	$175,200
$ 53,900	$ 2,300	(7)
$525,395	(8)	$ 27,300
$ 75,000	$ 27,400	(9)
(10)	$152,409	$322,222

Problem 2-2

Use the following information and headings:
1. Deposited $50,000 in bank as capital to start business.
2. Purchased a building by paying $10,000 in cash and signing a
   mortgage for $30,000.
3. Purchased furniture and supplies on account for $3,000.
4. Owner withdrew $1,000 cash for personal use.
5. Paid for the furniture and supplies.
6. Paid for installment on the mortgage ($2,000).
7. Placed $5,000 more cash into the business as additional capital.

ASSETS		LIABILITIES		OWNERS' EQUITY	
Dr(+)	Cr(−)	Dr(−)	Cr(+)	Dr(−)	Cr(+)

Required:
   a. Record the transactions by placing their amounts in the appro-
      priate columns.
   b. Compute the balance under each heading.
   c. Check the balance of the equation.

Problem 2-3

Activities of Thompson & Sons for their first month of business are summarized as follows:

1. Ken Thompson began business by contributing $20,000 cash, a building worth $30,000, and a delivery truck worth $1,000.
2. A new delivery truck was purchased for $4,000. Half of this amount was paid in cash, and the balance was to be paid in monthly installments.
3. The old truck was sold for $1,000.
4. The owner withdrew $3,000 to pay a personal debt.
5. Supplies were purchased in the amount of $500 on account.
6. The first $200 installment on the delivery truck was paid.
7. The owner contributed to the business a personal automobile with fair market value of $1,600.
8. $250 was paid on the supplies account (see item 5).

Required:

a. Set up the necessary T-accounts, and record the above transactions.
b. Key your entries.
c. After you have recorded all transactions, prove the accuracy by balancing the accounts and checking the equality of the accounting equation.

Problem 2-4

The following transactions occurred as Mr. Howe Long set up his plumbing service and repair business:

1. Mr. Long began his business by investing $1,200 in cash and the following additional assets: office equipment, $325; tools, $550; and truck, $1,300.
2. Purchased $175 worth of repair supplies on account from City Supply Company.
3. Traded an adding machine carried on the books at $45 for additional tools.
4. Paid $135 cash for a new adding machine to replace the one traded.
5. Paid City Supply Company one-half the amount owed to them.
6. Purchased additional plumbing tools for $20 cash.
7. Built a special, permanently attached box on the back of the truck to hold tools and supplies; total cost, installed, of $225 was paid in cash.

Required:

a. Set up the necessary T-accounts.
b. Record the transactions in the T-accounts. Use the transaction letters to key each debit and credit amount.

Problem 2-5

Art Anderson set up a small business and during the first month's operations engaged in the following transactions:

1. Mr. Anderson contributed $10,000 cash along with some land and a building. At date of contribution the land had an appraised value of $5,500. Mr. Anderson had recently been offered $18,250 for the building and the land.
2. Purchased furniture on account for $3,150.

3. Purchased a used truck for deliveries. A down payment of $500 is made, with the balance of $1,700 to be paid in installments over the next three years.
4. Invested $2,000 cash in U.S. Treasury notes.
5. Paid $900 on the furniture and supplies account.
6. Deposited all but $100 of the remaining cash in a bank account.
7. Deposited the last payroll check from Mr. Anderson's former employer, in the amount of $435, in the business bank account.
8. Purchased office supplies in the amount of $47 and issued a check to cover the purchase.

Required:

Record the above transactions in T-accounts, keying the debits to the credits in each transaction.

Problem 2-6

After the first month of operation, the accounts of the Franco Fixture Company appear as follows:

CASH		ACCOUNTS PAYABLE	
(1) 13,000 | (3) 5,000		(4) 600 | (2) 600	
(5) 8,000 | (4) 600		(7) 2,725 | (3) 7,750	
| (6) 1,250		| (6) 2,000	
| (7) 2,725			

MERCHANDISE		JIM FRANCO, CAPITAL	
(3) 12,750 |		| (1) 45,000	
		| (5) 8,000	

OFFICE SUPPLIES
(2)   600 |

FURNITURE
(6) 3,250 |

BUILDING
(1) 23,500 |

LAND
(1) 8,500 |

Required:

Analyze the T-accounts, and describe each transaction that has occurred.

Problem 2-7

R. U. Stone has decided to open up a small hardware store. The following transactions occur:

1. Mr. Stone contributes $38,000 cash.
2. A building and lot is bought by paying $7,000 down and taking a mortgage for $22,000. The land is appraised at $9,000.
3. The building is remodeled at a cost of $10,500 to accommodate a hardware store. Mr. Stone pays $5,000 in cash and puts the rest on account.
4. Store equipment and supplies are purchased from a liquidating hardware store in a nearby town. They are valued at $3,750, but Mr. Stone pays $2,000 cash for them.
5. Merchandise is purchased. Mr. Stone's supplier lists the total price at $7,900, but quotes Mr. Stone a "bargain price" of $7,500, which he pays in cash.
6. $500 is paid on the remodeling account (refer to number 3 above).
7. Mr. Stone finds it necessary to withdraw $2,000 from the business to pay his son's college tuition.

Required:

Record the transactions in the necessary T-accounts. Be sure to key each transaction and make sure that the accounting equation is kept in balance.

3

The
Recording
Process

One of the important functions of accounting is to record and classify data in a significant manner. In the early days of accounting these records were maintained primarily in handwritten form. As the volume of business transactions increased and the art of accounting developed, these handwritten records and the procedures which accompanied them were gradually revised. Technological change also played an important role in revising the accounting records. Adding machines, cash registers, bookkeeping machines, time clocks, and other mechanical devices were introduced to assist with chiefly clerical operations. Later, electronic data processing (EDP) was introduced, causing a complete revolution in accounting techniques.

ELECTRONIC DATA PROCESSING

The scope of this course will not permit extended discussion of electronic data processing. A brief discussion of the function of such systems will enable the student to appreciate the roles played by the computer and related equipment in freeing the accountant from bookkeeping routines. An electronic data processing system has five basic components: input, storage, calculation, control, and output.

Input

The basic accounting documents must be translated into a form which the machine can read and interpret. The most familiar form of input is probably a punch card such as the one shown in Figure 3-1. This card

Figure 3-1
THE PUNCHED CARD

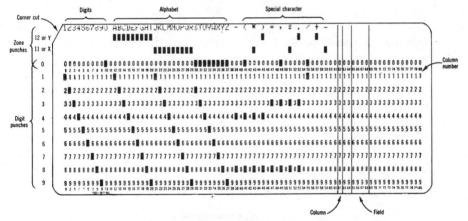

contains 80 vertical columns and 12 horizontal rows, giving a total of 960 separate punching positions. The rectangular punched holes in any particular column are "read" by the machine and interpreted as digits, letters, and symbols as shown at the top of the card illustrated. When a single digit is punched in one of the rows, it is interpreted as a digit. When a digit is punched in conjunction with a "zone" punch (one of the first three rows), this is interpreted as a letter; for example, row 12 in conjunction with row 1 is interpreted as the letter "a." The various symbols which provide instructions to the computer are entered by special combinations of two or three punches in a particular column.

Storage

Once the data have been entered into the machine system it can be stored for future calculation, recall, or other use. Since the input cards are bulky, the information contained thereon is usually stored on a magnetic tape, magnetic disc, or magnetic drum. In any case, the data on the card are recorded as magnetic impressions which can be recalled by the machine and translated back into the original form. All of the data contained on a single punched card can be stored on a piece of magnetic tape about one-tenth of an inch long. To get some idea of the volume of data that can be stored on these auxiliary storage devices, consider that the student records (i.e., grades and other transcript information) of a major university could all be stored on a single reel of magnetic tape about one inch thick and ten inches in diameter.

Control

The control function interprets the instructions and tells the computer exactly what to do. The instructions which guide the computer are known as a program. In an accounting system these programs must be established to account for each transaction properly and to summarize the results in the various accounts. The computer must be instructed through the program as to how the debit and credit transactions are to be interpreted in accordance with the accounting equation discussed in chapter 2.

The nature of an EDP program is illustrated in Figure 3-2. This oversimplified "block diagram" shows some of the decisions and actions which might constitute the process of getting up in the morning and preparing to leave for work. Note that the program asks the machine certain questions, and then depending on the answer, instructs the machine to proceed to the next step where another question is asked.

Calculations

One of the most important aspects of an EDP accounting system is the speed with which calculations can be made. Although calculations which would require several minutes to do manually can be done by modern mechanical equipment in seconds, an electronic computer is not limited by mechanical operations and is therefore capable of performing literally thousands of operations in a single *second*. The speed with which an account balance consisting of hundreds of debits and credits can be calculated is astounding. For example, a computer that operates in nano (one/billionth) seconds, the speed of the newest generation of computers,

Figure 3-2

BLOCK DIAGRAM: GET UP AND GO TO WORK ROUTINE

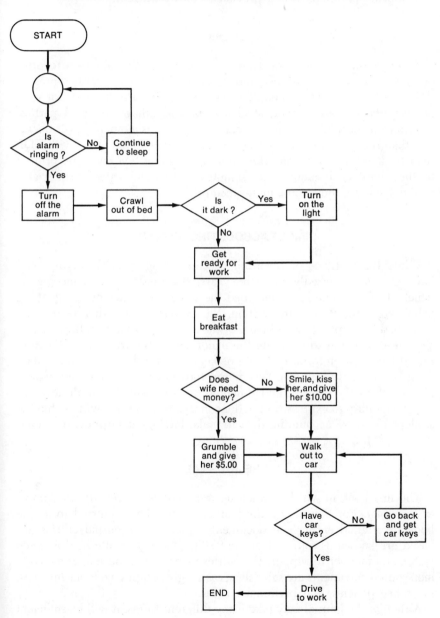

could perform 400,000 additions in a single second. The computer has thus been the means of freeing the accountant from many of the routine mechanical operations which previously burdened him.

Output

Through the program, the EDP equipment can be called on to print out any data which has been stored or calculated. These outputs represent the end products of the accounting system and provide the basis for various reports to management, stockholders, and other interested parties. Inasmuch as printing is a mechanical process, this is a much slower operation than is calculating; nevertheless it can be done much faster with EDP than by hand. For example, this entire accounting text could be printed by the computer in about fifteen minutes on a medium-speed printer and in about seven minutes on a high-speed printer.

SIMPLE ACCOUNTING SYSTEM

While the methods of recording, accumulating, and classifying data have changed markedly over the years, the fundamental concepts by which they are done have remained the same. The accounting equation, debits and credits, the transaction, the account, and other techniques described in chapter 2 are all parts of the most modern accounting system. We are now going to illustrate the major accounting records in the simplified handwritten form. It should be kept in mind that such handscribed records are rarely found in practice in today's dynamic business world. Nevertheless, the concept and functions are fundamental to all accounting. The ability to express transactions in this simple form will enable the student to utilize accounting data to make intelligent business decisions.

THE JOURNAL

The first book in which accounting transactions are recorded is known as a *journal*. For this reason the journal is sometimes referred to as the book of original entry. The documents upon which journal entries are based are known as source documents. These are generally filed in some systematic manner to support the entries made in the journal. Some common source documents are sales slips, cash register tapes, vendors' invoices, insurance policies, and premium notices.

Although the journal may take many different forms, it will be sufficient in this course to learn the mechanics of the two-column or general journal, an example of which is shown in Figure 3-3.

Figure 3-3

GENERAL JOURNAL

Date	Explanation	F	Debit amount	Credit amount
1970 Apl. 3	Cash		5000 —	
	Richard Tanner, Capital			5000 —
	To record investment by owner			
5	Office Equipment		255 39	
	Cash			255 39
	To record purchase of desk for office			
5	Office Supplies		53 82	
	Accounts Payable - Easy Office Supply			53 82
	To record purchase of supplies on account			
10	Land		2000 —	
	Cash			2000 —
	To record purchase of building site			
25	Delivery Equipment		2257 14	
	Note Payable			1800 —
	Cash			457 14
	To record purchase of delivery truck.			
May 7	Accounts Payable - Easy Office Supply		53 82	
	Cash			53 82
	To record payment on account.			
10	Richard Tanner, Drawings		400 —	
	Cash			400 —
	To record living allowance withdrawn by owner.			

A handwritten general journal may be prepared by observing the following rules:

1. Transactions are recorded in the journal chronologically.
2. In entering the date, the year and month are entered only the first time they occur, or at the top of each page. The day of the month, on the other hand, is repeated for each transaction.
3. Debits are always listed before credits in any given transaction. The debit account (or accounts) is listed against the left hand side of the explanation column. Credit accounts are indented approximately one inch.
4. There is no uniform method for entering the explanation. Some accountants write against the left hand margin (as with a debit

account), while others indent two inches. A common practice is shown in Figure 3-3 where the indentation is halfway between the debit and credit accounts (about one-half inch). The explanation should permit the reader to trace the entry to the source document if necessary.

5. The reference (folio) column is left blank at the time transactions are journalized. This column will be used when the transactions are posted, a process described later in the chapter.

6. In the two-column journal a separate column is provided for debits and credits. This enables the accountant to prove at a glance the equality of the debits and credits in each transaction.

7. Note the lack of punctuation in the journal. No decimals or commas are used because the journal paper is ruled in a manner which makes this unnecessary. Inasmuch as the journal is an internal record, no dollar signs are required. It is apparent to the accountant that dollars serve as the system of measure in this country. Some accountants prefer to use a dash in the cents column in lieu of two zeros.

8. A blank line is left between the end of the explanation of one transaction and the beginning of the next.

SPECIAL JOURNALS

When a given transaction occurs with enough frequency, it may be desirable to set up a special journal just to record that particular type of transaction. This practice saves considerable time by eliminating explanations and other information that otherwise would be repeated. Journals which are set up to record only one type of transaction are known as *special journals*. They are most commonly established to record cash receipts, cash disbursements, credit purchases, and credit sales. When special journals are utilized, the general journal is used only to record transactions that cannot be recorded in one of the special journals. Figure 3-4 shows a sales journal, one of the more common special journals.

Figure 3-4
SALES JOURNAL

Date	Account debited	Invoice number	F	Debit accounts receivable	Credit Sales	Credit Sales tax payable	Page 1
1970 Aug. 1	Arden Madour	Z-4329		11 33	10 95	38	
1	Robert C. Hatch	Z-4330		439 88	425 -	14 88	
3	Clair B. Moody	Z-4331		113 85	110 -	3 85	
4	R. Henry Staker	Z-4332		51 75	50 -	1 75	

We are not concerned in this course with the mechanics of special journals. It is important to realize, however, that the basic rules of debit and credit apply to all journals—that is, the debits must equal the credits for each transaction, regardless of the journal in which the particular transaction is recorded. Every transaction is first recorded in a journal. When special journals are used, it must be decided in which journal the transaction can be recorded most easily.

THE LEDGER

The student was introduced to the account in chapter 2. A *ledger* is simply a group of accounts arranged in some systematic manner. The journal does not replace the account, but merely precedes it in the recording process. Transactions are first recorded in the journal (the book of original entry) and later transcribed into the individual accounts which constitute the ledger. The process of copying amounts from the journal to the ledger accounts is known as *posting*. As each debit entry in the journal is posted to the respective ledger account, the "folio" or "reference" columns are completed. In the journal this reference serves two purposes. First, it indicates that the posting has been completed for that particular item. Should the bookkeeper be interrupted while posting, he could easily tell just where he was when he left off. Second, the reference indicates the account number to which the posting has been made, thus facilitating cross reference. The reference in the ledger accounts similarly cross refers to the particular journal page on which the transaction was initially recorded.

WHY A JOURNAL AND A LEDGER?

On the surface it may appear that the ledger duplicates what has already been recorded in the journal. This is not true. Each of these records has distinct advantages and serves a worthwhile purpose. The journal provides a complete record of transactions in chronological order. It is the only place where the accountant may find a complete record of the transaction in one place. Both the debit and credit are recorded on the same page; the whole story of a particular transaction is apparent at one glance.

The ledger, on the other hand, contains only half the story in a particular account. The cash account, for example, may contain a credit of $500. This tells management that cash has decreased, but does not explain what brought about the decrease. Was the cash used to buy merchandise, to pay salaries, or to buy a fur coat for the office manager's wife? The answer to this question can be found quickly by referring to the journal, but would require considerable searching if it were to be answered from the ledger.

What good then is the ledger? The ledger serves as a device to sort and collect like items. For example, transactions involving cash, which may be scattered over several journal pages, are all collected in one place in the ledger, the cash account. If management wants to know how much cash the company has at a particular time, it will seek the answer in the ledger rather than in the journal. The cash account would summarize all receipts and disbursements of cash, regardless of the purpose. Thus it is seen that both the journal and the ledger serve unique purposes.

THE TRIAL BALANCE

Periodically, each ledger account is balanced. This is done by computing the total debits and total credits, and then calculating the difference between these two amounts. The difference is termed the "balance" in the account and is described as a debit balance or a credit balance, according to which side of the account has the largest total.

As soon as all of the account balances have been calculated, a trial balance can be prepared.

A *trial balance* is merely an accounting tool used to test the equality of the debits and credits within the ledger at a specified point of time. It does not prove that the accounting process is without error, but merely assures that the sum of the debit balances equals the sum of the credit balances. The trial balance tests the mathematical accuracy of such things as footing journals (the process of totaling columns), posting to the proper side of the ledger, and balancing the ledger accounts.

EXTENDED ILLUSTRATION

The Kool Theatre Company was established by Martin Kool on August 1, 1970; the following events took place:

1. August 1, Mr. Kool invested $50,000, which he withdrew from a personal savings account, in the business.
2. August 1, Mr. Kool signed a one-year lease for the building, agreeing to pay $350 per month, payable the first of each month, beginning September 1, 1970.
3. August 4, the company purchased theater and projection equipment at a cost of $22,355. Paid cash.
4. August 4, a cash register was purchased for $417 cash.

5. August 7, purchased a candy display cabinet from Theatre Supply Company for $138. Although the cabinet was installed this date, the bill is not due for 30 days.

The above transactions would be recorded as shown in Figure 3-5.

Figure 3-5

KOOL THEATRE COMPANY
General Journal

Page 1

1970				
Aug. 1	Cash		50000 —	
	Martin Kool, Capital			50000 —
	To record investment by owner			
4	Theater and Projection Equipment		22355 —	
	Cash			22355 —
	To record purchase of equipment from Cinema, Inc. Their invoice #72394			
4	Office Equipment		417 —	
	Cash			417 —
	To record purchase of cash register.			
7	Concession Equipment		138 —	
	Accounts Payable - Theatre Supply Co.			138 —
	To record purchase of candy display cabinet. Terms: net 30 days			

Note that no entry is made for the second transaction (the signing of the lease) because no goods or services have yet changed hands. The lease is merely a contract whereby the parties agree to do certain things. Until one or the other (or both) of the parties actually performs on the contract, there is no accounting transaction. When the first month's rent is paid, on or about September 1, that amount will be recorded.

As soon as the transactions have been journalized, the amounts should be posted to the respective ledger accounts. As this is done, the account number should be entered in the folio column of the journal, indicating that the posting of the particular account is complete. At the same time, the folio column in each ledger account is filled in, indicating the source of the entry (J-1, meaning page 1 of the general journal). The ledger accounts after posting are shown in Figure 3-6.

Figure 3-6
KOOL THEATRE COMPANY
Ledger Accounts

A trial balance taken at this point would appear as shown in Figure 3-7.

Figure 3-7

KOOL THEATRE COMPANY
Trial Balance
August 7, 1970

Cash	27,228	
Martin Kool, Capital		50,000
Theater & Projection Equipment	22,355	
Office Equipment	417	
Concession Equipment	138	
Account Payable—Theatre Supply Co.		138
	50,138	50,138

REVENUES AND EXPENSES

In the previous chapter, the student was concerned only with asset, liability, and owners' equity accounts. These are known as *real*, or permanent, accounts, and they reflect the acts affecting the accounting equation. From these accounts, management can determine the firm's financial position at any moment of time. By comparing these accounts at two different dates, say one month apart, management could tell in general terms what happened during the intervening period. For example, if the owners' equity were $1,000 on July 1 and $1,500 on August 1 and no investments or withdrawals were made during the period, then the firm apparently enjoyed a $500 profit.

While a firm can determine its profitability by utilizing only real accounts, such a practice does not provide management with sufficient detail to enable them to exercise control over operations. Management is concerned with what *caused* the profit. This detail can be provided by setting up some temporary, or *nominal*, accounts. Such accounts are used to measure the operating activities of a particular period of time. The two main types of nominal accounts are revenue accounts and expense accounts.

Revenue accounts are established to measure the increases in owners' equity that arise from operating the business. Inasmuch as they measure increases to owners' equity, they have signs similar to those used in permanent owners' equity accounts, i.e., debits record *decreases* in revenue accounts, and credits record *increases* in revenue accounts. The most common forms of revenues are those earned by selling merchandise (called sales revenue) or by providing services (for example, cleaning revenue). Revenue accounts measure the gross inflow of assets coming into the business through its operations.

Expense accounts record the various costs incurred in producing revenues. These accounts measure the decrease in owners' equity that results from using up assets and incurring liabilities in order to generate the revenues. Since expenses record decreases in owners' equity, these accounts have signs opposite to those found in permanent equity accounts. In the case of expense accounts, debits record increases and credits record decreases (just the opposite of revenue accounts).

Profit (sometimes called income or earnings) is the difference between revenues and expenses in those instances where the revenues exceed the expenses. When the reverse is true, the difference is known as a *loss*. As was noted previously, profits and losses can be arrived at through the use of permanent (real) accounts only. Revenue and expense accounts, however, provide detail as to *what caused* the profit or loss.

The concept of revenues and expenses might be understood more clearly by referring to Figure 3-8. This diagram represents a cross section of a

Figure 3-8

NET ASSET FLOWS

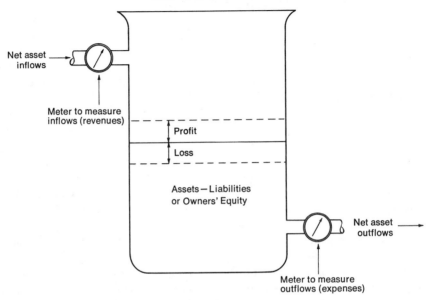

tank. The pipes on the left carry net assets (assets minus liabilities) into the tank. The pipes on the right carry net assets out of the tank. The level in the tank at any moment is the owners' equity or net assets. The profit or loss represents the net increase or decrease in the owners' equity during a given period.

If the tank contained a liquid, a calibrated dipstick could be inserted at two points of time. By comparing the readings on the dipstick, one could measure the increase (profit) or decrease (loss) that occurred during the period. This would be similar to calculating profits by utilizing only real accounts (assets minus liabilities equals owners' equity).

A better technique for measuring the profit or loss would be to install meters on each of the pipes. By recording the flow through the various pipes, one could better determine *why* the profit or loss occurred. Revenue accounts may be likened to the inflow meters; they are devices for measuring the inflow of net assets from operating the business. Expense accounts are similar to the meters measuring the outflow of net assets.[1]

Owners' equity changes are not always caused by profits or losses. The equity of the owners may be increased by additional *investments* or de-

---

[1] *Net assets* (assets minus liabilities) is synonymous with owners' equity because of the accounting equation. Assets equal liabilities plus owners' equity, or assets minus liabilities equals owners' equity.

creased by *withdrawals* of the owners. Sometimes temporary accounts are established to measure the amounts withdrawn by particular owners during an accounting period. Such accounts are called *drawing* or *withdrawal* accounts in a partnership or proprietorship, and *dividend* accounts in a corporation. These accounts are similar in most respects to expense accounts, except that they do not pertain to operations and, therefore, do not affect the profit or loss for the periods.

CLOSING ENTRIES

At the end of the accounting period it is necessary to close all nominal accounts. This is accomplished by transferring amounts recorded therein to the permanent owners' equity accounts. The revenues and expenses are generally first brought together in a profit and loss summary or income summary account. Revenue accounts are closed by debiting the respective revenue accounts and crediting the income summary account. Expenses are closed by debiting the Income Summary account and crediting the individual expense accounts. The balance in the Income Summary account represents the profit (if a credit balance) or the loss (if a debit balance) for the period. This amount is closed to the owners' capital accounts in a partnership or proprietorship, or to Retained Earnings in a corporation. The drawing accounts are also closed to the owners' capital accounts (partnership or proprietorship), or the dividend accounts are closed to Retained Earnings (corporation). When the closing process is complete, the nominal accounts all have zero balances, and only real accounts remain.

FINANCIAL STATEMENTS

At regular intervals the accountant summarizes the data in the various ledger accounts and prepares financial statements to assist management and other interested parties in making pertinent decisions. The two most common financial statements are the balance sheet and income statement. The latter statement sumarizes the revenues and expenses for the period and thereby shows the profit or loss as illustrated in Figure 3-9.

The balance sheet presents the firm's financial position as of a given date and is composed of real accounts only. This means it is prepared after all temporary accounts (revenues, expenses, drawings, dividends) have been closed. An abbreviated balance sheet is presented in Figure 3-10. Note that the statement is presented in the form of the accounting equation. In chapter 5 financial statements are discussed in greater detail.

Figure 3-9

NADTO COMPANY
Income Statement
Month of June 1970

Revenues:		
Commissions earned		$2,490
Consulting revenue		1,815
Total revenue		$4,305
Expenses:		
Building rent	$1,300	
Heat and power	500	
Insurance	120	
Salaries	1,880	
Supplies	100	
Travel	220	
Total expenses		4,120
Net income		$ 185

Figure 3-10

MOORE COMPANY
Balance Sheet
December 31, 1970

ASSETS		LIABILITIES	
Cash	$ 2,902	Accounts payable ... $ 3,800	
Receivables	4,200	Mortgage payable ... 12,000	
Inventories	3,920	Total liabilities	$15,800
Land	10,000	OWNERS' EQUITY	
Buildings	14,300	Michael Moore, capital .	$19,522
Total assets	$35,322	Total liabilities and owner's equity	$35,322

EXTENDED ILLUSTRATION

As the Kool Theatre opens for business on September 1, 1970, the following transactions occur:

6. September 1, paid first month's rent on building (see item 2).
7. September 15, receipts from paid admissions for the first half of month, $1,542.

8. September 30, paid employees' wages for month, $1,222.

9. September 30, paid the newspaper for advertising for month, $191.

10. September 30, receipts from paid admissions for second half of month, $1,853.

11. September 30, received an invoice from Film Rental, Inc., for films supplied during month, $1,449. The invoice is to be paid within 10 days.

12. September 30, Mr. Kool withdrew $400 from the business for personal living expenses.

13. September 30, concession revenue for month was $337.

Figure 3-11 shows how these transactions would appear in the journal.

Figure 3-11

KOOL THEATRE COMPANY
General Journal

Page 2

1970				
Sept. 1	Building Rent Expense		350 -	
	Cash			350 —
	Paid rent for month of September			
15	Cash		1542 —	
	Admission Revenue			1542—
	Admissions for period 9-1-70 to 9-15-70			
30	Wage Expense		1222 —	
	Cash			1222 —
	Paid wages for month of September.			
30	Advertising Expense		191 —	
	Cash			191 —
	Paid for newspaper advertising for Sept.			
30	Cash		1853 —	
	Admission Revenue			1853 -
	Admissions for period 9-16-70 to 9-30-70			
30	Film Rental Expense		1449 —	
	Accounts Payable - Film Rental Inc.			1449 —
	Film rentals for September, due 10 days			
30	Martin Kool, Drawings		400—	
	Cash			400 —
	Living allowance for September			
30	Cash		337 —	
	Concession Revenue			337—
	Concession revenue for September			

As soon as the journal entries have been posted, it is possible to close the books. All nominal or temporary accounts created in the preceding illustration should be closed. This may be accomplished in four steps. First, all amounts in revenue accounts (Admission Revenue) should be transferred to the Income Summary account. Second, all amounts in expense accounts (Building Rent Expense, Wage Expense, Advertising Expense, and Film Rental Expense) should be transferred to the Income Summary account. Next, the balance in the Income Summary account should be transferred to the owner's capital (Martin Kool, Capital). Finally, the owner's drawings (*Martin Kool, Drawings*) should be transferred to his capital account. The journal entries which accomplish this *closing process* are shown in Figure 3-12.

Figure 3-12

GENERAL JOURNAL

Page 3

1970				
Sept. 30	Income Summary	3212		
	Building Rent Expense			350
	Wage Expense			1222
	Advertising Expense			191
	Film Rental Expense			1449
	To close all expense accounts			
30	Admission Revenue	3395		
	Concession Revenue	387		
	Income, Summary			3782
	To close all revenue accounts			
30	Income Summary	520		
	Martin Kool, Capital			520
	To close profit for September to capital			
30	Martin Kool, Capital	400		
	Martin Kool, Drawings			400
	To close drawing for September to capital			

Figure 3-13 shows the ledger accounts as they would appear after posting all transactions, and Figure 3-14 shows a post-closing trial balance. The income statement for the month of September is shown in Figure 3-15 and the balance sheet as of September 30 in Figure 3-16.

Figure 3-13

KOOL THEATRE COMPANY
Ledger Accounts

Cash — Account Number 1

Date		Ref	Debit	Date		Ref	Credit
1970 Aug. 1		J-1	50,000 —	1970 Aug. 4		J-1	22,355 —
Sept. 15		J-2	1,542 —	4		J-1	417 —
30		J-2	1,853 —	Sept. 1		J-2	350 —
30		J-2	337 —	30		J-2	1,222 —
				30		J-2	191 —
	Balance. 28,797 —			30		J-2	400 —

Martin Kool, Capital — Account number 2

Date		Ref	Debit	Date		Ref	Credit
1970 Sept. 30		J-3	400 —	1970 Aug. 1		J-1	50,000 —
				Sept. 30		J-3	520 —
				Balance. 50,120 —			

Theater and Projection Equipment — Account Number 3

Date		Ref	Debit				
1970 Aug. 4		J-1	22,355 —				

Office Equipment — Account number 4

Date		Ref	Debit				
1970 Aug. 4		J-1	417 —				

Concession Equipment — Account Number 5

Date		Ref	Debit				
1970 Aug. 7		J-1	138 —				

Account Payable - Theatre Supply Co. — Account number 6

				Date		Ref	Credit
				1970 Aug. 7		J-1	138 —

Building Rent Expense — Account number 7

Date		Ref	Debit	Date		Ref	Credit
1970 Sept. 1		J-2	350 —	1970 Sept. 30		J-3	350 —

Wage Expense — Account Number 8

Date		Ref	Debit	Date		Ref	Credit
1970 Sept. 30		J-2	1,222 —	1970 Sept. 30		J-3	1,222 —

Advertising Expense — Account Number 9

Date		Ref	Debit	Date		Ref	Credit
1970 Sept. 30		J-2	191 —	1970 Sept. 30		J-3	191 —

Illustration 3-13 (cont.)

KOOL THEATRE COMPANY
Ledger Accounts

					Account Number 10
1970 Sept. 30		J-3	3395—	1970 Sept. 30	J-2 1542—
				30	J-2 1853—
			3395—		3395—

Film Rental Expense					Account number 11
1970 Sept. 30		J-2	1449—	1970 Sept. 30	J-3 1449—

Accounts Payable - Film Rental Inc.					Account Number 12
				1970 Sept. 30	J-2 1449—

Martin Kool, Drawing					Account Number 13
1970 Sept. 30			400—	1970 Sept. 30	J-3 400—

Concession Revenue					Account number 14
1970 Sept. 30		J-3	337—	1970 Sept. 30	J-2 337—

Income Summary					Account number 15
1970 Sept. 30		J-3	3212—	1970 Sept. 30	J-3 3732—
	30	J-3	520—		
			3732—		3732—

Figure 3-14

KOOL THEATRE COMPANY
Post-Closing Trial Balance
September 30, 1970

Cash	28,797	
Martin Kool, Capital		50,120
Theater & Projection Equipment	22,355	
Office Equipment	417	
Concession Equipment	138	
Account Payable, Theatre Supply Co.		138
Account Payable, Film Rental Inc.		1,449
	51,707	51,707

Figure 3-15

KOOL THEATRE COMPANY
Income Statement
Month of September 1970

Revenue:
Admissions revenue	$3,395	
Concession revenue	337	$3,732

Expenses:
Building rent expense	$ 350	
Wage expense	1,222	
Advertising expense	191	
Film rental expense	1,449	3,212

Net income .... $ 520

Figure 3-16

KOOL THEATRE COMPANY
Balance Sheet
September 30, 1970

ASSETS		LIABILITIES	
Cash	$28,797	Accounts payable	$ 1,587
Theater and projection			
equipment	22,355		
Office equipment	417	**OWNERS' EQUITY**	
Concession equipment .	138	Martin Kool, capital ...	50,120
	$51,707		$51,707

SUMMARY

One of the important functions of accounting is to record and classify data in a meaningful manner. Today's accountant is assisted in accomplishing this function by all sorts of modern accounting equipment. Nearly all accounting systems, whether machine oriented or manual, are based on the fundamentals of double entry accounting. The concepts on which modern accounting is based can best be understood by following through a simple, handwritten system and then proceeding to the more complex systems.

The first record in the accounting process is known as a journal. Although journals may take many different forms, each follows the basic principles of debit and credit presented in this chapter. Each transaction must be recorded so that the sum of the debits is equal to the sum of the credits. After the transactions have been entered chronologically in a journal, the amounts are posted to the respective ledger accounts. The ledger serves as a device for the accumulation and sorting of homogeneous data so that it can be summarized for management's use. Ledger accounts may be balanced periodically and a trial balance prepared to test the equality of the debits and credits. A balance sheet may also be prepared to determine the firm's financial position as of a given point in time.

Although double entry accounting can be accomplished utilizing only real accounts, the addition of certain nominal accounts makes the process more meaningful. Revenue accounts can be used to measure the inflow of net assets from operating the business, while expense accounts may be used to measure the outflows. The expenses are the costs incurred to produce the revenues. The revenue and expense accounts provide the information necessary to determine the firm's profit or loss of the period and to prepare the income statement. Drawing, or dividend, accounts can also be established to record withdrawals of assets by the owners. The revenue, expense, and dividend (withdrawal) accounts are closed at the end of the accounting period by transferring the amounts therein to permanent owners' equity accounts.

QUESTIONS

1. Electronic data processing has greatly reduced the need for handwritten records. What purpose then is served by the student learning how to record transactions in handwritten form?
2. List the five basic functions of an electronic data processing accounting system. How are these same functions performed in a handwritten system?
3. What is a journal? What purpose does it serve? List the most important rules for recording transactions in journals.
4. What is a ledger? What purpose does it serve? Is the ledger a duplication of the journal? Explain.
5. Describe what is meant by each of the following terms: posting, footing, balancing.
6. Distinguish between "real" and "nominal" accounts. What is the function of each?
7. Define the terms *revenue* and *expense*. What do revenue accounts measure? What do expense accounts measure?
8. What is a trial balance? When are trial balances prepared? If the trial balance is in balance, can the bookkeeper be sure that no errors have been made? Explain.
9. Can profits be measured without the use of revenue and expense accounts? If so, how? What purpose do the revenue and expense accounts serve?
10. Why are closing entries made? When are they made? What types of accounts are closed?

11. How are revenue accounts closed? Prepare the journal entries necessary to close the following accounts: Cleaning Revenue, $4,322; Pressing Revenue, $551; Laundry Revenue, $3,917.

12. How are expense accounts closed? Prepare the journal entries necessary to close the following expense accounts: Wage Expense, $3,296; Rent Expense, $1,907; Insurance Expense, $500; Delivery Expense, $2,444; Miscellaneous Expense, $841.

13. Assume that John Roundy is the proprietor of a laundry and that he withdrew $1,000 from the business during the accounting period. Refer to questions 11 and 12 and complete the closing entries for the business.

14. What purposes are served by special journals? What types of transactions would you expect to see recorded in special journals?

15. Where special journals are used, are transactions recorded in more than one journal?

PROBLEMS

Problem 3-1

On January 4, 1970, Paul Plane began the operation of the Plane Print Shop. During January the following transactions took place:

Jan. 4   Deposited $10,000 in the bank account of Plane Print Shop.

Jan. 5   Purchased printing machinery for $6,000, paying $2,000 cash and signing a ninety-day promissory note for the balance.

Jan. 5   Purchased on account from Printing Wholesalers $800 worth of supplies.

Jan. 8   Paid $100 cash to Advertising, Incorporated, for advertising during the month.

Jan. 10   Completed printing job for Boston Company and collected $300 cash.

Jan. 12   Paid $110 for January rent of print shop.

Jan. 15   Completed and delivered print job for Jackson & Jackson. Billed them for $450 (account receivable).

Jan. 15   Paid $175 for wages of two employees.

Jan. 17   Mr. Plane withdrew from the company's cash account $500 for his personal expenses and compensation.

Jan. 19   Signed a purchase order for a new printing machine at a price of $2,000, to be delivered and paid for next month.

Jan. 24   Paid $25 to Instant Delivery Service for delivery charges.

Jan. 25   Billed Smith & Company $150 for printing job.

Jan. 27   Paid $400 to Printing Wholesalers on account.

Jan. 28   Received $300 from Jackson & Jackson as payment on their account.

Jan. 31   Paid $175 for employees' wages.

Required:

   a. Journalize each transaction in good form, using two-column journal paper. Place an asterisk by the account title of each nominal account.

   b. Post these entries to ledger T-accounts.

   c. Prepare a trial balance.

   d. Prepare an income statement for the month of January.

Problem 3-2

William Watt, an electrician, has decided to start his own business as an electrical contractor. During the month of March he completed the following transactions:

March 2   Deposited $10,000 cash to the account of Watt Electrical Service and invested his small tools and equipment having a current fair market value of $3,000.

March 4   Traded an old pickup truck of his own (fair market value, $500) for a new truck especially equipped for use in his business. The cost was $3,500 plus his old truck. He gave $2,000 cash and signed a note for the improvements.

March 6   Decided to convert his garage into a shop to be used solely in his business. The fair market value of the garage was $2,500, and he paid $800 from the Watt Electrical Service account to make the necessary changes and improvements.

March 8   Completed an electrical job for Home Builders, Incorporated, and billed them for $600.

March 10   Purchased $300 of supplies on account from Electrical Suppliers.

March 13   Completed a wiring job for Suburban Homes and collected $300 cash.

March 15   Paid $200 for wages of two part-time helpers.

March 17   Paid $75 for repairs on his equipment.

March 18   Received a check for $600 from Home Builders, Incorporated, in full payment of their account.

March 21   Paid $200 to Electrical Suppliers to be applied on account.

March 24   Paid $75 to have his name and an advertising display painted on his truck (the paint job is expected to last as long as the truck).

March 26   Completed an electrical job for Smith Manufacturing and billed them for $650.

March 28   Paid $90 for gas and oil consumed during the month.

March 29   Paid for an ad that appears daily in the newspaper, $40 for March.

March 30   Paid $200 for helpers' wages.

March 31   Withdrew $500 for personal expenses.

Required:
   a. Prepare general journal entries in good form for each transaction, indicating which accounts are nominal.
   b. Post the transactions to T-accounts.
   c. Prepare a trial balance.

Problem 3-3

The following trial balance was taken from the Easy Service Company at the end of its annual accounting period.

EASY SERVICE COMPANY
Trial Balance
December 31, 1970

Cash	3,202.50	
Accounts Receivable	632.20	
Supplies	672.25	
Building	4,000.00	
Accounts Payable		1,010.00
Notes Payable		210.00
I.T. Easy, Capital		8,000.00
I.T. Easy, Drawings	2,035.00	
Service Revenues		3,132.35
Advertising Expense	285.30	
Office Expense	375.10	
Wages Expense	650.00	
Delivery Expense	300.00	
Miscellaneous Expense	200.00	
	12,352.35	12,352.35

Required:
   a. Prepare closing entries in general journal form.
   b. Prepare a post-closing trial balance.

Problem 3-4

Below are the post-closing trial balance and the closing entries prepared by the Sweet Company as of December 31, 1970.

SWEET COMPANY
Post-Closing Trial Balance
December 31, 1970

Cash	1,300.00	
Repair Parts	600.00	
Land	1,000.00	
Patents	800.00	
Accounts Payable		500.00
U. M. Sweet, Capital		3,200.00
	3,700.00	3,700.00

Closing Entries

1970   *190*

Dec. 31 Revenue from Services 1,985.00
         Revenue and Expense Summary.   1,985.00

     31 Revenue and Expense Summary 200.00
         Office Rent Expense 200.00

     31 Revenue and Expense Summary 250.00
         Miscellaneous Expense 250.00

     31 Revenue and Expense Summary 800.00
         Salaries Expense 800.00

     31 Revenue and Expense Summary 735.00
         U. M. Sweet, Capital 735.00

     31 U. M. Sweet, Capital 75.00
         U. M. Sweet, Drawings 75.00

Required:

Use the above data to construct a pre-closing trial balance.

Problem 3-5

On February 1, 1970, R. A. Hooker organized the Hooker Auto Repair Company. His transactions during February are given below:

Feb. 1 Contributed $6,000 cash and tools worth $350.

Feb. 1 Rented a garage in which to set up the business, paying $350 for February.

Feb. 2 Put ads in the local newspaper, $45 on account (the ads appeared during February).

Feb. 5 Did work on car for C. A. Dent amounting to $80. Dent paid $50 and promised to pay the balance in March.

Feb. 8 Finished work on truck for Speedy Delivery Company. Paid $75 in cash, and put the balance of $35 on account.

Feb. 9 Hired another employee.

Feb. 10 Paid the newspaper for advertising ordered earlier.

Feb. 12 Accepted from Speedy Delivery Company nine trucks for overhauls.

Feb. 15 Paid wages of $85 for the first half of the month.

Feb. 16 Withdrew $230 for personal living expenses.

Feb. 18 Received $30 on account from C. A. Dent.

Feb. 19 Purchased additional tools for $175.

Feb. 21 Received balance of amount due from Speedy Delivery Company for February 8 job.

Feb. 26 Finished work on nine trucks of Speedy Delivery Company, the bill amounting to $1,250.

Feb. 28 Paid $460 for parts used on repair jobs in February.

Feb. 28   Paid wages of $350 for the balance of the month.

Feb. 28   Withdrew $150 for personal living expenses.

Required:

  a. Journalize the transactions, including explanation.
  b. Post to T-accounts.
  c. Prepare a trial balance.
  d. Journalize and post closing entries.
  e. Take a post-closing trial balance.

Problem 3-6

The following errors in recording transactions on the Perfection Repair Company's books were discovered at the end of the month. Explain what effect each error will have on the trial balance taken at the month's end.

1. A $250 purchase of repair parts was recorded as a debit to cash and a credit to Repair Supplies.

2. A monthly insurance premium of $23 was erroneously posted as a debit both to Insurance Expense and to Cash (no credit posting).

3. A small machine costing $189 was purchased on account. The bookkeeper turned to the wrong page in the ledger and recorded the debit to Advertising Expense. (The corresponding credit was correct.)

4. A bill in the amount of $129 for advertising was recorded as a debit of $129 to Advertising Expense and a credit of $192 to Accounts Payable.

5. Wages of $1,260 were paid in cash near the end of the month, with a debit to Wages Expense and a credit to Wages Payable.

6. Rent in the amount of $120 was paid during the period. The transaction was recorded as a debit of $210 to Rent Expense and a credit of $210 to Cash.

7. Equipment that cost $237 was recorded as a credit both to Accounts Payable and to Equipment. No debit was made for this transaction.

8. Repair service performed by a Perfection Repair Company employee for a customer and billed at $134 was recorded by a debit to Repair Expense and a credit to Cash.

9. Revenue from repairs amounting to $262 was recorded as a debit of $262 to Cash and a credit of $226 to Repair Revenue.

10. Travel expenses of $122 were recorded as a debit of $12 to Travel Expense and a credit of $212 to Cash.

Problem 3-7

Following is a trial balance prepared at the end of the first month of operations of the No-Spot Cleaners.

NO-SPOT CLEANERS
Trial Balance
July 31, 1970

Cash	1,685.00	
Accounts Receivable	280.00	
Miscellaneous Supplies	165.00	
Equipment	1,335.00	
Accounts Payable		237.00
Lance Knowles, Capital		3,000.00
Lance Knowles, Drawings	165.00	
Sales Income		1,482.00
Rent Expense	105.00	
Salaries Expense	750.00	
Advertising Expense	136.00	
Miscellaneous Expense	98.00	
	4,719.00	4,719.00

Required:

Prepare journal entries to close the books.

Problem 3-8

The following trial balance was prepared by Stephen Black for the Black Watch Repair Company for the month of April.

BLACK WATCH REPAIR COMPANY
Trial Balance
April 30, 1970

Cash	351.00	
Accounts Receivable	431.00	
Tools	123.00	
Repair Parts	206.00	
Furniture and Equipment	489.00	
Accounts Payable		639.00
Stephen Black, Capital		1,000.00
Stephen Black, Drawings	235.00	
Watch Repair Revenue		624.00
Rent Expense	110.00	
Salaries Expense	215.00	
Advertising Expense	47.00	
Miscellaneous Expense	89.00	
	2,296.00	2,263.00

Mr. Black has just hired a new bookkeeper, and he is concerned because the trial balance is not in balance. You have been called in to reconcile the figures, and you discover the following information:

1. An advertising expense of $13 was recorded in the Salaries account.
2. A $36 repair job on a grandfather clock was recorded by debiting Cash and crediting Watch Repair Revenue, each for $63.
3. Salaries expense of $135 was recorded as a drawing.
4. An advertising expense of $21 was not posted (the credit was properly posted).
5. Tools were purchased for $28. The entry was properly recorded in the journal; in posting the debit to the tools account, however, the amount was recorded as $82.
6. A customer paid Mr. Black $13 in cash for a job completed; Accounts Receivable was debited.

Required:
   a. Prepare entries to correct the books.
   b. Prepare a corrected trial balance.

4

Income
Measurement

One of the major objectives of accounting is to measure periodic profits accurately. This would be a simple task if one could wait until the business were liquidated before doing an accounting. To be useful, however, the earning statements must be prepared to cover relatively short periods of time such as a month, quarter, or year. Many transactions simply do not fit these arbitrary accounting periods, and accordingly the accountant must make numerous estimates and judgments in order to determine the periodic profits.

RECOGNITION OF REVENUE

The first judgment that an accountant must make relates to *when* the revenue should be recognized. There are three acceptable methods of recognition actually employed in practice: the *accrual basis*, the *production basis*, and the *cash basis*.

The Accrual Basis

The most commonly accepted basis of revenue recognition is the *accrual method*. Where this technique is followed, revenues are recognized in the period in which the goods or services are delivered to the customer (the period of sale), regardless of when the cash is received. When cash is received before or after the date of sale, it is necessary to shift the recognition of the revenue to the period when the actual delivery takes place. For example, if a customer purchases some goods on credit during December but does not make payment for these goods until January, the revenue should be recognized during December. Under the accrual system the important factor is *when the goods or services are delivered* and not when they are paid for. Because receipts and payments are often made in periods other than when the revenue or expenses should be recognized, it is necessary to adjust the accounts to reflect these facts. The topic of adjustments under the accrual system is discussed later in this chapter.

The Production Basis

Sometimes it is argued that revenue should be recognized as being earned when the goods are produced, rather than as they are sold. In long-term construction contracts, for example, it may be more reasonable to recognize the revenue as the production progresses than to wait until the job is completed. The *production basis* relates the recognition of revenue to the period when the effort is expended. This method may be acceptable where the goods are being produced under contract and the selling price has been firmly established in advance. In most cases, however, the construction basis is not acceptable for one of the following reasons:

1. The *amount* of revenue obtainable is usually not known at the time the goods are produced. This figure will not be available until the goods are actually offered for sale in the marketplace, at which time the revenue will be determined through the interaction of supply and demand, and other factors.

2. Revenue may be regarded as only speculation until an actual sales agreement is reached. For most products, the sales effort represents a very significant part of the total effort required to earn revenue. It would not be proper to say that the revenue is earned when a major

portion of the work remains yet to be done. To do so would be to anticipate profits, a practice frowned upon by accountants.

The Cash Basis

The *cash basis* of revenue recognition may appropriately be employed where collection of a billed amount does not seem reasonably certain. For example, medical doctors often do not recognize revenue until the cash is collected because they cannot accurately predict how much of the billed amount will actually be realized. Likewise, when merchandise is sold on installment contracts the revenue is often recognized as collections are made because of the high rate of default and the difficulty of accurately predicting the amount ultimately collectible.[1]

Although the cash basis and the production basis are sometimes used to recognize revenue in very special circumstances, the overwhelming majority of business transactions is recorded on the accrual basis. In most instances, the collection rate can be predicted with reasonable accuracy, and the amount of revenue can be established at the time the sale is actually made. The accrual basis is the most widely accepted method of revenue recognition, largely because it recognizes the revenue when it is earned, regardless of when the payment is received.

THE MATCHING CONCEPT

Having arrived at a systematic manner of recognizing revenues, it becomes necessary to decide when to recognize an expense. Expenses have been defined as the costs of producing revenues. It would seem, then, that profit could best be measured by recognizing the expenses in the same period as the revenues which the expenses have helped produce. We should not be concerned, then, with when the cash payment is made, but rather with the period or periods that benefit from the expenditure. Advertising costs incurred for a sale made in December may be paid in advance, say in November. The salesman's commission may not be paid until January. Both of these, however, should be recognized as expenses in December, since that is when the expenditure contributed to the company's revenue. Our objective should be to match expenses with the appropriate revenues, a practice known as the *matching concept.*

---

[1]The installment sales method of accounting, an example of cash basis revenue recognition, is discussed in chapter 16.

ADJUSTMENTS

An adjustment is required when a transaction is recorded in one accounting period, but the recognition of that transaction's revenue or expenses must be made, in accordance with the matching concept, in another period. There are four kinds of adjusting entries, which may be summarized graphically as in Figure 4-1:

Figure 4-1
TYPES OF ADJUSTING ENTRIES

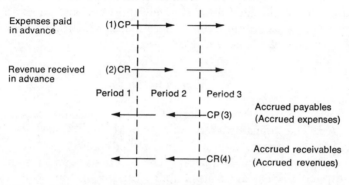

1. We may have a cash payment (CP) in one period which will benefit one or more later periods. The adjusting entry is necessary in order to show that the expense is recognized in the period of benefit, rather than in the period of payment. As shown by the arrow, the adjustment shifts the expense to a later period or periods. These types of adjustments may be referred to as *expenses paid in advance*.

2. When a cash receipt (CR) is collected in one period but will not be earned until a later period or periods, it constitutes *revenue received in advance*, or unearned revenue. In this case, an adjusting entry is necessary to defer the revenue so that it will be recognized in the period the goods or services are actually delivered.

3. Just as cash can be paid or received before the period of expense or revenue, so also it can be paid or received after that period. When this occurs and no transaction reflecting it has been recorded, it is necessary to *accrue* the revenue or expense. When services received in one period will not be paid for until a later period it is known as an *accrued payable* or *accrued expense*. Both terms may properly be used since the two accrue together. The accrual of an expense is always accompanied by the accrual of a liability (payable).

4. When a revenue is earned in one period through the delivery of goods or services, but cash will not be received (CR) until a later period, it may be necessary to *accrue revenue*. This, of

course, would only be necessary if the revenue has not already been recorded as a part of some other transaction. When an adjustment is made, it is known as an *accrued receivable* or *accrued revenue*. Again, either title may be appropriate in describing the adjustment, inasmuch as the accrual of a revenue is always accompanied by the accrual of an asset (receivable).

Expenses Paid in Advance

Expenses paid in advance must be properly allocated or apportioned out over the periods that will benefit from these expenditures. Those assets which are to be allocated over relatively short periods, usually a year or less, are known as *prepayments*. Those assets which have lives beyond one year are known as *fixed assets*.

Prepayments

Prepayments are generally charged to an asset account when they are purchased. The adjusting entry, then, would debit an expense account and credit the prepaid asset account for the "expired" or "used" portion at the end of each accounting period. This practice would leave the unused or unexpired portion as an asset to be carried on the books to future periods. Examples of prepaid (asset) accounts are Prepaid Insurance, Prepaid Rent, and Supplies on Hand.

To illustrate the accounting technique, let us assume that the Spartan Company closes its books monthly. On April 1, 1970, the company pays a fire insurance premium of $180 covering a one-year period beginning on that date. The entry to record the premium would be as follows:

Prepaid Insurance 180
    Cash in Bank   180

At the end of April, prior to the closing of the books, an adjusting entry would be required to record the allocation of one-twelfth of the premium ($15) to the month of April. This would be necessary inasmuch as the company received insurance protection during the month. Since the month of April received one-twelfth of the benefit, it should be charged with a corresponding fraction of the premium. The adjusting entry required at the end of April would be as follows:

Insurance Expense 15
    Prepaid Insurance   15

After posting the above entries, the accounts would appear as follows:

PREPAID INSURANCE		INSURANCE EXPENSE	
180	15	15	
Balance 165		Balance 15	

Alternate Method of Recording Prepayments.   An alternative method is sometimes followed for recording prepayments. The adjusting entry is also different, but the end result is identical to the above. Under this method the $180 premium would be recorded as an expense at the time it was paid, as follows:

    Insurance Expense   180
        Cash in Bank   180

At the end of the month the accountant would calculate the actual expense for the month (one-twelfth of $180, or $15) and compare this with the amount shown in the expense account ($180). He would conclude that $165 too much expense had been recorded and make the entry necessary to transfer this amount out of the expense account to the asset account as follows:

    Prepaid Insurance   165
        Insurance Expense   165

These accounts would appear as follows in the ledger after the adjusting entry had been posted:

PREPAID INSURANCE		INSURANCE EXPENSE	
165		180	165
Balance 165		Balance 15	

Note that both methods of recording the prepayment produce identical account balances after adjustment (Prepaid Insurance, $165, and Insurance Expense, $15).

Fixed Asset.   Fixed assets are long-lived assets (expected to last more than a year) which are *used* in the business. They may be either tangible (such as a building) or intangible (such as copyrights). They may have perpetual life (for example, land) or limited life (for example, machinery). Fixed assets which have limited life are subject to depreciation or amortization. Both of these terms refer to allocating or apportioning the asset's cost over the periods that benefit from its use.

Actually, this process is similar to the one followed in apportioning prepayments except that the period of time is longer. For example, if a company purchased for $2,400 a delivery truck that would last four years, after which time it would be worthless, the purchase would be recorded as follows:

Truck	2400	
Cash		2,400

Entries could be made at the end of each year to record depreciation as follows:

Depreciation Expense on Truck	600	
Truck		600

These accounts would appear in a ledger after posting as follows:

TRUCK		DEPR. EXPENSE ON TRUCK	
2,400	600	600	
Balance 1,800			

The adjusting entry would be repeated each year until the entire $2,400 cost had been apportioned to the benefiting periods.

Depreciation Is an Estimate. Depreciation is not as exact a process as implied in the preceding illustration. Rather, there are two key estimates: first, the useful life of the asset must be forecast, and second, its scrap value at the end of its useful life must be estimated. Both of these factors affect the amount of cost which should equitably be apportioned to each accounting period. Because depreciation is an estimate, accountants *do not credit the periodic depreciation directly to the asset account,* as was done in the previous illustration. Instead, a contra or negative asset account, Accumulated Depreciation, is used. The Accumulated Depreciation account is really part of the asset account to which it pertains. When the asset is shown, the accumulated depreciation is deducted from it to show the net unallocated asset cost. Credits made in the Accumulated Depreciation account are really amounts which should have been credited to the asset account. They are placed in a separate account only because the amounts have had to be estimated.

In practice it would not be possible for us to know that our delivery truck would last exactly four years. Nor is it likely that the asset would have no salvage value. If we *estimated* the truck would last four years, and we *estimated* it would be worth $400 at the end of that period, then we would record depreciation as follows:

Depreciation Expense, Truck	500	
Accumulated Depreciation, Truck		500

The accounts are shown below as they would appear after posting the above adjustment:

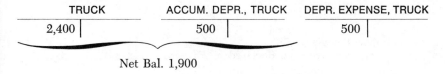

TRUCK	ACCUM. DEPR., TRUCK	DEPR. EXPENSE, TRUCK
2,400	500	500

Net Bal. 1,900

Revenues Received in Advance

When payment is received for goods or services prior to the time they are delivered to the customer, the payment does not represent revenue. Instead, this receipt of cash gives rise to a liability which might be called revenue received in advance. This liability represents an obligation to provide goods or services at some time in the future.

The situation where a company receives revenue in advance is complementary to that of its paying expenses in advance (prepayments). Refer again to the prepayment of a $180 insurance premium; this time view the prepayment from the standpoint of the insurance company (the company receiving payment) instead of that of the company paying the premium. The insurance company would record the transaction as follows:

Cash 180
    Premium Revenue Received in Advance 180

At the end of the first month they would record the expiration of one-twelfth of the premium. That is, they would record the fact that they have now provided one-twelfth of the service which they agreed to provide. The following adjusting entry would be appropriate at the end of the month:

Premium Revenue Received in Advance 15
    Premium Revenue 15

Alternate Method of Recording Revenue Received in Advance. Just as there was an alternate method for recording the prepayment, so also may the accountant elect one to record the premium's receipt. An equally effective means of recording this transaction would be:

Cash 180
    Premium Revenue 180

The above entry would, of course, necessitate a different adjusting entry. In this case the accountant would calculate the amount of revenue earned

($15), compare this with the amount shown in the premium revenue account ($180), and conclude that any difference ($165) should be removed from this account and transferred to the Premium Revenue Received in Advance account. This would be recorded as follows:

```
Premium Revenue ...................................   165
      Premium Revenue Received in Advance ............        165
```

Note that this alternate method produces results identical to those of the previous method. In both instances the Premium Revenue account has a credit balance of $15, and the Premium Revenue Received in Advance account has a credit balance of $165.

Accruals

Accruals bring about changes in various accounts through passage of time. The word "accrue" means to grow or increase. Certain assets and liabilities grow or increase as time passes, and this growth is accompanied by a growth in corresponding revenues and expenses. In order to match the revenues and expenses of a given period properly, it is necessary that the increment be recorded in the period of growth, rather than in the period the cash is paid or received.

Accrued Payables (Expenses). When services are received in one accounting period but are not to be paid for until some subsequent period, then an adjusting entry may be in order. It is necessary to recognize that the firm has incurred an expense by virtue of the fact that it has received services. It is also proper to reflect the fact that it has an obligation or liability to pay for these services. A common example of this type of situation would be the accrual of wages. Assume that an employee earns $25 per day and is paid for his five-day week each Friday. If the end of the accounting period falls on a Wednesday, it would be proper on that date to make the following entry:

```
Wages Expense .......................................   75
      Wages Payable ....................................        75
```

The result of this entry is to show the $75 wage expense in the period in which it was earned, although payment has not yet been made. Likewise, the balance sheet prepared as of that date would reflect the company's liability for these wages.

When payment is made on the subsequent Friday, the following entry would be appropriate:

```
Wages Expense .....................................    50
Wages Payable .....................................    75
    Cash .........................................          125
```

The adjusting entry sorts the $125 payment into the proper accounting periods. Note that $75 of expense is shown in period one, and $50 of expense is shown in period two.

Accrued Receivables (Revenues). In most instances procedures are set up to record revenue in the period in which the goods or services are delivered, and therefore no adjusting entries are required. Certain types of revenue, however, grow with time, and it would not be practical to record them each hour or day as the service is provided. In these instances, accountants either record the revenue when it is received, or else accrue the revenue at the end of the accounting period, whichever occurs first. As the revenue is recognized by accrual, so it is necessary also to record the asset which accompanies it.

An example of an accrued receivable is seen in the accrual of interest by a bank or other lender. Assume that a bank loans $1,000 at 6 percent interest on December 1, repayment of loan plus interest to be made in sixty days. If the bank closes its books on December 31, the accrued interest would properly be recorded on that date as folows:

```
Interest Receivable ................................    5
    Interest Earned ................................          5
```

When the loan is repaid on January 30, the following entries would be made:

```
Cash .........................................   1,000
    Note Receivable ..........................          1,000
    To record payment of note at maturity.

Cash .........................................      10
    Interest Receivable ......................             5
    Interest Earned ..........................             5
    To record payment of interest.
```

The adjustment sorted the interest revenue into the periods in which it was earned, one half ($5) in December and the other half in January.

SUMMARY

The process of measuring income is not an exact science because many transactions do not conveniently fit into the relatively short periods for which we must account. Just *when* should revenue be recognized as being earned, and to what periods should the expenses be charged? Revenue is most often recognized in the period the goods or services are delivered, although it is occasionally recognized as the goods are produced or sometimes as the proceeds from the sale are actually collected. An attempt is made in the accounting process to match the expenses with the revenues by recognizing these expenses in the period in which they help produce revenues.

Transactions often are recorded in some period other than the one in which the revenue or expense applies. This accordingly requires an adjusting entry to shift the recognition of the revenue or expense to the proper period. There are four basic kinds of adjusting entries:

1. *Expenses paid in advance* (pre-payments and fixed assets). These expenditures require an adjustment to apportion the expense to the periods which benefit therefrom.
2. *Revenue received in advance.* In this instance an adjustment is required to shift the revenue to the periods or period when the goods or services are delivered.
3. *Accrued payables* (accrued expenses). In this instance the adjustment is made before the transaction is recorded. Such an adjustment shifts the expense back to the period when the goods or services were actually received.
4. *Accrued receivables* (accrued revenues). These adjustments are also made prior to the transaction, but shift the revenue back to the period in which it was actually earned.

QUESTIONS

1. List three methods of revenue recognition and indicate under what circumstances each might be acceptable. Which method is most widely used? Why?
2. Describe the matching concept of accounting. Why is this such an important concept?
3. When are adjusting entries made? What circumstances make it necessary to prepare adjusting entries?
4. What are expenses paid in advance? What entry is made when the amount is paid? When is the adjustment made? What entry is made at the time of adjustment?
5. Describe the alternate method of recording expenses paid in advance and the corresponding adjusting entry required.
6. What is meant by revenue received in advance? Give an example of a transaction which would record the receipt of cash prior to the time that the revenue is regarded as earned. Give the adjustment that will be required when the revenue is recognized.
7. What entry is made to record the receipt of cash under the alternate method of recording revenue received in advance? What adjustment would be required under the alternate method?

8. What are accruals? When is the adjustment made under an accrual in relation to the time the cash is paid or received?

9. How is the cost of a fixed asset allocated to the periods that benefit from its use? Illustrate the entries required, assuming a machine cost of $4,000, salvage of $500, and useful life of five years.

10. The Thompson Boat Company closes its books annually on December 31. On August 1 the company pays $162.24 as the premium on a one-year fire insurance policy. Record the payment of the premium and the corresponding year-end adjustment, using two separate methods.

11. Beacher Bellows Company pays its four employees on Friday of each week. Each employee works five days per week and earns $32 per day. The company's accounting period ends on a Tuesday this year. Prepare the necessary year-end adjustment, together with the next Friday's payroll.

12. Why do some people say that depreciation is not an exact process? What impact does this have on the accuracy of a company's reported profits?

PROBLEMS

Problem 4-1

The transactions listed below are those of A. A. Archer, engineering consultant, who began business on April 1, 1970.

April 1 Invested $10,000 cash as initial capital.

April 2 Paid $250 for the use of office facilities for April and May.

April 2 Paid $130 premium on a one-year insurance policy for the office.

April 3 Purchased supplies for $150 on account.

April 5 Finished consulting job today and collected a fee of $300.

April 10 Delivered bill to B. B. McMullin in the amount of $625 for consulting work completed today. The customer agreed to pay within ten days.

April 10 Billed Mark Greene $300 for consulting work completed.

April 11 Paid $32 to Office Services Company for office expense.

April 12 Paid $50 for newspaper advertising that will appear during April.

April 18 Purchased land as a future building site, paying $2,000 cash and signing a mortgage for $4,000.

April 19 Received $625 from B. B. McMullin for work completed on April 10.

April 25 Paid $380 for salaries.

April 30 Received $500 from Richard Dillon, $100 for work completed today and the balance for work to be performed next week.

April 30 Mr. Archer withdrew $500 for personal use.

April 30 Received a bill from Office Services Company for office expenses of $47.

Additional Information
    1. Salaries of $75 had accrued as of April 30.
    2. Office supplies on hand as of April 30 amounted to $110.

Required:
    a. Journalize each transaction in general journal form, omitting explanations.
    b. Post to T-accounts.
    c. Prepare a trial balance.
    d. Journalize and post the adjusting and closing entries.
    e. Prepare a post-closing trial balance.

Problem 4-2
    Information taken from the Dicker Company is presented below.

Trial Balance Data as of December 31, 1970

Accumulated Depreciation, Office Furniture........	548.00
Accounts Receivable	1,740.00
Advertising Expense	350.00
Cash	985.00
Commissions Expense	1,620.00
Daniel Dicker, Capital	12,137.00
Interest Earned	40.00
Land	14,500.00
Notes Payable	870.00
Office Furniture	1,370.00
Office Rent	2,030.00
Prepaid Insurance	450.00
Salaries Expense	12,440.00
Service Revenue	23,890.00
U. S. Government Bonds	2,000.00

Adjusted Trial Balance Data as of December 31, 1970

Accumulated Depreciation, Office Furniture	685.00
Accounts Receivable	1,740.00
Advertising Expense	295.00
Cash	985.00
Commissions Payable	150.00
Commissions Expense	1,770.00
Daniel Dicker, Capital	12,137.00
Depreciation Expense	137.00
Insurance Expense	360.00
Interest Earned	66.00
Interest Expense	35.00
Interest Payable	35.00
Interest Receivable	26.00
Land	14,500.00
Notes Payable	870.00
Office Furniture	1,370.00
Office Rent	1,720.00

Prepaid Advertising	55.00
Prepaid Insurance	90.00
Prepaid Office Rent	310.00
Revenue Received in Advance	230.00
Salaries Expense	13,270.00
Salaries Payable	830.00
Service Revenue	23,660.00
U. S. Government Bonds	2,000.00

Required:

a. Compare the unadjusted and adjusted account balances, and prepare the adjusting entries made by the Dicker Company on December 31, 1970. (*Hint:* it will probably be helpful to first separate the debit and credit amounts and prepare two trial balances from those data given.)

b. Prepare the necessary closing entries.

Problem 4-3

Calculate each of the following:

a. What is the insurance expense for the year if (1) the balance of the Prepaid Insurance account at the beginning of the accounting period was $120; (2) an annual premium of $275 was paid this period; and (3) the Prepaid Insurance account had an ending balance of $93 after the adjustments?

b. What was the ending balance of the Prepaid Rent account after adjustments if (1) the rent expense for the period was $2,070; (2) the beginning balance of the Prepaid Rent account was $495; and (3) the rent payment made during the period was $2,200 and was to cover the next twelve months?

c. What was the amount of the payment made to the advertising agency if (1) the beginning balance of the Prepaid Advertising account was $79; (2) the ending balance (after adjustments) of the Prepaid Advertising account was $103; and (3) the advertising expense for the year was $690?

d. What was the balance of the Prepaid Magazine and Catalog Subscriptions account at the beginning of the accounting period if (1) the ending balance was $23; (2) the subscriptions expense for the period was $52; and (3) the cash payments made during the period for magazine and catalog subscriptions amounted to $44?

Problem 4-4

Data pertaining to the accounts of the Woodtap Publishing Company for the month of May follow:

1. An annual insurance premium of $264 had been paid on February 1.

2. The company had two presses. One had cost $9,350 with an estimated life of eight years and a salvage value of $150. The second press cost $5,825 and is expected to bring $125 in salvage at the end of its six-year estimated life.

3. The total daily payroll is $625, and employees are paid each Tuesday for all work done during the preceding week (assume a five-day week).

4. The company holds three $1,000 bonds that pay 6 percent annual interest.

5. Estimated tax expense for May was $110.

6. A customer paid a $100 deposit on May 26 for work yet to be done. This was included in income.

7. Work had been completed on an $800 job which had not been billed by May 31.

8. Repairs amounting to $275 had been done, but a bill had not been received by the company.

Required:

a. Prepare adjusting journal entries required on May 31 for the month of May.

b. Explain for each how the profit or loss for the month would be affected if the adjustment were not made.

Problem 4-5

Given the following data (assuming the company closes its books monthly):

1. An annual insurance premium of $276 is paid on March 2.

2. A new delivery truck was purchased at the end of July for $3,650. It is expected to last seven years, at which time its salvage value is estimated to be $150. The company records depreciation monthly.

3. Employees are paid on the fifth of each month (for the last half of the preceding month) and on the twentieth of each month (for the first half of the current month).

Payrolls for July and August were as follows:

EARNING PERIOD	AMOUNT EARNED
July 1–15	$2,600
July 16–31	2,600
August 1–15	3,000
August 16–31	3,000

4. A customer paid the company $840 in June for work which will be completed in October. It is estimated that during August about one-third of the job was completed.

5. The company has loaned a customer $1,000 at 5 percent interest annually, to be paid back next year.

6. The company pays for parking spaces for three months at a time. On August 1 it paid $261 for seventeen spaces.

Required:

a. Record each of the above items dealing with revenues and expenses under the assumption that the company uses the *accrual basis* of accounting.

b. Prepare adjusting entries that would be required at the end of August, assuming the company uses the *accrual basis* of accounting [refer to requirement (a) above].

c. Record each of the above items dealing with revenue and expense under the assumption that the company uses the *cash basis* of accounting.

d. Prepare adjusting entries that would be required at the end of August, assuming the company uses the *cash basis* of accounting [refer to requirement (c) above].

Problem 4-6

The beginning trial balance taken from the ledger of the Dart Detective Agency for the accounting year ending December 31, 1970, follows:

DART DETECTIVE AGENCY
Trial Balance
December 31, 1970

Cash	755.00	
Accounts Receivable	1,664.00	
Office Supplies	185.00	
Prepaid Insurance	1,020.00	
Office Equipment	840.00	
Accounts Payable		710.00
Revenue Received in Advance		1,200.00
Daniel Dart, Capital		1,400.00
Daniel Dart, Drawings	3,150.00	
Service Revenue		47,910.00
Salaries Expense	33,930.00	
Travel Expense	5,290.00	
Meals Expense	1,805.00	
Rent Expense	1,425.00	
Telephone Expense	836.00	
Miscellaneous Expense	320.00	
	51,220.00	51,220.00

The above trial balance was taken before any adjusting entries were made. Items that should have been considered are:

1. The office equipment was purchased on May 2, 1970, for $840. It is expected to be useful for ten years, with no salvage value.

2. The company pays its employees each Tuesday for the previous week's work. The daily payroll amounts to $130. The last day of the year falls on Sunday. Assume a regular, five-day work week.

3. D. Dart withdrew $280 on December 31; this was not recorded.

4. The company has not reimbursed two of its employees for travel expenses incurred during December; these total $138.

5. The company recently decided to insure all of its employees. The first annual insurance premium of $1,020 was paid on June 15, 1970.

6. Rent of $570 for six months was paid on October 1.
7. A large firm recently ordered the detective agency to do some work for them. Upon hiring the agency, the firm paid them $1,200 in advance. The work is now considered to be about one-fourth complete.

Required:
   a. Prepare the necessary adjusting entries.
   b. Prepare the closing entries.
   c. Take a post-closing trial balance.

Problem 4-7

C. A. Line has just begun the Line Realty Company, and he completed the following transactions during its first month of operation:

Feb. 1 Sold 100 shares of personally owned General Motors stock for $9,500 and deposited $9,000 of the proceeds in a checking account opened in the company's name.

Feb. 2 Purchased $72 of office supplies on account from Midtown Supply.

Feb. 3 Paid $420 for office rent three months in advance.

Feb. 4 Purchased $1,375 of office equipment, giving $1,000 in cash and a $375 promissory note. The equipment is estimated to last eight years with $32 salvage value at that time. Interest on the note for the month of February amounts to $2.50. The interest, however, will not be paid until maturity.

Feb. 9 Sold a house and collected $1,250 commission from the sale.

Feb. 11 Sent a local newspaper a $55 check in payment for advertising that had appeared.

Feb. 12 Paid the balance due on the office supplies purchased.

Feb. 17 Sold a house and collected a $950 commission from the sale.

Feb. 19 Received $50 from Gary Moore for property management services not yet performed.

Feb. 20 Mr. Line withdrew from the company's bank account $125 to pay for personal living expenses.

Feb. 26 Sold a duplex on which $1,380 commission is due. Line has not yet received this.

Feb. 28 Paid gas and oil expenses of $68.

Feb. 28 Paid office clerk's salary of $350.

Feb. 28 Paid $32 for the telephone and other utilities.

Feb. 28 Performed one-half of the property management services contracted with Gary Moore.

Feb. 28 Commissions earned by Line Realty salesmen during February amount to $450. None of this amount has been paid.

Required:
   a. Journalize the transactions.
   b. Post to ledger accounts.
   c. Prepare adjusting entries.
   d. Prepare closing entries.
   e. Prepare a post-closing trial balance.

5

Financial Statements

Most companies prepare two financial statements: an income statement and a balance sheet. These are normally prepared as soon after the end of the accounting period as the necessary information is available.

THE BALANCE SHEET

The balance sheet is sometimes referred to as a position statement. Its purpose is to show a firm's financial position as of a given moment of time, normally as of the close of business on the last day of the accounting period. It presents a picture of the business position as of an instant of time, just as a still camera takes a snapshot. The balances of all asset, liability, and owners' equity accounts ("real" accounts) are shown as of the closing date. These balances are taken *after* adjusting and closing entries have been posted and, therefore, no revenue or expense accounts are shown.

There are a variety of ways in which the various accounts might be classified on a balance sheet. The major asset classifications normally would include captions for current, fixed, and other assets. Liabilities are typically designated either current or long-term. The classification of owners' equity depends on the form of the business organization.

Current Assets

Current assets have been defined as follows:

> ... cash and other assets or resources commonly identified as those which are reasonably expected to be realized in cash or sold or consumed during the normal operating cycle of the business (usually one year).[1]

Current assets, then, could include cash, accounts receivable, notes receivable, inventories (raw materials, goods in process, finished goods and supplies), prepayments, and marketable securities (held for short term only). It is common practice to list current assets on the balance sheet in the order of liquidity, i.e., cash first and then those assets most readily convertible to cash.

Fixed Assets

Fixed assets are assets other than current assets which are *used* in the business. The word "used" is emphasized because this is the major factor which distinguishes fixed assets from investments or other assets.

Fixed assets may have perpetual or limited life, as well as be tangible or intangible in nature. A list of common tangible fixed assets would include land, land improvements, buildings, and machinery and equipment. Intangible fixed assets may include patents, copyrights, franchises, trademarks, and goodwill. It should be noted that the same basic rules are followed in showing intangible and tangible assets on a balance sheet. They are both carried at unamortized *cost*. The balance sheet normally does not reflect the value of fixed assets.

In listing fixed assets on the balance sheet, it is rather common to list the most permanent (perpetual life) assets first and move towards those

---

[1] *Accounting Research and Terminology Bulletins,* final ed. (New York: American Institute of Certified Public Accountants, 1961), p. 20.

that are less fixed in nature (depreciable). For example, land, building, and equipment would probably be listed in that order.

Other Assets

Any assets which are not current or fixed may be listed in the other asset classification. The most common type of other asset is long-term investments. This classification may include items such as investments in other companies' stocks or bonds, cash surrender value on insurance policies, and land held as a future building site.

Current Liabilities

Current liabilities are obligations that will be satisfied within a relatively short period of time. The AICPA cites the following definition:

> The term *current liabilities* is used principally to designate obligations whose liquidation is reasonably expected to require the use of existing resources properly classifiable as current assets, or the creation of other current liabilities. As a balance sheet category, the classification is intended to include obligations for items which have entered into the operating cycle, such as payables incurred in the acquisition of materials and supplies to be used in production of goods or in providing services to be offered for sale; collections received in advance of the delivery of goods or performance of service; and debts which arise from operations directly related to the operating cycle, such as accruals for wages, salaries, commissions, rental, royalties, and income and other taxes. Other liabilities whose regular and ordinary liquidation is expected to occur within a relatively short period of time, usually twelve months, are also intended for inclusion, such as short-term debts arising from the acquisition of capital assets, serial maturities of long-term obligations, amounts required to be expended within one year under sinking fund provisions, and agency obligations arising from the collection or acceptance of cash or other assets for the account of third persons.[2]

Thus, current liabilities include accounts payable, notes payable, revenues received in advance, and accrued payables (such as wages, salaries, commissions, interest, taxes).

Long-Term Liabilities

Those liabilities which mature beyond the period designated as current are known as long-term liabilities. For most companies this means debts

---

[2]Ibid., p. 21.

which are not due for at least one year. Long-term liabilities could include accounts such as Bonds Payable, Mortgage Payable, and Contracts Payable.

Other Liabilities

Although most liabilities can be classified as either current or long term, some might be more properly placed under another caption. The most common liabilities so classified are deferred credits. These represent amounts which have been designated as pertaining to future periods and which are being held in suspense until the appropriate time arrives.

Owners' Equity in the Balance Sheet

There are three major forms of business enterprise: sole proprietorship, partnership, and corporation. For the most part, all three forms are treated quite similarly in the accounts. Each is regarded as an economic entity, separate and apart from its owners. The accounting differences between the three forms are seen in the owners' equity section of the balance sheet.

The Proprietorship. The capital section of a sole proprietorship's balance sheet consists of one account—the owner's capital account. This single account reflects the net of all investments, withdrawals, and retained income. Sometimes accountants prefer to itemize on the balance sheet the changes that have taken place in the owner's capital account since the date of the previous balance sheet. Actually, this is better treated on a separate statement, since, strictly speaking, the balance sheet should show only ending balances.

The Partnership. Normally the balance sheet shows a separate capital account for each partner. Each of these accounts would be similar to the single capital account used in the proprietorship. In partnerships with a large number of partners, the balance sheet would probably show only one owners' equity caption—"partners' capital."[3]

The Corporation. Most corporations have several capital accounts, primarily because of certain legal restrictions such as those governing the payment of dividends. The two major corporate sources of owners' equity are paid-in capital and retained earnings.

The paid-in capital chiefly represents investments by owners, but is usually segregated into a number of different accounts specifying the

---

[3]Some partnerships have several hundred partners. For example, Peat, Marwick, Mitchell & Company, a large public accounting firm, reported 645 partners in 1970.

source or nature of the investment. Some paid-in capital accounts include Capital Stock, Common Stock, Preferred Stock, Premium on Stock (Paid-in Capital in Excess of Par Value), Discount on Stock (a negative owners' equity account representing the amount by which par value exceeds the amount paid in), and Treasury Stock (a negative owners' equity account representing reacquired stock).

Retained Earnings is normally shown in a single account representing the net amount retained in the business since the company's formation. Where the amount retained is negative (accumulated losses exceed accumulated profits), the account is referred to as a "deficit" and is shown as a deduction from paid-in capital.

Some companies prefer to "earmark" retained earnings by setting up several retained earnings accounts and indicating the reason why the earnings were retained (such as Retained Earnings Appropriated for Bond Retirement). Sometimes these accounts are referred to as reserves; for example, Reserve for Plant Expansion.

Do not be confused by the Retained Earnings account title. Retained Earnings is not an asset account, nor does this account reflect the amount of funds the company has. Remember that the asset side of the balance sheet shows the nature of the assets. The Retained Earnings account merely shows a portion of the owners' equity in those assets.

Balance Sheet Illustration

The balance sheet of the Gazuntite Paper Company is shown in Figure 5-1. The assets have been classified into three major headings: *Current, Fixed,* and *Other.* The liabilities are classified as *Current, Long-Term,* or *Other,* while the owners' equity has been classified as *Paid-in Capital* or *Retained Earnings.* A brief description of the various accounts shown in the Gazuntite balance sheet follows.

Cash as shown on the balance sheet generally includes all monies on hand, as well as those on deposit in various company bank accounts. Some companies prefer to show detailed classifications of cash, such as undeposited receipts, change funds, payroll bank accounts, and general bank accounts. Only cash which is available for use in the ordinary course of business should be included under the balance sheet heading, Cash. Sums which are not readily available, or those which will not be drawn upon in ordinary business transactions (such as the cash surrender value of life insurance policies or amounts held in sinking funds), should be listed as investments. Overdrafts in bank accounts (credit balances) should not be offset against debit balance accounts, but instead should be shown in the balance sheet as current liabilities.

Figure 5-1

GAZUNTITE PAPER COMPANY
Balance Sheet
December 31, 1970

ASSETS

CURRENT ASSETS:			
Cash			$35,443
Marketable securities			5,753
Accounts receivable	$75,194		
Notes receivable	5,200	$80,394	
Less: Allowance for doubtful accounts		890	79,504
Inventories:			
Raw materials		$22,590	
Goods in process		50,558	
Finished goods		11,094	184,242
Prepaid expenses			2,941
Total current assets			$307,883
FIXED ASSETS:			
Land			$72,000
Land improvements		$12,664	
Less: Accumulated depreciation		3,400	9,264
Buildings		$125,000	
Less: Accumulated depreciation		63,400	61,600
Equipment		$397,200	
Less: Accumulated depreciation		151,100	246,100
Intangibles			529
Total fixed assets			$389,493
OTHER ASSETS:			
Investments:			
Non consolidated subsidiary	$52,815		
Cash surrender value of life insurance	2,194		
Bonds of ...an't corporation	5,780	$60,789	
Deferred charges		63,011	
Total other assets			$60,789
Total assets			$760,387

LIABILITIES AND STOCKHOLDERS EQUITY

CURRENT LIABILITIES:			
Accounts payable			$25,728
Notes payable			1,251
Current portion of long-term debt			1,251
Accrued wages payable			6,534
Accrued interest payable			12,213
Federal and state income taxes payable			1,200
Taxes payable			23,831
Total current liabilities			$70,751
LONG-TERM DEBT:			
25-year 5% percent sinking fund bonds			$59,200
20-year 5% percent promissory notes			50,000
Mortgage payable			10,785
Total long-term debt			$119,985
OTHER LIABILITIES:			
Deferred federal income tax liability			$7,083
STOCKHOLDERS' EQUITY:			
Paid-in capital			
Preferred stock, par value $100			
Common stock, par value $10	$10,000		
Paid-in capital in excess of par	65,625		
Other paid-in capital	170,492		
Retained earnings	10,505	$256,622	
		311,717	
		$568,339	
Less: Treasury stock (at cost)		5,777	
Total stockholders' equity			$562,562
Total liabilities and stockholders' equity			$760,387

Marketable securities include stocks or bonds which have been acquired by the company and which will be held for a short term (generally less than a year). Companies generally invest in marketable securities in order to put excess cash to work. Funds accumulated in periods of low business activity often are invested in short-term securities. These securities are, in turn, liquidated as the funds are required to buy inventories and finance receivables during periods of high business activity. Marketable securities may consist of government or commercial obligations.

Accounts receivable constitute amounts due the company from the sale of goods or services in the ordinary course of business. These amounts are generally supported only by routine sales slips or sales invoices and generally do not earn interest. Receivables arising from sales to employees or to officers are generally shown separately in the balance sheet. In those industries where it is acceptable practice to sell goods on installment contracts, the receivables arising therefrom are generally treated as current assets, even though they may not be collected in full for some time. It would probably be desirable to designate such receivables as *installment accounts receivable* to distinguish them from ordinary accounts. As with cash, receivables which have credit balances should be shown as current liabilities and not be offset against those receivables which have debit balances.

Notes receivable are similar to accounts receivable, except that the notes generally bear interest and are supported by written promises to pay at a specified future date. Notes often arise in settlement of an account by a customer desirous of protecting his credit rating, but lacking the funds to make payment within the terms of sale.

It would not be reasonable to assume that all receivables will ultimately be collected. For this reason, most businesses set up an *allowance for doubtful accounts* to provide for losses arising from the failure of customers to pay their accounts. The allowance for doubtful accounts is a *contra* or negative asset and is deducted from the receivables on the balance sheet. The mechanics of accounting for bad debts are discussed in chapter 8.

Inventories include goods which have been acquired or produced for resale in the ordinary course of business. The balance sheet heading might include raw materials, goods in process, and finished goods. *Raw materials* are goods which have been acquired for use in the production process and which will be fabricated further prior to sale. *Finished goods* inventory consists of goods which have been produced and are now ready for sale. In the nonmanufacturing concern finished goods inventory is generally referred to as *merchandise inventory*. Both of these constitute completed goods which are ready to be sold. *Goods in process* inventory consists of goods which are in various stages of completion.

Prepaid expenses represent expenses which have been paid for in advance and which will normally be charged off as an expense in the next accounting period. The heading might include prepaid rent, prepaid insurance, prepaid advertising, office supplies, and similar items.

Land consists of sites for buildings, parking lots, and other property currently being used in the business. The fixed asset caption *land* should not include property being held for future plant sites or otherwise not currently being used. Land of this type should be designated as an investment.

Land improvements include sidewalks, asphalt paving, landscaping, and similar items which increase the value of the land. These improvements are generally shown separate from the land account because they have limited life and are subject to depreciation.

The fixed asset caption *buildings* should include only those buildings being used in the business such as office buildings, factory buildings, warehouse facilities, and sales floors.

Equipment might include machinery used in the factory, office equipment, materials handling equipment, and vehicles. The term machinery is often used to designate factory or production equipment.

Inasmuch as buildings, machinery, and equipment are subject to depreciation, we generally find an *accumulated depreciation* account in the balance sheet. This account, which may properly be termed a contra fixed asset account, represents the amount of the asset cost which has been amortized, or apportioned to past accounting periods. The difference between the asset account and the accumulated depreciation account (the unamortized cost) is referred to as the *book value* of the asset.

Intangibles are generally grouped together under one heading in the balance sheet. This caption might include copyrights, patents, trademarks, and goodwill. Keep in mind that intangible assets should be shown on the balance sheet at *cost* as are other assets. Where these assets have no cost, it may be desirable to record them at some nominal figure so that their existence, at least, will be recognized. This explains why we often find balance sheets with intangibles listed at $1.

Investments shown under the other asset caption are those which are held for long-term purposes. The *investment in nonconsolidated subsidiaries* would represent stock which the company has purchased in other concerns but in which the Gazuntite Paper Company does not yet hold a controlling interest. The *cash surrender value of life insurance* represents investments that the company can obtain only through cashing in the policies. Since the policies will not ordinarily be cancelled, the sums will not be available for use in the business and cannot, therefore, be properly shown as current assets.

The caption *deferred charges* basically covers long-term prepayments. These costs will be charged off against the income of future periods.

The *accounts payable* account is generally the most significant current liability. This account reflects the obligations the company has incurred by purchasing goods on credit. These obligations normally will be due in a relatively short period, possibly thirty to sixty days from the balance sheet date.

Notes payable represent short-term obligations wherein the company has borrowed funds for a relatively short period. These obligations usually bear interest and are supported by written promise to pay.

Current installments on long-term obligations should also be included as a current liability. For example, mortgages generally require installment payment. Those installments on the mortgage that will fall due within one year generally should be treated as current liabilities, whereas the remaining installments should be regarded as long-term liabilities.

Balance sheets often include a number of *accrued* liability accounts. The nature of these accounts was explained in chapter 4. Accrued liabilities might include accrued wages payable, accrued interest payable, accrued federal and state income taxes payable, and similar items.

Corporations often incur long-term debts in the form of *bonds.* The 5⅝ percent sinking fund bonds of the Gazuntite Paper Company are an example of a general credit bond. Long-term debts might also be incurred in the form of *promissory notes,* these latter obligations generally being incurred by borrowing from banks, insurance companies, or other financial institutions. The *mortgage payable* represents a long-term obligation for which the company has pledged certain fixed assets as collateral to assure the loans repayment.

Various deferred credits might be shown under the other liability caption. The *deferred federal income tax liability* shown on the Gazuntite Paper Company's balance sheet represents taxes that must be paid in future periods as a result of special tax concessions given to the company in past periods.

Paid-in capital consists of all amounts contributed by the owners on original and subsequent stock transactions. The *preferred stock* and *common stock* accounts are merely classes of capital stock. The amounts shown in these accounts have usually been determined by an arbitrary par value. The other paid-in capital account reflects amounts paid in which exceed the par value of the stock.

The *retained earnings* account reflects all amounts which have been earned and retained in the business.

Treasury stock consists of shares of the company which, having once been issued, have been reacquired. This account represents a negative stockholders' equity account and has, therefore, been subtracted to arrive at the net stockholders' equity.

THE INCOME STATEMENT

The income statement presents the results of a business' operations for a specified *period of time*. The income statement, by identifying specific revenues and expenses, tells us what has happened during the accounting period. Are we going forward or backward? Why? At what rate? What contributed to our progress? What held us back? These are just a few of the many questions which might be answered by an income statement. One might compare the income statement to a movie camera. Unlike the snapshot, which shows only position at a given moment, the movie shows just what took place along the way. Revenue and expense accounts are set up to measure the business activity during a particular period, and these accounts are summarized and presented in the income statement.

A Service Enterprise

The simplest form of income statement is probably found in a service enterprise. This type of organization earns revenue by offering various services to the public, whereas a merchandising firm earns revenue by selling goods. The income statement of the Speedy Car Wash is shown in Figure 5-2. In this statement all revenues have been itemized first, expenses have been deducted next to arrive at income before taxes, and finally the income taxes have been deducted to arrive at net income. This

Figure 5-2

SPEEDY CAR WASH
Income Statement
Month of June 1970

Revenue:		
Washing revenue	$1,552	
Waxing revenue	330	
Total revenue		$1,882
Expenses:		
Salary and wages expense	$ 817	
Water expense	145	
Insurance	22	
Supplies expense	107	
Depreciation expense	125	
Total operating expense		1,216
Net income before taxes		$ 666
Federal and state income taxes		205
Net income		$ 461

statement provides management with some useful data regarding operations. It can be seen, for example, that waxing cars provided only one-fifth as much revenue as did washing cars.

A Merchandising Concern

The income statement of a merchandising concern differs from that of a service enterprise primarily in the area known as the trading section. This may be seen by referring to the income statement of the Granite Stores, Inc., which appears in Figure 5-3. The trading section has been identified in the left hand margin to assist the student in focusing his attention on this key area.

Normally the most significant expense a merchandising company incurs is the cost of the merchandise it sells. Because of the significance of this expense (called *cost of goods sold*), it is deducted directly from the revenue to arrive at what is called "gross margin" or "gross profit." Actually, "gross margin" is nothing more than a subtotal representing that portion of the revenue which has not been exhausted in covering cost of goods sold. Often this one expense is greater than the sum of all other expenses combined. Because of this significance, the figures used to calculate the cost of goods sold, such as inventories, purchases, freight-in, and purchase returns, are shown in the trading section.

Notice also that certain deductions, called "contra revenues," are made directly from the gross sales (revenues from selling merchandise) to arrive at net sales. Another rather common practice of merchandising companies is to separate the expenses into selling and administrative classifications. Those expenses directly related to getting the goods from the shelves to the customer are classified as selling expenses; all others are administrative expenses.

The income statement of the Granite Stores, Inc., has another feature which differs from that of the simplified Speedy Car Wash presented previously. *Operating income* has been computed by considering only those revenues and expenses which are concerned with the normal business operations. Those items which do not pertain to operations (in this instance, interest income, dividend income, and interest charges) have been shown separately under the heading *nonoperating items*. This practice is often followed so that management may more accurately evaluate the profitability of operations.

The Manufacturing Enterprise

Manufacturing concerns produce the merchandise they sell rather than buying it in finished form as do merchandising firms. The income state-

Figure 5-3

GRANITE STORES, INC.
Income Statement
Year Ended December 31, 1970

Gross sales			$647,500
Less: Sales returns and allowances ...	$ 7,200		
Sales discounts	5,050	12,250	
Net sales			$635,250
Cost of goods sold:			
Merchandise inventory, 1-1-70		$ 87,741	
Purchases	$420,620		
Less: Purchase returns and allowances	15,040		
Net purchases	$405,580		
Freight-in	19,375		
Net cost of goods purchased		424,955	
Goods available for sale		$512,696	
Merchandise inventory, 12-31-70		97,852	
Cost of goods sold			414,844
Gross margin			$220,406
Selling expenses:			
Sales salaries and commissions	$ 40,400		
Depreciation expense, sales floor	15,300		
Depreciation expense, sales equipment	9,500		
Advertising expense	6,290		
Freight-out and delivery expense	3,298		
Sales supplies expense	2,492		
Total selling expense		$ 77,280	
Administrative expense:			
Office salaries	$ 20,250		
Executive compensation	39,155		
Insurance expense	5,272		
Depreciation expense, office bldg.	18,500		
Depreciation expense, office equip. ...	11,000		
Office supplies expense	7,210		
Total administrative expense		101,387	
Total operating expenses			178,667
Operating income			$ 41,739
Nonoperating items:			
Add: Interest income	$ 7,555		
Dividend income	12,240		
Total	$ 19,315		
Deduct: Interest charges	13,303		
Net nonoperating items			6,012
Net income before taxes			$ 47,751
Federal and state income taxes			22,400
Net income			$ 25,351

(vertical label along left: TRADING SECTION)

ments for the two types of concerns are similar except that the trading section lists "cost of goods manufactured" instead of "purchases." The cost of goods manufactured figure is supported by a separate schedule detailing manufacturing costs. A cost of goods manufactured schedule is illustrated in chapter 7.

NOTES TO FINANCIAL STATEMENTS

Most published financial statements are accompanied by numerous footnotes which explain various items presented in the body of the statements. Notes are also used to describe items that have been omitted from the financial statements in accordance with generally accepted accounting principles, but that nevertheless have an important bearing on the company's financial position and/or results of its operations. Some typical footnotes taken from a published report are quoted below.

> STOCK OPTIONS. On May 3, 1965, the shareowners approved a Stock Option Plan for key employees, including officers and directors, which provides for the granting of options for 500,000 additional shares of common stock during the period to April 30, 1970, at option prices per share which shall not be less than the fair market value of the common stock on the date the options are granted. No options had been issued at December 31, 1965, under this plan.
>
> At December 31, 1965, under the Stock Option Plan of 1958, 504,176 shares were under option to employees, including officers and directors, at prices ranging from $36.00 to $51.25 per share representing not less than 95 per cent of the quoted market price of the shares at the time the options were granted. These options may be exercised subject to continued employment and certain other conditions during an approximate four year period, starting one year after the options were granted. They expire at various dates to January 11, 1970. No additional options may be granted under this plan. During 1965 options for 197,154 shares were exercised at prices ranging from $36.00 to $51.25 per share.
>
> RETAINED EARNINGS. Under the terms of a bank loan agreement, as of December 31, 1965, the amount of retained earnings available for cash dividends and distributions on common stock was limited to $41,398,878.
>
> LEGAL MATTERS. In August, 1963 the Federal Trade Commission reversed in part its Hearing Examiner's decision which had dismissed all charges made against the Company and others in a complaint filed in 1958 charging violation of the Federal Trade Commission Act in the production and sale of antibiotics and in obtaining a patent on tetracycline. An order issued by the Commission in January, 1964, would require, among other things, the granting of royalty-bearing licenses by the Company to make, use and sell tetracycline, if it became effective. An appeal has been taken to the Federal courts and no decision was issued as of February 18, 1966.

The order is not in effect during the appeal. As to the Sherman Act antitrust suit filed in 1961 making charges similar to those in the F. T. C. proceeding, certain preliminary proceedings are being conducted in the case, but no date has been set for trial.

Lawsuits have been filed by Pfizer against a number of companies and individuals and against the City of New York for injunction and treble damages as a result of their infringement of Pfizer's tetracycline patent. Some of these defendants have made charges, in counterclaims or in separate actions, similar to those asserted in the Federal Trade Commission case and the Sherman Act antitrust suit mentioned above and have asserted claims for large amounts for alleged damages in some instances. Pfizer has denied and vigorously contests these charges. In the only patent infringement case to reach trial, a Federal Court in Florida ruled in March, 1965, that Pfizer's tetracycline patent is valid and enforceable, and was infringed by the defendant.

As to the antitrust suit filed in 1958 charging monopolization in the manufacture and distribution of citric acid and violation of Section 3 of the Clayton Act, the Federal Court in Brooklyn in May, 1965, ordered that the complaint be dismissed, finding that the Government had failed to prove its charges. The Government has filed a notice of appeal to the Supreme Court.[4]

SUMMARY

The two major financial statements prepared by most companies are the balance sheet and income statement. The balance sheet discloses a company's financial position as reflected in its asset, liability, and owners' equity accounts as of some instant of time. In preparing a balance sheet, the assets are generally classified as current, fixed, or other. The distinction between the first two of these is made primarily on the basis of time. Current assets are those that will normally be converted to cash, sold, or consumed within one year, while fixed assets generally have life beyond the current peiod. Other assets may be distinguished from fixed assets primarily on the basis of use. Fixed assets are used in the business, whereas other assets are not.

Liabilities may be similarly classified as current, long-term, or other, while the classification of owners' equity depends upon the form of business. Partnerships and proprietorships show all of a particular owner's equity in one account, whereas corporations normally distinguish between the contributed capital (paid-in capital) and the retained capital (retained earnings).

Income statements reflect the results of operations during a specified period of time. These statements differ somewhat between service, mer-

---

[4]Chas. Pfizer & Co.,Inc., and Subsidiary Companies, *1965 Annual Report.*

chandising, and manufacturing concerns. The most important distinction is probably seen in the trading section of a merchandising concern. Here details are shown regarding the cost of goods sold, because this expense is normally more significant than all other expenses combined. Expenses are usually classified as either selling or administrative expenses. Items of revenue and expense which do not pertain to the normal business operations are usually shown under a separate caption at the bottom of the statement.

QUESTIONS

1. Name the two primary financial statements prepared by most companies. What types of accounts are reported on each?
2. What are the major account classifications on a balance sheet? List some examples of each type of account.
3. What significant difference is there between the headings of a balance sheet and those of an income statement?
4. What is the purpose of a balance sheet? Of an income statement?
5. Distinguish between current, fixed, and other assets. Could a single item, such as land, appear under different classifications on two different balance sheets?
6. How should the current installment on a long term debt with serial maturity be classified on a balance sheet?
7. On the balance sheets of a partnership and a corporation, how do the owners' equity sections differ?
8. What is a *contra* asset account? Give several examples of contra asset accounts. How should such accounts be shown on a balance sheet?
9. What are deferred charges and deferred credits? Where are such items properly shown on the balance sheet?
10. What is the nature of the Retained Earnings account? Why don't partnerships and proprietorships have Retained Earnings accounts?
11. In what way does the income statement of a merchandising concern differ from that of a service enterprise?
12. Why do firms generally attach notes to published financial statements? What is the nature of the items disclosed therein?
13. What is the difference between the operating income and the net income of a firm?
14. What is gross margin? Why is this figure of such importance to a merchandising firm?
15. What accounts enter into the calculation of a company's cost of goods sold? In what section of the balance sheet does the Cost of Goods Sold account appear?
16. Assume that a company had cost of goods sold of $920,000, beginning inventory of $27,500, selling expenses of $89,900, and goods available for sale of $999,900. How much was its ending inventory?

17. Assume that a firm had cost of goods sold of $44,800, selling expenses of $7,820, administrative expenses of $9,870, and operating income of $4,973. What was the amount of the firm's net sales?

PROBLEMS

Problem 5-1

Using the classifications for various sections of the balance sheet and the income statement as described in this chapter, arrange the following accounts in proper statement form, disregarding amounts, and state on which statement and under which heading each would appear. Classifications for the income statement should include Revenues, Cost of Goods Sold, Administrative Expenses, Selling Expenses, Other Income, and Other Expense.

1. Copyrights
2. Accounts Receivable
3. Accounts Payable
4. Sales
5. Cash in Bank
6. Delivery Wages
7. Interest Earned
8. Mortgage Payable, 5-year
9. Capital Stock
10. Retained Earnings
11. Depreciation Expense, Office Building
12. Purchase Returns and Allowances
13. Land, Held for Future Use
14. Revenue Received in Advance
15. Accumulated Depreciation, Office Building
16. Patents
17. Current Installment on Mortgage
18. Dividend Income
19. Interest Payable
20. Equipment
21. Federal Income Tax Liability
22. Property Taxes, office building
23. Prepaid Rent
24. Unexpired Insurance
25. Ending Inventory
26. Long-term Investments
27. Accrued Salaries
28. Administrative Salaries
29. Land
30. Freight-in
31. Commissions Earned
32. Interest Expense
33. Freight-out
34. Salesmen's Commissions

Problem 5-2

The adjusted trial balance of Super Sales Corporation is shown below, with the accounts listed in alphabetical order.

SUPER SALES CORPORATION
Adjusted Trial Balance
December 31, 1970

Accounts Payable		22,320.00
Accounts Receivable	59,200.00	
Accumulated Depreciation, Building		15,350.00
Advertising Expense	5,920.00	
Building	250,000.00	
Capital Stock		200,000.00
Cash	12,922.00	
Depreciation Expense, Building	10,000.00	

Freight-out	2,300.00	
Insurance Expense	4,800.00	
Interest Expense	950.00	
Inventory (December 31, 1969)	22,489.00	
Land	40,000.00	
Long-term Investments	22,921.00	
Miscellaneous Expenses	3,200.00	
Mortgage Payable		20,000.00
Purchases	110,300.00	
Purchase Discounts		1,492.00
Retained Earnings		54,141.00
Sales		285,300.00
Supplies	3,255.00	
Supplies Used	11,111.00	
Taxes	7,300.00	
Transportation-in	1,995.00	
Wages and Salaries	29,940.00	
	598,603.00	598,603.00

Inventory, December 31, 1970: $ 29,585.00

Required:
    a. Income statement in good form.
    b. Balance sheet in good form.

Problem 5-3
    Part 1: Determine the missing amounts in the following sets of figures. Each vertical row represents a separate situation. Use a minus sign to indicate a loss.

	(a)	(b)	(c)	(d)	(e)	(f)	(g)	(h)
Sales	70,000	105,000	125,000	(8)	90,000	(14)	90,000	80,000
Beginning Inventory	40,000	45,000	60,000	40,000	(11)	40,000	30,000	40,000
Purchases..	30,000	(4)	(6)	70,000	60,000	50,000	55,000	(20)
Ending Inventory	(1)	55,000	40,000	35,000	45,000	30,000	(17)	45,000
Cost of Goods Sold	55,000	60,000	(7)	(9)	(12)	(15)	50,000	50,000
Gross Margin..	(2)	(5)	55,000	40,000	40,000	40,000	(18)	(21)
Expenses ..	20,000	25,000	35,000	35,000	(13)	(16)	15,000	(22)
Net Income (Loss)..	(3)	20,000	20,000	(10)	20,000	−5,000	(19)	20,000

    Part 2: The following account balances are found in the ledger of a merchandising concern: Sales $13,220; Purchases, $9,860; Sales Returns and Allowances, $420; Purchase Returns and Allowances, $160; Freight-in, $190; Freight-out, $320; Purchase Discounts, $130; Selling Expenses, $650;

Inventory, August 1, 1970, $5,140; Inventory, August 31, 1970, $5,560. Prepare the "trading section" of the income statement.

Problem 5-4

Following are the errors found in the December 31, 1970, adjusted trial balance of Gadgets Corporation:

1. Beginning inventory overstated, $1,000.
2. Purchase discounts omitted, $200 (counterbalancing error in Accounts Payable).
3. Ending inventory overstated, $2,000.
4. Sales discounts understated, $100.
5. Freight-out, $500, added to Freight-in in the Cost of Goods Sold section of the income statement.

Required:

a. Describe the effect (overstatement or understatement) of each error on the 1970 net income.
b. Describe the effect of each error on retained earnings reported at the end of 1970.
c. Explain which, if any, of the above errors, if not corrected, would affect the income reported for 1971. How?

Problem 5-5

The adjusted trial balance for the Bateman Manufacturing Company is presented below:

BATEMAN MANUFACTURING COMPANY
Adjusted Trial Balance
June 30, 1970

Cash	118,690.00	
Marketable Securities at Cost (market value, $125,870)...	123,950.00	
Accounts Receivable	86,430.00	
Allowance for Doubtful Accounts		9,760.00
Prepaid Insurance	1,840.00	
Investment in Stock of Lance Company[a]	98,650.00	
Land	57,130.00	
Buildings	148,960.00	
Accumulated Depreciation, Buildings		66,540.00
Equipment	251,720.00	
Accumulated Depreciation, Equipment		43,600.00
Goodwill	72,000.00	
Cash Surrender Value of Life Insurance on Company Officers	7,780.00	
Accounts Payable		40,930.00

Notes Payable		16,500.00
Accrued Wages and Other		
Expenses		21,370.00
Estimated Income Taxes		
Payable		25,900.00
Notes Payable, due June 30, 1972		350,000.00
Deferred Rental Revenue		1,850.00
Capital Stock, $10 par value		325,000.00
Premium on Stock		21,750.00
Retained Earnings		42,430.00
Gross Sales		1,253,800.00
Sales Returns and Allowances ...	18,180.00	
Sales Discounts	9,930.00	
Merchandise Inventory,		
July 1, 1969	148,640.00	
Purchases	771,460.00	
Purchase Returns and Allowances		18,800.00
Freight-in	20,930.00	
Salesmen's Salaries	36,800.00	
Advertising	17,890.00	
Shipping Department Expense ...	19,130.00	
Freight and Delivery Expense ...	16,720.00	
Depreciation, Store and		
Equipment	2,990.00	
Officers' Salaries	31,640.00	
Office Salaries	18,900.00	
Taxes	6,170.00	
Insurance	1,820.00	
Utilities	8,440.00	
Depreciation, Office and Office		
Equipment	4,350.00	
Interest and Dividends on		
Investments		5,250.00
Rent Revenue		4,800.00
Interest Expense	12,750.00	
Estimated Income Tax Charges...	134,170.00	
	2,248,060.00	2,248,060.00

Merchandise Inventory, June 30, 1970: $202,500.00

---

[a]Lance Company stock is being held as a long-term investment.

Required:
   a. Prepare a classified balance sheet in good form.
   b. Prepare an income statement in good form.

Problem 5-6
   The following data were taken from the accounts of the Standard Corporation. Except where otherwise noted, the figures all represent adjusted balances as of December 31, 1970.

Accounts Payable	$24,950.00
Accounts Receivable	41,490.00
Accrued Salaries	1,860.00
Accumulated Depreciation, Store Fixtures	2,790.00
Advertising	880.00
Allowance for Doubtful Accounts	7,090.00
Bad Debt Expense	870.00
Cash	8,690.00
Common Stock, par value $50	33,300.00
Depreciation Expense, Store Fixtures	780.00
Freight-out	730.00
Income Tax	1,500.00
Land	24,820.00
Long-term Investments	10,460.00
Merchandise Inventory, January 1, 1970	47,420.00
Merchandise Inventory, December 31, 1970	48,720.00
Mortgage Payable	26,280.00
Office Expenses	2,220.00
Office Salaries	11,540.00
Prepaid Rent	850.00
Purchases	23,360.00
Rent Revenue	1,960.00
Retained Earnings, January 1, 1970	44,550.00
Sales	82,680.00
Salesmen's Commissions	38,890.00
Store Fixtures	7,850.00
Store Rent	2,040.00
Transportation-in	1,070.00

Required:
  a. Prepare a classified balance sheet as of December 31, 1970, in good form.
  b. Prepare an income statement for the year ending December 31, 1970.

Problem 5-7

The following amounts were taken from the books of the Kendall Corporation. The accounts are listed in alphabetical order.

Advertising	$	680.00
Bad Debts Expense		210.00
Depreciation Expense, Delivery Equipment		300.00
Depreciation Expense, Office		1,600.00
Freight-out		960.00
Income Tax		8,960.00
Insurance Expense		70.00
Interest Earned		210.00
Interest Expense		70.00
Merchandise Inventory (beginning)		1,730.00
Miscellaneous Selling Expenses		270.00
Office Salaries		3,800.00
Purchase Returns and Allowances		2,000.00

Purchases $29,000.00
Rent Revenue 1,300.00
Sales ....   ?
Sales Discounts 300.00
Sales Returns and Allowances 200.00
Salesmen's Commissions and Salaries 2,700.00
Store Rent 2,450.00
Taxes (other than income) 380.00
Transportation-in 230.00

The net income after taxes was $13,400, and the ending merchandise
inventory was $1,850.

Required:
   a. Calculate the gross sales for the Kendall Corporation for the
      period.
   b. Prepare an income statement in good form.

Case 5
BIG SKY GAS

Mr. I. K. Knowitall is the sole owner of the Big Sky Gas station. Early
in January he decided to make an addition to his station and went to the
local bank to borrow the money. The banker, Mr. Bright, said, "We'd
be happy to do business with you, but we'll need to have a look at your
financial statements in order to agree on the amount and terms of the
loan. If you will bring me your balance sheet and income statement for
this past year, I'll look them over so we can talk further about the loan."

Mr. Knowitall had never had a balance sheet or income statement, but
didn't want the bank to know this so he replied, "O.K., Mr. Bright, I'll have
to dig them out of my files and that might take a little time. Will it be
all right to bring them to you next week?" Mr. Bright agreed, and Mr.
Knowitall went back to his station to "find" the balance sheet and income
statement.

Mr. Knowitall had taken bookkeeping in high school and so thought
he knew all there was about making financial statements. He rummaged
through old records and found he had bought the station for $25,000 just
two years earlier. He paid $5,000 cash and signed a fifteen-year mortgage
note for the balance. The station was expected to last twenty years with
no salvage value. When the business was formed (two years ago), Mr.
Knowitall also contributed an old tow truck which had a market value
of $2,500 at that date. He estimated the truck had an additional ten years
of useful life, with no expected salvage value. Additional tools and equipment for doing motor tune-ups and minor auto repairs were purchased
just one year ago at a cost of $1,500. This equipment should last five years
with no salvage value.

The annual statement from the mortgage company shows that $100 interest has accrued against the mortgage note. In addition, a $1,000 principal installment will be due in one month. The remaining $17,700 balance on the note will be paid off in installments which are payable from one to thirteen years hence. The business employs three full-time employees besides the owner. An examination of the cash records for the past year discloses the following:

Receipts:

Gas	$110,000
Lubrication	20,000
Oil and tires	40,000
Tune-ups	60,000

Disbursements:

Owner's drawings	$ 15,000
Employees' wages	30,000
Gas	100,000
Oil and tires	22,000
Grease	5,000
Parts	10,000
Utilities	3,600
Insurance	2,400

The cash account had a balance of $5,000 at year's end. Mr. Knowitall estimated inventories were about $15,000 at the end of each of the last two years. At year's end customers still owed balances in the amount of $10,000 on charge sales. No charge sales were made during the company's first year in business. Experience of other stations in the area shows that about 2½ percent of customers' accounts prove uncollectible. Of the $60,000 cash received for tune-ups, $10,000 represents advances from customers for repairs which have not yet been performed. This work is expected to be completed within two or three months. The $2,400 insurance premium was paid one year ago and covers a three-year period.

After much effort, Mr. Knowitall constructed the following balance sheet and income statement:

Exhibit 5-1

BIG SKY GAS
Income Statement
As of December 31

Revenues:

Gas	$120,000	
Oil and tires	40,000	
Lubrication	20,000	
Tune-ups and maintenance	60,000	
Total revenues		$240,000

Expenses:

Knowitall drawings	$ 15,000	
Employees' wages	30,000	
Cost of gas	100,000	
Cost of oil and tires	22,000	
Cost of lube	5,000	
Cost of tune-ups, maintenance and parts	10,000	
Utilities	3,600	
Insurance	2,400	
Total expenses		188,000
Profit		$ 52,000

Exhibit 5-2

BIG SKY GAS
Balance Sheet

Current Assets:			Current Liabilities:		
Cash	$ 5,000		Accounts payable	$ 4,000	
Accounts receivable	10,000		Accumulated		
Inventories on hand	15,000		depreciation	1,450	
Accrued interest on			Reserve for bad debts	250	
building note	100				
Fixed Assets:			Long-term Liabilities:		
Station	25,000		Current installment		
Equipment	1,500		on building note	1,000	
Other Assets:					
Tow truck	2,500		Owner's Equity:		
Prepaid insurance	2,400		Owner's equity	28,800	
	$61,500			$61,500	

As an afterthought, Mr. Knowitall decides that it might be a good idea to have an accountant check his balance sheet and income sheet before Mr. Bright sees them. As that accountant, answer the following questions:

1. Are the income statement and balance sheet correctly prepared?
2. Make any changes you feel necessary to correct the income statement and balance sheet.
3. How are contra assets handled? Contra liabilities? Depreciation?
4. As Mr. Bright, would you lend Mr. Knowitall money? Assume Mr. Bright's requirement for loan approval is a current ratio (Current Assets/Current Liabilities) of 5.0 or more. Show calculations.

6

Accounting
for Merchandise
Inventories

There are three major problems associated with accounting for inventories: how to arrive at quantities, how to value these quantities, and how to arrive at the cost of the inventories.

ARRIVING AT QUANTITIES

There are two common methods used to arrive at the quantity of goods on hand at any particular date: periodic physical count or perpetual records.

Periodic Inventory

Periodic inventory has the advantage of simplicity of record keeping. No accounting records of quantities on hand are maintained under this system. Rather, when this information is needed for preparation of financial statements, a physical count of all goods on hand is made. The taking of a physical count is no easy task, since operations must be stopped and everything from "wall to wall" counted. Inasmuch as taking a physical inventory is such a major task, it is normally not done very often. Most concerns perform this physical count only once each year at the end of the fiscal period. Companies which carry many line items of relatively low unit value typically use this physical inventory system.

Perpetual Inventory

Under the perpetual inventory system, running records which reflect at all times the quantity of goods on hand are maintained. Each time a purchase or sale is made, the change is recorded on a stock record card. This, of course, requires a rather extensive system of records and normally would be practical only where the unit value of the goods is relatively high. Physical counts are generally made at regular intervals to verify the accuracy of the perpetual records. Since these can be made at longer intervals and staggered by type of goods, the hardship is considerably less than would be the case with a complete "wall to wall" count. Inventory control and the ability to prepare interim statements may be cited as two of the chief advantages of the perpetual system.

VALUING INVENTORIES

Having arrived at the quantity of goods on hand at a given date by either the periodic or perpetual method, the next task is to price them. But at what value? At least four different values might be used: *cost, market, selling price,* or *standard cost.*

Cost

The American Institute of Certified Public Accountants has stated:

> The primary basis of accounting for inventories is cost, which has been defined generally as the price paid or considerations given to acquire an asset. As applied to inventories, cost means in principle the sum of the applicable expenditures and charges directly or indirectly incurred in bringing an article to its existing conditions and locations.[1]

---

[1] *Accounting Research and Terminology Bulletins,* final ed. (New York: American Institute of Certified Public Accountants, 1961), p. 28.

In short, this means that the cost of an inventory includes all expenditures made to get the goods onto the shelves and ready for sale. For a merchandising concern, this would be chiefly the invoice price plus freight-in. Storage costs could also be included where they are significant in amount. For a manufacturing concern, the cost would include all production costs: materials used, direct labor, and manufacturing overhead.

Cost or Market

The conservative principle of accounting dictates a departure from cost in those instances where the market price is lower than the original cost. The acceptable practice is to value inventories at "lower of cost or market."

> As used in the phrase *lower of cost or market*, the term *market* means current replacement cost (by purchase or by reproduction, as the case may be), except that:
> 1. Market should not exceed the net realizable value (i.e., estimated selling price in the ordinary course of business, less reasonably predictable costs of completion and disposal); and
> 2. Market should not be less than net realizable value reduced by an allowance for an approximately normal profit margin.[2]

The "cost or market" rule may be applied to each separate item in the inventory, the total of components of each major category, or the total of the inventory.[3]

In an economic climate featuring "creeping" inflation such as we have experienced in this country for several decades, the application of the cost-or-market rule poses no difficult problem. In the vast majority of cases, cost is the lower of the two and is, therefore, the common basis for valuing inventories.

Selling Price

Only in rare instances are inventories valued at their selling prices. Such practice may be justified if:

1. The company is unable to determine the appropriate approximate costs
2. The product has immediate marketability at quoted market price (marketing is no problem)
3. The product has the characteristic of unit interchangeability.

---

[2]Ibid., p. 31.
[3]Ibid., p. 32.

The most likely example of a product which might be valued at selling price is gold or some other precious metal.

Standard Costs

Many manufacturing concerns employ a system of accounting known as standard costing. This subject is discussed at greater length in chapter 17. Suffice it to say here that standard costs are not actual costs, but "should" costs. They are regarded as acceptable for pricing inventories, provided they are "adjusted at reasonable intervals to reflect current conditions so that at balance-sheet date standard costs reasonably approximate costs computed under one of the recognized bases."[4]

ARRIVING AT COST

While other bases for valuing inventory are sometimes used, one must conclude from the foregoing discussion that most inventories are valued at cost. The next question is, "Which cost?" If quantities of a given product are purchased at several different prices, then one must decide which of these cost figures is appropriate for pricing the inventory. There are four acceptable methods of arriving at cost: *first-in, first-out* (FIFO), *last-in, first-out* (LIFO), *weighted average,* and *specific identification.* An example of a physical flow paralleling each of these methods is cited in the following paragraphs. It should be noted, however, that the accountant is not as much concerned with the physical flow as he is with the cost flow. The major concern in choosing the appropriate cost method should be to select that method which best matches costs and revenues in a particular case. This might mean selecting FIFO costing even though the goods physically flow on a LIFO basis.

FIFO

First-in, first-out (FIFO) assumes that the earliest goods purchased are the first to be sold and, therefore, the costs which should be assigned to the unsold goods (ending inventory) are the *most recent costs.* For this reason, the FIFO method could be referred to as the *most recent invoice method* of pricing inventories. Perishable products in a grocery store, such as milk, would normally follow FIFO flow, i.e., the most recently purchased milk would be placed at the back of the cooler so that the customer would purchase the oldest milk first. Grocers are often cautioned to rotate their

---

[4]Ibid., p. 30.

stock. This is just another way of saying the physical flow should follow the FIFO method.

LIFO

Last-in, first-out (LIFO) assumes just the opposite flow, that is, that the customer always purchases the most recently acquired goods, always leaving the oldest goods unsold. This means that the inventory is priced from the oldest invoices. An example of LIFO physical flow would be a bin of bolts in a hardware store. As new bolts are purchased by the hardware store, they are emptied into the bin. When a customer purchases a bolt, he selects one of the most recently acquired ones from the top, leaving the oldest bolts in the bins. The ending inventory would always consist of old bolts, many of them the same, period after period.

Weighted Average

Weighted average assumes that each sale contains a weighted portion of the beginning inventory and of each of the purchases made during the period. Gasoline purchased at a service station is an example where the physical flow corresponds to the above assumption. Each time new gasoline is placed in the tank by the distributor, it mixes with the contents of the tank. Each gallon delivered from the tank includes a fraction of each of the quantities previously placed in the tank.

Specific Identification

Specific identification of units sold and on hand is usually accomplished by means of serial numbers or some sort of identification tags. New automobiles are easily inventoried in this manner by referring to the manufacturer's serial number. Documents related to both the purchase and sale of a new car refer to this serial number, thus making it easy to determine the costs associated with any particular unit.

Extended Illustration

With two methods of arriving at quantities and four methods of arriving at their costs, we have quite a variety of possible inventory values. In the discussion that follows, we shall illustrate some of these various possibilities.

Periodic Inventory Illustration

Let us assume the following facts:

DATE	PURCHASES
September 1	50 @ $50
September 3	75 @ $51
September 10	100 @ $52
September 25	60 @ $53

Physical count on September 30, 70 units.

The cost of the ending inventory utilizing the FIFO periodic assumption would be $3,700. Since the first units available have been sold, the most recently acquired are still on hand. The ending inventory would be calculated as follows:

$$60 \ @ \ \$53 = \$3,180$$
$$10 \ @ \ \$52 = \quad 520$$
$$\overline{\$3,700}$$

The cost of the ending inventory, utilizing the LIFO periodic assumption, would be $3,520. Under the periodic method we have no information on just when the goods were sold, so we assume that all the goods were available before any were disposed of. Since the last ones were sold first, the beginning ones would still be on hand. The ending inventory would be calculated as follows:

$$50 \ @ \ \$50 = \$2,500$$
$$20 \ @ \ \$51 = \quad 1,020$$
$$\overline{\$3,520}$$

The cost of the ending inventory under the weighted average periodic method would be $3,613.40, calculated as follows:

$$50 \ @ \ \$50 = \$ \ 2,500$$
$$75 \ @ \ \$51 = \quad 3,825$$
$$100 \ @ \ \$52 = \quad 5,200$$
$$60 \ @ \ \$53 = \quad 3,180$$
$$\overline{285 \qquad \$14,705}$$

Average cost, $51.62 ($14,705 ÷ 285 units).
Ending inventory, $3,613.40 (70 units @ $51.62).

Perpetual Inventory Illustration

Under the perpetual system, we would have details as to when specific quantities were sold. In addition to the facts regarding purchases used in the previous illustration, let us assume the following:

September 7	Sold 100 units
September 15	Sold 60 units
September 29	Sold 55 units

The cost of the ending inventory, utilizing the FIFO perpetual method, would be $3,700, the same as under the periodic FIFO method. Inasmuch as we cannot have negative quantities on hand, the FIFO periodic and the FIFO perpetual will aways give the same answer. The calculations of FIFO perpetual are shown in Figure 6-1.

Figure 6-1

FIFO PERPETUAL

DATE	PURCHASES	SALES	BALANCE ON HAND
Sept. 1	50 @ $50		50 @ $50
Sept. 3	75 @ $51		50 @ $50 75 @ $51
Sept. 7		50 @ $50 50 @ $51	25 @ $51
Sept. 10	100 @ $52		25 @ $51 100 @ $52
Sept. 15		25 @ $51 35 @ $52	65 @ $52
Sept. 25	60 @ $53		65 @ $52 60 @ $53
Sept. 29		55 @ $52	10 @ $52 60 @ $53

The cost of the ending inventory, utilizing the LIFO perpetual assumption, would be $3,595. The calculation of this amount is shown in Figure 6-2.

The cost of the ending inventory, utilizing the weighted average perpetual assumption, would be $3,663.80. Note in Figure 6-3 that a new weighted average is calculated after *each* purchase. This is done by averaging the cost of the units on hand at that time with the cost of the goods purchased.

Figure 6-2

LIFO PERPETUAL

DATE	PURCHASES	SALES	BALANCE ON HAND
Sept. 1	50 @ $50		50 @ $50
Sept. 3	75 @ $51		50 @ $50 75 @ $51
Sept. 7		75 @ $51 25 @ $50	25 @ $50
Sept. 10	100 @ $52		25 @ $50 100 @ $52
Sept. 15		60 @ $52	25 @ $50 40 @ $52
Sept. 25	60 @ $53		25 @ $50 40 @ $52 60 @ $53
Sept. 29		55 @ $53	25 @ $50 40 @ $52 5 @ $53

Figure 6-3

WEIGHTED AVERAGE PERPETUAL

DATE	PURCHASES	SALES	BALANCE ON HAND
Sept. 1	50 @ $50		50 @ $50.00
Sept. 3	75 @ $51		125 @ $50.60
Sept. 7		100 @ $50.60	25 @ $50.60
Sept. 10	100 @ $52		125 @ $51.72
Sept. 15		60 @ $51.72	65 @ $51.72
Sept. 25	60 @ $53		125 @ $52.34
Sept. 29		55 @ $52.34	70 @ $52.34

COMPARISON OF INVENTORY METHODS

In a period of stable prices, there would be little reason to advocate one method of inventory valuation over another. The differences in inventory values noted in the preceding examples can be attributed solely to the price changes. The total value of goods available for sale is the same in each case. The difference comes in how much of this cost is allocated to inventory and how much to goods sold. This may be seen more clearly in Figure 6-4. Note that, of the three methods, the LIFO method allocates the largest portion to cost of goods sold and the least to inventory. In periods of rising prices, LIFO will consistently charge proportionately more to the cost of goods sold. In periods of declining prices, on the other hand, LIFO will charge proportionately more to inventory.

Figure 6-4

COMPARISON OF METHODS OF ARRIVING AT INVENTORY COSTS UNDER PERIODIC INVENTORY METHOD

	FIFO	LIFO	WA
Cost of:			
Goods Sold	$11,005	$11,185	$11,092
Ending Inventory	3,700	3,520	3,613
Total Goods Available for Sale	$14,705	$14,705	$14,705

This phenomenon accounts for the increased popularity of LIFO in recent years. Many companies have switched from FIFO to LIFO during the last several decades in order to minimize their income tax liability. By increasing the cost of goods sold, LIFO reduces the company's profits, which in turn reduces the amount of income taxes assessed.

One of the weaknesses of LIFO inventory valuation is found in the effect it has on the balance sheet. This method can result in showing the inventories on the balance sheet in terms of costs prevailing many years earlier. While LIFO inventory valuation admittedly improves the income statement, it does so at the expense of the balance sheet. Although this distortion may not be serious at first, it becomes increasingly serious as time goes on. Each year the spread between the inventory cost as shown on the balance sheet and the current market price widens. This may be seen by referring to a specific example. Assume that the Center Lumber Company started carrying cement in one-hundred-pound bags in 1945, when the cost was $0.75 per bag. Each year since that date the company has sold five hundred bags during the year and has had a physical inventory of fifty bags at year end. The most recent purchases by the company were as follows:

100 bags @ $1.50
100 bags @ $1.51
100 bags @ $1.52
100 bags @ $1.53
100 bags @ $1.54
100 bags @ $1.55

Under LIFO inventory valuation, the fifty bags on hand at the end of the current year would be valued at $0.75 each, or a total of $37.50. This means that the inventory figure shown in the balance sheet would be stated in terms of the cost prevailing over twenty years ago. The three methods of inventory valuation for this specific situation are compared in Figure 6-5. Note that while the LIFO inventory method does give a slightly higher cost of goods sold (and, accordingly, a tax saving), it results in a very substantial undervaluation of inventory shown in the balance sheet.

Figure 6-5

COMPARISON OF METHODS OF ARRIVING
AT COST OF FIFTY BAGS OF CEMENT

	FIFO	LIFO	WA
Cost of Goods Sold	$762.50[a]	$765.00[b]	$763.50[c]
Cost of Ending Inventory	77.50[d]	37.50[e]	76.35[f]

[a] 50 @ 1.50	[b]100 @ 1.55
100 @ 1.51	100 @ 1.54
100 @ 1.52	100 @ 1.53
100 @ 1.53	100 @ 1.52
100 @ 1.54	100 @ 1.51
50 @ 1.55	

[c] 50 @ 1.50 =   75
100 @ 1.51 = 151
100 @ 1.52 = 152 $840 ÷ 550 = $1.527 average cost
100 @ 1.53 = 153
100 @ 1.54 = 154   500 × $1.527 = $763.50
100 @ 1.55 = 155
──   ───
550   840

[d]50 @ 1.55   [e]50 @ .75   [f]50 × $1.527 =
                                                    $76.35

LIFO and the Price Level Problem

Actually, the use of the LIFO inventory method is a partial attempt to solve a much broader problem. The real problem stems from the changing value of the dollar. Dollars of different buying power are all treated in the financial statements as though they were equal. It is this fact that causes the serious discrepancies between the various inventory methods just described. A similar problem is felt in other sections of the balance sheet. Depreciation allowances, for example, are inadequate in the fixed asset section for this same reason.

Because the problem affects much more than inventory valuation, the solution cannot come in a piecemeal manner. The solution must ultimately be achieved by attacking the overall problem. An approach to such a solution, the use of price level indexes, is discussed in chapter 21. LIFO, at best, is a stop-gap measure.

ESTIMATING INVENTORIES

Sometimes it is neither practical nor possible to calculate inventory as illustrated in the preceding paragraphs. In these instances, it may be necessary to estimate the value of the goods on hand at a particular date. There are two common methods of estimating inventories: the *gross profit method* and the *retail inventory method*.

The Gross Profit Method

The gross profit method utilizes the gross margin percentage from the prior period or the average gross margin from a number of prior periods to estimate the cost of goods sold. This figure is then deducted from the goods available for sale (beginning inventory plus net purchases) to arrive at the ending inventory. Basically, it assumes that there are only two things that can happen to acquired goods: they can be sold, in which event the costs are transferred to cost of goods sold; or they are still on hand. The gross margin percentage is used to estimate the cost of goods sold, and it is assumed that the remainder of the goods must still be on hand.

In order to illustrate the gross profit method, let us assume that the inventory of the Eleven-Seven Store is destroyed by fire the night of April 23, 1971. The company records, maintained in a fireproof safe, provide the following information:

	NET SALES	COST OF GOODS SOLD
1968	$ 55,000	$32,000
1969	62,000	37,000
1970	51,000	30,000
TOTAL	$168,000	$99,000

Sales, January 1, 1971, to April 23, 1971	$29,300
Purchases, January 1, 1971, to April 23, 1971	25,400
Freight-in, January 1, 1971, to April 23, 1971	1,100
Inventory, January 1, 1971	7,200

First of all, the figures from prior years may be utilized to determine the average gross profit experienced by the firm over the past several years. In examining these figures, we note that net sales have averaged $56,000 per year, while cost of goods sold has averaged $33,000 per year. This means that the cost of goods sold has averaged about 59 percent of net sales ($33,000/$56,000), and gross margin has averaged about 41 percent of net sales ($23,000/$56,000). Utilizing this past cost/selling price relationship, we can calculate the estimated value of the ending inventory as follows:

Beginning Inventory		$ 7,200
Purchases	$25,400	
Freight-in	1,100	
Net Purchases		26,500
Goods Available for Sales		33,700
Less Cost of Goods Sold		
(59 percent of $29,300 Net Sales)		17,287
Estimated Cost of Ending Inventory		$16,413

All of the figures necessary to calculate the goods available for sale are available directly from the company records. By first calculating that portion of the goods sold (utilizing the complement of the gross profit percentage), it is a matter of simple arithmetic to find the unsold portion (the ending inventory).

The Retail Inventory Method

Under the retail inventory method, records are maintained which indicate the cost and selling price of all goods available for sale. A rate is then calculated to determine the average percentage of the marked selling prices represented by cost. This percentage can be applied to the actual sales of the period to estimate the cost of goods sold. This latter figure can then be deducted from the goods available for sale (at cost) to estimate the cost of the ending inventory. The main difference between the gross profit and retail methods is that the former method utilizes the historical cost/selling price relationship (expressed as an average gross profit rate), whereas the latter utilizes the current or expected cost/selling price relationship.

A simple illustration of the retail inventory method follows:

	COST	SELLING PRICE
Beginning Inventory	$ 25,000	$ 45,000
Purchases	165,000	215,000
Freight-in	10,000	
GOODS AVAILABLE FOR SALE[a] .	$200,000	$260,000
Goods Sold at Retail (Sales)		180,000
ENDING INVENTORY AT		
RETAIL		$ 80,000
ENDING INVENTORY AT COST[b]	$ 61,600	

[a]Cost/selling price relationship = $200,000/$260,000 = 77 percent.
[b]The cost of the ending inventory is estimated to be 77 percent of the retail value of the inventory, based upon the cost/selling price relationship calculated above.

JOURNAL ENTRIES FOR MERCHANDISE

The preceding paragraphs have discussed problems associated with determining the dollar value of inventories. Let us now turn to the relatively simple task of recording merchandise transactions in the general journal.

Periodic Inventory Entries

Under the periodic inventory system, no running record is maintained of the merchandise inventory. Instead, details regarding merchandise are accumulated in a series of accounts until the end of the period, at which time the amounts are brought together and sorted according to goods sold (Cost of Goods Sold) and goods which remain unsold (Merchandise Inventory). These separate accounts are maintained to give management details regarding merchandise costs which may be helpful for control purposes. Separate accounts are used for merchandise inventory (this account reflects only beginning and ending balances), purchases, freight-in, purchase discounts, purchase returns, and purchase allowances. The use of these accounts under a periodic inventory system is illustrated by the following transactions:

1. Assume that the Cottonwood Merchandise Mart had on hand at the beginning of the accounting period merchandise which cost $4,000. This amount would appear as the opening balance in the Merchandise Inventory account.

2. The company purchased $23,000 of merchandise on account from Diagonal Wholesale.

   Purchases 23,000
       Accounts Payable, Diagonal Wholesale ..   23,000

3. Freight amounting to $500 was paid on the above shipment.

   Freight-in 500
       Cash   500

4. Some of the goods were improperly labeled, and the wholesaler made an allowance of $100 to the purchase price.

   Accounts Payable, Diagonal Wholesale 100
       Purchase Returns and Allowances   100

5. The balance of the account to Diagonal Wholesale was paid after deducting a cash discount of $458.

```
Accounts Payable, Diagonal Wholesale ......    22,900
     Purchase Discounts ..................                 458
     Cash ..............................              22,442
```

6. For $1,600 Cottonwood Merchandise Mart sold on account goods which cost $1,200.

```
Accounts Receivable ......................     1,600
     Sales ...............................                1,600
```

At the end of the accounting period it is necessary to bring together all the amounts pertaining to merchandise available during the period. Because most of the goods have been sold by the end of the accounting period, this can be accomplished by closing all of the "merchandise" accounts to Cost of Goods Sold, as follows:

```
Cost of Goods Sold .........................   26,942
Purchase Discounts .........................      458
Purchase Returns and Allowances .............      100
     Merchandise Inventory (beginning) .........              4,000
     Purchases ............................              23,000
     Freight-in ...........................                500
```

The above entry charged all merchandise costs off as an expense. Since some of the goods are still on hand, an adjustment is required to record the ending inventory. If a physical count revealed $2,500 worth of goods on hand at the end of the period, the ending merchandise inventory would be recorded as follows:

```
Merchandise Inventory (ending) .................  2,500
     Cost of Goods Sold .......................              2,500
```

The net effect of the preceding entries has been to charge off cost of goods sold, in the amount of $24,442 ($26,942 debit, less $2,500 credit), as an expense of the current period. The remaining $2,500 would appear on the balance sheet as merchandise inventory.

PERPETUAL INVENTORY ENTRIES

Only one account is maintained for merchandise under the perpetual inventory system. This account, known as Merchandise Inventory, is debited with the total cost of merchandise acquired, including the purchase price and the freight-in. The account is likewise credited for any cost reduction, such as purchase discounts and purchase returns. When merchandise is sold, the Merchandise Inventory account is credited with the cost of goods sold, at which time this amount is charged to expense. Thus, the Merchandise Inventory account shows the net cost of the goods on hand at all times. The journal entries required under a perpetual system are shown below, utilizing the same facts as the preceding illustration.

1. Beginning inventory of $4,000.00. This amount would appear in the Merchandise Inventory account at the beginning of the period.
2. Purchase of merchandise for $23,000.00.

Merchandise Inventory	23,000	
Accounts Payable, Diagonal Wholesale ...		23,000

3. Freight-in on the above shipment, $500.00.

Merchandise Inventory	500	
Cash		500

4. Purchase allowance of $100.00.

Accounts Payable, Diagonal Wholesale	100	
Merchandise Inventory		100

5. Payment of the balance due within the discount period.

Accounts Payable, Diagonal Wholesale	22,900	
Merchandise Inventory		458
Cash		22,442

6. Goods which cost $1,200 are sold for $1,600 on account.

Accounts Receivable	1,600	
Sales		1,600
Cost of Goods Sold	1,200	
Merchandise Inventory		1,200

Note that under the perpetual system two entries are required at the time of sale: the first, to record the sales revenue; and the second, to record the cost of goods sold. After the above transactions have been posted, the Merchandise Inventory account would appear as follows:

MERCHANDISE INVENTORY

Beginning Balance	4,000	Purchase Allowance	100
Purchase	23,000	Purchase Discount	458
Freight-in	500	Cost of Goods Sold	1,200

Under either the perpetual or the periodic inventory system it is, of course, necessary to close the Cost of Goods Sold account to Income Summary, as is the case with all other expense accounts.

INVENTORY MANAGEMENT

One of the more significant assets of most business concerns is their inventory. The inventories are the lifeblood of most business organizations because they are the major source of revenue. Controlling the level and cost of these inventories is one of the major concerns of management. If the inventory levels become too low, the entire production process may be stopped for the lack of a single part; or, in other cases, customers may become dissatisfied and turn to competitors who carry a more complete stock. If the inventory levels are too high, on the other hand, excessive "carrying costs" such as costs of storage, spoilage, and capital are incurred.

Selecting and maintaining the best inventory level is indeed a difficult and complex task that taxes the imagination of the most astute management. For many years, the problem of inventory management seemed to be approached according to a "feelin' in the bones." Management would periodically look over the stock and order whatever seemed to be needed, based upon a very superficial review of the stock levels. Often, management learned of the items most in demand by attempting to satisfy a customer's request and then finding the item out of stock: "We can order one of those for you if you'd like, but it will take two or three weeks." This "stock out" method was a common means of arriving at the inventory needs and often seemed adequate for the small business.

Recent years have seen a marked trend toward scientific inventory management techniques. This move has been prompted by a number of factors. First of all, as business units have grown in size and complexity, the *need* for scientific management of inventory has become more apparent. Second, the buyer in our society seems to have become much more sophisticated and well informed. Where a buyer once was content to "wait it out" when informed of a stock out, today he is more likely to turn to a competitor. His dissatisfaction seems to be more lasting as well. Often, a lost sale means a lost customer.

The most important factor prompting a move to scientific inventory control has probably been the development of new methods and machines. In recent years advanced mathematical and statistical techniques which have made certain inventory information available for the first time have been developed. The use of electronic data processing and modern communication devices has helped make this information available at lightning speed. A part needed by a customer in one sector of the country can now be located, ordered, and shipped across the entire nation within hours. Computers with vast memories can report the quantity and location of goods stored in hundreds of locations, then calculate the fastest and least expensive method of shipment, and even automatically prepare a requisition to replace the item in inventory. The possibilities of these modern tools are almost overwhelming. Many companies are now managing their inventories by utilizing these scientific methods and machines.

SUMMARY

There are three major problems associated with accounting for inventories: how to arrive at the quantities, how to value these quantities, and how to arrive at the cost of the inventories. A company may arrive at the quantity of goods on hand at a particular date either by physical count or by the maintenance of perpetual inventory records. The quantities so arrived at should normally be valued at the lower of cost or market value.

Where the cost is used to value the inventory and where the goods have been purchased at a variety of prices, the paramount question becomes which costs to use to value the inventory. Four methods are regarded as acceptable for apportioning the cost of goods available between the goods sold and the goods on hand. First-in, first-out (FIFO) assigns the most recent cost to the inventory and the balance to the goods sold. Last-in, first-out (LIFO) assigns the oldest costs to inventory and the more recent costs to the goods sold. The weighted average method averages the costs and then apportions these costs to the inventory and the goods sold at the same rate. The specific identification method identifies the specific goods on hand or sold with their actual cost.

Sometimes it is necessary to estimate the value of the inventories at a particular date. This may be done by either the gross profit method or retail inventory method. Both of these utilize the cost/selling price relationship to arrive at a usable rate for estimating the inventory.

Because inventories are such a significant asset and the key to the profitability of many business enterprises, their proper management and control are vital. The development in recent years of advanced mathematical and statistical techniques has greatly increased the interest in scientific inventory management. Many progressive companies have coupled these techniques with modern electronic data processing and communications equipment to provide fast, efficient, and economical inventory management.

QUESTIONS

1. Distinguish between the two major methods of determining the quantity of merchandise on hand at a particular date.

2. What is the "cost or market" rule used in valuing inventories? Name three ways in which the rule could be employed.

3. What are the two primary methods used to estimate inventories? Why is it sometimes necessary or desirable to use these methods? What do both methods have in common?

4. What are the four methods used to arrive at the cost of an inventory? Cite an example of the physical flow of goods for each of these methods. What is the primary criterion for selecting a method of arriving at an inventory's cost?

5. Assume that a company purchased a single commodity at three different prices: $5, $6, and $7 per unit, in that sequence. At the end of the period, one unit was on hand. At what price should this be valued if the company uses FIFO costing? LIFO? Weighted Average?

6. Why do the LIFO periodic and LIFO perpetual methods usually give different inventory valuations? Why do FIFO periodic and FIFO perpetual give the same inventory valuation?

7. The Central Furniture Company had a fire on September 3. The goods available for sale to the date of the fire were $185,000; the sales to that date were $212,000; and the customary gross margin rate was 40 percent. What was the approximate value of the firm's inventory at the time of the fire?

8. Which inventory costing method best matches current costs with current revenue? Does this method always produce the "best" matching? Explain.

9. Which inventory costing method do you feel is best from the standpoint of the balance sheet? Why?

10. Is it ever acceptable to value inventories at their current selling price? If so, under what circumstances?

11. Explain why LIFO inventory valuation has been so popular in recent years. What problem is LIFO really trying to overcome?

12. Why is inventory management important? What tools do modern managers have to assist them in this crucial task?

13. How do the inventory accounts differ under the perpetual and periodic inventory methods? What difference does this make in the adjusting and closing entries at the end of the period?

PROBLEMS

Problem 6-1

Part 1: Ace Sporting Goods closes its books quarterly and maintains a perpetual inventory system. The following information is available for the first quarter of 1971:

	QUANTITY	UNIT PRICE
Beginning inventory	150	$2.00
Purchases:		
January 15	150	1.90
February 12	75	2.00
March 8	100	2.10
March 29	100	2.20
Sales:		
January 8	100	
January 20	125	
February 18	50	
March 13	100	
	375	

Required:

Compute the cost of the ending inventory and the cost of goods sold under each of the following methods:

a. FIFO
b. LIFO
c. Moving average

Part 2: A physical count at the end of the quarter verified the perpetual records as correct. Mr. Ace, however, feels that the perpetual records are too cumbersome. He wishes to abandon them, but is concerned about the effect this would have on his financial statements.

Required:

Using the same figures, compute for him the cost of the ending inventory and cost of goods sold under each of the three above assumptions, assuming further that he had NOT maintained perpetual records for the first quarter.

Part 3: Assume that all sales were made at $3.00 per unit, and that operating expenses for the period were $300. Compute his net profit under:

Required:

a. Perpetual FIFO
b. Perpetual LIFO
c. Periodic FIFO
d. Periodic LIFO

Part 4: Your calculations in Part 3 should indicate to you the significant effect on income which the choice of inventory valuation methods can have.

Required:

Explain the significance of the choice between FIFO and LIFO under periodic and under perpetual. What is the cause of the variations?

Problem 6-2

On the night of April 14 of the current year, Arnold Anderson's store caught fire. Everything except the accounting records, which were kept in a fireproof vault, was destroyed. Mr. Anderson filed an insurance claim listing an inventory loss of $38,000. As a fire insurance adjuster you called on Mr. Anderson to verify this claim. From the accounting records the following information is available:

1. Merchandise inventory on January 1 of the current year $ 21,820
2. Sales from January 1 through April 14   108,840
3. Purchase returns for the same period   3,460
4. Purchases from January 1 through April 14   57,910
5. Freight-in from January 1 through April 14   2,160
6. Sales returns for the same period   2,175
7. The company indicates that gross profit this year is expected to be about the same as the average for the previous five years.
8. Facts from prior years:

YEAR	NET SALES	COST OF GOODS SOLD	OPERATING EXPENSE
1965	$ 80,000	$47,000	$30,000
1966	100,000	61,000	44,000
1967	120,000	80,000	56,000
1968	90,000	53,000	42,000
1969	110,000	70,000	51,000

Required:

Indicate your estimate as to the cost of the inventory at the time of the fire. Show your computations.

Problem 6-3

During the month of March, the Shady Sales Company completed the following transactions:

March 2   Purchased 500 widgets at a cost of $3,000 on account from Widget Company.

March 5   Sold sixty widgets (our cost, $360) for $600 on account to Wilson Company.

March 8   Returned ten damaged widgets (cost, $60) to Widget Company for credit.

March 14 Sold 100 widgets (cost, $600) to Jones Company for $900 cash.

March 17 Wilson Company returned ten widgets for credit.

March 21 Purchased 200 widgets from Widget Company for $1,200 on account.

March 24 Sold 240 widgets (cost, $1,440) on account to Adams Company for $2,000.

The inventory at March 1 was valued at $600, and a count on March 31 valued it at $2,400.

Required:

a. Prepare journal entries to record the above transactions, assuming a periodic inventory method is used. Prepare entries necessary to adjust and close the accounts.

b. Prepare journal entries and closing entries, assuming a perpetual inventory is maintained.

Problem 6-4

The Campus Bookstore suffered a fire on December 17, 1970 (the final day of test week), that caused extensive damage. The building and its contents were covered by insurance. You are asked to prepare a report to be submitted to the insurance company to support the claim for merchandise destroyed. A physical count indicates that books and other goods which cost $29,350 were not damaged by the fire, but that the balance of the goods on hand at the time of the fire was completely destroyed. The bookstore has followed the practice of marking all merchandise to sell at a price 25 percent above cost. From the bookstore's records, which were maintained in the vault of an adjoining building, you gather the following facts:

Inventory	Dec. 31, 1969	$172,391
Purchases	Jan. 1, 1970 to Dec. 17, 1970	524,300
Purchase Returns	Jan. 1, 1970 to Dec. 17, 1970	10,200
Sales	Jan. 1, 1970 to Dec. 17, 1970	825,400
Sales Returns	Jan. 1, 1970 to Dec. 17, 1970	12,700

Required:

Prepare a report indicating the cost of the goods destroyed by the fire with detailed supporting computations.

Problem 6-5

The data below were taken from the September 15, 1970, inventory records of the Campus Corner Clothing Store.

	QUANTITY	PER UNIT COST	PER UNIT MARKET PRICE
Women's Apparel			
Blouses	75	$ 4.45	$ 4.63
Dresses	125	18.75	18.31
Coats	32	38.17	37.48
Skirts	60	6.00	6.28
Sport Pants	58	8.50	8.22
Men's Apparel			
Suits	28	38.40	38.32
Shirts	81	3.95	4.03
Pants	43	6.15	6.23
Shoe Department			
Women's Shoes	108	8.35	8.64
Men's Shoes	72	12.92	12.75

Required:

Price the above inventory, using the lower of cost or market method, applied

a. item by item
b. to categories of inventory, and
c. to total inventory.

Problem 6-6

On December 31, 1970, the Fuller Card Shop took a physical inventory which was valued at a cost of $276.24. Mr. Fuller thinks this inventory is much lower than it should be and fears that there has been some theft involved. He furnishes you with the following data:

Inventory, January 1, 1970	
Cost	$ 31,620
Selling Price	45,675
Purchases	
Cost	284,450
Selling Price	562,110
Purchase Returns	
Cost	8,940
Selling Price	15,635
Transportation-in	18,553
Sales	520,875
Sales Returns	6,460

Required:

Calculate how much, if any, has been lost by theft, by using the retail inventory method.

Problem 6-7

Echo Electric Corporation has the following inventory record for 1970 on part C6-10, which they purchase to use in making tubes. The inventory on January 1, 1970, was 53,200 units at a price of $0.20. (Where purchases and sales occur on the same day, assume that the purchases occurred first.)

		PURCHASES		
		UNITS	COST	UNITS SOLD
January	20	140,000	$30,800	96,100
March	4	100,000	23,500	85,450
April	10			62,300
May	31	80,000	19,200	55,400
July	3			56,300
August	26	130,000	32,500	82,540
October	1	140,000	35,700	86,600
November	20	130,000	33,150	90,410
December	21			94,300

Required:

a. Assume that the company uses the periodic inventory method and that the physical count agrees with the balance on hand shown on the inventory record card. Calculate the cost of the inventory at December 31, 1970, using
   1. FIFO method
   2. LIFO method
   3. Weighted average method
b. Prepare a perpetual inventory card through May 31, assuming that the company uses the FIFO inventory method.

Problem 6-8

The following trial balance was taken from the records of Ajax Company:

AJAX COMPANY
Trial Balance
December 31, 1990

Accounts Payable		10,133
Accounts Receivable	13,980	
Administrative Expense	1,608	
Cash	14,656	
Common Stock		25,000
Freight-in	1,682	
Merchandise Inventory	16,120	
Purchases	68,403	
Purchase Discounts		1,365
Purchase Returns and Allowances		160
Retained Earnings		6,000
Sales		76,223
Sales Returns and Allowances	326	
Selling Expense	2,106	
	118,881	118,881

The merchandise inventory on December 31, 1990, was $14,783.

Required:

Prepare the journal entries to close the books of Ajax Company.

Case 6
ACE SPECIALTY COMPANY

Mr. Sharp and Mr. Grant are partners in Ace Specialty Company, a firm formed in 1966 to wholesale inexpensive flashlights. Because the flashlights are manufactured in Japan, it is necessary to buy in large quantities to get favorable prices and shipping rates. For this reason, the company makes one purchase per year, based upon the sales forecast for the coming year. The flashlights are sold for seventy-five cents each to retailers as promotional sales items or to firms as advertising give-aways.

In January 1971 the bookkeeper presented the income statement for the previous calendar year to the owners for their review. They were happy to note that profits had increased to $14,470 from the previous year's $12,700. This came as a complete surprise, since the company's salesman had previously reported the number of flashlights sold had decreased slightly, from 240,000 units in 1969 to 239,000 units in 1970. Physical counts showed 20,000 flashlights were on hand December 31, 1969, and 21,000 flashlights were on hand December 31, 1970. The selling and administrative expenses remained about the same during the two-year period. Selling expenses were $32,500 in 1969 and $32,000 in 1970, while administrative expenses were $10,000 in 1969 and $10,500 in 1970. Apparently, the profit increase was attributable to an increase in gross profit. "How could gross profit go up when our sales price has remained unchanged?" asked Mr. Grant.

The more the two partners studied the income statements, the more puzzled they became. Finally they called in Mr. Newly, the firm's part-time bookkeeper, for an explanation. A very heated discussion followed, and finally Newly said, "As you know, I've been here for a little less than a year now. I have priced the inventory in the only correct way I know, at the price we paid during this last year. How else could one price it? Check it yourself, if you're so darn smart!" After throwing the following summary of purchases on the desk, Mr. Newly stamped out of the office.

YEAR	UNITS PURCHASED	UNIT COST (in cents)
1966	200,000	42
1967	210,000	44
1968	230,000	48
1969	240,000	52
1970	240,000	52

Mr. Sharp and Mr. Grant know very little about inventory cost accounting, but they don't like Mr. Newly's attitude. Accordingly, they decide to hire an independent accountant to review their books and determine whether Newly is trying to put something over on them. As the independent accountant, answer the following questions:

1. What caused the sudden decrease in Cost of Goods Sold? Support your answer with income statements for the two years and necessary calculations.
2. Is the cause a legitimate method of inventory cost accounting? Can the firm continue to use this method?
3. Does a firm have a choice of inventory costing methods when preparing annual income statements? Is the choice limited?
4. In an inflationary economy (declining dollar value), which method of inventory costing would you recommend to Mr. Sharp and Mr. Grant? Why?

7

Accounting
for Manufacturing
Inventories

Since a merchandising firm purchases products which are already in a completed and marketable form, it has only one type of inventory. This is usually referred to as *merchandise inventory*, but it could just as well be called *finished goods inventory*, inasmuch as it represents goods which are ready and available for sale. Manufacturing enterprises also have finished goods inventories; however, these are manufactured or at least partially manufactured by the company itself, rather than purchased in finished form. In addition to carrying inventories of finished goods, manufacturing concerns usually have some unprocessed goods known as raw materials inventory and some partially completed products known as goods in process (work in process) inventory. It should be noted that the term "raw materials" does not refer only to natural resources, such as iron ore, but to any product which the manufacturing concern purchases from someone else and intends to process further. Thus, what is a finished good to one firm may be a raw material to another.

Goods in process are all partially completed goods—everything between the raw materials which have not yet been issued to production and the finished product which is ready for sale.

THE MANUFACTURING INCOME STATEMENT

The income statement of a manufacturing concern is similar to that of a merchandising firm. The major difference is found in the cost of goods sold section where a new account, Cost of Goods Manufactured, is shown. This account appears in place of the net purchases (purchases, freight-in, purchase returns and allowances, purchase discounts) because the manufacturer produces his own finished goods inventory, rather than procuring it from an outside firm. Because the cost of goods manufactured is so important, the details are shown on a separate statement known as the "Schedule of Cost of Goods Manufactured."

SCHEDULE OF COST OF GOODS MANUFACTURED

All normal costs incurred in the factory are production costs. Note that they are *not* expenses, but costs. The distinction is important. Production costs become a part of the total inventory costs. In the strictest sense they are asset costs. They will become expenses in the period the inventory is sold and at that time will appear on the income statement as cost of goods sold. Production costs are generally classified under three major headings: *raw materials used, direct labor,* and *manufacturing overhead.* The two most significant costs for most manufacturing concerns are raw materials and direct labor. All other production costs are thrown together under the heading "manufacturing overhead."

A schedule of cost of goods manufactured is shown in Figure 7-1. Note the three classifications of cost: raw materials, direct labor, and manufacturing overhead. The first two of these are itemized separately because of their relative importance. The overhead is a "catch-all" heading which covers all factory costs except raw materials and direct labor. The sum of the three cost elements represents the total manufacturing costs incurred during the period. Since some goods were in process at the beginning of the period, the value of these partially completed goods must be added. Similarly, the value of the goods in process at the end of the period must be subtracted to arrive at the total cost of goods manufactured and should correspond with the amounts so designated on the income statement.

Figure 7-1

SPARTAN MANUFACTURING COMPANY
Schedule of Cost of Goods Manufactured
For the Year Ended December 31, 1970

Raw Materials Used:
Raw materials inventory, Jan. 1, 1970 . .		$ 25,500	
Raw materials purchased	$192,300		
Less: Returns and allowances	4,200		
Net raw materials purchased	$188,100		
Freight-in	9,320		
Net cost of raw materials purchased		197,420	
Raw materials available for use		$222,920	
Raw materials inventory, Dec. 31, 1970 . .		37,410	
Raw materials used			$185,110
Direct labor costs			229,750
Manufacturing overhead costs:			
Depreciation of factory building		$ 65,000	
Depreciation of factory equipment		47,000	
Indirect labor costs		29,500	
Heat, light, and power		24,322	
Repairs and maintenance		19,740	
Factory insurance expired		12,000	
Factory taxes		8,900	
Factory supplies used		6,205	
Patent amortization		5,000	
Total manufacturing overhead			217,667
Total manufacturing costs this period			$632,927
Add: Work in process, Jan. 1, 1970 . .			21,952
Total costs in process during year			$654,879
Deduct: Work in process, Dec. 31, 1970			37,777
Cost of goods manufactured			$617,102

COST ACCOUNTING

When goods are purchased from another enterprise, it is a relatively simple task to determine the unit cost, calculate the value of the inventories, and control the cost of goods sold. When we engage in production ourselves rather than buying our merchandise, the situation becomes more difficult. How do we measure the cost of a unit of output? What is the value of a goods in process inventory when we have thousands of items, each at a different stage of completion? How do we control the costs of production? These are a few of the important questions which a cost accounting system is set up to answer. There are two major types of cost accounting systems: *job order cost* and *process cost*.

Job Order Cost Accounting

Under a job order cost accounting system, the costs are accumulated by job on subsidiary records known as job orders or work orders. As any given project passes through the various stages of completion, the costs applicable to that project are posted to the job order. Summary entries are entered in the journal to record the sum of all amounts which have been posted to the individual job orders. As jobs are completed, the costs assigned to them are transferred from the Work in Process account to the Finished Goods account; and as the jobs are delivered to the customers, the costs are transferred to the Cost of Goods Sold account.

Job order costing is generally used where the goods are being produced to order, and the requirements differ significantly from job to job. The publisher of this textbook used a job order system to accumulate the costs on this particular project. No two books published would require the same outlay of time or materials. Each is a separate and distinct project, and a cost accounting system has been set up to accumulate the costs of production in the manner that will be most meaningful.

Process Cost Accounting

No attempt is made under a process system to keep a record of the actual costs incurred on each job or item produced. Instead, costs are accumulated by process or "cost center." These costs are then assigned on an average basis to the individual units of output that pass through each of these processes. Process costing is used most often for companies that mass produce homogeneous products. It would be difficult for General Motors, for example, to maintain a job order system which would keep track of the exact cost of producing each separate automobile. Since they produce thousands of units of each model, it would be much more practical for them to calculate the average cost of producing each type or model. They could do this with an effective process cost accounting system.

Predetermined Overhead

Under either a process or job system, it is a relatively simple task to determine the quantity of direct labor and material used in production and to identify these with a particular process or job. Overhead, on the other hand, is quite a different problem. It is really not one cost but many costs, each being used in production in a different manner and at a different rate. To keep track of each of these costs individually and then to identify it with a specific product or job would be an almost impossible task. For this reason, overhead is generally allocated to production at some pre-determined rate. There are several ways in which the predetermined overhead might be allocated to production:

1. On a direct labor hours basis,
2. On a direct labor cost basis,
3. On a direct material cost basis,
4. On a prime costs (material costs plus direct labor costs) basis, or
5. On a machine hour basis.

Management should select the method or methods that it feels produces the most accurate allocation. There is no universally *best* method since each company's circumstances are different. A company that is highly automated may find the machine hour basis best, while a company which utilizes a great deal of direct labor and few machines may find the direct labor hour basis is best. Probably the most widely used are the direct labor hour and the direct labor cost bases.

The predetermined overhead rate is established by estimating the total overhead costs for a specified period (usually one year). This total is then divided by the estimated base (hours or costs) to arrive at a rate. To illustrate, let us assume that a shoe manufacturer allocates overhead on the basis of direct labor hours. The company forecasts overhead costs of $355,500 and direct labor of 150,000 hours. The overhead rate of $2.37 per direct labor hour may be calculated as follows:

$$\text{Overhead rate per direct labor hour} = \frac{\text{estimated overhead cost}}{\text{estimated direct labor hours}}$$

$$= \frac{\$355,500}{150,000 \text{ hours}} = \$2.37 \text{ per hour}$$

Where a process system is used, separate overhead rates may be calculated for each process. For simplicity, the single rate has been used in the illustrations presented later in this chapter.

Cost Flows

Before we look at the various forms of cost accounting systems, it may be helpful to study the flow chart shown in Figure 7-2. The chart summarizes the flow of various costs from the time the expenditures are made until they appear on the income statement as expenses.

The first six steps are not peculiar to the manufacturing enterprise, but occur to varying degrees in all profit-making enterprises. Journal entries

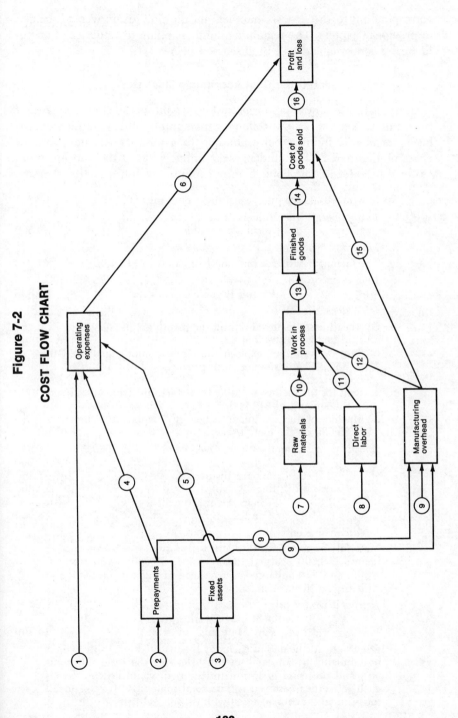

Figure 7-2

COST FLOW CHART

corresponding to the first six numbers on the flow chart were discussed in previous chapters. The remaining numbers relate to activities of manufacturing concerns and will be discussed below.

Job Order Cost Accounting Illustrated

In order to see how a job order system would work, a simple series of transactions is given in the following paragraphs. Each transaction has been assigned a number corresponding to a number on the cost flow chart of Figure 7-2. The student will probably grasp the concept more easily if he refers to the flow chart and follows each transaction thereon.

7. Raw materials are purchased on account for $20,500.

  Journal entry: Raw Materials   20,500
                  Accounts Payable   20,500

  Job order: No entry

8. The factory payroll for the month amounts to $15,325.

  Journal entry: Factory Payroll   15,325
                  Payroll Payable   15,325

  Job order: No entry

9. Overhead costs incurred during the month are as follows:
   a. Paid factory power bill $2,300.
   b. Factory insurance expired during the month amounted to $1,450. The insurance has previously been recorded as prepaid.
   c. Rent for the factory building for the month is due but unpaid in the amount of $12,000.
   d. Machinery and equipment (factory) depreciation amounts to $5,000 for the month.

  Journal entry: Manufacturing Overhead   20,750
                  Cash   2,300
                  Prepaid Insurance   1,450
                  Rent Payable   12,000
                  Accum. Depr., Machinery
                    and Equip.   5,000

  Job order: No entry

10. Materials costing $14,100 were issued from the storerooms as follows: $8,000 charged to job #501; $6,000 charged to job #502; and $100 charged to overhead (could not be identified with any particular job).

  Journal entry: Work in Process   14,000
                  Manufacturing Overhead   100
                  Raw Materials   14,100

  Job order: At the end of each day the material issue slips would be tabulated by job, and an entry showing the issue slip numbers and the costs of the materials used would be entered on each job order cost sheet. The total materials charged to all jobs should, of course, agree with the journal entry.

11. Job time tickets are summarized for the month as follows:

    Job number 501:   1,500 hours; labor cost $7,500
    Job number 502:   1,400 hours; labor cost $7,000
    Unassigned time: 165 hours; labor cost $ 825

    Journal entry: Work in Process   14,500
                   Manufacturing Overhead   825
                   Factory Payroll   15,325

    Job order: The time tickets would be tabulated by job number and posted to the respective job order cost sheets. The total charged to all job orders should agree with the debit to Work in Process in the above entry. Note that unassigned time is charged to Manufacturing Overhead.

12. Overhead is charged to production at the rate of 150 percent of direct labor costs.

    Journal entry: Work in Process   21,750
                   Manufacturing Overhead . . $21,750

    Job order: As direct labor costs are posted to the job order cost sheets in transaction (11) above, 150 percent of this amount would also be posted as overhead costs.

13. Job number 501 is completed and transferred to the warehouse.

    Journal entry: Finished Goods   26,750
                   Work in Process   26,750

    Job order: The job order is removed from the "in process" file and placed in the "completed" file. The total job cost as recorded on the job order cost sheet serves as the basis for the above entry.

14. The completed job (number 501) is delivered to the customer. The customer is billed for the selling price of $55,000.

    Journal entry: Accounts Receivable   55,000
                   Sales   55,000
                 To record sale.
                 Cost of Goods Sold   26,750
                   Finished Goods   26,750
                 To record cost of sale.

    Job order: The job order is removed from the "completed" file and placed in the "delivered" file. The total on the job order cost sheet serves as the basis for the above entry.

15. At the end of the accounting period, the Manufacturing Overhead account generally has some balance. This is true because actual overhead costs have been recorded as debits and only estimated costs of overhead used have been recorded as credits. The difference between the debits and credits in this account is called "underapplied overhead" (debit balance) or "overapplied overhead" (credit balance). In theory, this balance should be disposed of by closing some portion to Work in Process, some to Finished Goods, and some to Cost of Goods Sold, in relation to the overhead which has been left in these accounts as it has flowed through the system. Because most overhead has found its way to Cost of Goods Sold by the end of the period, it is

more expedient to charge the entire under- or overabsorbed amount directly to Cost of Goods Sold. In the previous illustration, the Manufacturing Overhead account has a credit balance of $75.

Journal entry: Manufacturing Overhead   75
              Cost of Goods Sold   75

Job order: No entry

16. The Cost of Goods Sold is an expense account and is closed in the same manner as all other expenses.

Journal entry: Income Summary   26,675
              Cost of Goods Sold   26,675

Job order: No entry

Process Cost Accounting Illustrated

The flow of costs under a process cost system is similar to that for a job order system, except that there is a separate work in process account for each distinct process. Materials, labor, and overhead flow through the various work in process accounts to finished goods. In addition to these three cost elements, the various work in process accounts may be charged with "prior department" costs. These latter costs are the total material, labor, and overhead accumulated in the previous process. As the goods move from process to process, so also are the costs of production transferred in the accounts.

The journal entries to record the acquisition of materials (7), labor (8), and overhead (9) are the same with process or job order cost accounting. The difference comes as the goods are *used*. At this point, the costs are associated with a particular department or process, rather than with a particular job. Again, let us follow the transactions on the flow chart. Since the transactions would be recorded in the same manner, let us assume that entries (7), (8), and (9) have been recorded just as they were under the job order illustration.

10. The summary of materials used discloses that materials have been issued to production as follows:
    Department A $8,500
    Department B   2,000
    Department C   3,500
    Jointly to all departments   100

    Journal entry: Work in Process A   8,500
                 Work in Process B   2,000
                 Work in Process C   3,500
                 Manufacturing Overhead   100
                    Raw Materials   14,100

11. Employees are assigned to a particular department or process for the entire month, and all their time is charged to that par-

ticular process. In the event that an employee is loaned from one department to another, an interdepartmental transfer form is prepared to notify the accounting department of the change so that the proper process can be charged. The labor summary for the month (after giving consideration to interdepartmental transfers) is as follows:

Department A .... $ 3,000
Department B 7,000
Department C 4,500
Unassigned (serve all departments) 825

Journal entry: Work in Process A 3,000
Work in Process B 7,000
Work in Process C 4,500
Manufacturing Overhead 825
Factory Payroll 15,325

12. Overhead is assigned to production at the rate of 150 percent of direct labor.

Journal entry: Work in Process A 4,500
Work in Process B 10,500
Work in Process C 6,750
Manufacturing Overhead . 21,750

13a. During the month, department A completed and transferred to department B goods which have been assigned costs of $13,200.

Journal entry: Work in Process B 13,200
Work in Process A....... 13,200

13b. During the month, department B completed and transferred to department C goods which have been assigned costs of $29,000. Note that the costs assigned to Goods in Process B include not only material, labor, and overhead costs charged to that process, but also the "prior department" costs transferred from Process A.

Journal entry: Work in Process C 29,000
Work in Process B 29,000

13c. During the month, goods which have been assigned costs of $41,400 were completed and transferred to the finished goods inventory.

Journal entry: Finished Goods 41,400
Work in Process C 41,400

14. Goods which cost the company $25,000 to produce were sold for $37,000 on account.

Journal entry: Accounts Receivable 37,000
Sales 37,000
Cost of Goods Sold 25,000
Finished Goods 25,000

15. The overapplied overhead of $75 is closed to Cost of Goods Sold (as was done under the job system).

Journal entry: Manufacturing Overhead 75
Cost of Goods Sold 75

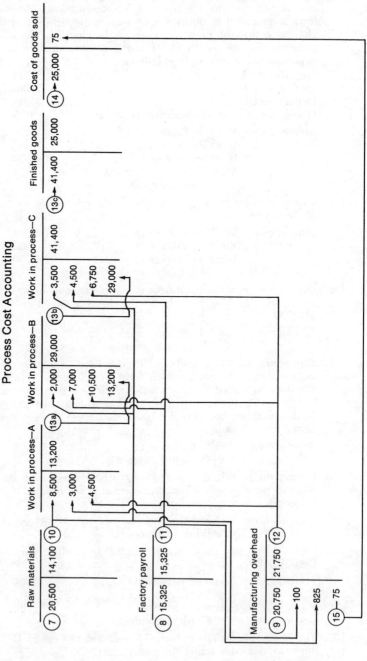

Figure 7-3

COST FLOW

Process Cost Accounting

It will be helpful at this point to look at the pertinent part of our flow chart with entries (7) through (15) posted. This is shown in Figure 7-3. Note how the various costs flow through the accounts. The balances in Raw Materials ($6,500), Work in Process A ($2,800), Work in Process B ($3,700), Work in Process C ($2,350), and Finished Goods ($16,400) represent quantities of inventory which are still on hand at the various stages of completion.

The balance in the Manufacturing Overhead account (under- or over-applied overhead) is closed to the Cost of Goods Sold account.

Equivalent Units

In the preceding illustration the amounts transferred from process to process were given. The student might question how these amounts were arrived at: i.e., how does the accountant determine how many dollars should be assigned to the goods transferred and how many dollars pertain to the goods still in process? Under the process system this is usually determined by calculating the equivalent units of production.

Based upon estimates provided by the foreman as to stages of completion, the accountant estimates the equivalent finished production. Unit costs are then calculated so that a dollar value can be assigned to the goods transferred. The technique assigns costs to various units according to their status in the manufacturing process. For example, a unit which is 50 percent complete will have only half as much labor cost charged to it as one which is 100 percent complete.

In order to see how equivalent units are used in cost accounting, let us assume the following facts regarding a manufacturing process:

1. Materials are all added at the beginning of the process.
2. Work in process at beginning of period was 600 units, one-third complete as to labor and overhead.
3. Work in process at end of period was 1,000 units, one-fourth complete as to labor and overhead.
4. 10,000 units were completed during the period.

The Work in Process account appears below:

WORK IN PROCESS

Beginning Balance	1,870	Cost of Goods Completed	??
Raw Materials Used . . .	26,000		
Direct Labor	30,150		
Manufacturing OH	39,195		

Our task is to determine the costs that should be assigned to the 1,000 incomplete units still on hand and the costs to be assigned to the 10,000

units completed and transferred. This will enable us to fill in the amounts
for the following entry:

Finished Goods .... ?
Work in Process .... ?

Because the goods are at different stages of completion regarding
materials, labor, and overhead, two equivalent units schedules must necessarily be prepared. The equivalent units schedules are shown in Figure
7-4. The top schedule tells us that we have used sufficient materials to
produce 10,400 completed units. The second schedule tells us that we
have used sufficient labor and overhead to produce 10,050 completed units.
In other words, if all work done this period had been applied to the full
processing of units which were begun and finished within the period, it
would have produced 10,050 units of product. As it was, we had to use
some of our effort to finish up the 600 units on hand, partly done, at the
first of the period, and we used some effort to start the 1,000 units still
incomplete at the end of the period.

Figure 7-4

SCHEDULE OF EQUIVALENT UNITS: MATERIAL

	PHYSICAL UNITS	FRACTION ADDED THIS PERIOD[a]	EQUIVALENT PRODUCTION
Beginning inventory	600	—0—	—0—
Started and completed[b]	9,400	1	9,400
Ending inventory	1,000	1	1,000
	11,000		10,400

[a]Inasmuch as materials are all added at the beginning of the period, no materials were
added to the 600 units already in process, and 100 percent was added for the 10,400
units started this period.
[b]If 10,000 units were completed (given) and 600 of these were on hand at the beginning of the period (given), then 9,400 were started and completed this period.

SCHEDULE OF EQUIVALENT UNITS: LABOR AND OVERHEAD

	PHYSICAL UNITS	FRACTION ADDED THIS PERIOD	EQUIVALENT PRODUCTION
Beginning inventory	600	2/3[a]	400
Started and completed	9,400	1	9,400
Ending inventory	1,000	1/4	250
	11,000		10,050

[a]The beginning inventory was one-third complete at the beginning of the current
period, which means we added the other two-thirds of the labor and overhead during
the period.

Utilizing these equivalent unit figures we can now calculate the various costs as follows:

$$\frac{\$26,000 \text{ (Raw Materials Used)}}{10,400 \text{ (Equivalent Material Units)}} = \$2.50 \text{ per unit}$$

$$\frac{\$30,150 \text{ (Direct Labor Cost)}}{10,050 \text{ (Equivalent Labor Units)}} = \$3.00 \text{ per unit}$$

$$\frac{\$39,195 \text{ (Overhead Applied)}}{10,050 \text{ (Equivalent Overhead Units)}} = \$3.90 \text{ per unit}$$

The amounts charged to the Work in Process account can now be apportioned as follows:

		GOODS COMPLETED		
	AMOUNT	BEGINNING INVENTORY	STARTED COMPLETED	ENDING INVENTORY
Beginning Balance	$ 1,870	$1,870	–0–	–0–
Raw Material Used	26,000	–0–	$23,500[a]	$2,500[b]
Direct Labor	30,150	1,200[c]	28,200[d]	750[e]
Manufacturing Overhead . .	39,195	1,560[f]	36,660[g]	975[h]
	$97,215	$4,630	$88,360	$4,225

$$\$92,990$$

---

[a]9,400 equivalent units $\times$ $2.50 unit cost
[b]1,000 equivalent units $\times$ $2.50 unit cost
[c]400 equivalent units $\times$ $3.00 unit cost
[d]9,400 equivalent units $\times$ $3.00 unit cost
[e]250 equivalent units $\times$ $3.00 unit cost
[f]400 equivalent units $\times$ $3.90 unit cost
[g]9,400 equivalent units $\times$ $3.90 unit cost
[h]250 equivalent units $\times$ $3.90 unit cost

We can now complete the journal entry transferring the costs from the Work in Process account to the Finished Goods account:

Finished Goods   92,990
     Work in Process   92,990

Joint Products and By-products

Sometimes several products are manufactured simultaneously from common raw materials. These may be referred to as multiple products, and they present a special accounting problem in that the costs incurred up to the point of separation must be shared by the various products. All costs incurred after the products are separated, of course, can be accounted for as is done with single products.

Multiple products may be classified as *joint products* or *by-products*, according to their relative importance. Each joint product is a major product in that it makes a significant contribution to the company's revenue. By-products, on the other hand, are relatively insignificant in value and are produced as an incidental part of the manufacturing process. The main products (joint products) would be produced even if the by-products did not "happen" to result. The distinction between joint and by-products is often difficult to make, and some firms actually see the classification change from year to year. A product may start out as a by-product and evolve into a main product.

Accounting for By-products.   Generally, accountants do not assign any of the joint costs to the by-products; instead, the entire amount is apportioned to the main products. The by-products are, of course, charged with any costs incurred by them after the point of separation.

There are two methods which might be employed to account for the proceeds from the sale of by-products. First, the net amount received from the sale might be regarded as other income. In this event, the proceeds are added at the bottom of the income statement, as is generally done with interest or dividend income. Under the second alternative, the net proceeds from the sale are treated as a reduction of the cost of the main products. In this event, the amount is subtracted from the cost of goods manufactured and does not appear as a separate item in the income statement. In the first instance, the by-product revenue increases profits in the period the *by-product* is sold, and in the second instance the profits are increased in the period the *joint products* are sold.

Accounting for Joint Products.   We have previously noted that joint products must share the costs incurred up to the point when the products are separated. The most common basis for sharing these costs is the relative sales value of the joint products. To illustrate this joint cost allocation, let us assume that the Economy Slaughterhouse purchases a 900-pound steer for $200. Production records indicate that the following end products are produced from the steer:

PRODUCT	PERCENT OF LIVE WEIGHT	WHOLESALE PRICE PER POUND
Steaks	10	$0.95
Roasts	30	0.75
Hamburger	40	0.40
Waste	20	0.00

The $200 joint cost may be allocated to the end products according to their relative sales value as follows:

PRODUCT	REVENUE CONTRIBUTION	PERCENT OF TOTAL REVENUE	COST ALLOCATION
Steaks	$ 85.50[a]	19.8	$ 39.60
Roasts	202.50[b]	46.9	98.80
Hamburger	144.00[c]	33.3	66.60
Waste	–0–	–0–	–0–
	$432.00	100.0	$200.00

[a] 0.10×900 lbs. $\times$ $0.95 = $ 85.50
[b] 0.30×900 lbs. $\times$ $0.75 = $202.50
[c] 0.40×900 lbs. $\times$ $0.40 = $144.00

The cost per pound can be calculated by dividing the portion of the cost allocated to each product by the number of pounds produced. Thus, the cost per pound of steak would be $39.60 $\div$ 90 lbs. = $0.44; roast, $93.80 $\div$ 270 lbs. = $0.347; and hamburger, $66.60 $\div$ 360 lbs. = $0.185. None of the cost would be assigned to the waste.

DEPARTMENTAL ANALYSIS

There are many overhead costs that cannot economically be identified with a particular department or process. In a sense, these also are joint costs since they, too, must be allocated. For example, the rent cost of a factory building represents a joint cost which must be shared by all the departments occupying space in the building.

Basis for Allocation

One of the most difficult problems in distributing these joint overhead costs is selecting the basis for allocating them to the respective departments. Each element of overhead should be analyzed separately and a basis that seems fair and equitable selected. While each case must be decided according to actual conditions, some common overhead accounts are listed below, together with a suggested basis for allocation.

Heat—cubic feet of floor space heated.
Light and power—allocated according to engineering studies on power used by various machines, etc.
Telephone—monthly rental according to number of telephones; toll charges direct.
Property taxes—assessed value of property.
Fire insurance—insurable value of property.
Payroll taxes—in ratio of direct labor charges.
Depreciation of building—according to square footage occupied.

Building repairs and maintenance—major repairs on work order
basis to department in which repair or maintenance was done;
others on square footage basis.
Depreciation of machinery—direct, according to investment in
machinery.
Supplies—direct, according to estimated usage.
Superintendency—allocated on basis of number of employees.
Custodial—according to square footage occupied.

Allocating Service Department Costs

All departments of a manufacturing concern may be classified as either
production or service departments. The production departments actually
alter the product physically, while the service departments merely contribute services which aid indirectly in the production process. A cabinet
mill, for example, might include cutting, assembly, and finishing as production departments, and maintenance and stock room as service departments.

Inasmuch as all normal factory costs must ultimately be borne by the
end product, service department costs are generally allocated to the production departments. These costs first are assigned to the service departments, and then are redistributed to the departments that benefit from
their services. Where these departments render services to one another,
we have a problem of reciprocal benefits. The allocation could be made
in such a case by utilizing simultaneous equations, but generally such
accuracy is not necessary. A more common procedure is to close out the
service departments one at a time, starting with that department which
receives the least benefit from other service departments. Once a department has been closed, no more costs are assigned to it—in effect, we assume
that the closed departments receive no benefit from the remaining departments. In this manner, the service departments are closed out one at a
time, in order, beginning with that department receiving the fewest
reciprocal services and progressing to that receiving the most.

An overhead cost distribution worksheet is shown in Figure 7-5. Once
the actual overhead costs have been distributed, a comparison can be
made with the budgeted overhead as follows:

	TOTAL	CASTING DEPT.	GRINDING DEPT.	FINISHING DEPT.
Actual Overhead (per worksheet)	$249,165	$82,918	$ 97,931	$68,316
Budget Overhead (per budget)	253,000	81,000	102,500	69,500
Over (under) Budgeted Amount	($ 3,835)	$ 1,918	($ 4,569)	($ 1,184)

Figure 7-5

Overhead Cost Distribution Worksheet
For the Year Ended December 31, 1970

COST	BASIS OF ALLOCATION	FACTORY OFFICE	CUSTODIAL AND MAIN-TENANCE	MATERIALS HANDLING	CASTING DEPT.	GRINDING DEPT.	FINISHING DEPT.	TOTAL
Indirect Labor	Direct	$45,000	$40,000	$52,000	$18,000	$12,000	$14,000	$181,000
Heat	Cubic Feet	1,000	500	2,000	2,000	3,000	3,500	12,000
Light and Power	Engineering Study	2,000	1,000	1,000	3,000	10,000	5,000	22,000
Telephone	Number of Phones	3,500	100	500	300	300	300	5,000
Factory Depreciation	Square Feet	1,300	1,100	1,500	3,200	8,900	5,000	21,000
Supplies	Direct	250	890	110	400	380	1,300	3,330
Property Taxes	Assessed Value	50	40	60	150	400	300	1,000
Fire Insurance	Appraised Value	10	8	12	30	80	75	215
Other Factory Costs	Indirect Labor Ratio	900	800	1,040	360	240	280	3,620
Totals		$54,010	$44,438	$58,222	$27,440	$35,300	$29,755	$249,165
Redistribute Factory Office	Number of Employees	<54,010>	2,701	5,401	13,502	18,904	13,502	
			$53,501	$63,623				
Redistribute Materials Handling	Direct Materials Used		6,362	<63,623>	31,811	15,906	9,544	
			$53,501					
Redistribute Custodial and Maintenance	Square Feet		<$53,501>		10,165	27,821	15,515	
					$82,918	$97,931	$68,316	$249,165

135

Departmental Analysis

The preceding illustration of cost allocation deals with the overhead of a manufacturing concern. Many nonmanufacturing enterprises have similar problems with which this type of analysis can be useful. A department store, for example, may wish to make departmental income statements to evaluate the various operations. Since many costs, such as building rent, are not incurred directly by the departments, they must be allocated in a manner similar to that used in the preceding illustration.

SUMMARY

Because manufacturing firms produce the products they sell, as opposed to buying the goods in finished form, they have the special problem of accounting for this production. A system that accounts for the factory operations and determines the cost of the goods produced is known as a *cost accounting system*. All normal factory costs are considered inventory costs and are accordingly charged to the product. These production costs may be classified as raw materials used, direct labor, or manufacturing overhead. The overhead includes all factory costs except materials and direct labor, the latter two being itemized separately because of their relative importance. The costs associated with factory operations are summarized on a statement known as the *schedule of cost of goods manufactured*.

There are two major types of cost accounting systems: *job order* and *process*. Under the first of these, the costs are accumulated by specific job, and the cost of each job is calculated separately. The job order system is generally used in those instances where each job is different.

Under the process cost system, the costs are accumulated by process or department and then assigned to the goods produced on an average basis. The process system is generally used for companies that mass produce homogeneous products. The equivalent units produced each period must be calculated under the process system in order to determine how the costs should be apportioned between the goods sold and those still on hand.

When products are produced simultaneously from common raw materials, they are known as multiple products. Each product that makes a significant contribution to revenue is known as a *joint product*, while those that make little or no contribution to revenue are termed *by-products*. The joint costs incurred in multiple product operations are generally assigned to the main (joint) products on the basis of the relative sales value of the units produced.

QUESTIONS

1. Which inventory of a manufacturing enterprise corresponds to the merchandise inventory of a nonmanufacturing concern?

2. Discuss the appropriateness of the following account titles: Factory Depreciation Expense; Direct Labor Expense; Materials Used Expense. Suggest better account titles.

3. On which statement or statements would the ending inventories of raw materials, goods in process, and finished goods appear?

4. What are production costs? Which production costs are generally most significant?

5. What is the difference between the total manufacturing costs incurred during the period and the cost of goods manufactured during the same period? What difference is there between the latter and the cost of goods sold?

6. Name the two major types of cost accounting systems. What types of manufacturing concerns would you expect to use each system?

7. What is predetermined overhead? What are some bases which might be used to allocate the overhead costs to production?

8. If a company applies overhead on the basis of direct labor hours and estimates overhead costs of $212,000 and direct labor hours of 50,000, what is the overhead rate?

9. At what point in the flow of production costs are these costs recognized as expenses? Do you feel this practice assists in matching revenues and expenses? Why?

10. How much would a company's direct labor costs be if that of raw material used were $58,500; raw materials purchased, $52,000; manufacturing overhead costs, $72,761; and total manufacturing costs during the period, $194,333?

11. Assume an overhead rate of 200 percent of direct labor costs and a balance in the goods in process account of $429. Job number 3096 is the only job in process, and it has been charged with direct labor of $75. How much material was used on job 3096?

12. How do journal entries differ under the job order and process systems? In what way does the accumulation of costs differ under the two methods?

13. What is the equivalent production during the period if the beginning inventory consists of 600 units one-third complete, 6,000 units started, and 6,100 units completed, and the ending inventory is one-half complete?

14. Why is it necessary to calculate equivalent units under a process cost system? Under what circumstances can one prepare a single equivalent unit schedule to cover material, labor, and overhead costs?

15. Distinguish between joint products and by-products. How are "joint costs" allocated to each of these products?

16. How should the proceeds from the sale of by-products be shown in the financial statements?

17. What types of overhead costs must be allocated? Name several such costs and indicate what you feel would be a fair basis for allocation.

18. Distinguish between service departments and production departments. In what order should service costs be reallocated to users?

PROBLEMS

Problem 7-1

Below is the adjusted trial balance of the Mill Manufacturing Company. Accounts are listed in alphabetical order.

MILL MANUFACTURING COMPANY
Adjusted Trial Balance
December 31, 1970

Accounts Payable		15,400
Accounts Receivable	17,000	
Accumulated Depreciation, Factory Machinery		34,200
Accumulated Depreciation, Office Equipment		1,800
Advertising	5,400	
Cash	19,200	
Common Stock		98,000
Depreciation, Factory Machinery	9,600	
Depreciation, Office Equipment	700	
Direct Labor	95,600	
Factory Heat, Light, and Power	8,400	
Factory Insurance Expired	500	
Factory Machinery	175,800	
Factory Supplies	8,900	
Finished Goods Inventory	33,600	
Freight-in	1,200	
Goods in Process Inventory	18,700	
Indirect Labor	18,700	
Machinery Repairs	9,300	
Office Equipment	6,800	
Office Rent	3,300	
Office Salaries	10,600	
Officers' Salaries	19,700	
Other Factory Overhead Costs	12,000	
Prepaid Factory Insurance	5,500	
Raw Materials Inventory	21,200	
Raw Materials Purchased	81,400	
Retained Earnings		47,500
Sales		419,400
Sales Returns	2,000	
Sales Salaries	31,200	
	616,300	616,300

Physical inventory on December 31, 1970, disclosed the following goods on hand:

Raw Materials	$20,000
Goods in Process	14,000
Finished Goods	35,000
Factory Supplies	1,200

Required:
  a. Prepare a schedule of cost of goods manufactured.
  b. Prepare an income statement.

Problem 7-2

The Super Soap Manufacturing Company utilizes a process cost accounting system. On January 1, the following account balances appeared on the books:

Raw Materials Inventory	$10,000
Work in Process A	2,000
Work in Process B	4,000
Finished Goods Inventory	12,000

During the month of January the following costs were assigned to production in each department:

	MATERIALS	DIRECT LABOR
Department A	$6,000	$4,000
Department B	8,000	6,000

Overhead is applied at a rate of 150 percent of direct labor.
During the month, goods with assigned costs of $14,000 were transferred from department A to department B. Goods with assigned costs of $35,000 were completed in department B and transferred to Finished Goods. Goods with assigned costs of $38,000 were sold on account for $60,000.
Raw material were purchased during the month at a cost of $10,000. Actual overhead costs totalled $14,500 (credit various accounts).

Required:
Keying your entries to the flow chart shown in the chapter, prepare all necessary journal entries for January pertaining to the production and sale of goods, including the closing entries.

Problem 7-3

The Wonder Widget Manufacturing Company uses process cost accounting. On January 1, department B had a beginning work in process inventory of $20,000, consisting of 8,000 units 60 percent complete as to labor and overhead and 40 percent complete as to materials. Production on 75,000 units was begun during the month, with $52,000 worth of materials added and $140,000 worth of direct labor and overhead added.

The work in process inventory of department B on January 31 consisted of 3,000 units, 25 percent complete as to materials, labor, and overhead. No units were lost in process.

Required:
  a. Determine the equivalent units of production for materials.
  b. Determine the equivalent units of production for labor and overhead.
  c. Determine the unit costs for materials, labor, and overhead.
  d. Determine the total dollar amount assignable to the ending inventory and to the goods completed.

Problem 7-4

Corbin and Collier form a partnership to speculate on land. They purchase an undeveloped ten-acre tract on the east bench at a cost of $52,000. They pay closing costs and title fees of $1,000 and hire an architect to lay out a subdivision on the property. The architect's fees and the costs of filing for the subdivision amount to $2,000. Since a main highway goes past the front of the property, an irrigation canal runs through the middle, and the back is covered with natural scrub oak, there is a great deal of variation in the value of the lots. A competent real estate appraiser assists Corbin and Collier in fixing the following list prices for the lots.

TYPE OF LOT	NUMBER OF PARTICULAR TYPE	LIST PRICE PER LOT
Choice	5	$15,000
Medium	9	9,000
Fair	6	7,000

Required:
Determine the amount of the joint cost which should be assigned to each lot.

Problem 7-5

The trial balance for Century Manufacturing Company is presented below.

CENTURY MANUFACTURING COMPANY
Adjusted Trial Balance
June 30, 1971

Accounts Payable		43,092
Accounts Receivable	63,124	
Accumulated Depreciation, Machinery and Equipment		78,128
Advertising	14,352	
Cash	29,612	
Common Stock		160,000
Depreciation, Machinery and Equipment	19,532	
Direct Labor	142,395	
Factory Heat, Light, and Power	10,823	
Factory Insurance Expired	18,676	
Factory Rent	75,000	
Factory Supplies	5,320	
Finished Goods Inventory	18,135	
Freight-in	1,458	
Goods in Process Inventory	25,600	

Indirect Labor	21,942	
Machinery and Equipment	292,975	
Machinery Repairs	14,608	
Miscellaneous Factory Expense	10,863	
Office Rent	10,400	
Office Salaries	24,600	
Prepaid Insurance	4,845	
Purchases, Raw Materials	68,580	
Raw Materials Inventory	10,120	
Retained Earnings		41,250
Sales		588,830
Sales Salaries	28,340	
	911,300	911,300

The inventories at June 30, 1971, were:

Finished Goods Inventory	$ 22,684
Goods in Process Inventory	34,175
Raw Materials Inventory	14,721
Supplies Inventory	428

Required:

Prepare a schedule of cost of goods manufactured.

Problem 7-6

The Work in Process account of the Widget Works Manufacturing Company showed the following amounts:

Work in Process, January 1, 1985	$ 36,450
Materials Used	230,650
Direct Labor	165,727
Manufacturing Overhead	45,052

At the beginning of the year there were 4,500 units in the work in process inventory; each unit was two-thirds complete as to labor and overhead. During the year, 35,000 units were started in the manufacturing process. On December 31, 1985, the work in process inventory contained 5,400 units; each unit was one-fifth complete as to labor and overhead. All the materials were put into the process at the start of production.

Required:

   a. Make a schedule of equivalent units of production for materials and a second schedule for labor and overhead.
   b. Make a schedule showing how the above costs should be distributed to the units in the beginning inventory, the goods started and completed during the period, and the goods in the ending inventory.
   c. Prepare journal entries to transfer the appropriate costs from Work in Process to Finished Goods.

Problem 7-7

Data related to the Wangsguard Manufacturing Company overhead costs for the first quarter (January–March) of 1971 are summarized as follows:

	NUMBER OF EMPLOYEES	FLOOR SPACE	NUMBER OF PHONES	DIRECT MATERIAL USED	DIRECT OVERHEAD CHARGES
Custodial	6	4,000	3	$ 8,000	$ 8,400
Maintenance	9	10,000	6	10,000	9,450
Factory Office	15	16,000	15	12,000	23,250
Department A	45	30,000	6	60,000	10,400
Department B	50	25,000	8	40,000	8,325
Department C	25	20,000	4	30,000	6,309
Department D	50	35,000	8	40,000	16,611
	200	140,000	50	$200,000	$82,745

	BASE FOR ALLOCATION	TOTAL AMOUNT TO BE ALLOCATED
Heat	Floor space	$ 18,000
Light and Power	Floor space	48,000
Telephone	Number of phones	12,000
Factory Depreciation	Floor space	35,000
Supplies	Rate of direct material used	6,800
Property Tax	Floor space	4,600
Fire Insurance	Floor space	6,000
Other Factory Costs	Number of employees	16,600
Total		$147,000
Custodial	Direct material used	
Maintenance	Floor space	
Factory Office	Number of employees	

The company allocates service department costs in the following order: (1) factory office, (2) maintenance, (3) custodial.

Required:

a. Prepare a schedule of overhead allocation. First allocate the above overhead costs to the various departments, and then reallocate the service department costs to the production departments.

b. Evaluate the appropriateness of the bases used for overhead allocation and suggest bases you think might be more equitable.

Problem 7-8

The Efficiency Company uses a job order cost system. At the beginning of the month, order number 410 was in process with a total cost of $4,654.

The following costs were incurred in April:

ORDER NUMBER	MATERIALS USED	DIRECT LABOR
410	$1,620	$4,500
411	2,308	7,084
412	952	1,648
413	1,475	3,070

At the end of April, order number 413 was still in process. Manufacturing overhead is applied to production at the rate of 75 percent of direct labor costs.

Orders 411 and 412 were sold for $22,400 and $6,805 respectively.

Required:
   a. Prepare the journal entries to record all of the transactions for the month of April.
   b. Prepare job costs sheets showing the charges to each job.

Case 7

BRIDGER MANUFACTURING COMPANY

The Bridger Manufacturing Company makes alarm clocks. The several different models offered for sale are basically all variations of one "standard" and one "deluxe" model, with several different trim features. For many years the firm was operated as a partnership by Mr. Cant and Mr. Wilson. Recently, Mr. Hood was admitted to the firm as a partner. The three partners decided that it would be advantageous to incorporate the business and thereby avoid some of the risks of partnership. They also felt a need for a good accounting system to provide information regarding their costs. You are hired to set up a cost accounting system for the company and to determine the unit cost of alarm clocks produced during October. After searching the records, you find the following information.

The company completed twenty thousand clocks during the month of October, of which 40 percent were deluxe models. Each clock consisted of a molded plastic case and three molded knobs manufactured in the molding shop, the clock works, manufactured in the stamping shop, and faces and hands produced in the assembly department. The parts were assembled into finished clocks by the assembly department and then stored and shipped by the materials handling department. Clean-up, machine servicing, and other miscellaneous services common to all shops and departments were handled by the service shop.

Materials costing eighty-five cents per clock were used in producing a case for each standard model, and materials costing ninety-five cents per clock were used in producing a case for each deluxe model. The material used to produce each knob cost three cents.

The stamping shop used $1.15 of sheet steel and steel rod, $0.35 of spring steel, $0.75 of phosphorous bronze, and $0.50 worth of sheet brass on each clock assembly. The assembly department added the face, hands, and various screws. Unit costs for materials used in the assembly department have not been calculated. However, materials which cost $16,160 were used by the department during the month. During that period 20,000 clocks were completed, of which 2,000 were in process (one-fourth complete) at the beginning of the period. There were 3,500 units one-fifth complete at the end of the month.

Direct labor in all shops was paid at the rate of $3.90 per hour. It took 0.3 hours to mold a standard case; 0.4 hours to mold a deluxe case; 0.1 hours to mold three knobs; 0.3 hours to stamp the gears for each clock; 0.2 hours to make the springs for each clock; 0.5 hours to make the shafts; 0.75 hours to assemble the clock works; 0.2 hours to install the case and put on the face and hands.

Overhead costs incurred during the month of October were as follows:

Molding	$ 30,000
Stamping	50,000
Assembly	60,000
Materials handling	14,000
Service	16,000
	$170,000

The service department's overhead costs are allocated equally to the other four departments, after which the material handling costs are allocated to the molding, stamping, and assembly departments in the ratio 3:2:1.

Overhead costs in the production departments (including that portion allocated from service departments) are assigned to the clocks on the basis of actual direct labor hours worked. During October, 8,800 direct labor hours were worked in the molding shop, 20,000 hours in the stamping shop, and 19,000 hours in the assembly shop.

QUESTIONS

1. What was the unit cost of each deluxe clock? What was the unit cost of a standard clock?
2. What kind of cost accounting system would you recommend for this company? Why?
3. If the company manufactures toys out of scrap plastic left over from molding clock cases, what costs should be charged to the toys (assume the plastic cannot be used in production of clocks)? What are such products called?
4. What is the hourly overhead rate in each of the departments?
5. What was the equivalent production during the month in the assembly department? How much was the materials cost per clock in the assembly department?

8

Accounting
for
Current Assets

In defining current assets in chapter 5, reference was made to the operating cycle. This is the cycle in which current assets are converted to cash (or consumed), and, in turn, the cash is used to acquire other current assets. This operating cycle flow may be summarized graphically as follows:

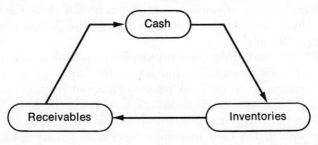

The operating cycle is the revenue-producing phase of a business. In order to maximize this revenue, management typically tries to minimize the length of each operating cycle. Other things remaining equal, the more turns it can get in an accounting period, the more revenue it will enjoy.

ACCOUNTING FOR CASH

Most companies try to operate with a minimum of cash on hand, placing as much as they can spare in inventories and other productive assets. Some cash, of course, is needed at all times to act as a reservoir from which day-to-day operations can be financed. The size of the cash balance required is determined largely by the regularity and rate of the cash inflows and outflows.

It is very important that controls be established within a company to safeguard the cash, so that all monies due the company are actually received and disbursements are made only for legitimate purposes. Cash has universal usage and can easily be misappropriated and concealed. It must, therefore, be subject to more strict control than that governing other assets.

As a means of control, most concerns maintain the bulk of their cash in checking accounts. A minimum of cash is maintained on hand in order to make change for customers (change funds) and to provide funds to make small cash purchases (petty cash funds). All cash received exclusive of these amounts is normally deposited in the bank on a daily basis. All disbursements are then made by check, except for very small sums which may be paid from the petty cash fund. Procedures normally require that every check be signed by two persons, each of whom is required to check carefully the disbursement's validity. The bank account thereby becomes the center of control over cash.

There are two records maintained to reflect the amount of cash a concern may have in the bank. The first is the company's Cash in Bank ledger account. As cash is received and deposited in the bank, the amounts are entered as debits to the account. As checks are written to satisfy the company's obligations, the amounts are entered as credits to the Cash in Bank account. The balance in this account is termed the "balance per books" as of any particular date.

The second record of the company's cash in the bank is one maintained by the bank. This account is a liability to the bank and is called Customers' Deposits. When the bank receives a deposit from a customer, the amount is entered as a credit to his account. As checks which have previously been written by the customer clear the bank, these amounts are entered as debits. The bank may enter other transactions in this account according to agreements with the customer. For example, the bank may act as agent for the customer in collecting a note, in which event the amount collected would also be credited to the customer's account. The balance in this account is known as the "balance per bank." At regular intervals (usually monthly), the bank sends the company a statement which summarizes all entries made in the account since the last statement. It also reflects the balance remaining in the account, according to the bank's records, at the end of the statement period. A sample bank statement from Zions First National Bank is shown in Figure 8-1.

Because both of these accounts cover the same funds, they should agree at all times. For a number of reasons, they normally do not; thus, the accountant must "reconcile" the two balances. There are only two reasons why the balances might not be in agreement: first, the company may have properly recorded items that the bank has not yet recorded; second, the bank may have recorded items that the company has not yet properly recorded. Because either of these may be either positive or negative, a bank reconciliation consists of four parts as follows:

Balance per books: xxx
   Items bank has recorded properly, company has not:
   1. Additions (e.g., collection of note by bank) xxx
                                                  xxx
   2. Deductions (e.g., bank service charge) xxx
     Adjusted balance per books xxx
Balance per bank: xxx
   Items company has properly recorded, bank has not:
   3. Additions (e.g., deposits in transit) xxx
                                                   xxx
   4. Deductions (e.g., outstanding checks) xxx
     Adjusted balance per bank xxx

Both bank and book balances are adjusted to the correct or true cash balance. Adjusting journal entries must be made on the company's books in order to adjust the ledger account to this corrected figure.

Illustration of Bank Reconciliation

In order to illustrate a bank reconciliation, let us assume the following set of facts. The bank statement from the Dodge National Bank covering the account of Color TV Sales Company for the month of November shows a balance at November 27 (the date of the last entry on the statement) of $435.44. The Cash in Bank account in Color TV Sales Company's ledger has a debit balance of $129.82 at the end of November. The company books indicate that a deposit of $420.00 was made on November 29. The following checks written during November were not returned by the bank: number 4084, $600.00; number 4094, $92.45; number 4095, $138.20;

Figure 8-1

BANK STATEMENT

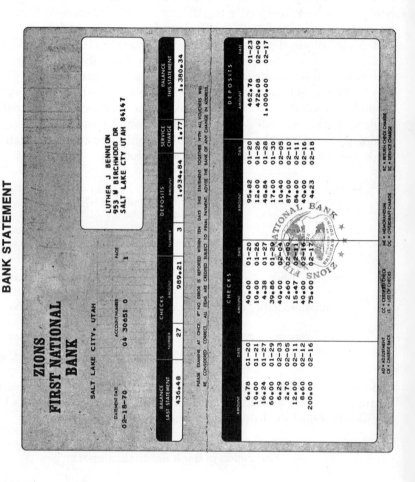

148

number 4097, $22.72. Also, check number 3884, written in August in the amount of $37.00, has still not cleared the bank. The items returned by the bank include:

1. A debit memo for $3.75 for bank service charges;
2. A debit memo for $15.00 for safety deposit box rental for one year, beginning December 1 of this year;
3. A credit memo for $78.00, which represents the net proceeds from collecting an $80.00, noninterest-bearing note after deducting a $2.00 collection charge;
4. An unnumbered check for $53.00 written to RCA Distributor for some merchandise;
5. A check written by Color TV Repair for $171.00 and charged in error to the account of Color TV Sales.

A bank reconciliation for the Color TV Sales at the end of November is shown in Figure 8-2.

Figure 8-2

COLOR TV SALES
Bank Reconciliation
as of November 30, 19xx

Balance per books		$ 129.82
Addition:		
Credit memo for collection of note:		
Face amount	$ 80.00	
Less: collection fee	2.00	78.00
		$ 207.82
Deduction:		
Debit memo for service charge	$ 3.75	
Debit memo for safety deposit box rental	15.00	
Unrecorded check	53.00	71.75
Adjusted balance per books		$ 136.07
Balance per bank		$ 435.44
Addition:		
Deposit of Nov. 29 in transit	$420.00	
Check of color TV repair charged in error	171.00	591.00
		$1,026.44
Deduction:		
Outstanding checks:		
#3884	$ 37.00	
#4084	600.00	
#4094	92.45	
#4095	138.20	
#4097	22.72	890.37
Adjusted balance per books		$ 136.07

Inasmuch as the books now show a balance of $129.82 and the reconciliation shows the correct cash balance to be $136.07, the following adjusting entries are necessary on the company's books:

Cash	78.00	
Bank Service Charges	2.00	
Notes Receivable		80.00
Bank Service Charges	3.75	
Prepaid Safety Deposit Box Rental	15.00	
Purchases	53.00	
Cash		71.75

One compound entry could be used instead of the above adjusting entries to reflect the corrected balance in the books, as follows:

Cash	6.25	
Bank Service Charges	5.75	
Prepaid Safety Deposit Box Rental	15.00	
Purchases	53.00	
Notes Receivable		80.00

ACCOUNTING FOR INVENTORIES

The subject of accounting for inventories, the second phase in the operating cycle, was discussed in the two preceding chapters. Chapter 6 dealt with accounting for inventories of merchandising concerns and chapter 7 with accounting for inventories of manufacturing enterprises. The major difference noted between these two types of businesses was the fact that the former purchased their inventories in finished form ready for sale, whereas the latter produced their finished inventories by consuming materials, labor, and overhead. One might expect that this production process would lengthen the time required to complete the inventory phase of the operating cycle. Other things being equal, we could expect to find a manufacturing firm utilizing more time to complete a cycle than might be used by a merchandising firm. Management's goal, of course, would be to keep the time required to complete the inventory phase of the cycle to a minimum. This can best be accomplished through utilizing scientific inventory management.

ACCOUNTING FOR RECEIVABLES

As inventories are sold, receivables are created, and the final phase of the operating cycle is ushered in. The time required to complete this phase of the cycle will depend on the company's credit terms and collection experience. The credit terms are influenced heavily by industry practices, while the collection policies are set by management. No matter how carefully management grants credit or how diligently it pursues collection, some receivables will never be collected. One of the major problems in accounting for receivables is making adequate provision in the accounts for these bad-debt losses. All businesses that grant credit must expect some of the accounts to go bad. In fact, even businesses that sell for cash only will have some bad-debt losses through bad checks. Although it is hoped that bad-debt losses can be held to a minimum, the fact that some will occur necessitates that provisions should be made.

Bad debts constitute an expense. According to the matching concept, these expenses should be charged to the period in which the sales revenue was recorded. Because the bad accounts are unknown at the time of the sale, it is necessary to estimate the bad-debt expense prior to the time when the bad account is actually written off.

Providing for Bad Debts

If an account is recognized as being bad during the same accounting period in which the sale is recorded, then it is appropriate to write the account off directly to the Bad-Debt Expense account as follows:

Bad-Debt Expense xxx
    Account Receivable—J. James   xxx

It would not be common for the above situation to occur. Normally it takes some time to recognize an account as being bad. For this reason, it is generally advisable to estimate the bad-debt expense in the period of sale and at that time make the following entry:

Bad-Debt Expense xxx
    Allowance for Bad Debts   xxx

In a subsequent period when the bad accounts are recognized, they are written off against the allowance as follows:

Allowance for Bad Debts xxx
    Accounts Receivable—I. M. Swindler   xxx

It can be seen that the Allowance for Bad Debts account is merely a suspense account in which the credits are held until it is known which customer's account is bad. This credit is then transferred to the appropriate accounts receivable account. The balance in the Allowance for Bad Debts account is shown on the balance sheet as a deduction from Accounts Receivable. It may be classified as a "contra" or negative asset account. This presentation serves to show that the company does not expect to collect all of the receivables.

Methods of Estimating Bad Debts

There are three primary methods used to estimate bad debts; each of them utilizes past experiences with bad-debt losses to arrive at rates applicable to current figures. The methods are discussed briefly in the following paragraphs.

Percent of Sales. A rate is developed from prior periods' bad-debt losses and sales figures (or sometimes credit sales figures). This rate, when multiplied by the current period's sales, will give the company an estimate of the bad-debt expense for the same period. The rate is multiplied by an income statement account (Sales); therefore, the product is also an income statement account (Bad-Debt Expense).

Percent of Accounts Receivable. Under this method a rate is developed by comparing former bad-debt losses with year-end accounts receivable balances. This rate is applied to the current year-end accounts receivable balance as an estimate of the total amount of accounts that will not be collected. This method does not provide the amount of the expense directly because provision may have been made in prior periods for some of these same accounts to go bad. The amount of expense is determined by taking the product of the above calculation and adding (debit balance) or subtracting (credit balance) the balance already in the Allowance for Bad Debts account. Inasmuch as the rate is applied to a balance sheet account (Accounts Receivable), it seems logical that the product will also reflect the balance of a balance sheet account (Allowance for Bad Debts). If the accountant failed to give consideration to the existing balance in the allowance account he might be providing for the same account to go bad several times, since an account receivable balance could remain on the books for several periods. It is not necessary to give consideration to the allowance balance under the first method, since the rate is applied only to the sales of one period. Any balance which might remain in the account is assumed to pertain to previous periods' sales.

Aging Accounts Receivable. This is just a refinement of the second method, percent of accounts receivable. Instead of having one rate for the total accounts receivable, several rates are developed according to the age of the particular receivable. Normally, experience will indicate that the longer the account remains unpaid, the less likely is ultimate collection. Recognizing this fact, the accounts receivable balances are sorted according to age, and a separate rate is applied to each age based on past experience. For example, a company might find that only 0.5 percent of balances that are less than thirty days old will go bad, whereas 50 percent of those over 120 days will go bad.

Since this method is only a refinement of the previous method, it also provides the amount desired as the balance in the allowance account. Again, consideration must be given to the existing balance in the allowance account before arriving at the amount of expense for the period.

Accounting for Notes

In some instances, promissory notes are given in payment of accounts. Promissory notes are written agreements to pay a fixed sum of money at a specified date. These notes may be interest-bearing or noninterest-bearing. Figure 8-3 shows a sample form used for an interest-bearing note.

We should not be overly concerned here with the problems of accounting for notes. Our major reason for discussing the subject is to note some simple rules for calculating interest. The student should recall the discussion of adjusting entries in chapter 4, and note that interest on notes accrues and generally will require adjustment at the end of the period.

If a 6 percent, sixty-day note in the amount of $600 is received December 1 as payment on account, the following entry would be appropriate:

Notes Receivable	600	
Accounts Receivable		600

At the end of December, when the company closes its books, the following adjustment would be made:

Accrued Interest Receivable	3	
Interest Earned		3

When the note and interest are paid on January 30, the following entry would be recorded:

Cash	606	
Notes Receivable		600
Accrued Interest Receivable		3
Interest Earned		3

Figure 8-3

PROMISSORY NOTE
(INDIVIDUALS AND PARTNERSHIPS)

_____, UTAH

$ _____   _____, 19___

_____ AFTER DATE, FOR VALUE RECEIVED, THE UNDERSIGNED, JOINTLY AND SEVERALLY, PROMISE TO PAY TO THE ORDER OF ZIONS FIRST NATIONAL BANK, A NATIONAL ASSOCIATION, AT ITS _____ OFFICE IN _____, UTAH, THE SUM OF

_____ DOLLARS

IN LAWFUL MONEY OF THE UNITED STATES WITH INTEREST THEREON IN LIKE MONEY AT THE RATE OF _____ PER CENT PER ANNUM,

BOTH BEFORE AND AFTER JUDGMENT, PAYABLE _____ FROM DATE UNTIL PAID.

If the holder deems itself insecure, or if default be made in payment of the principal, or if the interest be not paid when due, time being the essence hereof, then the entire unpaid balance, with interest as aforesaid, shall at the election of the holder hereof, and without notice of said election, at once become due and payable.

If this note becomes in default as aforesaid, the undersigned, jointly and severally, agree to pay to the holder hereof collection costs, including reasonable attorneys' fees and legal expenses, in addition to all other sums due hereunder.

The undersigned and all endorsers, sureties and guarantors hereof hereby jointly and severally waive presentment for payment, demand, protest, notice of protest and of non-payment and of dishonor, and consent to extensions of time, renewal, waivers or modifications without notice.

No. _____ Due _____ Renewed _____

P. O. _____ Phone _____

CL-1 Rev. 6-69 2M

DISCLOSURE STATEMENT (COMMERCIAL CONSUMER LOAN)

NAME _____

1. LOAN PROCEEDS	_____	$ _____
2. OTHER CHARGES	_____	$ _____
3. AMOUNT FINANCED (1 + 2)	_____	$ _____
4. FINANCE CHARGE	_____	$ _____
5. TOTAL OF PAYMENTS (3 + 4)	_____	

PAYMENTS IN AMOUNTS AND DUE AS PROVIDED IN ATTACHED PROMISSORY NOTE OF EVEN DATE.

6. ANNUAL PERCENTAGE RATE _____ %

7. IF ANY DEFAULT OCCURS, BANK MAY OFFSET AGAINST THIS LOAN ANY BANK ACCOUNT OR OTHER AMOUNTS OWED BY BANK IN ANY CAPACITY TO BORROWER. REASONABLE ATTORNEYS' FEES AND LAWFUL COLLECTION COSTS INCURRED AFTER DEFAULT MAY ALSO BE IMPOSED.

8. THIS LOAN IS SECURED BY (LIST BOTH DOCUMENT(S) AND COLLATERAL): _____

(Reference is made to security document(s), if any, listed above for additional information.)

RECEIVED THIS STATEMENT AND PROMISSORY NOTE, WITH ALL BLANKS COMPLETED, BEFORE SIGNING ANY DOCUMENT EVIDENCING THIS LOAN.

DATE: _____   _____ BORROWER

Accounting for Interest

The formula for calculating interest on a note is as follows:

Face of note × Rate of interest × Period of time

In calculating interest the following rules are normally applied:

1. Unless specified otherwise, the rate on a note represents the rate *per annum*. A 6 percent, sixty-day note, for example, does not earn 6 percent in sixty days. It earns interest at the rate of 6 percent *per annum* for a sixty-day period.
2. In order to simplify the calculations, a 360-day year is used in calculating interest. Again referring to a 6 percent, sixty-day note, the time period would be referred to as 60/360 or 1/6.
3. In calculating the due date of a note, the first day is not counted, but the last day is counted. A sixty-day note dated December 1 will fall due January 30, not January 29.

A short-cut method of calculating interest known as the "6 percent method" is sometimes used. This simply recognizes that the interest on a 6 percent, sixty-day note works out to be exactly 1 percent of the face of the note. The interest on a 6 percent, sixty-day note in the amount of $7,295 is $72.95. Notice how the formula cancels out to 1/100, or 1 percent.

$$7,295 \times \frac{\overset{1}{\cancel{6}}}{100} \times \frac{\overset{1}{\cancel{60}}}{\underset{\underset{1}{\cancel{6}}}{\cancel{360}}} = 72.95$$

This technique can be utilized quickly for notes with different lengths of maturity. For example, a 6 percent, ninety-day note would be one and one-half times the interest of a sixty-day note, thus:

6 percent, ninety-day note in the amount of $3,720:

Interest on 6 percent, sixty-day note (1 percent)	$37.20
Add one-half (ninety days is one-half greater than sixty days)	18.60
Interest on 6 percent, ninety-day note	$45.80

Likewise, the technique can be used for different interest rates. For example, an 8 percent, sixty-day note would be one and one-third times the interest of a 6 percent note, thus:

8 percent, sixty-day note in the amount of $8,430:

Interest on 6 percent, sixty-day note (1 percent)	$ 84.30
Add one-third (8 percent is one-third greater than 6 percent)	28.10
Interest on 8 percent, sixty-day note	$112.40

With different interest rates and different lengths of maturity, the 6 percent method might still be a useful and time-saving technique, as is seen in the following illustration:

8 percent, ninety-day note of $1,550:

Interest on 6 percent, sixty-day note (1 percent)	$15.50
Add one-half (ninety days is one-half greater than sixty days)	7.75
	23.25
Add one-third (8 percent is one-third greater than 6 percent)	7.75
Interest on 8 percent, ninety-day note	$31.00

SUMMARY

All businesses which sell goods go through an operating cycle: utilizing cash to buy or produce inventories, selling these inventories (usually on credit), and collecting the accounts receivable arising therefrom. This operating cycle is self-generative and is repeated over and over again in the life of a business. Most business enterprises complete several cycles per year. For some, it may take several years to complete a single revolution. In this chapter, some of the procedures associated with the accounting for cash and receivables have been discussed. Accounting for inventories was discussed in chapter 6 (for a merchandising concern) and in chapter 7 (for a manufacturing enterprise).

Cash is the reservoir from which operations are financed. It is generally desirable to keep the level of cash to a minimum and to invest the excess in productive assets. Control over cash is maintained in part from depositing most sums in the bank and then making all but petty expenditures by check only. The balance of the Cash in Bank account must be reconciled monthly with figures shown on the bank's statement.

Credit may be granted to customers on open account or by promissory notes. The receivables created by this practice constitute the final phase of the operating cycle. Regardless of the care exercised by management, some receivables will prove to be uncollectible. Proper matching of revenue and expense, as well as more accurate balance sheet valuations, are accomplished by providing for these uncollectibles in advance. Where this is done, an estimate is made in the period of sale to establish an allowance for bad debts. When the accounts are found in fact to be bad, usually in a later accounting period, the uncollectible account is then written off against the allowance.

QUESTIONS

1. Why is it important that a company control the size of its cash balance? Can a company have too much cash?
2. List some of the important internal controls which a company might adopt to safeguard its cash.
3. What two cash records must be reconciled at the end of each month? What are some of the reasons these two records might not agree?
4. How should a customer's N.S.F. (nonsufficient funds) check that has been returned by the bank be treated in a bank reconciliation?
5. What are outstanding checks? How would a person go about compiling a list of outstanding checks?
6. What are deposits in transit? How are such items shown in a bank reconciliation?
7. Can bad debts arise on cash sales or only on credit sales? Explain.
8. Why is it customary to set up a provision for bad debts in advance, rather than waiting until the account is actually known to be bad?
9. What type of an account is the Allowance for Bad Debts? How should this account be shown in the balance sheet?
10. Determine the amount of bad-debt expense, assuming the company estimates 2 percent of the receivables balances will prove uncollectible and has the following account balances: Accounts Receivable, $29,490 (debit); Allowance for Doubtful Accounts, $120 (credit); Accounts Payable, $30,300 (credit); Sales $229,400 (credit).
11. Refer to the facts in question 10 and determine the amount of bad-debt expense, assuming the company estimates that one-half of 1 percent of sales will be uncollectible.
12. Determine the amount of interest on a seventy-five-day, 5 percent note in the amount of $1,325.
13. Use the 6 percent method to determine the amount of interest on a forty-two-day, 6 percent note in the amount of $425.

PROBLEMS

Problem 8-1

The books of Hogan's Hatrack showed accounts with the following balances on December 31:

Sales .... $74,000 credit
Accounts Receivable .... 17,000 debit
Allowance for Doubtful Accounts ....   100 credit
Sales Returns ....   700 debit

The bookkeeper has prepared the following aging of the accounts receivable.

| | DAYS OLD | | | |
	0-30	31-60	61-90	over 90
Amount	$8,000	$4,000	$3,000	$2,000
Estimated percent uncollectible	1	5	10	50

Required:
  a. Based on the aging schedule and the estimated percentages of
     bad debts, prepare the adjusting journal entry to record the bad-
     debt expense for the year.
  b. Assuming that the schedule had not been prepared and that bad
     debts are estimated at one percent of net sales, prepare the ad-
     justing entry to record the expense.
  c. On January 10 of the following year, it was decided that the
     $1,000 account of J. D. Prestwitch, now six months old, was
     uncollectible. Prepare the entry to write it off.
  d. On January 21 a check was received from J. D. Prestwitch for
     $500 on account. No further payments are expected. Make the
     appropriate journal entries.

Problem 8-2

	FACE OF NOTE	RATE OF INTEREST (PERCENT)	PERIOD OF TIME (DAYS)
a.	$22,340	6	42
b.	8,268	9	60
c.	15,287	4	90
d.	4,619	7	84
e.	3,042	8	72
f.	48,507	3	132

Required:
Using the 6 percent method, calculate the interest on the above notes.

Problem 8-3

The Valley Company received an 8 percent, forty-two-day note dated June
20, in the amount of $9,556, from Mr. Beaumont as payment on his account.
On June 30 the company closed its books. Valley Company received full
payment from Mr. Beaumont on August 1.

Required:
Prepare all journal entries that should be made on Valley Company books.

Problem 8-4

An analysis of the records of Baja Corporation on December 31, 1969, revealed the following information:

Sales	$2,583,000 credit
Accounts Receivable	342,600 debit
Allowance for Doubtful Accounts	1,809 debit

The manager of the company has decided that the estimate for bad debts should be at a higher rate than in the past.

Required:

Assume that the company has been using the percent of sales method and prepare journal entries to record the following:

a. The bad-debt expense for the year if the new rate to be used is one-half of 1 percent of sales.

b. On February 3, 1970, it was determined that W. Wilson would probably not pay his account of $1,425.

c. On March 1, 1970, a check for $925 was received from W. Wilson as partial payment of his account. (He indicated the balance would be forthcoming.)

Assume that the company has been using the percent of accounts receivable method (rather than the percent of sales method assumed above) and prepare journal entries to record:

d. The bad-debt expense for the year if the new rate is 2½ percent of accounts receivable.

e. The write-off of the W. Wilson account.

f. The subsequent reinstatement and payment by W. Wilson.

Problem 8-5

An examination of the records of Superior Company revealed the following information:

Cash Deposits

DATE	AMOUNT
Nov. 1	$1,220.60
4	418.09
12	132.68
15	2,489.82
19	142.18
23	503.35
25	1,340.82
27	275.48
28	216.12
29	313.16
30	1,142.85
	$8,195.15

Checks Written

CHECK NUMBER	DATE	AMOUNT
913	Nov. 2	$ 195.00
914	8	1,470.88
915	14	351.75
916	16	568.90
917	20	1,184.25
918	21	308.10
919	23	411.68
920	25	1,008.34
921	28	148.52
922	30	321.27
		$5,968.69

A bank account is held with the National City Bank. An examination of the bank statement revealed the following information:

CHECKS RETURNED	DEPOSITS RECEIVED BY THE BANK
$ 195.00	$1,220.60
62.25 N.S.F.	418.09
568.90	2,489.82
1,470.88	142.18
148.52	132.68
1,008.34	503.35
411.68	1,340.82
4.48 service charge	275.48

The balance per books on November 1, 1970, was $2,168.57. There were no outstanding checks or deposits in transit on October 31, 1970. The November 30 balance shown on the bank statement was $4,821.54. The N.S.F. check was previously received from Atlas Company as a payment on their account.

Required:

a. Prepare Superior Company's bank reconciliation.
b. Make any necessary adjusting journal entries.

Problem 8-6

The following information was taken from the records of Colorado Corporation on August 31, 1999.

1. An examination of the returned checks revealed that the following had not cleared:

NUMBER	AMOUNT
3521	$ 347.50
3535	23.09
3547	1,425.11
3549	69.83
3552	133.16
3555	833.57

6

2. An unrecorded check made out to Management Company for $1,560.70 cleared the bank. This was a payment on accounts payable.
3. Check #3528 in the amount of $255.20 was erroneously recorded as $220.55. The offsetting debit was to interest expense.
4. Deposits in transit on July 31, 1999, amounted to $8,700.44.
5. Deposits in transit on August 31, 1999, amounted to $13,316.50.
6. A debit memo for $12.16 represented the bank service charges.
7. The balance on the bank statement as of August 31 was $44,199.76.

Required:
   a. Calculate the balance per books at August 31, 1999.
   b. Prepare a bank reconciliation.
   c. Record all necessary adjusting entries on Colorado Corporation books.

Problem 8-7
   The following information was taken from the bank statement and the books of Barton Engineering Company on May 31, 1970.
   1. The balance on the bank statement as of May 31, 1970, is $5,261.75.
   2. The balance per books as of May 31, 1970, is $3,621.57.
   3. An examination of the returned checks revealed that the following had not cleared:

NUMBER	AMOUNT
589	$232.16
603	420.45
611	325.89
614	129.50
616	239.50

   4. Check number 609, issued as partial payment of an account payable, was recorded for $194.50. The actual amount on the check was $149.50.
   5. An unrecorded check, paying Oliver and Company for supplies purchased on account for $461.90, has cleared the bank.
   6. A check written by Braton Engle, Incorporated, for $255.21 was charged in error by the bank to Barton Engineering Company's account.
   7. An examination of the deposits received by the bank showed that the company's deposit of $250 had not been recorded on the books.
   8. A deposit of $195.37 made by Burton Equipment Company was added by the bank to the Barton Engineering Company's account.
   9. A deposit of $1,490.60 was in transit at the end of May.
   10. A credit memo for $2,141.25 represents the net proceeds from the collection of a $2,125.00 note and $21.25 interest after deducting a $5.00 collection charge.

p

℃ ☞ 11. A check for $125.47 received from N. O. Money as payment of his account was returned to Barton Engineering Company marked N.S.F.

℃ 𝒟 12. A debit memo for $5.76 represented the bank's service charge.

Required:

    a. Prepare a bank reconciliation in good form.

    b. Record all necessary adjusting entries on Barton Engineering Company's books.

Case 8
KORNER'S GROCERY STORE

Mr. A. O. Korner is the sole owner of the Korner's Grocery Store. He started the business from scratch and built it up to the point where he is now doing a sizable business. His store is located next to the B.S.U. Campus, and much of his business is with college students and faculty members.

Mr. Korner had always run his store on a cash basis, paying his creditors as they delivered the merchandise he ordered. For some time he worried over the substantial amounts of cash that accumulated during the week. He first tried taking the cash home at night, but then began to worry that he might be robbed as he closed the store after dark. He asked one of his customers, a member of the B.S.U. accounting faculty, what he should do about the excess cash on hand. The accounting professor suggested that Mr. Korner open a business checking account and that he pay his creditors only by check. He could maintain a small change fund and then deposit his cash receipts on a daily basis.

Mr. Korner took the advice and went to the Planter National Bank to open an account. Several weeks later he received his first statement from the bank, showing a month end cash balance of $389.12. At first he thought the bank had made a mistake since his checkbook showed a balance of only $383.92. He then sat down and compared the checks returned by the bank against his own record of checks written, finding that the following checks had not been returned: number 104 to Aston Wholesale for $96.45; number 107 to Easyway Dairies for $76.18; number 111 to Lurkind's Bakeries for $26.12; and number 113 to Bozeman Distributing Company for $87.95. In addition, check number 115, written for $49.50, had been recorded in the checkbook at $45.90. He found another check drawn on the Korner Furniture Company for $65.15 included in his returned checks, and there was a notice on the statement that his account had been billed $2.25 for the monthly service charge. The deposits shown on the statement were short of the amount shown in the checkbook, and careful analysis showed the bank had not recorded deposits in the amounts of $100.75 and $183.25. He had also turned over to the bank for collection a $200, 6 percent, five-month note owed to him by Mr. I. M. Lake. The bank statement indicated the note and interest had been collected. A charge of $2.50 had been deducted by the bank for the services rendered. Mr. Korner noted that three customers' checks, totaling $129.00, had been returned by the bank marked "N.S.F."

After considerable manipulation, Mr. Korner prepared the following reconciliation:

Mr. Korner's Checkbook Balance		$383.92
+ Checks Outstanding	$286.70	
		$286.70
− Service Charge	2.25	
− Note Service Charge	2.50	
− Check Charged in Error	65.15	
− Error on Check Number 115	3.60	
		$ 73.50
Adjusted Checkbook Balance		$597.12
Bank Statement Balance		$389.12
+ Deposits since Statement	$284.00	
+ N.S.F. Checks	129.00	
		$413.00
− Note Collected	$205.00	
		$205.00
Adjusted Bank Statement Balance		$597.12

While his bank reconciliation did balance, he was concerned about how to handle the N.S.F. checks since bad checks had always been a problem. In the past he had turned all checks over to a collection agency which charged him 3 percent of the gross amount of the checks collected. Checks which could not be collected within a six-month period were returned by the collection agent to Mr. Korner, who wrote them off as a bad-debt expense as soon as they were returned. Mr. Korner estimates that about 40 percent of his sales are now paid for by check and that approximately 5 percent of the amount of checks he receives prove uncollectible.

Mr. Korner thinks his bank reconciliation is all right, but his concern about the N.S.F. checks prompts him to show the reconciliation to the accounting professor. As the professor, answer the following questions:

1. Is Mr. Korner's bank reconciliation correct? Why?
2. What adjusting entries should Mr. Korner make, assuming he is now closing his books?
3. What rules could you suggest to Mr. Korner to assist him in preparing future reconciliations?
4. How would you suggest Mr. Korner account for N.S.F. checks? Assuming his sales for the past year were $102,000 and that N.S.F. checks written off (all pertaining to this year's sales) amount to $12,00, prepare entries to account for the N.S.F. checks.

9

Accounting
for
Fixed Assets

Fixed assets represent relatively long-lived assets which are used in the business. Some of these assets have perpetual life and will remain on the books without change as long as the business is in existence. Most of them, however, will be useful to the business for only a limited period of time.

ACQUISITION OF FIXED ASSETS

Fixed assets are initially recorded on the books at cost. The cost figure includes all expenditures incurred in getting the assets on the premises, in place, and ready to use. An asset's cost includes the invoice price, sales taxes, freight and transportation costs, installation costs (including wages paid a company's own employees), special modification costs, testing costs, and any other expenditure associated with getting the asset ready to use. As a matter of expediency, some of these costs may be charged off as an expense where the amounts are immaterial.

By the same token, all price reductions or discounts should be treated as reductions to the cost of the asset. A cash discount on a new machine, for example, should be credited to the asset account. Similarly, the proceeds from razing an old building from the site of a new building should be treated as a reduction in the cost of the land.

Expenditures pertaining to an asset which are made after the asset has been placed in operation may fall into one of three categories: routine maintenance and repairs, extraordinary repairs that extend the asset's life beyond original expectation, and extraordinary repairs that do not extend the asset's life. Admittedly, the line between these is often difficult to draw. Routine maintenance and repairs are called *revenue expenditures* because they are charged off as expenses (offset against revenues) during the period in which they are incurred. Any expenditure that might be expected to occur in the ordinary course of an asset's life would be considered as a revenue expenditure. Replacing spark plugs, oil filters, tires, and similar items on a delivery truck would all be examples of typical revenue expenditures.

All expenditures that are not expensed must be capitalized. When an expenditure is capitalized it is charged to an asset account and then amortized over the accounting periods that benefit from the expenditure. These capitalized expenditures may be of two types: those that *do* extend the original asset's life and those that *do not* extend the original asset's life. The former type is capitalized by debiting the accumulated depreciation account. This type of expenditure may be regarded as cancelling part of the previous depreciation. Replacing an engine in an old delivery truck would be an example of such an expenditure.

Those capital expenditures that *do not* extend the asset's life, but nevertheless serve to improve or better the asset, should be charged directly to the asset account. For example, the installation of a heavy-duty bumper on a delivery truck should be charged to the asset account. Such an expenditure would increase the usefulness of the truck, but would in no way influence its life span.

METHODS OF DEPRECIATION

Nearly all expenditures ultimately will be recognized as expenses. Those that are capitalized in the current period must ultimately be apportioned to the various accounting periods that use the particular asset. The process of allocating the cost of a fixed asset to the various periods is known as *depreciation* (in the case of tangible fixed assets), or *depletion* (in the case of "wasting" fixed assets), or *amortization* (in the case of intangible fixed assets). This allocation is done in accordance with the matching concept, which specifies that expenses should be matched with the revenues they help produce. In chapter 4, depreciation was allocated on a straight-line basis, that is, in a manner which provided for equal charges to each period. In some instances, straight-line depreciation results in proper matching, but in many cases the amount or quality of service received from an asset varies greatly from period to period. For this reason, we find several different methods of depreciation used in practice. The four most common depreciation methods are *straight-line, units of production, sum-of-the-years'-digits, and declining balance.*

Straight-Line

Straight-line depreciation should be used in those instances where passage of time is the most important factor relating to use. The assumption is, of course, that each period receives services of equal value from using the asset. The formula for straight-line depreciation is

$$\frac{C - S}{N^t} = D$$

where C = Cost of asset

S = Scrap value or salvage value

N^t = Life of asset expressed in terms of time (number of accounting periods)

D = Depreciation per period

Units of Production

The units of production method is similar to the straight-line method, except that the asset's life is measured in units of output rather than periods of time. For example, the life of a taxicab might be estimated as 100,000 miles, because in measuring the benefit derived from using the cab, mileage is probably a more important factor than time. The formula for units of production depreciation is

$$\frac{C - S}{N^u} = D^u$$

where N^u = Life of asset expressed in terms of units of output

D^u = Depreciation per unit of output

To get the depreciation for a particular period of time, the depreciation per unit (D^u) would be multiplied by the total output for the period. In the case of the taxicab, the depreciation per mile would be multiplied by the number of miles driven during the particular period.

Accelerated Depreciation

It can be argued that instead of apportioning the depreciation on an equal basis, the early periods of an asset's life should be charged with more depreciation and the later periods with less. Such a practice is known as *accelerated depreciation*, because the depreciation takes place at a faster rate in the early years.

There are two major arguments for accelerated depreciation. First, in many cases the value of the service rendered is not the same in the first year, when the machine is new and efficient, as in the last year, when it is nearly broken down. For example, a precision lathe will produce fewer rejects when it is new than when it is old. A new apartment building will command higher rent and greater occupancy when it is new than it will when it is old.[1]

The second argument in favor of accelerated depreciation relates to the cost of maintaining an asset. It is noted that the total cost of using the asset consists of depreciation charges plus maintenance costs. Since maintenance costs tend to increase as the machine gets older, a more uniform total charge would occur if the depreciation followed the opposite pattern. This may be seen more clearly by referring to the diagrams shown in Figure 9-1. The first diagram plots the costs under straight-line depreciation, while the second diagram uses one of the accelerated techniques. Notice how much more uniform the total costs are in the second diagram.

Figure 9-1
COMPARISON OF COSTS UNDER STRAIGHT-LINE
AND ACCELERATED DEPRECIATION METHODS

Assumptions:
    Machine cost: $25,000
    Machine life: 5 years
    Maintenance charges: year 1, $500; year 2, $1,200; year 3, $2,200; year 4, $3,500; year 5, $5,000.

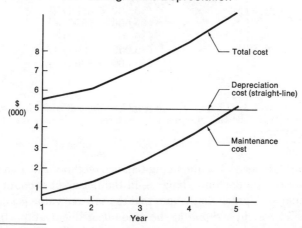

Straight-line Depreciation

[1] Ignore for the time being the complications caused by inflation and the changing value of the dollar. These problems are discussed in chapters 19 and 21 of this text.

Sum-of-the-Year's-Digits Depreciation

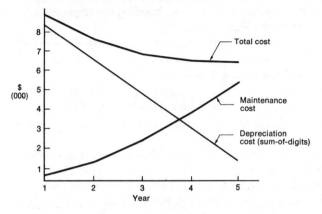

There are two major methods of calculating accelerated depreciation: sum-of-the-years' digits, and declining balance. Although the two methods do not produce identical results, both give the desired result of charging more depreciation in the early years and less in the later years.

Sum-of-the-Years'-Digits. The digits representing each accounting period are summed, and then used in reverse order to calculate the fraction of the total depreciation (cost less salvage) that should be charged in a particular period. For example, assume a machine that cost $5,000 will last six years, at which time it is expected that it will have an $800 salvage value. The depreciation calculation under the sum-of-the-years'-digits method is shown below.

YEAR	FRACTION		(C − S)	ANNUAL DEPRECIATION
1	6/21	×	($5,000 − $800) =	$1,200
2	5/21	×	($5,000 − $800) =	1,000
3	4/21	×	($5,000 − $800) =	800
4	3/21	×	($5,000 − $800) =	600
5	2/21	×	($5,000 − $800) =	400
6	1/21	×	($5,000 − $800) =	200
21ᵃ				$4,200

ᵃFor assets with long lives, where it would be difficult to actually sum all the digits, the following formula may be used to calculate the divisor: $S = \frac{N(N+1)}{2}$, where S = sum of digits N = number of accounting periods.

Declining Balance. The declining balance method utilizes a rate which is multiplied by the declining balance in the net asset account (asset less the accumulated depreciation). Note that the salvage value is *not* deducted from the asset cost in arriving at the amount of depeciation. Instead, the salvage value is taken into consideration in establishing the rate; but, once the rate is set up, the salvage value is no longer used in the calculations.

There are two methods that might be followed to establish the rate to be used. The theoretically correct method would be to use the rate that, when multiplied by the declining balance in the asset account, would leave the amount of the salvage in the asset account at the end of the last year. The formula to calculate this theoretical rate is

$$\text{Depreciation rate} = 1 - \sqrt[n]{\frac{\text{salvage}}{\text{cost}}}$$

The second method of establishing the rate is to double the straight-line rate. There is no theoretical justification for this method, which is borrowed from the income tax law.[2] Since depreciation is only an estimate anyway, the tax method is probably just as accurate as the theoretical method.

To illustrate the declining balance method, assume the following:

Asset cost: $5,000
Asset salvage value: $500
Asset life: five years

Since the asset life is five years, the straight-line rate is 20 percent (100 percent ÷ 5 years) and the declining balance rate (tax method) is 40 percent. The depreciation is calculated as follows:

(A) YEAR	(B) NET BALANCE IN ASSET ACCOUNT PRIOR TO CURRENT DEPRECIATION	(C) DEPRECIATION FOR YEAR (40 PERCENT OF COLUMN B)	(D) REMAINING BALANCE IN ASSET ACCOUNT AFTER CURRENT DEPRECIATION
1	$5,000	$2,000	$3,000
2	3,000	1,200	1,800
3	1,800	720	1,080
4	1,080	432	648
5	648	259	389

Revising Depreciation

It has previously been noted that depreciation is the product of several estimates. When it becomes apparent that an estimate made in a previous period is in error and the depreciation in turn has been misstated, the depreciation should be revised. There are two methods used to revise depreciation: counterbalancing errors, and revising past profits.

The first of these methods simply offsets the erroneous charge that has been made in the past with counterbalancing errors in the future. To illustrate, assume that an asset originally cost $10,000 and that the asset's

---

[2] The maximum rate allowable under accelerated depreciation for federal tax purposes is double the straight-line rate [Sec. 167(b), par. 2 of *1954 Internal Revenue Code*.]

life was estimated at ten years with a $1,000 salvage value. After four years it becomes apparent that the machine will last only a total of eight years with a $400 salvage. The depreciation can be revised by merely calculating the remaining balance to be depreciated, and then recomputing a rate for the remaining years of the asset's life. This could be done as follows:

Original cost	$10,000
Less depreciation to date (four years at $900 per year) ..	3,600
Net	$ 6,400
Less new salvage value	400
Remainder to be depreciated	$ 6,000
Depreciation for remaining years ($6,000 ÷ 4)	$ 1,500

The depreciation for the entire eight-year life may be summarized as follows:

YEAR	DEPRECIATION
1	$ 900
2	900
3	900
4	900
5	1,500
6	1,500
7	1,500
8	1,500
	$9,600

This method results in substantially higher depreciation charges in the last four years. An overcharge of depreciation is made in the last four years to offset the undercharge which was made in the first four years.

Under the second method, the depreciation rate is revised to reflect what the depreciation should have been, based upon the new set of facts. The accumulated depreciation account is then revised to reflect the proper balance with an offsetting entry being made to retained earnings as a revision of past periods' depreciation. Referring to the previous set of facts, we could calculate the revised depreciation and the amount of the necessary adjustment as follows:

Asset cost	$10,000
Revised estimate of salvage value	400
Net amount to be depreciated	$ 9,600
Revised depreciation per year ($9600 ÷ 8 years)	$ 1,200
Desired balance in the allowance for depreciation account (4 years × $1200)	$ 4,800
Actual amount in the allowance for depreciation account (4 years × $900)	3,600
Adjustment required	$ 1,200

The books could be corrected by the following entry:

Retained Earnings (Revision of Prior Years' Profits).	1,200	
Accumulated Depreciation		1,200

The remaining years would then be charged depreciation at the revised rate of $1,200 per year.

DEPLETION

Wasting assets are natural resources, such as mineral deposits, timberlands, and similar properties, that lose their value to the business as the resources are depleted. These assets are accounted for in a manner similar to that followed under the units of production method of depreciation. The "life" of the property is usually stated in terms of expected economical production. Generally, the accountant must rely on estimates of experts, such as geologists or engineers, in order to establish the potential output of these properties. A geologist, for example, might be called upon to estimate the total barrels of oil that might economically be pumped from a given well. The cost of developing the well would then be assigned to various accounting periods on the basis of the relative quantity of oil pumped. The process of allocating the cost of wasting assets to the various accounting periods is known as *depletion*. Suppose, for example, that it is estimated that a given oil well will produce one million barrels of oil and that the well will cost $50,000 to develop. The depletion rate in this instance would be $0.05 per barrel ($50,000 ÷ 1 million barrels). If 85,000 barrels were pumped in a given period, the depletion expense would be recorded as follows:

Depletion Expense   4,250
    Accumulated Depletion of oil properties   4,250

The Accumulated Depletion account would be treated as a contra asset to the property account.

AMORTIZATION

Amortization is the term used to describe the allocation of intangible asset costs such as patents or copyrights. The process is identical to that used in depreciating tangible fixed assets. It is simply a matter of terminology. Depreciation is the process of allocating the cost of tangible fixed assets, whereas amortization is the process of allocating the cost of intangible fixed assets.[3]

Intangibles may be amortized in a variety of manners (straight-line, units of production, or accelerated basis), as is the case with tangible fixed assets.

DISPOSAL OF FIXED ASSETS

Fixed assets may be disposed of through sale, trade-in, destruction, or retirement. In most instances, this does not occur exactly at the end of an

---

[3]The term *amortization* is also used to describe other allocations, such as the amortization of bond discounts and premiums as described in chapter 10.

accounting period, and so it is necessary to record depreciation for the fractional period. The disposition of the fixed asset cannot properly be recorded until the depreciation is brought up to date.

Depreciation for Fractional Periods

Most companies follow the practice of rounding depreciation to the nearest whole month. If an asset is acquired after the middle of the month or disposed of prior to the middle of the month, then no depreciation is charged for that month. On the other hand, when an asset is acquired during the first half of the month or disposed of during the last half of the month, a full month's depreciation is charged.

There are many other methods of rounding depreciation. Some companies go so far as to charge depreciation only on year-end balances. This has the effect of charging a full year's depreciation in year of acquisition and no depreciation in year of disposition. The practice of rounding depreciation can be justified on the grounds that deprecation is not an exact process anyway, but merely an estimate.

Where depreciation is recorded for a fractional period, it is normally calculated on a straight-line basis for this shorter period, regardless of the method of depreciation used for the full accounting period. To illustrate, let us assume the following about the asset:

Cost: $500
Acquired: January 2, 1968
Estimated life: four years
Estimated salvage value: $100
Method of depreciation: sum-of-the-years'-digits
Disposed of: April 13, 1970

Depreciation for the full third year (1970) would be $80 (2/10 × $400). Depreciation to April 13, 1970, would be one-fourth of this amount, or $20. For fractional periods, then, the depreciation is first calculated for the full accounting period under the appropriate method of depreciation and then apportioned to the fractional period on a straight-line basis.

Retirement, Sale, or Destruction

When a company continues to use fully depreciated fixed assets, it should continue to carry the asset account and the accumulated depreciation account on the books, even though no depreciation is being charged. When the asset is scrapped or retired from use, the asset account and accumulated depreciation account should be closed and the difference recorded as a loss.

Normally, when a fixed asset is disposed of, it has some value and is either sold or traded in on another asset. When it is sold, the cash received reduces the loss or adds to the gain. The entry to record the sale of an asset would be:

Depreciation Expense xxx

    Accumulated Depreciation xxx

   To record depreciation for fractional period

Cash xxx

Accumulated Depreciation xxx

Loss on Sale of Fixed Asset xxx

    or

    Gain on Sale of Fixed Asset xxx

    Asset xxx

The gain or loss on the sale of a fixed asset is a forced figure. If a debit is needed to bring the transaction into balance, then the company has sustained a loss. If a credit is needed, then the company has realized a gain. The amount of this gain or loss may be checked by comparing the proceeds from the sale with the book value of the asset (asset account less accumulated depreciation account).

The destruction of a fixed asset is really just a forced sale and, therefore, the entries are similar to the above. Many fixed assets are insured and, in this event, the insurance company's claim may be debited instead of cash.

Trade-ins: Theory Method

When an old asset is traded in on a new one, the new asset should be recorded at cost and a gain or loss on the trade recognized. Cost consists of the fair market value of everything given up—that is, the cash paid, plus the fair market value of the old asset. Note that it is the fair market value, not the trade-in allowance, that is pertinent. Trade-in allowances are often "puffed" to appear attractive when offset against inflated selling prices. Such allowances do not represent true values; where better figures, such as bona fide cash offers, are available, the latter should be used.

In recording a trade, the cost of the new asset should be recorded first. The balance of the entry is similar to a sale, except that cash is normally credited rather than debited. An illustration of a trade-in follows:

Machine Number 1

Cost: $500
Acquired: January 2, 1968
Estimated life: four years
Estimated salvage value: $100
Trade-in date: April 13, 1970
Depreciation method: straight-line
Fair market value at date of trade: $215
Company closes books annually at December 31

Machine Number 2

List price: $850
Trade-in allowance on old machine: $250
Balance: cash

Entries to record the trade:

Depreciation Expense	25	
Accumulated Depreciation, Machine 1		25
Machine 2ª	815	
Accumulated Depreciation, Machine 1	225	
Loss on Tradeᵇ	60	
Cash		600
Machine 1		500

To record trade-in of Machine 1 on Machine 2

ªMachine number 2 is recorded at cost: cash paid, $600 (list price, $850, less trade-in allowance of $250), plus the fair market value of the old asset, $215.
ᵇLoss is forced, but can be checked by comparing book value of the old asset ($500 asset, less $225 accumulated depreciation = $275) with the fair market value of the old asset (given as $215).

Trade-ins: Tax Method

The Internal Revenue Code does not recognize gains or losses on trade-ins for tax purposes at the time of the trade. Instead, the loss is added to (or the gain deducted from) the basis of the property. The net effect is that gains are recognized over the life of the new asset in the form of reduced depreciation charges, and losses are recognized over that period through increased depreciation charges.

Where the theory method and the tax method produce "substantially similar" results, then it is acceptable accounting practice to use the tax method in the books. Note that in doing so, a company violates the cost principle, because the new asset is recorded at a forced figure (cost plus a loss or cost less a gain) rather than at actual cost. Where the amounts involved are not material, such a deviation is acceptable.

The trade-in cited previously would be recorded as follows if the tax method were used:

Depreciation Expense	25	
Accumulated Depreciation, Machine 1		25
Machine 2	875	
Accumulated Depreciation, Machine 1	225	
Cash		600
Machine 1		500

SUMMARY

Fixed assets may be tangible or intangible and may have limited or perpetual life. It is customary to record all fixed assets at their total cost, including all costs associated with getting the asset in place and ready to operate. Those assets that have limited life are subject to depreciation (tangible fixed assets), depletion (wasting fixed assets), or amortization (intangible fixed assets). In each case, the cost of the asset is apportioned to the periods that benefit from its use. This allocation may be accomplished on the straight-line basis, the units of production basis, the sum-of-the-year's-digits basis, or the declining balance basis. The last two of these methods are known as accelerated depreciation, because they charge a larger proportion of the cost to the earlier periods.

Fixed assets may be disposed of by sale, destruction, or trade. In each case, the depreciation should be recorded for the fractional period prior to recording the disposition. Gains or losses are properly recorded on the disposition of fixed assets as the difference between the book value (asset cost less accumulated depreciation) and the proceeds. When one fixed asset is traded in on another, the cost of the new asset should include the fair market value of the old asset. Such a practice generally gives rise to a gain or loss on the trade. This amount is not deductible for tax purposes, but increases (if a loss) or decreases (if a gain) the tax basis in the property.

QUESTIONS

1. At what figure should a fixed asset be placed on the books? What are some of the typical charges included in this amount?
2. Why should fixed assets, which have limited life, be recorded in separate accounts from those that enjoy perpetual life?
3. Distinguish between capital expenditures and revenue expenditures. Give several examples of each.
4. What happens to an accumulated depreciation account when an asset is disposed of?
5. Distinguish between depreciation, depletion, and amortization. What is the accounting objective of each?
6. What is accelerated depreciation? Name the common methods of accelerated depreciation. What arguments might be presented in favor of accelerated depreciation?
7. What fraction would be used to calculate the third year's depreciation of a building with a forty-year life if the sum-of-the-years'-digits method of depreciation were used?
8. What is the general rule for recording depreciation for fractional periods?
9. Under the declining balance method of depreciation, what consideration is given to the salvage value of the asset? Why is the rate not multiplied by (cost − salvage) as in other methods of depreciation?
10. What is the difference between the figures at which an asset would be recorded under the tax method and under the theory method of recording a trade?

11. Describe two procedures that may be followed to revise depreciation if it becomes apparent that the original estimates of useful life and salvage value are erroneous.

12. What are "wasting" assets? How are such assets accounted for over their life? How is the useful life of these assets arrived at?

PROBLEMS

Problem 9-1

    a. State the major purpose of depreciation.

    b. Discuss the basic theory underlying each of the methods of depreciation: straight-line, units of production, sum-of-the-years'-digits and declining balance. For each method give two examples of depreciable items that theoretically are dealth with by that method.

    c. What variables are involved in the estimation of depreciation? Of what significance is this estimation to the degree of accuracy of figures reported on financial statements, as discussed in chapter 1?

Problem 9-2

A machine costing $7,300 was installed by the Andrews Manufacturing Company on April 6, 1970. Freight-in and installation charges amounted to $1,400. The machine has an estimated useful life of six years or 72,000 units of product, with an estimated trade-in value of $300 at the end of this time. The machine produced 5,000 units in 1970, and 12,000 in 1971.

Required:

Calculate and record the journal entry for the depreciation in 1970 and 1971 under each of the following methods:

    a. Straight-line

    b. Sum-of-the-years'-digits

    c. Units of production

    d. Declining balance (tax method)

Problem 9-3

A machine was purchased by the Ash Company on June 3, 1968, at a cost of $12,000. Its estimated useful life was five years, after which it was expected to have a scrap value of $800. The company adopted the double declining balance method of depreciation (for book and tax purposes).

On September 2, 1970, it was decided to purchase a more efficient machine at a price of $16,000. A competitor offered to purchase the old machine for $4,500, but the company decided instead to trade it in on the new one, for which they were allowed $5,000 off the purchase price. It was decided that the trade-in allowance in this case was probably the best indication of the fair market value of the old machine.

Required:
    a. Record the depreciation for 1968.
    b. Record the trade-in under the theory method.
    c. Record the trade-in under the tax method.

Problem 9-4

On June 30, 1969, Kaputi Truck Line purchased a tandem axle tractor. The invoice price was $19,500. The freight charge for transporting the tractor from the factory to Kaputi was $250. Break-in costs necessary to get the tractor fully operational amounted to $350. The company figures the useful life of the tractor to be eight years or 400,000 miles, and its scrap value to be $1,500. In 1969, 1970, and 1971 the tractor logged 25,000, 42,000, 61,000 miles, respectively.

Required:

Make a depreciation schedule for the years 1969, 1970, and 1971 using the following depreciation methods (round to nearest dollar):
    a. Straight-line
    b. Sum-of-the-years'-digits
    c. Declining balance
    d. Units of production

Which method do you feel would be best for Kaputi to use? Why?

Problem 9-5

On March 30, 1962, Snake Oil Corporation purchased machine A for an invoice price of $15,000; freight and installation costs were $3,000. Snake Oil estimated the useful life of machine A to be ten years with no scrap value. On June 30, 1965, Snake Oil purchased machine B. The list price, including freight and installation, was $25,000. Snake Oil used machine A as a trade-in and paid cash in the sum of $12,000 to acquire machine B. It was estimated that machine B would have a useful life of five years with a scrap value of $5,000. On December 20, 1967, Snake Oil replaced machine B with machine C because the latter machine had a production rate double that of machine B. The list price of machine C, including freight and installation, was $29,500. The machine dealers gave Snake Oil a trade-in allowance of $10,000 and the balance was paid in cash. The corporation uses straight-line depreciation on all equipment and closes its books annually on December 31.

Required:

Record the acquisition of machines A, B, and C and the disposition of machines A and B, using
    a. The theory method
    b. The tax method.

Problem 9-6

On January 3, 1969, Moffat Company purchased for cash a new machine for its foundry. The machine, the concrete platform, and various connections cost $22,000 and had an estimated service life of ten years with a salvage value of $2,000. In the first part of January 1975, the machine was rebuilt at a cost of $5,000. The betterment materially increased the efficiency of the machine, although it did not increase the useful life or the salvage value of the asset. On September 29, 1977, the machine was destroyed by fire. The insurance company settled the claim with a check in the amount of $5,000.

Required:

Prepare the following entries:
   a. The purchase of the new machine
   b. The first year's depreciation, assuming a straight-line method of depreciation
   c. The cost of rebuilding the machine
   d. Depreciation for the year 1975, assuming a straight-line depreciation method
   e. The destruction of the machine and the receipt of the insurance company's check

Problem 9-7

A machine costing $32,000 was purchased by the Atom Company. Freight-in and installation costs amounted to $3,600. Its estimated useful life was 100,000 units of product. The salvage value of the machine was estimated to be $3,200.

YEAR	UNITS OF PRODUCT
1	5,600
2	16,400
3	14,700

Before the books were closed in the third year, it was estimated that the total useful life of the machine would only be 70,000 units of product. The new salvage value was determined to be $3,800.

Required:

Calculate the necessary revision to adjust depreciation, and make the proper journal entries using first the counterbalancing error method and then the revision of past profits method.

Problem 9-8

The Able Company has purchased a small computer for use in its business. The invoice price of the computer is $192,000. The cost to move the computer to the Able Company offices was $16,435. The company hired a technician at $14 an hour to get the computer installed. After twenty-eight and one-half hours the technician said the computer would be ready for service as soon as it had been tested. The costs for testing came to $4,980. The computer manufacturer gave Able Company a 2½ percent cash discount on the invoice price for paying within the discount period.

Required:

Determine the cost at which the Able Company should record the computer.

Case 9
JORDAN WRIGHT CONTRACTOR

Jordan Wright is a plumbing contractor whose principal business activity is installing private sewer laterals. As sewer mains are installed in the suburbs or as new homes are constructed, Mr. Wright bids on private lines connecting the homes to the sewer mains.

In January 1970, Mr. Wright purchased a duplex for $52,000. He converted one apartment (one-half of the building) into an office for his business at an additional cost of $4,000. The other apartment is currently being rented to a young married couple for $185 per month. Although Mr. Wright has had no trouble renting the apartment to date, he has been advised by other landlords in the area that it is necessary to lower rentals every two or three years in order to keep apartments occupied. A competent real estate appraiser has advised Mr. Wright to plan to keep the building for thirty years, at which time it is expected to have a salvage value of $5,000.

On July 1, 1969, Mr. Wright purchased a new Case tractor, complete with backhoe and loader, for a total contract price of $10,340. An old tractor which had originally cost $8,205 and which had accumulated depreciation of $6,100 was traded in on the new tractor. Mr. Wright was given a trade-in allowance of $1,800 on the old machine and paid the balance in cash. The trade-in allowance was regarded as a good indication of the old machine's fair market value. The new tractor is equipped with a chronometer which records the number of hours the tractor is operated. Mr. Wright has found that maintenance costs become excessive after a tractor is operated more than 100,000 hours and accordingly plans to trade the tractor in on a new one when 100,000 hours are accumulated. Experience shows salvage value of trade-ins averages about 20 percent of original cost. The chronometer reading at December 31, 1969, was 5,329 hours, and at December 31, 1970, was 17,077 hours.

Mr. Wright has a number of small tools and other relatively low-cost assets for which he keeps no detailed accounts. When new assets are acquired they are charged to the Small Tool account. When these items are disposed of, the original cost is removed from the Small Tool account and the corresponding accumulated depreciation is removed from the Small Tool Accumulated Depreciation account. Depreciation on these assets is calculated as 20 percent of the year-end balance in the Small Tool account. Pertinent data regarding small tools follows:

Small Tool account balance, Dec. 31, 1969^a	$5,295
Small Tool Accumulated Depreciation balance,	
Dec. 31, 1969^a	2,005
Small Tool purchases during 1970	1,400
Original cost of small tools sold during 1970	800
Accumulated depreciation on small tools sold during 1970	720
Proceeds from small tool sales during 1970	110

^aAfter closing books at December 31, 1969.

Mr. Wright desires to have as accurate a measurement of net income as possible and asks you, an accountant, the following questions:

1. What method of depreciation should be used for each asset to provide the best "matching" of depreciation expense with associated revenues? Why?
2. What journal entries would have been made on July 1, 1969, to record the acquisition of the new Case tractor (assume the good accounting theory method is used to record trades)?
3. Do you feel the duplex purchased should be regarded as a single asset or as two separate assets? Why?
4. Prepare a depreciation schedule for the year 1970, showing for each asset the cost, depreciation taken in prior years, depreciation for 1970, method of depreciation, and rate of depreciation. Use the methods of depreciation which you selected as best in question 1.
5. What method of depreciation is being used for small tools? Do you approve of using the year-end asset account balance for the purpose of computing annual depreciation? How much depreciation would be charged during 1970 for an asset which originally cost $500 (purchased January 2, 1968) which was sold December 2, 1970? Justify the amount of depreciation charged.
6. What was the gain or loss on small tools sold during 1970? Prepare journal entries to summarize the small tool transactions for the year 1970.

10

Accounting
for
Liabilities

Most liabilities are incurred through the acquisition of goods or services on credit. Where this is true, the recording of the liability is automatically linked to the acquisition of the asset or service. The major problem with this type of transaction is to assure that the corresponding debit is charged to the proper asset or expense account. If the debit is properly recorded, it is unusual to find an error in the recording of the corresponding liability. Thus, most liabilities present no special accounting problems and, accordingly, need not be discussed individually. Attention will be focused here on three types of liabilities that do require special treatment in the accounts: *accounts payable, various payroll liabilities,* and *bonds.*

ACCOUNTS PAYABLE

Accounting for current liabilities is closely related to the safeguarding of cash, because many of the cash payments made by any company are to satisfy these claims. A system must be set up to assure that all claims paid are legitimate, that the amounts are disbursed in accordance with the terms of purchase, and that payments are made in a timely manner. The procedures which provide this control are part of the company's internal control system, a subject discussed in more detail in chapter 14.

One important control in dealing with accounts payable is to provide a system that will assure the proper accounting for discounts. The two major types of discounts are discussed below.

Trade Discounts

Trade discounts merely represent adjustments to the posted or published price and are generally offered only to persons in a particular trade or business. All other customers must pay the list price. Trade discounts are a vehicle by which suppliers can quote different prices to various classes of customers. For example, a lumber company may sell to both do-it-yourself customers and licensed contractors. Because of his business, a contractor may be given a discount of 10 percent of the list price, which means that the contractor's price is 10 percent less than the do-it-yourself price. Following this practice is certainly easier than publishing a catalogue containing two or more sets of prices. Also, the trade discounts improve customer relations by not offending customers who pay higher prices because, most often, they are not aware of the fact that others can buy at more favorable prices.

Because trade discounts are nothing more than reductions in the purchase price, purchases that are subject to trade discounts should be recorded at the "net" cost. These discounts are not recorded separately on the books. The purchase and the account payable are recorded at list price less the trade discount. If a $100 item is purchased subject to a trade discount of 10 percent, then it would be recorded at $90, with no record made of the discount.

Cash Discounts

A cash discount is offered by the vendor as an incentive for early payment of the amount owed. The credit terms specify the rate of discount and the time within which the bill must be paid in order to take advantage of the discount. For example, the term "2/10, n/30" indicates that a discount of 2 percent may be taken if the bill is paid within ten days of the invoice date, but that the full amount is due within thirty days ("net 30"). These discounts represent a "bonus" to the creditors that pay early.

A firm should make every effort to take advantage of cash discounts. Generally, it would even be wise to borrow, if necessary, in order to take the discount. If a company can earn 2 percent in just twenty days by paying within ten days instead of thirty, it is the equivalent of earning 36 percent per annum—a pretty healthy rate of interest in anyone's book.

Inasmuch as cash discounts are contingent upon prompt payment and are not always taken, a system of accounting for these discounts must be established. Two methods are found in practice: the *gross method* and the *net method*.

The Gross Method.   To illustrate the gross method of accounting for purchase discounts, let us assume that on February 3 a company purchases $550 worth of merchandise (terms: 2/10; n/30). The transaction would be recorded as follows:

Purchases	550	
Accounts Payable		550

Note that the cash discount is not recorded at the time of the above entry. Instead, the discount is recorded only when and if the discount is taken. If payment is made within the discount period, the following entry would be appropriate:

Accounts Payable	550	
Purchase Discounts		11
Cash		539

If payment is made after the ten-day discount period, then the payment would be recorded as follows:

Accounts Payable	550	
Cash		550

Note that when the company does allow the discount to lapse, no record of the discount is made. This constitutes a weakness in the gross method. The Purchase Discounts account indicates the amount of discounts taken, but no mention is made of the discounts lost. Thus, management has no way of knowing how effective payment procedures are.

The Net Method.   The net method recognizes that cash discounts normally should be taken and assumes that they will be. Accordingly, when the purchase is recorded it is done "net" of the discount, as shown below:

Purchases	539	
Accounts Payable		539

In the event that the discount is taken as it should be, the account payable already reflects the net amount owed. In this event, the journal entry would appear as follows:

Accounts Payable	539	
Cash		539

Under this method, no record is made of the discounts taken. Instead, emphasis is placed on those that are *not* taken. This enables management to operate by the "exception" principle, focusing their attention on discounts only in the event that they are forfeited. The entry to record payment after the discount period has expired gives rise to an account called Purchase Discounts Lapsed:

Accounts Payable	539	
Purchase Discounts Lapsed	11	
Cash		550

PAYROLL LIABILITIES

There are a number of liabilities which arise by virtue of a company's payroll. Most important are those that exist because of taxes levied against the earnings of employees. Some of these taxes are imposed on the employer and represent operating expenses to the company. Other taxes are levied on the employee. These latter taxes are *not* expenses of the company; however, the company is required by law to act as a government agent in collecting these taxes. Even though the indirect expense involved in collecting these taxes is considerable, the company is given no compensation for acting as tax collector. All amounts collected must be promptly remitted to the government agencies. From the time collection is made until the sums are remitted, these amounts represent liabilities to the company.

Taxes on Employers

There are presently three major payroll taxes which are levied against the employer. These are *F.I.C.A.* (Federal Insurance Contribution Act) *taxes, federal unemployment insurance tax,* and *state unemployment insurance tax.* Each of these represents expenses to the employer and results in a debit to an expense account and credit to a liability account. The entry to record the payroll taxes levied against the employer is as follows:

Payroll Tax Expense xxx
    F.I.C.A. Taxes Payable   xxx
    Federal Unemployment Tax Payable   xxx
    State Unemployment Tax Payable   xxx

Employer F.I.C.A. Tax.   In recent years, Congress has passed a number of bills that have had a rather strong impact on the F.I.C.A. tax. Legislation is pending at the present time that will likely provide further changes. The effect of this legislation has been to increase greatly the amount of the F.I.C.A. tax. The maximum tax that the law requires the employer to pay for each employee has risen from $120 per year in 1959 to $406 per year in 1971, an increase of over 238 percent in this short period. This appears modest in terms of legislation already on the books and other proposals now before Congress. These tax increases have been accomplished in two ways: first, the rate has increased from 2.5 percent to 5.2 percent; and second, the basis upon which the tax is computed has increased from the first $4,800 to the first $7,800 of wages paid each employee. Legislation that has already been signed into law provides for rate increases up to 5.9 percent by 1987.

Federal Unemployment Insurance Tax.   The state and federal governments have a joint program for compensating workers who are unemployed but "willing and able" to work. The funds to pay the federal portion of administering the program are derived from the federal unemployment tax. These tax monies are not used to pay unemployment benefits but, instead, are used to pay the cost of administering these joint state and federal programs.

The federal unemployment tax is paid by the employer, based upon the earnings of his employees. The current federal rate is 0.4 percent of the first $3,000 of wages paid to each employee each year. This rate has varied only slightly since the program was first inaugurated.

State Unemployment Insurance Tax.   Each state has its own unemployment program, which is supported largely by taxes levied on employers. These state programs came into existence primarily because of a federal program, inaugurated in the thirties, that provided assistance to states that established their own qualifying programs. Accordingly, there is a great deal of similarity among the various state laws and close alignment with the federal program. The federal government provides the funds for administering the program, while the state raises the money to pay the unemployment benefits through a state unemployment tax. A "merit-rating" plan that provides various tax rates according to employment experience is followed. The employers with "level" employment (same number of employees throughout the year) pay lower rates than those employers who experience seasonal peaks. This tax break encourages employers to stabilize employment. An example of a merit rating plan may be seen in the Utah state law that currently prescribes rates varying from 1.1 percent to 2.7 percent of the first $4,200 earned by each employee each calendar year. The latter is the maximum rate being paid by those employers who have not demonstrated a favorable pattern of employment.

Taxes on Employees

Employees are subject to two federal payroll taxes: the F.I.C.A. tax and the withholding tax. In many states, employees are also subject to a state withholding tax, and, in a few states, are subject to an unemployment tax. With each of these taxes, the employer, acting as an agent of the government, withholds the amounts from the employee's check and remits the entire amount to the appropriate government agency. These taxes *do not* represent direct expenses to the employer.

Employee F.I.C.A Tax.   The Federal Insurance Contribution Act provides for two separate taxes, one levied against the employer and an equal one levied against the employee. The rates and the basis for calculating the two taxes are identical. In this respect, the employer and employee "share and share alike" in the Social Security program. As noted previously, the current annual F.I.C.A. rate is 5.2 percent of the first $7,800 earned by each employee. This gives a total rate of 10.4 percent, half of this being paid by the employer and half by the employee.

Although these taxes are very similar in many respects, their treatment in the accounts is very different. Remember that the employer's F.I.C.A. tax is *an expense* to the company while the employee's F.I.C.A. tax is *not*. Both result in a liability to the same agency and, accordingly, are credited to the F.I.C.A. Taxes Payable account. The employee's F.I.C.A. tax, however, *does not* result in a debit to the Payroll Tax Expense account, as does the employer's share of the tax.

Federal Withholding Tax.   In order to accelerate income tax collections and, indeed, to insure that they are collected at all, the withholding tax was inaugurated. Under this system, the employer deducts a specified sum from the employee's pay and remits this to the Internal Revenue Service at regular intervals. Each year, the employee is furnished with a W-2 form which shows the total tax withheld during the year. This form, when filed with the employee's tax return, serves as a basis for credit against the employee's income tax liability.

The amount of withholding tax to be withheld is generally determined from a table furnished by the Internal Revenue Service. The amount is based upon the number of exemptions claimed by the employee and the level of his income. A portion of a table for 1970 for a monthly payroll is shown in Figure 10-1.

Congress has made attempts in recent years to revise the withholding system in an attempt to bring the withholding more in line with the ultimate tax liability.

Figure 10-1

WITHHOLDING TABLE
Monthly Payroll for Married Persons

And the wages are—		And the number of withholding exemptions claimed is—										
At least	But less than	0	1	2	3	4	5	6	7	8	9	10 or more
		The amount of income tax to be withheld shall be—										
$440	$460	$64.50	$55.50	$47.20	$39.20	$31.20	$22.80	$12.30	$1.80	$0	$0	$0
460	480	68.10	59.10	50.40	42.40	34.40	26.40	16.50	6.00	0	0	0
480	500	71.70	62.70	53.70	45.60	37.60	29.60	20.70	10.20	0	0	0
500	520	75.30	66.30	57.30	48.80	40.80	32.80	24.80	14.40	3.90	0	0
520	540	78.90	69.90	60.90	52.00	44.00	36.00	28.00	18.60	8.10	0	0
540	560	82.50	73.50	64.50	55.50	47.20	39.20	31.20	22.80	12.30	1.80	0
560	580	86.10	77.10	68.10	59.10	50.40	42.40	34.40	26.40	16.50	6.00	0
580	600	89.70	80.70	71.70	62.70	53.70	45.60	37.60	29.60	20.70	10.20	0
600	640	95.10	86.10	77.10	68.10	59.10	50.40	42.40	34.40	26.40	16.50	6.00
640	680	102.30	93.30	84.30	75.30	66.30	57.30	48.80	40.80	32.80	24.80	14.40
680	720	109.50	100.50	91.50	82.50	73.50	64.50	55.50	47.20	39.20	31.20	22.80
720	760	116.70	107.70	98.70	89.70	80.70	71.70	62.70	53.70	45.60	37.60	29.60
760	800	124.30	114.90	105.90	96.90	87.90	78.90	69.90	60.90	52.00	44.00	36.00
800	840	132.70	122.20	113.10	104.10	95.10	86.10	77.10	68.10	59.10	50.40	42.40
840	880	141.10	130.60	120.30	111.30	102.30	93.30	84.30	75.30	66.30	57.30	48.80
880	920	149.50	139.00	128.50	118.50	109.50	100.50	91.50	82.50	73.50	64.50	55.50
920	960	157.90	147.40	136.90	126.40	116.70	107.70	98.70	89.70	80.70	71.70	62.70
960	1,000	166.30	155.80	145.30	134.80	124.30	114.90	105.90	96.90	87.90	78.90	69.90
1,000	1,040	174.70	164.20	153.70	143.20	132.70	122.20	113.10	104.10	95.10	86.10	77.10
1,040	1,080	183.10	172.60	162.10	151.60	141.10	130.60	120.30	111.30	102.30	93.30	84.30
1,080	1,120	191.50	181.00	170.50	160.00	149.50	139.00	128.50	118.50	109.50	100.50	91.50
1,120	1,160	199.90	189.40	178.90	168.40	157.90	147.40	136.90	126.40	116.70	107.70	98.70
1,160	1,200	208.30	197.80	187.30	176.80	166.30	155.80	145.30	134.80	124.30	114.90	105.90
1,200	1,240	216.70	206.20	195.70	185.20	174.70	164.20	153.70	143.20	132.70	122.20	113.10
1,240	1,280	225.10	214.60	204.10	193.60	183.10	172.60	162.10	151.60	141.10	130.60	120.30
2,280	2,320	506.80	491.30	475.80	460.30	444.80	429.30	413.80	398.30	382.80	367.30	353.50
2,320	2,360	519.20	503.70	488.20	472.70	457.20	441.70	426.20	410.70	395.20	369.70	364.20
2,360	2,400	531.60	516.10	500.60	485.10	469.60	454.10	438.60	423.10	407.60	392.10	376.60
2,400	2,440	544.00	528.50	513.00	497.50	482.00	466.50	451.00	435.50	420.00	404.50	389.00
		31 percent of the excess over $2,440 plus—										
$2,440 and over		550.20	534.70	519.20	503.70	488.20	472.70	457.20	441.70	426.20	410.70	395.20

Source: Supplement to Circular E, Employer's Tax Guide, Internal Revenue Service, Publication 15 (Rev. January 1970), p. 20.

State Withholding Tax.   Many states have recognized the advantages to the state of the withholding system and have passed laws similar to the federal statute. These taxes are collected by the employer, remitted to the state, and applied to the individual's state tax liability in the same manner as federal taxes.

Other Payroll Deductions

Many other organizations and agencies, and even employees themselves, have seen advantages to having the employer make payroll deductions. Such a practice assures that the designated organization will get the funds before the employee spends them elsewhere. Also, the cost of the collection process is most often shifted from the organization requesting the withholding to the employer. For these reasons, unions have often required withholding of union dues, and employees have elected withholding for purposes such as savings bonds, retirement programs, club dues, and charity drives. In each of these instances, the employer merely acts as agent in collecting the particular obligation. The amounts withheld, of course, are liabilities to the company until such time as they are transmitted to the proper organization.

Illustration of Payroll Liabilities

The student can imagine the volume of detailed payroll records that must be maintained by the employer to account for the various payroll taxes and deductions. These records are largely clerical in nature, and a detailed knowledge of their operation is not necessary in this course. We will be concerned here only with the general journal entries that are prepared in conjunction with payroll accounting. Assume the following facts regarding a company's payroll:

> F.I.C.A. Rate: 5.2 percent on employers and employees (up to $7,800)
> Federal Withholding Rate: 14 percent
> State Withholding Rate: 2 percent
> Federal Unemployment Rate: 0.4 percent (up to $3,000)
> State Unemployment Rate: 2.7 percent (up to $4,200)

The payroll for the period amounts to $15,000, of which $4,000 is paid to employees who have earned less than $3,000; $6,000 is paid to employees who have earned less than $4,200; and $14,000 is paid to employees who have earned less than $7,800. Of the $15,000 payroll, $10,000 pertains to office employees and the balance to salesmen.

The general journal entries to record the payroll and the associated payroll taxes follow:

Sales Salaries Expense	5,000	
Office Salaries Expense	10,000	
F.I.C.A. Tax Payable		728
Federal Withholding Tax Payable		2,100
State Withholding Tax Payable		300
Payroll Payable		11,872
To record payroll for the month.		

Payroll Tax Expense 906
    F.I.C.A. Tax Payable 728
    Federal Unemployment Tax Payable 16
    State Unemployment Tax Payable 162
    To record payroll tax expense for the month.

The entry to record the payment of employees' wages would appear as follows:

Payroll Payable 11,872
    Cash 11,872

Note that of the $15,000 which employees earned, only $11,872 was actually paid to them. The balance was retained in the company's cash account. Because this amount does not belong to the company and because the company will be required to pay it soon to the respective government agencies, it represents a liability to the company.

BONDS PAYABLE

Bonds are a form of long-term borrowing that enables corporations to borrow large sums of money by breaking the obligation down into small segments. Each bond has a "face value" which represents only a small fraction of the total offering. For example, a company may raise $2,000,000 by issuing 2,000 bonds, each in $1,000 denominations. In this manner, companies are able to borrow sums that probably could not be borrowed from banks because of their legal "debt ceilings." Also, bonds spread the risk among many lenders, each one willing to bear part of the risk, but unwilling or unable to bear it all.

Premiums and Discounts

Because it is difficult to predict market interest rates for a given bond issue, the effective interest rate is not specified on the bond itself. Instead a "coupon rate" is printed on the bond, and it is sold to yield that interest rate which the market feels is proper.[1] This is accomplished by selling the bond at a "premium" or a "discount." If the coupon rate is too low, then the price of the bond is dropped until the yield becomes attractive enough for someone to buy. In this case, the bond is said to have sold at a discount.

---

[1]The yield is calculated by comparing the amount of interest received with the amount invested.

On the other hand, if the coupon rate is too high, buyers will rush to purchase this "bargain" and will bid the price up until the yield is competitive with similar risks. In this case, the bond will sell at a price greater than its face value and may be said to have sold at a premium.

Inasmuch as premiums and discounts really represent interest rate adjustments, they should be amortized over the life of the bond as an adjustment to the interest expense. The "effective yield" method of amortization is probably the most accurate because it records interest expense at the "effective yield" rate. Because calculating the effective yield involves techniques not yet discussed, we will follow the straight-line method here. This latter method is sufficient to illustrate the fact that premiums and discounts do not give rise to gains and losses, but merely represent adjustments of interest.

Premium Illustrated. The Gardner Manufacturing Company authorizes $5,000,000 of 5 percent, ten-year bonds. The issue is dated January 1, 1971, and pays interest each June 30 and December 31 through maturity. The entire issue is sold at 102 (meaning 102 percent of face value) on January 1, 1971. The sale would appear as follows on Gardner's books:

```
Cash  .................................   5,100,000
    Bonds Payable ....................                5,000,000
    Premium on Bonds Payable ..........                 100,000
```

Inasmuch as the $100,000 premium represents an adjustment of interest, the entire amount should be spread over the life of the bond issue. On a straight-line basis, this would amount to $5,000 per interest period (ten years with two interest payments per year). The entry to record this amortization would be made with the regular interest payment on June 30, as follows:

```
Interest Expense ........................   120,000
Premium on Bonds Payable ...............     5,000
    Cash ................................                125,000
```

Note that the premium amortization reduces the interest expense and that at maturity the entire premium will have been amortized. Although $125,000 is paid out each six months, $5,000 of this is not an expense but merely repayment of a portion of the extra $100,000 that was received by the company at date of issue.

Discount Illustrated. Assume the same set of facts regarding the Gardner Manufacturing Company bonds, except that they were issued at 98 rather than 102. The entry on January 1, 1971, to record the issue would be:

```
Cash ................................   4,900,000
Discount on Bonds Payable ..............   100,000
    Bonds Payable ....................              5,000,000
```

In this instance, the discount would be amortized along with interest payments as follows:

```
Interest Expense .........................   130,000
    Discount on Bonds Payable .............              5,000
    Cash ..............................              125,000
```

In this instance, the interest expense is *increased* by the amortization of the discount.

Premium and Discount in the Balance Sheet.   There are two possible ways of showing the balance in a premium or a discount account on the balance sheet. The first is to add or deduct these amounts from the Bonds Payable account in the long-term liability section. Thus a premium would be shown:

```
Long-term Liabilities:
    5 percent bonds payable, due 1991 . .  $2,000,000
    Plus: Unamortized premium .......       13,500    2,013,500
```

A discount could be shown in a similar manner:

```
Long-term Liabilities:
    6 percent bonds payable, due 1985 . .  $5,000,000
    Less: Unamortized discount ........        2,300   4,997,700
```

An alternative to the preceding presentation is to show the discount or premium separate from the bonds payable. In this event, the bonds payable are shown as a liability at their face value. A premium is then shown under a separate caption called Deferred Credits, and a discount is shown under Deferred Charges.

Issuance between Interest Dates

The coupon rate printed on the bond provides for fixed sums of interest to be paid on fixed dates. Most bonds provide for semiannual interest payments. If a bond is issued on one interest date, then the entire interest paid at the next interest date will be earned and no special accounting is required. But what if a bond is issued between interest dates, say halfway? In this case, only half of the interest will be earned, although the contract provides for the full amount to be paid. This problem is solved by accruing the interest at the time the bond is sold. In effect, the company calculates the amount of interest *not earned* at time of sale and charges this amount extra above the price of the bond itself. The bond is said to sell "plus accrued interest." This extra amount received at the time the bond is sold is offset against the excessive interest that will be paid at the next interest date so that the bondholder will only "net" the amount of interest actually earned.

To illustrate the issuance of bonds between interest dates, let us assume that a company authorizes the issuance of $1,000,000, 6 percent, twenty-year bonds, dated January 1, 1971, and paying interest January 1 and July 1. If the bonds are not sold until March 1, 1971, then two months will have gone by in which no interest was earned. In this instance, the buyer would be required to pay $10,000 accrued interest in addition to the regular price of the bonds. If the bonds were sold at par on March 1, 1971, the following entry would be appropriate:

Cash	1,010,000	
Accrued Interest Payable		10,000
Bonds Payable		1,000,000

The first interest payment would be recorded as follows:

Interest Expense	20,000	
Accrued Interest Payable	10,000	
Cash		30,000

Note that the bondholder paid an extra $10,000 at the time of purchase (two months' interest at 6 percent per annum), but that this was offset by an equal overpayment by the company on July 1. The interest expense was charged with only four months' interest.

Extended Bond Illustration

In the illustration that follows, the problem of issuing bonds between interest dates is combined with the problem of a discount. Also, the need for year-end accruals and the associated year-end amortization of the discount are shown.

Moody Glass Manufacturing Company authorized the issuance of 1,000 bonds, each of $1,000 face value. The bonds were dated April 1, 1971, and matured ten years from that date. Interest at 6 percent per annum was payable in equal installments on October 1 and April 1 of each year. The company closed its books annually on December 31. On August 1, 1971, ten of the bonds were sold for $9,536 plus accrued interest. The journal entries pertaining to the bonds for the years 1971 and 1972 are shown in Figure 10-2. A series of explanatory notes follows the journal entries to assist the student.

Figure 10-2

EXTENDED BOND DISCOUNT ILLUSTRATION

1971

Aug. 1	Cash[a]	9,736		
	Discount on Bonds Payable[b]	464		
	6 percent Bonds Payable		10,000	
	Accrued Interest Payable[c]		200	
	Issuance of ten bonds			
Oct. 1	Interest Expense	108		
	Accrued Interest Payable	200		
	Cash		300	
	Discount on Bonds Payable[d]		8	
	Paid semiannual bond interest			
Dec. 31	Interest Expense	162		
	Accrued Interest Payable		150	
	Discount on Bonds Payable[e]		12	
	Accrued 3 months' interest			

1972

Apr. 1	Interest Expense	162		
	Accrued Interest Payable	150		
	Cash		300	
	Discount on Bonds Payable		12	
	Paid semiannual bond interest			
Oct. 1	Interest Expense	324		
	Cash		300	
	Discount on Bonds Payable		24	
	Paid semiannual bond interest			
Dec. 31	Interest Expense	162		
	Accrued Interest Payable		150	
	Discount on Bonds Payable		12	
	Accrued 3 months interest			

---

[a]$9,536 for bonds, plus $200 accrued interest.

[b]$10,000 face value, less $9,536 received for the bonds.

[c]Interest for the four months (April 1 to August 1) that the bonds were *not* outstanding:

$$\frac{6}{100} \times \frac{4}{12} \times \$10,000 = \$200$$

[d]The bonds will be outstanding a total of 116 months (ten years less four months that they were not outstanding). The amortization is $4 per month ($464 discount ÷ 116 months).

[e]Interest is accrued at year end in the normal manner. In addition, it is necessary to amortize the discount so that the interest expense will be properly shown.

Figure 10-3 summarizes the entire amortization procedure. Notice that at the maturity date the entire discount has been amortized, and the balance in the discount account is zero. The discount is not regarded as a loss, in which event the entire amount would have been charged to the period when the issue was repaid, but instead as an adjustment of interest. The interest expense of each period has been increased for a share of the discount. At maturity only the Bonds Payable account remains, and this represents the total liability at that date. As the bonds are repaid, an entry debiting bonds payable and crediting cash is made to record the liquidation of the liability.

Figure 10-3

SUMMARY OF JOURNAL ENTRIES
Ten-year, 6 percent bonds, dated 4-1-71, issued 8-1-71[a]

	CASH	DISCOUNT	INTEREST EXPENSE	BONDS PAYABLE
August 1, 1971	9,536	464		(10,000)
October 1, 1972	(100)	(8)	108	
April 1, 1972	(300)	(24)	324	
October 1, 1972	(300)	(24)	324	
April 1, 1973	(300)	(24)	324	
October 1, 1973	(300)	(24)	324	
April 1, 1974	(300)	(24)	324	
October 1, 1974	(300)	(24)	324	
April 1, 1975	(300)	(24)	324	
October 1, 1975	(300)	(24)	324	
April 1, 1976	(300)	(24)	324	
October 1, 1976	(300)	(24)	324	
April 1, 1977	(300)	(24)	324	
October 1, 1977	(300)	(24)	324	
April 1, 1978	(300)	(24)	324	
October 1, 1978	(300)	(24)	324	
April 1, 1979	(300)	(24)	324	
October 1, 1979	(300)	(24)	324	
April 1, 1980	(300)	(24)	324	
October 1, 1980	(300)	(24)	324	
March 31, 1981	(10,300)	(24)	324	10,000
TOTALS	(6,264)	–0–	6,264	–0–

(credit)

[a]The above summary ignores the accrual of interest and annual closing in order to simplify the illustration. This in no way affects the entries related to the amortization of the discount. Note that over the life of the bonds the entire discount is amortized (balance in the account at maturity is zero).

SUMMARY

Generally, liabilities are recorded as part of an entry recording the acquisition of goods or services. The difficult part in recording most of these transactions is to be sure that the proper asset or expense account is charged. Correct recording of the liability is almost automatically linked to the recording of the corresponding debit.

Several special problems pertaining to liabilities should be noted. Liabilities normally are recorded *net* of any trade discounts. With cash discounts, the liability may be recorded at either net or gross as the management chooses. The "net" method does have the advantage of focusing attention on the discounts lost, an account which indicates someone has "goofed."

There are many special problems associated with the recording of payrolls. Most of these are related to withholding procedures required by various tax laws. Withholding is also sometimes required by contract (such as a labor contract), or is instituted as an employee service at the request of the employee.

The accounting for bonds is complicated by the fact that the effective interest rate is rarely printed on the face of the bond. Instead, a coupon rate is specified, and the bonds are then sold at a premium or at a discount in order to yield the market rate. This premium or discount represents an adjustment of the interest expense and should properly be amortized over the life of the bond issue.

QUESTIONS

1. What is the purpose of trade discounts? How are these discounts treated in the accounting records?
2. Why do many companies offer cash discounts? Explain the meaning of 2/15; n/60.
3. Under which method of recording cash discounts is the account Purchase Discounts Lapsed used? What signifiicance does this account have for the management of a firm?
4. What major payroll taxes are levied against employers? What is the current rate and limit of each tax?
5. What major payroll taxes are levied against employees? How are these taxes paid to the respective government agencies?
6. How does a "merit rating plan" affect the state unemployment insurance tax rate in states that employ such a program?
7. Name several deductions, other than for payroll taxes, that might be made from an employee's pay check. How would arrangements be made for such deductions? What is the employer's role in regard to all payroll deductions?

8. Why do most bond issues sell at either a discount or a premium rather than at their face value? What does the premium or discount actually represent?

9. When a bond is issued between interest dates, what arrangements are made to be sure the bondholder receives the proper amount of interest?

10. What is meant by "amortizing" a bond premium or discount? Over what period is the premium or discount amortized when the bonds are issued several months after they are dated?

11. How should bond premium and bond discount accounts be shown in the financial statements?

12. Is there normally a gain or loss when a bond that was originally issued at a discount is retired at maturity? Explain.

PROBLEMS

Problem 10-1

a. Distinguish between trade discounts and cash discounts.

b. What is the primary distinction between the gross method and the net method of accounting for cash discounts, and what is its significance to management?

c. On January 3 the Bluebell Company purchased merchandise at an invoice price of $2,000, less a 25 percent trade discount, terms 2/10; net 30. On January 5 goods were purchased from another supplier at an invoice price of $1,000 less a 20 percent trade discount, terms 1/10; net 30. The first invoice was paid on January 11 and the second on January 18. Give journal entries to record the purchase and subsequent payment on both invoices, using the gross method.

d. Assuming the same facts as in (c) above, give journal entries using the net method.

e. Where would the account Purchase Discounts Lapsed appear on the company's financial statements?

Problem 10-2

a. List separately those payroll taxes which are an expense to the employer and those which must be accounted for but are not an expense to the employer. What account is debited in each case when such taxes are accrued on the books?

b. Smith and Smythe Management Consultants employ three salaried office workers, two of whom are paid $800 per month, and one $600 per month. Also, two part-time clerical workers are employed twenty hours per week, each at $1.50 per hour. Pay periods end on the fifteenth and last day of the month, payable on the tenth and twenty-fifth. The following rates, in percents, are applicable to payroll taxes:

Federal Withholding	14
State Withholding	2
F.I.C.A. (on employers and employees)	5.2 (up to $7,800)

Federal Unemployment . .   0.4 (up to $3,000)
State Unemployment . . . .   2.7 (up to $4,200)

Assuming that all employees have worked the entire year, and that each pay period in October consisted of two weeks, record all entries related to the accrual and payment of the payroll for October. Do not include the September 30 payroll.

Problem 10-3

The Raine Manufacturing Corporation was authorized to issue $1,000,000 of 6 percent, fifteen-year bonds dated February 1, 1970. Interest is payable on February 1 and August 1 of each year. The entire issue is sold on July 1, 1970, at 103½, plus accrued interest.

Required:

    a. Assuming that the company is on a calendar year basis, record all journal entries from the date of issue through December 31, 1971.

    b. Show the bonds and premium as they would appear on the balance sheet, December 31, 1971.

    c. Assume the same facts as in (a), except that the bonds were sold at 96½ plus accrued interest. Prepare all entries from date of issue through February 1, 1971.

    d. Make a rough approximation of what the market rate of interest might have been in situation (a); in situation (b).

Problem 10-4

The Rich Development Company was authorized to issue $2,000,000 of 5 percent, twenty-year bonds dated April 1, 1971. Interest is payable on April 1 and October 1. The company closes its books on December 31.

Required:

    a. Assuming that the issue is sold at 100 on April 1, 1971, record all journal entries for 1971.

    b. Assuming that the issue is sold at 102½ on April 1, 1971, record all journal entries for 1971.

    c. Assuming that the issue is sold at 98½ on April 1, 1971, record all journal entries for 1971.

Problem 10-5

The Bluffs Company was authorized to issue $2,000,000 of 4 percent, seven-year bonds dated July 1, 1970. Interest is payable semiannually on January 1 and July 1. The entire issue was sold on September 1, 1970, at 108.2 plus accrued interest.

Required:

    a. Record all journal entries for 1970 and 1971, assuming that the company closes its books on a calendar year basis.

    b. Prepare the entry that would be made at maturity.

Problem 10-6

The Sweetwater branch office of Houston Company employs three office employees and a branch manager. The branch manager is paid $950 per month. The office employees are each paid $625 per month. Two of the office employees have been with the company for several years, but one was hired April 1 of this year. The following tax rates, given in percents, are to be used for payroll taxes:

Federal Withholding	14
State Withholding	2
F.I.C.A. (on employer	
and employees)	5.2 (up to $7,800)
Federal Unemployment . .	0.4 (up to $3,000)
State Unemployment . . .	2.7 (up to $4,200)

Assuming that each employee is paid at the end of the month, prepare all necessary journal entries to record the payroll payment and applicable taxes on August 31.

Problem 10-7

The Wind Corporation was authorized to issue $1,500,000 of 5½ percent, ten-year bonds dated February 1, 1971. Interest is payable on February 1 and August 1. The entire issue was sold on June 11, 1972. The company's accounting period closes on October 31.

Required:

a. Assuming that the issue sold at 103 plus accrued interest, prepare all journal entries through October 31, 1973.

b. Assuming that the issue sold at 98 plus accrued interest, prepare all journal entries through October 31, 1973.

Case 10

AJAX INCORPORATED

Mr. J. Williams and Mr. H. Bender are vice presidents of Ajax, Inc., a large conglomerate. Ajax is a diversified company having annual sales of over $25,000,000. The major portion of the company's income comes from two sources: wholesaling of replacement automobile parts and manufacturing of plumbing supplies.

Recently, Ajax decided to expand their previously all-metal plumbing supply line to include plastic pipe and other nonmetallic plumbing items. To accomplish this, Ajax authorized a $5,000,000 issue of 6½ percent bonds on January 1, 1969. Inasmuch as the interest rates in the bond market were climbing, Ajax was able to sell only $2,500,000 worth of bonds on March 1, 1969, at the coupon rate. The rest of the bonds did not sell until they were offered for a price of 97 on July 1, 1969. The bonds mature January 1, 1989, and pay interest semiannually on January 1 and July 1.

Early in 1970, after they had received the prior year's financial statements, Mr. Williams and Mr. Bender were very much disturbed by two items which appeared in the financial statements: purchase discounts and discount on bonds payable. Mr. Bender noted that purchase discounts were very low. The dollar value of wholesale items purchased during the year exceeded $8,000,000, and yet the purchase discounts amounted to only $50,000. Mr. Bender remarked to Mr. Williams, "Jack, there is something wrong with our purchasing system. I know that most of the auto part manufacturers we buy from offer discounts of 2/10; n/30; yet we apparently took discounts only in the amount of $50,000 for the whole year."

Mr. Williams replied, "That's not all, Hal. If you'll look at this figure for discount on bonds payable, you'll see that it is $73,077. That is absolutely ridiculous! What on earth is that controller thinking of? A company with Ajax' reputation shouldn't have to offer a discount like that."

Agreeing that the matters should be cleared up immediately, the two men went to the financial vice president, Mr. J. Adams, and asked if he could explain where the figures came from. Mr. Adams said, "Well, the purchase discounts are simple enough. When the company takes a discount, we merely record that amount in the Purchase Discounts account. As for the discount on bonds payable, that figure represents the amount of discount offered to bondholders. It is customary to just amortize this over the life of the bond issue. Both of these methods are accepted accounting practices, so I don't see where you have anything to quarrel about."

Mr. Bender didn't understand, but not wanting to appear stupid, said, "Thank you, John, for the information. Jack and I were a little concerned over the figures, but we're sure you know what you're doing." Still concerned about the matter, the two asked a friend of theirs, a partner in a CPA firm, the following questions which you should answer, also.

QUESTIONS

1. What is the matter with the Purchase Discounts account? What changes would you recommend in the method of recording purchase discounts?
2. What does the discount on bonds payable really represent? Do you think the controller made a mistake by offering the bond-holders this discount? How was the $73,077 amount arrived at? Where would it appear on the balance sheet?
3. Reconstruct all entries made during 1969 regarding the bonds.
4. Assume all suppliers do offer terms of 2/10; n/30, gross sales of $8,000,000, and that payments on accounts payable amounted to $7,000,000. Reconstruct all entries made regarding purchases, purchase discounts, and accounts payable. Prepare alternate entries which the company could have used to record these data.

11

Accounting
for
Owners' Equity

Transactions affecting the owners' equity vary according to the legal form of the business. There are few problems relating to accounting for the owner's equity in a proprietorship, because there is but one owner and a single account reflecting his equity. On the other hand, the partnership and the corporation do have some transactions that require special treatment. Some of the more important of these transactions are discussed in this chapter.

THE PARTNERSHIP

A partnership is an association of two or more persons who have contracted to do business together under a company name. This business relationship is much less formal than that of a corporation. In fact, the partnership is given little formal recognition by the law. The partnership cannot contract, cannot sue or be sued, and is not subject to taxation. Instead, all transactions that are conducted by the business are interpreted by the law as acts of the owners. The law views a partnership as though it were a proprietorship with several owners. For this reason, accounting for owners' equity is very similar to a proprietorship, except that a separate account is maintained for each owner.

We will be concerned here with three types of transactions related to the partnership form of business: *division of profits, admission of new partners*, and *withdrawal of partners*.

Division of Profits

Partners can agree to divide profits in almost any way they choose. In the absence of any agreement, the profits are divided equally among the partners. If an agreement specifies how profits are to be divided but says nothing about losses, then the losses are distributed according to the same plan as the profits.

There are a number of factors that partners ought to consider in working out an equitable method of profit distribution. The profit-sharing agreement should consider the relative capital contributions, the degree of time spent in the business, and a variety of intangible factors such as the talent, ability, reputation, and goodwill contributed by each partner. A separate provision can be made in the agreement as compensation for each of these factors. For example, salaries may compensate for time and special abilities, while interest[1] might compensate for capital contributions.

Where profit-sharing agreements require a number of calculations, it may be helpful to prepare a schedule of distribution of profits similar to the one shown in Figure 11-1. The schedule was prepared assuming the following facts: Goodbody, Hogle, Irving, and Jones are partners. They agree that Goodbody, Irving, and Jones are to be allowed salaries of $4,000, $6,000, and $10,000, respectively. Since Hogle is inactive, it is agreed that he will receive no salary. Interest is to be credited on the partners' capital accounts as of the beginning of the year at the rate of 10 percent, and all drawings, regardless of the date of withdrawal, are to be charged interest at the 10 percent rate. Jones is to be allowed a bonus of 10 percent of the profits for acting as managing partner. The bonus is to be figured before any of the foregoing allowances are deducted. Any balance is to be distributed to Goodbody, Hogle, Irving, and Jones in the ratio of 4:3:2:1.

---

[1]Salaries and interest allowed as compensation to the partners are not considered as expenses of the business, but as distributions of profits.

The net income for the year was $45,000, and the following information was compiled from the accounts:

	GOODBODY	HOGLE	IRVING	JONES
Beginning of Year Capital Balances	$10,000	$60,000	$5,000	$15,000
Drawings During Year	500	700	200	1,400

Figure 11-1

GOODBODY & ASSOCIATES
Schedule of Distribution of Profits
For the Year Ended December 31, 1970

PROVISIONS IN AGREEMENT	GOODBODY	HOGLE	IRVING	JONES	TOTAL
Salary	$4,000	$ –0–	$6,000	$10,000	$20,000
Interest on capital	1,000	6,000	500	1,500	9,000
Interest on drawings	(50)	(70)	(20)	(140)	(280)
Bonus to manager	–0–	–0–	–0–	4,500	4,500
Balance in ratio 4:3:2:1 .	4,712	3,534	2,356	1,178	11,780
Totals	$9,662	$9,464	$8,836	$17,038	$45,000

(Deductions)

In preparing the schedule, the various provisions of the partnership agreement are listed in order down the left side of the schedule, and the amounts allowed each partner are entered in the appropriate column. The total profit is next entered on the last line in the far right column. The figure necessary to balance the total column (in the above instance, $11,780) is "forced" and distributed to the partners as agreed (equally, in the absence of an agreement). The balancing figure may be either positive or negative, whichever is necessary to cause the total column to sum to the net profit of the period. The journal entry to close the Income Summary account in accordance with this agreement follows:

```
Income Summary ...........................   45,000
     Goodbody, Capital ......................          9,662
     Hogle, Capital ..........................          9,464
     Irving, Capital ..........................          8,836
     Jones, Capital ..........................         17,038
```

In the previous example, the profits were sufficiently high so that the balance was a positive figure. Figure 11-2, assuming a net profit of only $5,000, requires a negative balancing figure.

Figure 11-2

GOODBODY & ASSOCIATES
Schedule of Distribution of Profits
For the Year Ended December 31, 1970

PROVISIONS IN AGREEMENT	GOODBODY	HOGLE	IRVING	JONES	TOTAL
Salary	$4,000	$ –0–	$6,000	$10,000	$20,000
Interest on capital	1,000	6,000	10,000	1,500	9,000
Interest on drawings . .	(50)	(70)	(20)	(140)	(280)
Bonus to manager	–0–	–0–	–0–	500	500
Balance in ratio 4:3:2:1	(9,688)	(7,266)	(4,844)	(2,422)	(24,220)
Totals	($4,738)	($1,336)	$1,636	$9,438	$ 5,000

(Deductions)

Once the balancing figure has been computed and distributed to the partners, the columns can be totaled and cross-footed to assure accuracy. A journal entry can then be made to distribute the profits as shown by the last line of the schedule. The entry required to support the schedule shown in Figure 11-2 would be as follows:

Income Summary	5,000	
Goodbody, Capital	4,738	
Hogle, Capital	1,336	
Irving, Capital		1,636
Jones, Capital		9,438

Note that while the partnership enjoyed a $5,000 profit, two of the partners sustained losses and the other two gained as a result of the profit-sharing agreement.

Admission of Partners

A new partner may be admitted to an existing partnership either by his investing in the partnership (contributing new assets to it) or acquiring an interest from one or more of the old partners. The former may be called an *investment* in a partnership and the latter, the *purchase of an interest* in a partnership.

Purchase of an Interest.   No new assets flow to a partnership when an interest is purchased. The total assets and total owners' equity remain the same. The transaction is really a personal one between the old and new partners, and the only entry on the partnership books is to transfer equity from one (or more) owner's capital account to the new partner's capital account. The entry is the same regardless of the purchase price. To illustrate, let us assume Madsen, Nelson, and Olsen are partners with capital balances of $80,000, $20,000, and $60,000 respectively, and that Olsen decides (with permission of the remaining partners) to sell his interest to Kaspar. The entry on the partnership books—regardless of whether Kaspar paid $50,000 or $150,000—would be

Olsen, Capital	60,000	
Kaspar, Capital		60,000

Investment.   When a new partner invests in an existing partnership, new assets *do* flow to the firm, and the total assets and the total equity increase accordingly. The possible situations that may arise under an investment are as follows:

1. Asset contribution equals new partner's capital
2. Assets contributed are greater than new partner's capital
   a. Goodwill is recorded
   b. Bonus to old partner
3. Assets contributed are less than new partner's capital
   a. Goodwill is recorded
   b. Asset writedown
   c. Bonus to the new partner

Assets Contributed Equal New Partner's Capital.   Where the new partner is allowed a capital credit exactly equal to the assets he contributes, the entry is simply a debit to cash (or other assets) and a credit to the new owner's capital account. There are no special accounting problems presented by such a transaction.

Assets Contributed Greater than New Partner's Capital: Goodwill. When a new partner is not given credit for as much as he contributes, it may be implied that the existing firm has unrecorded goodwill. In this event, the goodwill may be placed on the books. To illustrate, let us assume that, instead of purchasing an interest in the Madsen, Nelson, and Olsen partnership, Kaspar invests $50,000 and acquires a one-fifth interest in the firm. If Kaspar is willing to pay $50,000 for a one-fifth interest, then he apparently feels the business is worth $250,000 (if $\frac{1}{5}X = \$50,000$, then $X = \$250,000$). Since the tangible assets will amount to only $210,000 and the business appears to be worth $250,000, this difference of $40,000 must represent goodwill. This goodwill existed prior to Kaspar's admission and, therefore, should be divided among the old partners according to their profit-and-loss-sharing ratio. The entry to record the goodwill and the admission of the new partner follows:

```
Goodwill ..................................    40,000
    Madsen, Capital ........................              13,333
    Nelson, Capital .........................              13,333
    Olsen, Capital ..........................              13,334
Cash .......................................    50,000
    Kaspar, Capital ........................              50,000
```

Note that, although the goodwill is credited to the old partners, the amount of the goodwill is determined by the valuation of the firm implied by the *new partner's* capital contribution.

Assets Contributed Greater than New Partner's Capital: Bonus.   If it does not seem desirable to record goodwill as was done in the above example, then the difference between the new partner's cash contribution and the capital credit can be recorded as a bonus to the old partners. Again, assume that Kaspar is given a one-fifth interest by investing $50,000, but that no goodwill is to be recorded. The entry follows:

```
Cash .......................................    50,000
    Kaspar, Capital .........................              42,000
    Madsen, Capital ........................               2,666
    Nelson, Capital .........................              2,667
    Olsen, Capital ..........................              2,667
```

The credit to Kaspar's capital account is determined by taking one-fifth of the total capital of $210,000, since he is to have a one-fifth interest in the new capital. The difference between the credit to his capital account of $42,000 and the debit to cash of $50,000 represents a bonus of $8,000. This amount is credited to the old partners in their profit-and-loss-sharing ratio.

Assets Contributed Less than New Partner's Capital: Goodwill.   When a new partner is given a capital credit in excess of the tangible assets he contributes, then it may be implied that he is also bringing some goodwill to the firm. In this instance, however, it is the old partners' contribution to the new firm that must be used to determine the amount of goodwill. To illustrate, let us assume that Kaspar is admitted to the firm of Madsen, Nelson, and Olsen by investing $50,000, but that he is given a one-third interest. This means that the old partners are contributing $160,000 (their present capital balances) in order to obtain a two-thirds interest in the new firm. If they are willing to pay $160,000 for a two-thirds interest, then presumably they would be willing to pay $240,000 for the entire business (if $\frac{2}{3}X = \$160,000$, then $X = \$240,000$). Since the new firm will have tangible assets of only $210,000 ($160,000 contributed by Madsen, Nelson, and Olsen, and $50,000 contributed by Kaspar), but has an implied value of $240,000, then Kaspar must be bringing goodwill of $30,000 as well as cash to the firm. Kaspar's admission would be recorded as follows:

Cash	50,000	
Goodwill	30,000	
Kaspar, Capital		80,000

Assets Contributed Less than New Partner's Capital: Asset Writedown. In the preceding illustration, the contribution of the old partners was used to determine the value of the enterprise and, in turn, the amount of goodwill to be recorded. The contribution of the new partner might just as appropriately be used to value the enterprise, in which case there is an implication that the existing assets are overvalued. If Kaspar is willing to pay $50,000 for a one-third interest, then apparently the existing assets are not worth $160,000, but only $100,000 (if $\frac{1}{3}X = $50,000$, then $X = $150,000$; $150,000 - $50,000 = $100,000$). Thus, a writedown of certain assets would be in order:

Madsen, Capital	20,000	
Nelson, Capital	20,000	
Olsen, Capital	20,000	
Various Assets		60,000
Cash	50,000	
Kaspar, Capital		50,000

Assets Contributed Less than New Partner's Capital: Bonus. Where the new partner's contribution is less than the amount of capital he is allowed, a third alternative would be to treat the difference between the two amounts as a bonus. In this event, no goodwill is recorded, but, instead, amounts are transferred from the old partners' accounts to the new partner's account. If Kaspar were given a one-third interest by contributing $50,000 and the bonus method were followed, the entry would be:

Cash	50,000	
Madsen, Capital	6,666	
Nelson, Capital	6,667	
Olsen, Capital	6,667	
Kaspar, Capital		70,000

Withdrawal of a Partner

The number of partners in a business may be reduced for several reasons, including death, retirement, or incompatibility. When a partner does withdraw, it is necessary to settle with him or his estate. In those instances where ample cash is available and the partners agree that capital balances reflect equity fairly, then the transaction is easily recorded by a debit to the retiring partner's capital account and a credit to cash. In many instances, however, the partner is allowed to take more or less than his capital balance. Whether he takes more or less is largely a matter of leverage. Are the other partners anxious to see him leave, or is he so anxious to withdraw that he is willing to do so at a sacrifice?

Where the capital account does not coincide with the agreed upon amount that will be withdrawn, the difference must be accounted for. Some accountants have argued that the difference implies unrecorded goodwill, and advocate placing goodwill on the books, as may be done when a new partner is admitted. Such a practice seems hard to justify on two grounds. First of all, the withdrawal may not be an "arms length" transaction and a fair judge of the value because of underlying circumstances which cause the withdrawal. For example, a partner may be so anxious to get out that he is willing to make a financial sacrifice to do so. The premium he pays to be released from his contract could not properly be called goodwill. Second, it is difficult to see how one could argue that goodwill is acquired at the time a partner withdraws. In fact, quite the opposite might be true if a prominent partner retires: the goodwill may, indeed, decrease.

It would seem that the preferable way to treat any difference arising in such circumstances would be to record it as a bonus to the retiring partner or to the remaining partners, depending on whether the retirement withdrawal amount was more or less than the retiring partner's capital account balance on the books. For example, if A, B, and C had capital balances of $10,000, $50,000, and $20,000, and C withdrew by taking $24,000, the transaction could be recorded as follows:

C, Capital	20,000	
A, Capital	2,000	
B, Capital	2,000	
Cash		24,000

In this instance, the bonus was from the remaining partners to the retiring partner. If C had withdrawn by taking $16,000, the bonus would have been reversed as follows:

C, Capital	20,000	
A, Capital		2,000
B, Capital		2,000
Cash		16,000

THE CORPORATION

A corporation is a multiple owner organization that is recognized as a separate legal entity by the law. Unlike the partnership, the corporation does have sufficient legal status to enable it to contract and to sue or be sued. Its legal status serves as a barrier to protect the owners from losses beyond the amount of their investment. Because of this special status, the corporation is able to raise large sums of capital, experience wide ownership, and enjoy perpetual life. On the other hand, being an artificial person makes the corporation subject to taxation.

Unlike the partnership or proprietorship, the corporation does not maintain separate equity accounts for each owner. Instead, the owners' equity is classified according to how it was obtained: as capital contributed by shareholders (*Paid-in Capital*), or as capital accumulated through earnings or other gain and loss transactions (*Retained Earnings*). If it were not for certain legal distinctions and accounting niceties, we could simply group all transactions under one or the other of these headings. For most financial reporting purposes they are adequate. But in order to provide for "fuller disclosure" as to sources of capital, availability for dividends, etc., it is customary to provide finer breakdowns by more precise labeling of the capital category portions.

Paid-in Capital

The owners of a corporation are issued certificates which indicate their interest in the enterprise. These documents are known as stock certificates and are the means by which a transfer in ownership takes place. A sample stock certificate is shown in Figure 11-3. When these certificates change hands, we say that the stock has been bought or sold. In reality, someone has bought or sold an interest in a corporation, and the stock certificate is merely evidence of the interest acquired.

One finds a wide variety of types of capital stock in practice, each type of stock having been designed to appeal to a particular type of investor and to complement the balance of the company's capital structure. Some of the more common features of capital stock are discussed in the following paragraphs.

Par Versus No-Par Stock. True no-par stock is stock which has no dollar value shown on its face. It is issued at the prevailing market price, and the entire proceeds are credited to the capital stock account. Most stocks do have an arbitrary value which is fixed either by the charter or by the board of directors. Such stock may be designated as having a par value or stated value. The journal entry to record the issuance of such

Figure 11-3

SAMPLE STOCK CERTIFICATE

stock must separate the credit into two accounts. To illustrate, let us assume that a company issued 1,000 shares of common stock with a $100 par value at a market price of $104 per share. The entry to record this transaction would be:

```
Cash  ...............................   104,000
      Common Stock, $100 Par Value .......              100,000
      Paid-in Capital in Excess of Par .......             4,000
```

The amount paid in excess of par is sometimes called a *premium on capital stock*. Where the amount is a debit, it may properly be termed a *discount on capital stock*. It is rare to find a stock issued at a discount, inasmuch as the original buyer of such stock may be held personally liable up to the amount of said discount.

In states where laws permit, no-par shares may be issued because the par or stated value is only a fiction with little relationship to the real value of the shares. The latter is set by the price which investors are willing to pay, rather than by an arbitrary valuation set upon it.

Common Versus Preferred Stock.   Many companies have several different classes of stock with each class having some special feature. When a firm has only one class of stock it is generally called *common stock* or *capital stock*. When there is more than one class, the other issues are usually described as *preferred stock*. Generally, this type of stock is given a prior claim on dividends. Not even preferred stock, however, is guaranteed a dividend. These are paid only when and if the board of directors declare them. The preference merely means that if a dividend is declared on the common stock, it can be legally done only after declaring one on the preferred. While one finds many preferred stocks in existence today, it is rather uncommon to find a new preferred issue.

Cumulative Versus Noncumulative Stock.   Preferred stock may be cumulative or noncumulative. With cumulative stock, dividends missed in any particular year must be made up before the common stock can be paid a dividend. These dividends that have been passed are sometimes called *dividends in arrears*. The directors are not obligated to pay dividends in arrears on noncumulative stock. Once these dividends are passed, they are lost.

Participating Versus Nonparticipating Stock.   Generally, the dividend on a preferred stock is expressed as a percent of its par value. When the preferred stock has no par value the dividends are stated as so many dollars per share. With nonparticipating stock the indicated dividend rate acts as a ceiling. Participating stock, on the other hand, is able to share in increased dividends no matter how high a dividend is paid to the common stockholder. Such stockholders are entitled to the same *rate* of dividend as is paid to the common stockholders in the event that such payment exceeds the regular preferred dividend rate.

Convertible Versus Nonconvertible Stock. Sometimes preferred stock has a provision which enables the stockholder to convert from preferred to common stock. Such conversion is done at the option of the stockholder.

Treasury Stock. Corporations sometimes reacquire shares of their own stock. If these shares are kept alive and held with the idea that they may be reissued again at some future date, they are designated as treasury stock. During the time the shares are held in the treasury they are registered in the company name, but no dividend is paid on them. When a company purchases treasury stock it is *not* acquiring an asset, but merely reducing the equity of the owners. At the time the company issues the stock, it increases owners' equity; when it reacquires these same shares, it reduces owners' equity. Because the reduction is only temporary, it is recorded in a separate account called treasury stock. Although this account has a *debit* balance, it is *not* an asset. Treasury stock is a contra or negative owners' equity account and should be shown as such on the balance sheet.

Treasury Stock Transactions. To illustrate, let us assume that a company issues 2,000 shares of common stock, $50 par value at $55 per share. The entry to record the stock issue would be as follows:

```
Cash ....................................  110,000
      Capital Stock .........................              100,000
      Paid-in Capital in Excess of Par ..........           10,000
```

Five years later the company reacquires ten of these shares in the open market at a price of $72 per share. The purchase of these treasury shares would be recorded as follows:

```
Treasury Stock ..............................  720
      Cash ...................................              720
```

If the company later sells five of these shares at a price of $85 per share, the following entry would result:

```
Cash ........................................  425
      Treasury Stock ..........................              360
      Paid-in Capital, Treasury Stock Transactions ...       65
```

If the remaining shares were sold at a price of $70 per share, the following entry would be made:

Cash	350	
Paid-in Capital, Treasury Stock Transactions	10	
Treasury Stock		360

Note that we do *not* recognize a gain or loss on treasury stock transactions. Any excess over the purchase price is treated as paid-in capital. When the stock is reissued at a price below the purchase price (as in the second instance), any deficiency is charged against the Paid-in Capital, Treasury Stock Transactions account to the extent of the account balance. When the Paid-in Capital, Treasury Stock Transactions account balance is exhausted, the excess is charged against Retained Earnings.

Retained Earnings

We have been concerned to this point with the permanent, or paid-in capital, portion of the owners' equity. This may be referred to as permanent capital because generally these amounts are not legally available for dividends. The other major type of owners' equity arises from the retention of income. Although these amounts generally are legally available for dividends, most companies do not pay out the entire amount because much of the earnings has been reinvested in equipment, inventories, and other assets, and is not in money form. Typically, corporations pay out as dividends anywhere from 40 to 70 percent of earnings, and the rest is invested in corporate assets for further growth. The retention of earnings has been one of the major means of growth for many United States corporations. In fact, the retained earnings often account for a greater portion of the owners' equity than does the paid-in capital. For example, General Motors reported retained earnings of about $7.2 billion and paid-in capital of only $1.5 billion in their 1966 annual report.

Appropriations of Retained Earnings.   Many companies have only one retained earnings account, while others prefer to appropriate or earmark a portion thereof. The main reason for appropriating retained earnings is to show why the amounts are being retained and not being paid out in dividends. For example, earnings may be retained for plant expansion or the retirement of bonds. Appropriations of retained earnings are sometimes called *reserves*. The entry to record an appropriation for plant expansion might be:

Retained Earnings	xxx	
Retained Earnings Appropriated for Plant Expansion ...		xxx

It should be noted that the above entry *does not* provide the cash necessary for plant expansion. It merely informs the stockholder why his dividend is not larger. The retained earnings appropriated for plant expansion is really an owners' equity account, *not* an asset account. A footnote to the balance sheet may be just as meaningful in showing why earnings were retained in the business, and this latter method seems to be less confusing than formally appropriating the retained earnings.

Cash Dividends. Dividends are payments made to stockholders as a return on their investment in the firm. There are two conditions that must be met before a dividend can legally be paid: the company must have unrestricted retained earnings in the amount of the dividend, and sufficient cash must be available to cover the payment. In order to give the stock transfer agent sufficient time to make the necessary cutoffs, dividends are usually declared as of one date, payable to stockholders of record on a second date, and actually paid on a third date. When a dividend is declared, the following entry is made:

```
Retained Earnings ...................................   xxx
     Dividends Payable ..............................           xxx
```

At this point, the dividend is a legal liability and would be shown on the balance sheet as a current liability. When the dividend is actually paid, the entry is similar to that made when other liabilities are paid:

```
Dividends Payable .........................'..............   xxx
     Cash  .........................................           xxx
```

Some companies prefer to debit a dividend account at the time the dividend is declared. In this event, the dividend account should be closed directly to retained earnings at the end of the accounting period.

Stock Dividends. Sometimes companies declare dividends that are settled by issuing shares of the company's own stock. These are known as stock dividends. Actually, the stockholder receives nothing when a stock dividend is distributed. His relative interest in the corporation remains the same as before, except that he now has more pieces of paper (stock certificates) to show an identical interest. A court decision ruling on whether or not stock dividends were income stated:

> A stock dividend really takes nothing from the property of the corporation and adds nothing to the interest of the stockholders. Its property is not diminished and their interests are not increased ... the proportional interest of each shareholder remains the same. The only change is in the evidence which represents that interest, the new shares and the original shares together representing the same proportional interests that the original shares represented before the issue of the new ones.[2]

---

[2]Eisner versus Macomber, 252 U.S. 189.

Theoretically, the market value of stock will fall proportionally when a stock dividend is declared. For example, if a person owned one hundred shares of stock which were selling for $50 per share before a 10 percent stock dividend was declared, he could expect the shares to drop to about $45.50 per share after the date of record. It might be argued that the stock price will not fall proportionately because some of the stockholders might *think* they are getting something. This seems hard to believe in a day of enlightened investors. The entry to record a stock dividend is simply a debit to the Retained Earnings account and a credit to Capital Stock account.[3] The effect is to convert retained earnings (temporary capital) to capital stock (permanent capital).

Stock Split. A company may call in its shares of stock which were originally issued at one par value and issue a proportionate number of another par value. For example, if a corporation originally issued 100,000 shares of $100 par value stock, they could call these shares in and reissue 200,000 shares of $50 par value stock in place thereof. Such a transaction would be described as a *2-for-1 stock* split and would be recorded by the following entry:

Common Stock, $100 par value   10,000,000
   Common Stock, $50 par value   10,000,000

Stock splits are usually initiated in order to lower the market price of the stock. One would expect that the preceding stock split would cause the market value of the stock to drop to half the price that prevailed before the split. A company may similarly increase the market price by going through a reverse stock split.

Corporate Financial Statements

Because of the large number of owners' equity accounts, the stockholders' equity section of a corporate balance sheet is usually more complex than that illustrated in chapter 5. A more complete stockholders equity section is shown in Figure 11-4.

---

[3]Accountants are not in agreement as to how much the charge to retained earnings should be; in other words, whether the par or market value of the stock should be used. The American Institute of Certified Public Accountants in *Accounting Research and Terminology Bulletin, final ed.*, indicates that where the dividend is less than 20–25 percent, the market value of the stock should be used to determine the charge to retained earnings. If the stock dividend is greater than 20–25 percent, then the par value of the stock should be used. The apparent logic of the American Institute's position is that small stock dividends may be "looked upon" as having a value equal to the market value of the shares distributed in the dividend.

Figure 11-4

STOCKHOLDERS' EQUITY

Paid-in Capital:
Common stock $1 par value, authorized
  8,000,000 shares, issued 6,000,000 shares,
  held in treasury 15,000 shares . . . . $ 6,000,000
5 percent cumulative convertible preferred
  stock, $100 par value, 20,000 shares
  authorized, issued and outstanding 2,000,000
Paid-in capital, excess over par of common stock 3,300,000
Paid-in capital, excess over par of preferred
  stock 800,000
Paid-in capital, treasury stock transactions 23,000
   Total paid-in capital $12,123,000
Retained Earnings:
Appropriated retained earnings:
  Retained earnings appropriated
   for plant expansion $2,500,000
  Retained earnings appropriated
   for treasury stock
   purchases 175,500
   Total Appropriated Retained Earnings . . $ 2,675,500
  Unappropriated retained earnings 14,259,407
   Total retained earnings   16,934,907
   Total $29,057,907
Less: Common stock in treasury, at cost   175,500
   Total stockholders' equity $28,882,407

Note the two major sections, Paid-in Capital and Retained Earnings, and the variety of accounts within each section. Inasmuch as treasury stock is a contra owners' equity account, it is shown as a deduction from the total stockholders' equity at the bottom of the statement.

Statement of Retained Earnings. Most corporations prefer to prepare a separate schedule to itemize the changes that have taken place in the retained earnings account during the period. The most simple statement of retained earnings would consist of only four items: the beginning account balance, the net income for the period, the dividends declared during the period, and the ending account balance. Such a statement would be prepared under the "all-inclusive income statement" concept (sometimes called "clean surplus" concept). All unusual, nonrecurring items (such as gains and losses from the disposing of fixed assets) would be shown in the income statement for the same period. An income statement and a retained earnings statement prepared under the "all inclusive" concept are shown in Figure 11-5.

Figure 11-5

All-Inclusive Income Concept
TARBOX SOUND COMPANY
Income Statement
For the Year Ended December 31, 1970

Net Sales		$1,213,949
Cost of goods sold		857,535
Gross margin		$ 356,414
Selling expenses	$123,802	
Administrative expenses	159,637	283,439
Net profit from operations		$ 72,975
Income taxes		25,000
Net profit before nonrecurring charges		$ 47,975
Deduct: Nonrecurring charges		
Loss of building by fire (net of tax)	$ 29,000	
Adjustment of prior periods' depreciation (net of tax)	5,500	34,500
Net profit		$ 13,475

TARBOX SOUND COMPANY
Retained Earnings Statement
For the Year Ended December 31, 1970

Retained earnings, Dec. 31, 1969	$425,429
Net income for year, per income statement	13,475
Total	$438,904
Dividends	24,000
Retained earnings, Dec. 31, 1970	$414,904

Some accountants argue that the income statement should only include items related to current operations and that the unusual, nonrecurring items should be charged or credited directly to retained earnings. By doing so, the comparability of reported net income from period to period and firm to firm is enhanced. The reported net income is thereby freed from one-time fluctuations extraneously caused. Where the "current operating concept" is followed, the unusual, nonrecurring items must be shown in the retained earnings statement. An abbreviated income statement and statement of retained earnings prepared under the "current operating" concept are shown in Figure 11-6.

In an attempt to make financial statements more uniform and to prevent firms from "burying" extraordinary items in the statement of retained earnings, the Accounting Principles Board of the American Institute of Certified Public Accountants has supported the all-inclusive concept. In a recent opinion they state:

The Board has concluded that net income should reflect all items of profit and loss recognized during the period with the sole exception of the prior period adjustments .... *Extraordinary items* should, however, be segregated from the results of ordinary operations and shown separately in the income statement, with disclosure of the nature and amounts thereof.[4]

Figure 11-6

Current Operating Concept
TARBOX SOUND COMPANY
Income Statement
For Year Ended December 31, 1970

Net sales		$1,213,949
Cost of goods sold		857,535
Gross margin		$ 356,414
Selling expenses	$123,802	
Administrative expenses	159,637	283,439
Net profit before taxes		$ 72,975
Income taxes		25,000
Net profit after taxes		$ 47,975

TARBOX SOUND COMPANY
Retained Earnings Statement
For Year Ended December 31, 1970

Retained earnings, Dec. 31, 1969			$ 425,529
Additions:			
Net income for year, per income statement			47,975
Total			$ 473,404
Deductions:			
Dividends		$ 24,000	
Nonrecurring charges:			
Loss of building by fire (net of tax) ..	$29,000		
Adjustments of prior periods'			
depreciation (net of taxes)	5,500	34,500	58,500
Retained earnings, Dec. 31, 1970			$ 414,904

Consolidated Statements.   Many large corporations have a number of subsidiaries in which they own controlling interests. For example, Ford Motor Company recently acquired controlling interest in Philco Corporation. When a parent corporation controls a subsidiary in this manner, in

---

[4]"Reporting the Results of Operations," *Opinions of the Accounting Principles Board No. 9* (New York: American Institute of Certified Public Accountants, 1967), pp. 112–13.

an economic sense they are one business entity. If Philco sells some radios to Ford Motor Company for installation in automobiles, then there really has been no transaction with outsiders. Inventory has merely shifted from one part of the company to another. A company cannot earn revenue by making sales to itself.

In order to reflect the economic facts inherent in this kind of situation, most corporations prepare consolidated financial statements. Each separate legal entity (such as Philco Corporation) keeps a separate set of books, records transactions, and prepares financial statements just as though they were independent economic units. At the end of the accounting period, the parent or controlling corporation assembles the financial statements from its many subsidiaries. Transactions which occurred between inter-related companies (such as between Philco Corporation and Ford Motor Company) are eliminated, and consolidated financial statements are prepared. The balance sheet presented in Ford Motor Company's Annual Report has a heading such as "Ford Motor Company and Consolidated Subsidiaries." The cash reported on this statement, for example, includes all that was held by the parent company or any of its consolidated subsidiaries. Generally, the individual subsidiaries' statements are not made available to the public, but, instead, the "net effect" of all of them is summarized in the parent's consolidated report.

The specific rules by which consolidated statements are prepared are extremely complex and are a subject for a more advanced text. It is sufficient to note here the general conventions by which they are prepared.

SUMMARY

The method of accounting for transactions affecting owners' equity varies, depending upon the legal form of business. In the proprietorship, all transactions involving the owner are recorded in a single capital account.[5] In a partnership, a separate account is maintained for each owner. The corporation, by contrast, does not maintain separate accounts for each owner, but, instead, classifies the equity according to source: paid-in capital or retained earnings.

There are unlimited ways that partners may agree to distribute profits or losses. Any agreement, however, should attempt to compensate the various parties according to differences in their investments of capital, time, ability, and other factors. In most cases, it is helpful to prepare a schedule of profit distribution to be sure that each partner's capital account is debited or credited as agreed.

---

[5]Except for withdrawals that are closed to the owner's capital account.

New partners may be admitted to an existing enterprise either by investment or by purchase of an interest. When the new partner invests, the
assets of the firm are increased. The amount he invests may be equal to,
greater than, or less than the amount of his capital credit, according to the
leverage exerted by the various parties. Where there is a difference between the amount invested and the capital credit, the transaction may be
recorded as implying goodwill, implying an overvaluation of assets, or a
bonus between partners. In the event that a difference arises upon withdrawal of a partner, this amount is generally treated as a bonus.

A corporation is a legal entity created by law and thereby has certain at-
tributes peculiar to that form of business. From an accounting standpoint
this status requires special recognition in the accounts. When a corporation
is organized (and sometimes thereafter as well), certificates known as capital stock are issued to the owners as evidence of ownership. There are numerous classifications and options of capital stock, including par or no-par,
common or preferred, cumulative or noncumulative, participating or nonparticipating, and convertible or nonconvertible. When a corporation reacquires its own previously issued shares they are known as treasury stock.

Retained earnings have been an important source of growth for most
American corporations, as these companies have adopted policies of paying only a fraction of their earnings out in dividends. Generally, the earnings so retained are carried in a single account. Some companies, however,
prefer to earmark part of these earnings by appropriation. Where this is
done, dividends may be declared only out of the free, or unappropriated,
portion.

Most corporations prepare a statement of retained earnings to summarize the changes which have taken place in this account during the
accounting period. Accountants are not in agreement as to whether certain unusual, nonrecurring items should be shown on this statement, or
whether they should be shown on the income statement of the same period.
The advocates of the "all-inclusive" concept prefer to disclose them on the
income statement, while the advocates of the "current operating concept"
favor showing them on the retained earnings statement. The American
Institute of CPAs has taken a position favoring the all-inclusive income
statement except for "... those rare items which relate directly to the
operations of a specific prior period or periods."[6]

QUESTIONS

1. How are the profits of a partnership divided in the absence of a specific
   agreement? If there is an agreement regarding the division of profits but
   none regarding the division of losses, how are the losses divided?

---

[6]*Opinions of the Accounting Principles Board no. 9*, op. cit.

2. List several important factors that should be taken into consideration in drawing up a profit-and-loss-sharing agreement. How would you provide compensation for each of these factors?

3. Is it possible for a partnership to show a profit for a particular period and for one or more of the partners to show a loss from the partnership for the same period? Explain.

4. Distinguish between a new partner's being admitted to an existing firm by purchase of an interest, and his admittance by investment.

5. How is the amount of the goodwill arrived at when the new partner's contribution exceeds his share of the tangible capital?

6. How should a bonus between partners be distributed, where the bonus is going from the new partner to the old partners?

7. What are some of the significant differences between partnerships and corporations?

8. Distinguish between common and preferred stock. What is the par value of a stock? Do all stocks have a par value?

9. What is treasury stock? How are treasury stock "purchases" recorded? How should the Treasury Stock account be shown in the balance sheet?

10. When treasury stock is reissued at a price higher than the price at which it was reacquired, to what account should the difference be credited?

11. Why do some companies appropriate portions of retained earnings? Is there some other means of accomplishing this objective?

12. What benefit does a stockholder receive when a stock dividend is distributed? How are stock dividends recorded? What is accomplished by declaring and distributing a stock dividend?

13. Compare a stock split with a stock dividend. What difference can be seen in the stockholders' equity in each case?

14. What items are included in an "all inclusive" income statement, but excluded from a "current operating" income statement? What treatment do you prefer? Why?

15. What is the objective of preparing consolidated statements? What types of transactions are eliminated prior to consolidation?

PROBLEMS

Problem 11-1

Martin, Lark, Price, and Smith are in a partnership. They ask you as their accountant to prepare a schedule of distribution of profits for them. According to the partnership agreement, Martin, Lark, Price, and Smith are to be allowed salaries of $10,000, $15,000, $25,000, and $35,000 respectively. The partners are to be allowed 8 percent interest on their capital balances at the beginning of the year and are to be charged interest against their respective drawings at the rate of 10 percent. Martin and Price are to receive a $5,000 bonus each. The remaining net income is to be divided among the partners, according to their capital ratio, after withdrawals for the year are deducted, but prior to any current distribution of income.

	M	L	P	S
Capital at beginning of year	$50,000	$20,000	$15,000	$15,000
Withdrawals during the year	5,000	2,000	3,000	6,000

The partnership net income for the year was $200,000.

Required:
   a. Make a schedule of distribution of profits for the year (round to nearest dollar).
   b. Prepare general journal entries necessary to close the income summary and drawings accounts.

Problem 11-2

Francis, Bunning, and Saathoff are partners in a small bootlegging firm. Their capital accounts are $5,000, $15,000, and $20,000 respectively, and they distribute profits equally among themselves. Capone, upon approval of the existing partners, is to be admitted as a partner to the firm. Capone is contributing $10,000 in cash to the partnership and will receive one-fourth interest in the firm.

Required:
   a. Record Capone's entrance on the partnership's books under the condition that goodwill is to be recognized.
   b. Record Capone's entrance on the partnership's books under the assumption that a bonus is to be recognized.
   c. Record the admission of Capone, assuming that his contribution implies that the firm's existing assets are overvalued (credit "various assets").

Problem 11-3

On January 1, 1971, Easy Corporation was organized and incorporated in the state of Hawaii. The following transactions took place thereafter:

January 1, 1971 Received a charter of articles of incorporation from the state authorizing Easy to issue 100,000 shares of $5 par common stock.

January 3, 1971 Sold 50,000 shares of $5 par common stock for $6 cash per share.

March 15, 1971 Sold 10,000 shares of $5 par value common stock for $9 cash per share.

March 30, 1971 Recorded a net income after taxes of $100,000 for the first quarter ending March 30 (close the Income Summary account).

April   1, 1971 The board of directors of Easy Corporation declared a $1 per share cash dividend to be paid June 1, 1971, to all holders of record as of May 1, 1971.

May   15, 1971 Sold 20,000 shares of $5 par value common stock for $15 cash per share.

June   1, 1971 Paid the cash dividend declared April 1, 1971.

June   30, 1971 Easy Corporation recorded a net loss of $10,000 for the second quarter of 1971 (close the Income Summary account).

Required:
Record the above transactions in the journal of Easy Corporation.

Problem 11-4

A, B, and C are partners in a small firm. The individual owners have the following credit balances in their capital accounts: A, $25,000; B, $35,000; and C, $40,000. D is to be admitted to the firm by contributing $30,000 in cash and is to receive one-fifth interest in the new partnership. The old partners share profits in ratio of 1:1:2.

Required:

    a. Record the entrance of D into the partnership if it has been determined that goodwill exists.

    b. Record the entrance of D into the partnership if it has been decided that no goodwill exists in the old partnership.

    c. Prepare the journal entries which would be made if D were admitted to the firm by purchasing B's interest in the firm for $30,000.

Problem 11-5

Tom, Dick, and Harry are engaged in a partnership and have asked you as their accountant to prepare a schedule of distribution of profits for them for the calendar year 1970. They supply you with the following information:

1. Net income for the year was $25,000.
2. Tom, Dick, and Harry are to be allowed the following salaries: Tom, $3,000; Dick, $10,000; and Harry, $7,000.
3. Interest is to be credited to each partner in the amount of 10 percent of his capital balance as of the beginning of the year.
4. Because Tom is the managing partner, he is to receive a bonus of $6,000 for the year.
5. The remaining income is to be divided in the ratio of the beginning capital balance.

	TOM	DICK	HARRY
Capital at beginning of year	$25,000	$15,000	$20,000
Withdrawals during year	2,000	3,000	5,000

Required:

    a. Prepare a schedule of distribution of profits for the partnership.

    b. Prepare journal entries necessary to close the partnership books.

Problem 11-6

Goldbrick Corporation has outstanding 3,000 shares of $100, 6 percent preferred stock and 15,000 shares of $25 par value common stock. No dividends were in arrears as of December 31, 1961. During a six-year period the corporation paid the following amounts in dividends:

YEAR	AMOUNT
1962	$25,000
1963	30,000
1964	–0–
1965	65,000
1966	55,000
1967	50,000

Required:

a. Prepare a form with columnar headings as follows:

YEAR	TOTAL PAID TO PREFERRED	TOTAL PAID TO COMMON	DIVIDEND PER SHARE PREFERRED	DIVIDEND PER SHARE COMMON

b. Complete the schedule assuming the preferred stock is cumulative but nonparticipating.
c. Prepare and complete a second form according to the foregoing directions under the assumption that the corporation's preferred stock is noncumulative and nonparticipating.
d. Prepare and complete a third form according to the foregoing directions under the assumption that the corporation's preferred stock is cumulative and fully participating.

Problem 11-7

Rowley Corporation is a fast-growing, profitable company. During the ten years of its existence, Rowley Corporation has retained all of its earnings for its future growth and development. The company feels that it should distribute to the stockholders some evidence of the prosperity it has enjoyed since formation. Inasmuch as the corporation needs all of its funds for expansion, the directors decide to declare a 15 percent stock dividend. The dividend is declared as of January 1, 1971, and is to be distributed as of March 1, 1971. On January 1, 1971, the stock of Rowley Corporation is selling at $10 per share, and the owners' equity section of the balance sheet appears as follows:

Common stock, $5 par value, authorized
    500,000 shares, issued and outstanding 300,000 shares. . . . $1,500,000
Paid-in capital in excess of par value   300,000
Retained earnings   725,000
Total stockholders' equity $2,525,000

After provision for income taxes the Rowley Corporation had a first-quarter net income of $86,000. On April 10, 1971, the board of directors declared a 5 percent stock dividend to be distributed on May 1, 1971. On April 10, 1971, the common stock of Rowley Corporation was selling for $15 per share. The net income (after taxes) for the second quarter of 1971 was $59,000. On July 1, 1971, the company's stock was split on a 2-for-1 basis.

Required:

    a. Prepare all journal entries required on the Rowley Corporation books from January 1, 1971, through July 1, 1971.

    b. Prepare in good form the stockholders' equity section of the Rowley Corporation's balance sheet as of July 1, 1971, after giving consideration to all of the foregoing transactions.

Problem 11-8

Selected data on the Granite Corporation for the year ended December 31, 1970, appear below:

Dividends	$ 75,000
Salaries expense	98,700
Cost of goods sold	986,215
Income tax expense	125,000
Lawsuit judgment against company for patent infringements for years 1958, 1963, inclusive[a] ...	100,000
Advertising expenses	21,000
Fire loss of uninsured building (May 10, 1970)[a]	89,000
Depreciation, plant and equipment	8,980
Adjustment for overcharge of prior years' depreciation[a]	8,500
Administrative expenses	78,000
Net sales	1,652,193
Rent expense	9,670
Retained earnings, December 31, 1969	24,350

[a]Net of tax.

Required:

    a. Prepare in good form an income statement and a statement of retained earnings under the assumption that the company prefers the "current operating" concept.

    b. Prepare in good form an income statement and a statement of retained earnings under the "all-inclusive" income statement method.

Problem 11-9

At the beginning of the period Junk Corporation had 100,000 shares of $10 par common stock outstanding. The Paid-in Capital in Excess of Par account had a balance of $500,000 at that date. On June 15, Junk Corporation reacquired 50,000 shares of its outstanding common stock at a cost of $20 per share. On June 30, the corporation declared a $2 cash dividend on its outstanding common stock to be paid July 15. On August 1, the company reissued 25,000 shares of stock held in the treasury at a price of $25 per share. On November 15, the corporation reissued the remaining shares of its treasury stock at a price of $14 per share.

Required:
Record the above transactions in the journal of Junk Corporation.

Problem 11-10

Mano, Otto, and Pero are partners with capital balances of $80,000, $65,000, and $45,000, respectively. They presently share profits in the ratio 20 percent to Mano, 30 percent to Otto, and the balance to Pero. The partners have agreed to admit Zero to the firm upon payment of $50,000. Prepare general journal entries to record the admission of Zero under each of the following assumptions:

1. Zero purchases a one-fourth interest in the firm by acquiring one-fourth of each of the existing partners' capital.
2. Zero invests in the firm, is given a one-fourth interest, and goodwill is recorded.
3. Zero invests in the firm, is given a one-fourth interest, and *no* goodwill is recorded.
4. Zero invests in the firm, is given a one-sixth interest, and goodwill is recorded.
5. Zero invests in the firm, is given a one-sixth interest, and *no* goodwill is recorded.
6. Zero invests in the firm and receives a one-fourth interest, but his investment implies that the firm's assets are overvalued. The partners agree that the Land account should be written down.

Case 11
JAKIDELL ENTERPRISES

Jason, Killroy, and Loddell are partners operating under the name, Jakidell Enterprises. The business was formed February 22, 1966, and since that date the partners have shared profits according to the following provision contained in the partnership agreement:

Partners are to be allowed monthly salaries as follows: Jason, $1,000; Killroy, $700; and Loddell, $300. Interest is to be credited to the partners at the rate of 10 percent per annum on the capital balances as of the beginning of the year. Any withdrawals by partners during the year in excess of the agreed salaries are to be charged interest at the rate of 20 percent per annum. Jason, as managing partner, is to be credited with a bonus of 10 percent of the firm's net profits remaining after the deduction of partners' salaries but before deduction of any other allowances or charges to partners. The balance of profits is to be divided equally among the partners. Profits are to be calculated on a yearly basis in accordance with generally accepted accounting principles as of each December 31.

Negotiations are underway to admit Mr. John Mason to the firm. It has been agreed that Mr. Mason will be admitted to the partnership upon investment of $41,600, for which he is to be given a one-fourth interest in the total capital of the new firm. The books for the current year, as summarized in Exhibit 11-1, are to be closed prior to Mason's admission, but after giving consideration to the following adjustments. It is agreed that a provision for bad debts in the amount of $1,200 should be established and that obsolete inventory should be written down in the amount of $2,300.

After recording Mason's admission, it is agreed that the business is to be incorporated. Each of the partners is to receive one hundred shares of $10 preferred stock in exchange for $1,500 of equity in the old firm. The balance of each partner's equity is to be satisfied by issuing common stock ($1.00 par value) at par.

Exhibit 11-1

JAKIDELL ENTERPRISES
Trial Balance
December 31, 1971

Cash	13,200	
Accounts Receivable	38,900	
Inventories	59,100	
Equipment	45,000	
Accumulated Depreciation, Equipment		5,400
Accounts Payable		22,300
Sales		222,900
Cost of Goods Sold	129,400	
Selling Expenses	33,800	
Administrative Expenses	48,600	
Jason, Drawing[a]	12,000	
Killroy, Drawing[a]	10,400	
Loddell, Drawing[a]	3,600	
Jason, Capital		50,500
Killroy, Capital		30,100
Loddell, Capital		62,800
	394,000	394,000

[a]Each of the partners withdrew the agreed salary as of the beginning of each month. In addition to these amounts, Killroy withdrew $2,000 as of May 1, 1971.

QUESTIONS

1. What was the partnership profit or loss for the year 1971? How should this be divided among the partners?
2. What are Jason's, Killroy's, and Loddell's capital balances after the 1971 closing entries have been posted?
3. Does it make any difference whether the bonus or goodwill method is used to record Mason's admission? Which method would you prefer if you were Mason?
4. How many shares of each class of stock will each of the owners hold in the new corporation?

12

Statements
Analysis

Financial analysis is an art requiring expert judgment and skill. Unfortunately, there exists no mystical crystal ball into which the analyst can gaze and clearly watch the future unfold before his eyes. In spite of this apparent handicap, financial analysis need not be a "fly-by-the-seat-of-your-pants" proposition. There are certain tools to which the experienced analyst can wisely turn. Three of these techniques are discussed in this chapter: *horizontal statement analysis, vertical statement analysis,* and *financial ratio analysis.*

Some of the material in this chapter is adapted from A. Tom Nelson, *The Impact of Leasing on Financial Analysis* (East Lansing, Mich.: Bureau of Business and Economic Research, Michigan State University, 1963).

HORIZONTAL ANALYSIS

A great deal can be learned by comparing a particular component in a financial statement with the same item as shown in another statement. The comparison generally is most meaningful when it relates figures of the same company of successive periods. This type of analysis may also be used to compare the current year's figures with some standard or base year. Generally, the two years are listed in adjoining columns, with the current figures listed first. A net dollar change column is then shown, followed by a percentage change column. The percentage change is calculated by dividing the net dollar change by the older of the two figures.

The balance sheet of the Majestic Oil Company, analyzed in this manner, is shown in Figure 12-1. The change columns indicate the net changes in balance sheet accounts that have taken place during the year 1970. The first of these columns shows the change in dollar amounts and the second in percentage terms. These latter figures are often useful in placing the change in proper perspective. For example, we note a 46 percent increase in the current assets of the Majestic Oil Company during a period when the total assets increased only 27 percent. This would indicate a change of major proportions in the ratio of current assets to total assets. Further analysis discloses the fact that the Short-term Investment account is the only current asset that increased at a rate greater than that experienced with either the total current assets or the total assets. Although the change in the investment account does explain the increase in current assets, the rate is somewhat misleading (892 percent) because of the low base figure. The student should recognize the fact that sometimes percentages can be misleading.

The income statement of the Majestic Oil Company is shown in Figure 12-2. This statement has also been analyzed in a horizontal manner. It is often informative in such a statement to relate the percentage change in sales to other changes. For example, Majestic Oil Company experienced only a 10 percent increase in sales during 1970 and yet enjoyed a 24 percent increase in net income. Analysis of changes in other items discloses that depreciation remained almost constant and selling, general, and administrative expenses increased only 6 percent. These figures indicate that the company increased its profit rate by coupling an increase in sales with a less than proportionate increase in expenses.

Space will not permit a detailed analysis of the Majestic Oil Company statements. It would be wise, however, to analyze these statements carefully by asking: What is the meaning of this change? What would cause these relationships to occur? Careful analysis of the change in these statements would give management considerable insight into trends, as well as areas of possible strength and weakness.

Figure 12-1

MAJESTIC OIL COMPANY
Horizontal Analysis of Balance Sheets
at December 31, 1969 and December 31, 1970

ASSETS

	AT DECEMBER 31		CHANGE	
	1970 ($000's)	1969 ($000's)	($000's)	PERCENT
Current Assets:				
Cash	42,494	47,630	− 5,136	− 10.79
Short-term investments, at cost	129,777	13,077	+116,700	+892.40
Accounts and notes receivable	140,142	119,242	+ 20,900	+ 17.53
Inventories of crude oil and refind products	68,393	75,718	− 7,325	− 9.67
Materials and supplies	21,392	18,174	+ 3,218	+ 17.71
Work in process	6,739	7,144	− 405	− 5.67
Total current assets	408,937	280,985	+ 127,952	+ 45.54
Long-Term Receivables and Investments:				
Notes receivable from sale of properties	22,037	24,806	− 2,769	− 11.16
Securities of affiliated companies, at cost	45,199	51,580	− 6,381	− 12.37
Other investments, at cost or less	9,747	4,881	+ 4,866	+ 99.69
Total long-term investments	76,983	81,267	− 4,284	− 5.27
Properties, Plants and Equipment:	1,318,444	1,161,371	+157,073	+ 13.52
Less depreciation and depletion	610,007	576,288	+ 33,719	+ 5.85
Net properties	708,437	585,083	+123,354	+ 21.08
Deferred Charges:	11,426	5,932	+ 5,494	+ 92.62
Total assets	1,205,783	953,267	+252,516	+ 26.49

LIABILITIES AND STOCKHOLDERS' EQUITY

	AT DECEMBER 31			
Current Liabilities:				
Accounts payable and accrued liabilities	86,451	78,517	+ 7,934	+ 10.10
Notes and bonds payable..	6,689	1,647	+ 5,042	+306.38
Taxes, other than income..	32,637	32,137	+ 500	+ 1.56
Income taxes	31,144	23,337	+ 7,807	+ 33.45
Total current liabilities..	156,921	135,638	+ 21,283	+ 15.69

	1970 ($000's)	1969 ($000's)	CHANGE ($000's)	PERCENT
Long-Term Debt:				
Sinking fund debentures ..	100,000	—	+100,000	—
Notes payable to banks ...	50,000	—	+ 50,000	—
Convertible debentures ...	11,597	—	+ 11,597	—
Notes and bonds payable ..	465	2,699	− 2,234	− 82.77
Total long-term debt ...	162,062	2,699	+159,363	+5,904.52ª
Deferred Credit	35,597	30,699	+ 4,878	+ 15.88
Stockholders' Equity:				
Common stock, $1.00 par.	50,000	50,000	—	—
Retained earnings	801,203	734,211	+ 66,992	+ 8.54
Total stockholders' equity	851,203	784,211	+ 66,992	+ 8.54
Total liabilities and stockholders' equity	1,205,783	953,267	+252,516	+ 26.49

The financial statements presented in this chapter differ in format from those of earlier chapters. The student should note that few rigid rules exist relating to format and that classification used and the presentation followed should be those that will make the particular statement most meaningful to the user.

ªBecause of the small base figure and the large increase, a percentage such as this is not too meaningful.

Figure 12-2

MAJESTIC OIL COMPANY
Horizontal Analysis of Income Statements
For Years Ended December 31, 1969 and 1970

	1970 ($000's)	1969 ($000's)	CHANGE ($000's)	PERCENT
Revenues:				
Sales	925,243	838,295	+86,948	+ 10.40
Other income	16,793	11,802	+ 4,991	+ 42.29
Total revenues	942,036	850,097	+91,939	+ 10.82
Costs and expenses:				
Costs of products sold	529,997	479,314	+50,683	+ 10.57
Selling, general and administrative expenses	141,102	133,327	+ 7,775	+ 5.83
Income taxes	88,698	78,343	+10,355	+ 13.22
Intangible development costs ...	37,027	32,067	+ 4,960	+ 15.47
Depreciation	57,221	57,705	− 484	− .84
Interest	3,084	754	+ 2,330	+309.02
Other costs	72	80	− 8	− 10.00
Total expenses	857,201	781,590	+75,611	+ 9.67
Net income	84,835	68,507	+16,328	+ 23.83

VERTICAL ANALYSIS

Financial statements may also be analyzed vertically. Such statements may be referred to as *common-size* statements because each item is expressed in terms of a percentage of a common base. In a balance sheet each component is expressed as a percentage of the total assets, while in an income statement net sales is used as the base. This type of analysis is particularly useful for comparing several companies within the same industry, or for comparing different divisions within a company. Even though these companies or divisions may vary greatly in size, the comparison can be meaningful because the common-size analysis has placed them on comparable terms.

The common-size balance sheet of Majestic Oil Company is shown in Figure 12-3, and the common-size income statement of the same company is shown in Figure 12-4. Actually, these statements are nothing more than a series of ratios. It may be noted, for example, that only 3½ percent of Majestic's assets at December 31, 1970, were in the form of cash, while 59 percent of the firm's assets at the same date were tied up in property, plant, and equipment. How do these figures compare with those of other companies in the industry? Does Majestic Oil Company have too large a proportion of its total assets invested in fixed assets? The same questions could be raised about any item in the balance sheet as various companies are compared or as various divisions within a company are compared. Does the company (or division) have too high a ratio of current assets to total assets? Does the firm have excess liquid funds? Why the large investment in current assets? Is too much (or too little) tied up in inventory? These questions can at least partially be answered by a vertical analysis.

Vertical analysis is particularly useful in comparing the performance of various companies or branches. If advertising costs represent 2 percent of net sales in one branch and 5 percent of net sales in another branch, there may be some significance in the difference. Management's attention is thereby called to areas which may need investigation.

FINANCIAL RATIOS

A financial ratio is merely a comparison, in ratio or percentage form, of two significant figures taken from financial statements. Actually, much of the vertical and horizontal analysis discussed in the previous sections falls under the heading of financial ratios. For example, expressing cash as a percent of total assets, as was done in vertical analysis, might just as

Figure 12-3

MAJESTIC OIL COMPANY
Consolidated Balance Sheet
Vertical Analysis, December 31, 1970

ASSETS

	($000's)	PERCENT
Current Assets:		
Cash	42,494	3.52
Short-term investment, at cost	129,777	10.76
Accounts and notes receivable	140,142	11.62
Inventories, crude oil and refined products	68,393	5.62
Material and supplies	21,392	1.77
Work in process	6,739	0.57
Total current assets	408,937	33.91
Long Term Receivables and Investments:		
Notes receivable from sale of property	22,037	1.83
Securities of affiliated companies, at cost	45,199	3.75
Other investments, at cost or less	9,747	0.81
Total long-term receivables and investments	76,983	6.39
Property, plant and equipment	1,318,444	
Less depreciation and depletion	610,007	
	708,437	58.75
Deferred charges	11,426	0.95
Total assets	1,205,783	100.00

LIABILITIES AND STOCKHOLDERS' EQUITY

	($000's)	PERCENT
Current Liabilities:		
Accounts payable and accrued liabilities	86,451	7.17
Notes and bonds payable	6,689	0.55
Taxes, other than income taxes	32,637	2.71
Income Taxes	31,144	2.58
Total current liabilities	156,921	13.01
Long-Term Debt:		
Sinking fund debentures	100,000	8.29
Notes payable to banks	50,000	4.15
Convertible debentures	11,597	0.96
Notes and bonds payable	465	0.04
Total long-term debt	162,062	13.44
Deferred credits	35,597	2.96
Stockholders' Equity:		
Common stock, $1.00 par	50,000	4.14
Retained earnings	801,203	66.45
Total stockholders' equity	851,203	70.59
Total liabilities and stockholders' equity	1,205,783	100.00

Figure 12-4

MAJESTIC OIL COMPANY
Consolidated Income Statement
Vertical Analysis
For Year Ended December 31, 1970

	($000's)	PERCENT
Revenue:		
Sales and other operating revenue	925,463	98.24
Other income	16,573	1.76
Total revenues	942,036	100.00
Cost and Expenses:		
Costs of products sold	529,997	56.26
Selling, general and administrative expenses..	141,102	14.98
Income taxes	88,698	9.42
Intangible development costs	37,027	3.93
Depreciation	57,221	6.07
Interest	3,084	.33
Other costs	72	.00
Total costs and expenses	857,201	90.99
Net income	84,835	9.01

well be called the "ratio of cash to total assets." The number of financial ratios possible is almost limitless. We will consider here only some of the more important ones.[1]

Limitation of Ratios

A word of caution about ratios in general seems in order at this point. Ratios must be used for what they are: financial tools. Too often they are looked upon as ends in themselves rather than as the means to an end. No ratio may be regarded as good or bad per se. It may be an indication that a firm is weak or strong, but it must never be taken as proof of either one. Ratios may be likened to railroad signals: they tell the analyst to stop, look and listen.

Another weakness in financial ratios stems from the fact that they are normally computed directly from a company's certified financial statements without any adjustments being made by the analyst. For ratio use, conventional financial statements prepared in accordance with generally accepted accounting principles have a number of serious weaknesses that

[1]Most of the ratios discussed here are included in Dun & Bradstreet's *Key Business Ratios.*

the analyst must consider if the ratios are to be meaningful.[2] For example, accepted accounting practice *does not* provide for inclusion of leased properties as assets, nor of obligations arising from long-term leases as liabilities in the financial statements. Ratios calculated from published financial statements of companies that lease extensively could be grossly misleading, unless the analyst takes this deficiency in accounting practice into consideration in his analysis. Financial analysts have developed several techniques to take into account the estimated assets and liability values arising from long-term leases.

A second weakness in conventional reporting stems from the problem generated by the changing value of the dollar: the old monster, inflation. Conventional financial statements are prepared under a constant dollar assumption which, in fact, is not valid. Ratios taken from conventional statements can be grossly in error because they have failed to consider the changing value of the dollar. Some attempts to deal with this problem are discussed in chapter 21.

Because of the limitations of financial ratios and the uncertainties surrounding the general business climate, some analysts refuse to use ratios and, instead, rely solely on their own intuition. Like the rheumatic weather forecasters, these analysts disregard available signs, gauging a company's financial position solely by a "feeling in their bones." The following statement relegates this "hunch" method to its proper place.

> A man may say, if he likes, that the moon is made of green cheese: that is an hypothesis. But another man who has devoted a great deal of time and attention to the subject, and availed himself of the most powerful telescopes and the results of the observations of others, declares that in his opinion it is probably composed of materials very similar to those of which our own earth is made up; and that is also only an hypothesis. But I need not tell you that there is an enormous difference in the value of the two hypothesis. That one which is based on sound scientific knowledge is sure to have a corresponding value; and that which is a mere hasty random guess is likely to have little value. Every great step in our progress in discovering causes has been made in exactly the same way as that which I have detailed to you . . . It is in these matters as in the commonest affairs of practical life: the guess of the fool will be folly, while the guess of the wise man will contain wisdom. In all cases you see that the value of the result depends on the patience and faithfulness with which the investigator applies to his hypothesis every possible kind of verification. . . .[3]

---

[2]An article by the author illustrating the misleading nature of conventional ratio analysis, entitled "Capitalizing Leases—The Effect on Financial Ratios," appeared in the July 1963 issue of the *Journal of Accountancy*.

[3]Thomas Henry Huxley, as quoted by Roger E. Ballard and Allan A. Gilbert in "How to Quantify Decision-Making," *Business Horizons* 1 (Winter 1958): 79.

So it is also with the task of financial analysis. The analyst is still working only with hypotheses to which he must apply every available test. While ratios may never transform an hypothesis into a fact, they may well distinguish the "fool" from the "wise man." Granted, ratios have certain weaknesses; but if the limitations are properly discounted, ratio analysis can be a most useful tool. There will probably never be a substitute for skilled judgment in the field of financial analysis. Nevertheless, the successful analyst will continue to utilize every available tool in exercising his judgment.

Statement analysis is meaningful only when approached from the standpoint of the individual who is taking a particular action (investing, promoting, firing, etc.). What information can the reader glean from the statements that will be meaningful in relation to a specific decision? What is the person trying to learn about the company or branch that he is attempting to evaluate? What ratios might assist him in this evaluation? The student should refrain from merely memorizing or applying a "cookbook" technique to the ratios cited here; instead, in each case he should ask himself who might use this ratio and what the user would be trying to learn.

The discussion of ratios in this chapter is centered around the second question: what are the ratios designed to measure? The major questions that may be partially answered by ratio analysis are

1. What is the firm's current debt-paying ability?
2. How profitable is the firm?
3. How effectively is the working capital being utilized?
4. How well balanced is the company's equity structure?

The data from the financial statements of the Majestic Oil Company, presented in Figures 12-1 through 12-4, have been used to calculate the illustrative ratios which follow. Year-end ratios have been calculated as of December 31, 1970, and period ratios for the year 1970.

Ratios to Measure Current Debt-Paying Ability

One important consideration in evaluating a company's financial position is its ability to meet obligations as they mature. Probably the best way to evaluate a firm's debt-paying ability is to prepare a projected cash-flow statement, a procedure described in the next chapter. A more common practice, however, is for financial analysts to use ratios to give a crude idea of current debt-paying ability. Three ratios commonly used for this purpose are the *current ratio* (working capital ratio), the *quick ratio* (acid-test ratio), and the *ratio of current debt to inventory*.

Current ratio. Probably the most widely known financial ratio is the current ratio. Its purpose is to measure the firm's general debt-paying ability within the near future, generally one year from date of computation. The current ratio is calculated by dividing the current assets by the current liabilities. For example, if a firm has current assets of three million dollars and current liabilities of one million dollars, its current ratio is three to one. If the ratio is less than one to one the firm is thought to be verging on insolvency. To the extent that the ratio exceeds one to one, there exists some cushion of current assets over current liabilities.

Almost as well known as the ratio itself is the often suggested rule of thumb ideal: the two-to-one ratio. Such rules of thumb are to be discouraged, since financial analysis is an individual matter, and a ratio which is perfectly acceptable in the case of one company or industry may be totally inadequate for another.

Because it has been so widely used and because of the stereotype imposed by the application of rule of thumb standards, the current ratio has been the subject of much abuse. To begin with, it has been implied that the higher the ratio, the sounder the company. Actually, this is far from the truth. A ratio may be too high as well as too low. A management which accumulates excess cash and cash equivalents will soon build up a high current ratio. This may well be a sign of stagnation rather than of astute management. During the post–Second World War era, for example, Montgomery Ward accumulated large amounts of cash in anticipation of a depression which never occurred. In this instance the high current ratio was probably not a sign of an alert and progressive management.

Another possible misuse of the current ratio is the analysts' failure to go beyond the ratio to the items which compose it. This is really not a weakness of the ratio itself, but of the analyst, and is an example of confusing the means with the end. An increased current ratio may well be a sign of a business slowdown as excess inventory is accumulated and the collection of accounts receivable slows up. On the other hand, the inventories may have been accumulated intentionally, to provide a basis for enlarged volume in the future. Again the analyst must be reminded to stop, look, and listen, and then proceed with extreme care.

The current ratio for Majestic Oil Company as of December 31, 1970, may be calculated as follows:

$$\frac{\text{Current assets}}{\text{Current liabilities}} = \frac{\$409}{\$157} = 2.6$$

Quick Ratio. The quick ratio, sometimes called the acid-test ratio, is an even finer measure of a company's ability to meet current debts. It is similar to the current ratio except that instead of total current assets, only those assets that are considered liquid or that can be readily converted into cash are included. Those assets most generally treated as "quick" are cash, receivables, and temporary investments. Excluded from this classification are current assets such as inventories and prepaid items which cannot, in the ordinary course of business, be converted into cash in a short time.

The quick ratio is calculated by dividing the total quick assets by the total current liabilities as follows:

$$\frac{\text{Quick assets}}{\text{Current liabilities}} = \frac{\$312}{\$157} = 1.99$$

Current Debt to Inventory. Actually, the quick ratio is concerned only with the very immediate ability to meet current obligations. As the operating cycle continues, current debts are incurred in the form of accounts payable in acquiring more inventory. This inventory, in turn, serves as the basis for eventually providing cash with which to liquidate the liabilities. The ratio of current debt to inventory indicates the extent to which a company relies on its inventory as a source of funds to meet its current debts. The ratio is calculated by dividing the current liabilities by the year-end inventory, as shown below:

$$\frac{\text{Current liabilities}}{\text{Year-end inventory}} = \frac{\$157}{\$96} = 1.64$$

Profitability

Probably the most important consideration of investors and potential investors, so far as a company's financial affairs are concerned, is that of profitability—not just how much profit the company makes, but how much these profits are in relation to some meaningful yardstick. There are many such comparisons: *net profits to net sales, net profits to net working capital, net sales to net worth, plant turnover, return on total assets, return on owner's equity, earnings per share, price-earnings ratio,* and *yield.*

Net Profits to Net Sales. This is one of the ratios that can be read directly from a common-size income statement. It is calculated by dividing the net profits (after taxes) by the net sales. The purpose of sales is to earn profits, and this ratio indicates how well management is achieving that objective. The ratio of net profits to net sales is probably most meaningful when compared with that of other companies in the same industry or with some similar standard.

The 1970 ratio of net profits to net sales for Majestic Oil Company may be calculated as follows:

$$\frac{\text{Net profits}}{\text{Net sales}} = \frac{\$85}{\$925} = .09$$

Net Profits to Net Working Capital. A firm's working capital is computed by subtracting its current liabilities from its current assets. The resulting amount represents a cushion available to the business in financing current operations. The ratio of net profits to net working capital is obtained by dividing net profits (after taxes) by the net working capital.

A certain amount of working capital is required to operate any business. If the working capital is properly managed, the concern should earn a profit. As more money is invested in working capital, one would expect a corresponding increase in the profits. The ratio of net profits to net working capital is computed to help measure how effectively the working capital is being managed.

This ratio, also, has been widely misused. It implies that profits are earned on working capital only, and that all other assets are nonproductive parasites. A great deal of promotional literature has implied that fixed assets are frozen, and that only working capital is essential for profitable operations. While the importance of working capital cannot be denied, it is nevertheless only one of the factors that contributes to profit. All of the resources of a firm, whatever the source of supply, generate profits jointly; a relationship that implies otherwise is faulty, and actually may be misleading.

The ratio of net profits to net working capital for Majestic Oil Company may be calculated as follows:

$$\frac{\text{Net profits}}{\text{Current assets–current liabilities}} = \frac{\$85}{\$409\text{–}\$157} = .34$$

Net Sales to Net Worth. The ratio of net sales to net worth[4] measures the turnover of invested capital. It is calculated by dividing net sales by the total owners' equity. This ratio is really more a measure of sales volume than of profitability. The net sales to net worth for Majestic Oil Company may be calculated as follows:

$$\frac{\text{Net sales}}{\text{Owners' equity}} = \frac{\$925}{\$1,206} = .77$$

---

[4]Many analysts prefer to use "tangible net worth" instead of "net worth." The former is calculated by subtracting the intangible assets from the total owners' equity. This practice dates back to the 1920s, when it was common to place intangible assets on the books at market values. Today the generally accepted practice is to show intangible assets on the books at cost (the same as is done with tangible assets) and, therefore, no reason is seen for excluding the intangibles from ratios. Throughout this chapter the author will use total net worth rather than tangible net worth.

Plant Turnover. The ratio of sales to net plant (sometimes called the *plant turnover*) is computed by dividing the sales by the total fixed assets (net of depreciation and amortization). The result is the dollar of sales during the year per dollar of plant investment. The objective of the ratio is to measure the efficiency with which fixed assets have been administered. Two major advantages of high plant turnover have been cited:

1. The larger the volume of business with respect to investment, the less is the percent of new profit on sales required to earn a given rate of return on investment.
2. The company with a low ratio is presumably obliged to spread the fixed expenses resulting from the use of the fixed assets, such as depreciation and interest, and generally insurance and taxes, over a relatively smaller volume of business, and consequently is likely to be at a disadvantage from a competitive standpoint.[5]

The ratio of sales to net plant may fail to measure accurately management's efficiency in administering fixed assets because of

1. *Price level changes.* Sales tend to vary with changes in the level of prices, but plant usually remains on the books at cost until its parts are worn out or discarded and new units entered at the going level of prices.
2. *Operating functions assumed.* Sometimes two concerns are engaged in apparently the same business, but upon closer scrutiny it is found that one performs more functions than the other—a fact that justifies additional investment.
3. *Depreciation reserves.* If the net fixed assets after the deduction of depreciation are used in this ratio, two concerns with equal plant costs but of different ages might show, as a result, different plant turnovers.[6]

The plant turnover for Majestic Oil Company may be calculated as follows:

$$\frac{\text{Net sales}}{\text{Fixed assets}} = \frac{\$925}{\$708} = 1.31$$

Return on Total Assets. The return on total assets (return on total capital) is studied as a measure of a firm's general earning power. It measures the return from utilizing a bundle of assets without considering whether these assets were financed by debt or equity funds. The return on total

---

[5]Harry G. Guthmann, *Analysis of Financial Statement* (Englewood Cliffs, N. J.: Prentice-Hall, 1953), p. 162.
[6]Ibid., pp. 10–11.

assets is computed by dividing the net operating income (income before interest, taxes, and dividends) by the total assets. The ratio attempts to isolate the return from operations from the return that has come about through "trading on the equity." It is a measure of management's effectiveness in employing the resources intrusted to them from whatever source.

Some writers have questioned the advisability of including liabilities, such as accounts payable and accrued liabilities, in the above calculations.[7] The reason for their concern is the fact that these sources of capital do not represent explicit rights to share in earnings. Regardless of the claims these creditors may or may not hold, the liabilities nevertheless represent an important source of assets that management must effectively employ, and they should be included in the firm's total capital in computing the previous ratio.

The return on total assets for Majestic Oil Company may be calculated as follows:

$$\frac{\text{Operating income}}{\text{Total assets}} = \frac{\$177}{\$1,206} = .15$$

Return on Owners' Equity. This ratio is calculated by dividing net profits after taxes by the total owners' equity. The ratio is designed to indicate how profitable the company is to the owners. The weakness is that it relates current profits to the book value of the stock. Often, the market value of a share is far in excess of the book value, and so this ratio will not reflect the true rate of return that a potential investor might expect to earn. The return on owners' equity ratio may be useful as a general guide of profitability when used for comparative purposes rather than as an absolute rate. It could be useful, for example, in comparing the return of two companies within the same industry which have assets of somewhat comparable ages. The return on owners' equity for Majestic Oil Company may be calculated as follows:

$$\frac{\text{Net profits}}{\text{Owners' equity}} = \frac{\$85}{\$851} = .10$$

Earnings per Share. One of the most frequently quoted ratios in investment circles is the earnings per share. This is calculated by dividing the net profits after taxes by the average number of shares of stock outstanding during the year. Outstanding stock refers only to shares held by stockholders and does not include unissued or reacquired shares. Where the

[7]William A. Paton and William A. Paton, Jr., *Corporation Accounts and Statements* (New York: Macmillan Co., 1955), pp. 49–97.

company has more than one class of stock, separate calculations are made for each class. Earnings per share on preferred stock is calculated by using the preferred dividends instead of profits, and earnings per share on common stock is then calculated on profits less the preferred dividends.

Because earnings per share data are so widely used in financial circles, the Accounting Principles Board of the American Institute of Certified Public Accountants has recently issued opinions which place new requirements on the calculation of this ratio. The first requirement is that "earnings per share amounts should ... be presented for (a) income before extraordinary items and (b) net income. It may also be desirable to present earnings per share amounts for extraordinary items, if any."[8]

The second requirement provides for dual earnings per share calculations—primary earnings per share and fully diluted earnings per share—for firms with complex capital structures. Firms with complex capital structures are companies that have "... potentially dilutive convertible securities, options, warrants or other rights that upon conversion or exercise could in the aggregate dilute earnings per common share."[9] It is important that investors recognize the dilute effect of these securities and thus the reason for the dual earnings per share requirement.

The 1970 earnings per share for Majestic Oil Company may be calculated as follows:

$$\frac{\text{Net profits}}{\text{Average common shares outstanding}} = \frac{\$84,835}{50,000 \text{ shares}} = \$1.70 \text{ per share}$$

Price-earnings Ratio. The price-earnings ratio is another index of profitability commonly used in investment circles. It is calculated by dividing the current market price per share of stock by some earnings per share figure, most frequently the last twelve months' earnings per share. Sometimes this ratio is calculated based upon expected future earnings. The price-earnings ratio has real meaning to the investor or potential investor because it relates earning power to current investment. It tells the investor what kind of return he can expect on his investment. Unlike the return on total capital (which theoretically is designed to measure the same thing), this ratio uses the current market value rather than the historical book value.

If the market price of Majestic Oil Company common stock was $28 per share on December 31, 1970, the price-earnings ratio would be calculated as follows:

$$\frac{\text{Current market price}}{\text{Earnings per share}} = \frac{\$28}{\$1.70} = 16.5$$

---

[8]"Earnings Per Share," *Opinions of the Accounting Principles Board No. 15* (New York: American Institute of Certified Public Accountants, 1969) pp. 220–221.
[9]Ibid, p. 221.

Yield. The yield on a stock is calculated by dividing the annual dividend per share by the current market price per share. This ratio tells the stockholder how much return he will receive on his investment. Many companies "plow back" or retain a large portion of their earnings for growth and do not declare dividends equal to total earnings. The price-earnings ratio indicates how much is *earned* in relation to the market price, while the yield indicates how much is *paid out* in relation to market price.

Although the dividends for Majestic Oil Company are not shown directly on the financial statements, the amount may be calculated by comparing the net income ($84,835,000) with the increase in retained earnings during the year ($801,203,000–$734,211,000, or $66,992,000). This difference ($17,843,000), amounting to $0.36 per share ($17,843,000÷50,000,000 shares), apparently represents the dividends paid during the year. With this dividend figure and the assumed market price of $28 per share, the yield may be calculated as follows:

$$\frac{\text{Dividends per share}}{\text{Current market price}} = \frac{\$0.36}{\$28} = .01$$

Productivity of Working Capital

A company's working capital consists of the current assets less the current liabilities (sometimes called net working capital). This working capital is the primary basis upon which the company performs its operating cycle. Merchandise is purchased on credit, and cash is utilized to pay the liabilities thus created. The merchandise is sold (either for cash or on credit), the receivables are collected, and the cycle repeats itself. This cycle is the lifeblood of a business enterprise. Generally speaking, the faster this cycle occurs, the better. If a company can shorten the cycle or increase the number of cycles per year, while holding profit margins and expenses constant, it will increase its profitability. For most merchandising companies, the control and movement of working capital are the keys to profitability.

There are a number of ratios designed to measure the effectiveness with which management controls the working capital. Some of the more important ones are *inventory turnover, net sales to inventory, accounts receivable turnover, average collection period, inventory to net working capital,* and *net sales to net working capital.*

Inventory Turnover. The inventory turnover may be used as a guide to evaluate the effectiveness of inventory management. The ratio is calculated by dividing the cost of goods sold by the average inventory and is usually expressed in turns per year. It indicates how many times the average inventory has been replenished. The ratio is most accurate when the average inventory is calculated from monthly balances, since inventory levels generally fluctuate greatly during the year. In fact, most companies deliberately end their fiscal period at a point when inventories are at their lowest levels. This means that an average calculated from year-end balances only would be abnormally low and show too high an inventory turnover. Generally, the analyst must work from published statements which do not reflect monthly inventory figures. When the inventory turnover is calculated from year-end figures, the resulting ratio should properly be discounted.

Generally, management strives to get as many turnovers of inventory as possible. The more sales that can be produced from a given investment, the better. In evaluating inventory turnover, however, the analyst must be careful to evaluate also the cause of the turnover. A company can increase its turnover in a number of unfavorable ways. For example, the inventory will move faster if marked to sell at half price, a practice which may result in serious losses. Heavy advertising may increase turnover, but increased revenue may be more than offset by the increased advertising costs. This points out again the importance of looking at a ratio in the light of other ratios.

The inventory turnover for Majestic Oil Company for the year ended December 31, 1970, may be calculated as follows:

$$\frac{\text{Cost of goods sold}}{\text{Average inventory}} = \frac{\$530}{\$99} = 5.35$$

Net Sales to Inventory.   The ratio of net sales to inventory is designed to measure the same thing as the inventory turnover: how well the inventory is managed. It is calculated by dividing the net sales by the average inventory. This ratio is often used instead of the inventory turnover where financial statements do not detail the cost of goods sold. This ratio does *not* yield the actual inventory turnover, but is merely an indication of the dollar sales produced from the average inventory. Where relevant data are available, the inventory turnover is probably a more effective tool.

The 1970 net sales to inventory for Majestic Oil Company may be calculated as follows:

$$\frac{\text{Net sales}}{\text{Average inventory}} = \frac{\$925}{\$99} = 9.34$$

Receivables Turnover.   The receivables turnover is calculated by dividing net sales by the average balance of notes and accounts receivable. This ratio is used as a guide in evaluating the relative collectibility of receivables. A company usually strives for as many turnovers as possible in order to tie up a minimum of funds in receivables. The 1970 receivables turnover for Majestic Oil Company may be calculated as follows:

$$\frac{\text{Net sales}}{\text{Average receivables}} = \frac{\$925}{\$129.5} = 7.14$$

Average Collection Period. Probably the best measure of account movements is found in the average day's sales uncollected (average collection period). This average collection period can be calculated by dividing the number of days in the period by the receivables turnover. This ratio expresses the average time it takes to collect an account and, like the receivables turnover, is designed to analyze the collectibility of accounts. By expressing the collection period in terms of days, the ratio makes it easy to compare this with a company's sales terms. Comparing the average collection period with the company's terms of sales is an effective evaluation of the success of a company's credit policy. For example, a company that offers credit terms of 2/10, net thirty days and has an average collection period of sixty days, is not being very successful in granting credit and collecting its accounts.

The average collection period for Majestic Oil Company during the year 1970 was fifty-one days, as shown below:

$$\frac{\text{Number of days per period}}{\text{Receivables turnover}} = \frac{365 \text{ days}}{7.14} = 51 \text{ days}$$

Inventory to Net Working Capital. The ratio of inventory to net working capital is calculated by dividing the year-end merchandise inventory by the net working capital at that same date. The purpose of the ratio is to measure the proportion of working capital tied up in unsold inventory. If the ratio becomes too high, the firm is likely to experience difficulty in meeting its current obligations. This ratio would be most meaningful when used in connection with the inventory turnover and the current ratio.

The inventory to net working capital for Majestic Oil Company as of December 31, 1970, may be calculated as follows:

$$\frac{\text{Inventory (end)}}{\text{Current assets}-\text{current liabilities}} = \frac{\$97}{\$409-\$157} = .38$$

Net Sales to Net Working Capital. The ratio of net sales to net working capital (sometimes called *working capital turnover*) is computed by dividing the net sales by the net working capital. The ratio recognizes that there is a direct relationship between sales and the amount of working capital required. It indicates whether increased sales are being financed largely by payables or from increased working capital. The ratio is subject to all of the criticism of the current ratio mentioned above. Its limitations are summarized in the following statement:

If the business suffers from a relatively high current debt—that is, has a low current ratio—the business will show a relatively higher ratio of sales to working capital. A high working capital turnover may reflect efficient receivables and merchandise turnover, but it may just as well reflect a dangerously low current ratio. But a ratio which can tell either of such opposite stories is a blur of a number of relationships.[10]

The net sales to net working capital for Majestic Oil Company may be calculated as follows:

$$\frac{\text{Net sales}}{\text{Current assets}-\text{current liabilities}} = \frac{\$925}{\$409-\$157} = 3.67$$

Balance of Equity Structure

One of the most important areas of financial analysis is concerned with the relative proportions of debt and equity in a firm's capital structure. There is no magic formula to determine the proper balance, but most companies find it desirable to have some debt in order to utilize the principle of *trading on the equity*, or *financial leverage*. Financial leverage simply means that profits or losses are amplified by the existence of debt in a firm's capital structure. If a company can borrow money at 5 percent interest and invest it at 10 percent interest, the difference represents a gain to stockholders. The principle is made clearer by referring to Figure 12-5. Company L has a debt-to-total-capital ratio of 50 percent and, therefore, employs "financial leverage." Company U, on the other hand, has a debt-to-total-capital ratio of zero. Notice that the common stock of the levered company (Company L) makes a greater return during years when profits (before interest and after taxes) exceed $10,000. However, in years when profits are less than this breakeven point, the common stockholders' earnings are reduced by unfavorable leverage.

The following ratios are used by financial analysts in appraising the degree of balance in a company's equity structure: *debt to equity, debt to total capital, times interest charges earned, current debt to net worth, funded debt to net working capital,* and *fixed assets to net worth.*

Debt-to-Equity and Debt-to-Total-Capital Ratios. The debt-to-equity ratio and the debt-to-total-capital ratio probably show most clearly the extent to which a company is levered. The two ratios are really just different methods of expressing the same thing. Both attempt to measure the relative proportion of total assets supplied, respectively, by the owners and creditors. The debt-to-equity ratio is computed by dividing the total liabilities by the total stockholders' equity. The debt-to-total-capital ratio is computed by dividing the total liabilities by the total assets (which is the same as the total of the liabilities and the stockholders' equity).

---

[10]Guthmann, op. cit., p. 122.

Figure 12-5

FINANCIAL LEVERAGE

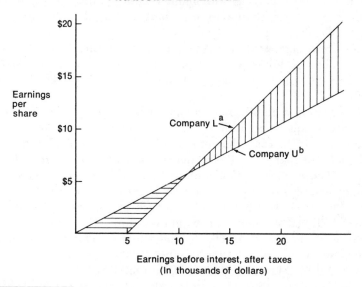

^a Company L: 1,000 shares of $100 par value common stock; $100,000 5% mortgage bonds.
^b Company U: 2,000 shares of $100 par value common stock; no debt.
   Gain from favorable leverage.
   Loss from unfavorable leverage.

As with other financial ratios, it is neither possible nor desirable to establish a rule of thumb by which one can determine the acceptable debt ceiling. This is a matter that must be determined by careful, considered judgment on the analyst's part, and will vary widely from firm to firm and from industry to industry. However, the primary basis for the determination consists of the level and the stability of corporate earnings. The higher and more stable the earnings, the higher the ratio of debt to equity that is permissible.

The debt-to-equity ratio and the debt-to-total-capital ratio for the Majestic Oil Company as of December 31, 1970, are calculated below:

$$\text{Debt to equity} = \frac{\text{Liabilities}}{\text{Owners' equity}} = \frac{\$335}{\$851} = .42$$

$$\text{Debt to total capital} = \frac{\text{Liabilities}}{\text{Assets}} = \frac{\$355}{\$1,206} = .29$$

Times Interest Charges Earned.   Another important ratio that is closely related to the debt-to-equity ratio is the times interest charges earned. The objective of this ratio is to measure the extent of cushion available to the funded debt in case future earnings do not meet expectations. A firm with a long history of relatively high and stable earnings could tolerate a lower ratio than could a company with highly volatile earnings. Thus, the number of times the interest charges must be earned varies directly with the instability of the firm's earnings.

The ratio is computed by dividing the net operating income by the bond interest charges. For example, if the net operating income is $40,000 and the interest on the bonds is $10,000, the interest charges have been earned four times.

The situation is slightly more complex when there is more than one issue of bonds because a separate computation must be made for each issue. Where such is the case, the net operating income is divided by the sum of the interest charges on the particular issue, *plus the interest charges on all prior issues*. Such a calculation will reflect the fact that the fortune of a junior issue is linked closely to that of the senior issues. For example, assume an issue of $1,000,000 of 4 percent first mortgage bonds and an issue of $500,000 of 5 percent general debentures. If the company had net operating income of $200,000, the times interest charges earned on the senior issue would be 5.00 ($200,000 ÷ $40,000), and those on the junior issue would be 2.11 [$200,000 ÷ ($40,000 + $25,000)].

Sufficient detail is not given in the Majestic statements to enable us to make separate times-interest-earned calculations for each long-term obligation. The overall ratio, however, shows ample earnings cushion:

$$\frac{\text{Operating income}}{\text{Interest charges}} = \frac{\$177}{\$3} = 59 \text{ times}$$

Current Debt to Net Worth. The ratio of current debt to net worth is obtained by dividing the current debt by the total stockholders' equity. This is another of the many ratios designed to measure the relationship of debt to equity and to assure that an adequate proportion of the funds is supplied by the owners. Dun & Bradstreet cautions that "ordinarily a business begins to pile up trouble when this relationship exceeds 80 percent."[11]

The current debt to net worth for Majestic Oil Company of 18 percent looks good compared to this Dun & Bradstreet standard. The calculation follows:

$$\frac{\text{Current liabilites}}{\text{Owners' equity}} = \frac{\$157}{\$851} = .18$$

---

[11]Dun & Bradstreet, Inc., *Key Business Ratios in 125 Lines 1965* (New York: Dun & Bradstreet, Inc., 1966), p. 22.

Funded Debt to Net Working Capital. An extension of the current ratio to the needs of the bondholders is found in the ratio of funded debt to net working capital. The funded debts are all long-term obligations, as represented by mortgages, bonds, debentures, term loans, serial notes, and other types of liabilities maturing more than one year from statement date.

It may be difficult to see the relationship between net working capital and funded debt, since the bonds are often secured by a lien on the fixed assets rather than on current assets. In answer to this alleged inconsistency, one writer states:

> Actually, the bondholders are recognizing two important factors; namely, (1) the greater ease of valuing the current assets as compared with the fixed assets, and (2) the virtue of a strong working capital in supporting interest charges during a period when earnings are temporarily inadequate.[12]

Certainly it cannot be denied that a firm's current position has a direct bearing on the security of the bondholders. The current ratio is an indication of the extent to which working capital may be available to meet interest charges and other pressing requirements during the period when earnings are temporarily inadequate. The ratio of funded debt to net working capital attempts to go one step further by recognizing that the greater the funded debt, the greater the cushion which may be required as a hedge against contingencies.

The ratio of funded debt to net working capital has some drawbacks, however. First, since it is so closely related to the current ratio, the weaknesses noted there are also applicable here. We cannot say that a high ratio is necessarily good or bad per se. Further, it is difficult to see any direct relationship between working capital and funded debt. Though this ratio may deserve an occasional glance, there are other ratios which might command more of the bondholder's attention.

The funded-debt-to-net-working-capital ratio for Majestic Oil Company as of December 31, 1970, may be calculated as follows:

$$\frac{\text{Long-term liabilities}}{\text{Current assets}-\text{current liabilities}} = \frac{\$162}{\$409-\$157} = .64$$

Fixed Assets to Net Worth. The ratio of fixed assets to net worth is computed by dividing the fixed assets (net of depreciation and amortization) by the stockholders' equity. The purpose of the ratio is to determine the extent to which the firm has tied up its investment in fixed assets, thereby limiting the funds available to meet working capital requirements. Dun & Bradstreet has suggested the following as a guide:

[12]Guthmann, op. cit., p. 161.

The relationship between Fixed Assets and Tangible Net Worth should not exceed 100 percent for a manufacturer, and 75 percent for a wholesaler or a retailer. Beyond these limits, so disproportionate an amount of capital is frozen into machinery or "bricks and mortar" that the necessary margin of operating funds for carrying receivables, inventories, and day-to-day cash outlays, as well as maturing obligations, becomes too narrow. This not only exposes the business to the hazards of unexpected developments, such as sudden change in the business climate, but creates possible drains on income in the form of heavy carrying and maintenance charges should a serious portion of Fixed Assets lie idle for any length of time.[13]

The fixed assets represent 83 percent of the net worth of Majestic Oil Company as of December 31, 1970, as shown below:

$$\frac{\text{Fixed assets}}{\text{Owners' equity}} = \frac{\$708}{\$851} = .83$$

COMPARATIVE DATA

Financial analysis is often most meaningful when the figures of one company are compared with those of other companies in the same industry. There are a number of sources to which one can turn to get the necessary figures, including agencies of the federal government, trade associations, and private financial advisory companies. For many years Dun & Bradstreet, Inc., has put out an annual publication, *Key Business Ratios*. For each industry, Dun & Bradstreet shows the upper quartile, the median, and the lower quartiles for each of fourteen key ratios in different lines of business. The ratios are calculated from the sampling of corporations with owners' equity in excess of $35,000.[14]

SUMMARY

In this chapter the student has been introduced to some of the tools of financial analysis: horizontal analysis, vertical analysis, and ratio analysis. These techniques can be useful tools if they are properly used and if their weaknesses are fully understood. The techniques described here must be used as what they are: financial tools. No ratio may properly be viewed as being good or bad per se; rather, each must be considered one of many indicators to be evaluated together.

---

[13]Dun & Bradstreet, Inc., *Fourteen Important Ratios in 72 Lines of Business* (New York: Dun & Bradstreet, Inc., 1961), p. 71.

[14]A current copy of this publication can be obtained by writing Dun & Bradstreet, Inc., Public Relations and Advertising, 99 Church Street, New York, N. Y. 10007.

The student should attempt to view each particular financial ratio from the standpoint of the user of the financial statement, be he manager, stockholder, creditor, potential investor, potential lender, or someone else. What information does the reader seek? What ratios might assist him in reaching the required decision? Ratio analysis can be meaningful only if it is approached in this manner. The ratios discussed in this chapter may assist in answering the following questions:

1. What is the firm's current debt-paying ability?
2. How profitable is the firm?
3. How effectively is the working capital being utilized?
4. How well balanced is the company's equity structure?

QUESTIONS

1. What is a financial ratio? Are financial ratios always expressed in ratio forms?
2. It has been said that a current ratio should not fall below two to one. Comment on the danger of using rules of thumb such as this.
3. In evaluating a company's inventory turnover, what are some of the other ratios that might be useful?
4. What danger do you see in using "year-end" figures to calculate the average inventory to be used in computing the inventory turnover?
5. In vertical analysis, which items on the balance sheet equal 100 percent? Which item on the income statement equals 100 percent?
6. In comparing the change between year 19X1 and 19X2, which year is used as the base year? If an item appeared at $75 in 19X1 and $100 in 19X2, what was the percent change?
7. Which assets are "quick assets"? Which current assets are not considered "quick assets"?
8. What do yield and the price-earnings ratio have in common? What is the main difference between what is shown by these two ratios?
9. What are the differences in the procedures for constructing horizontal and vertical analytical statements? What is the special purpose of each?
10. What are the relative advantages of presenting changes in percentage terms as opposed to presenting them in absolute figures? What are the disadvantages of using percentages?
11. What is the working capital of a firm? Of what importance is the working capital?
12. The current ratio of Armore Company is three to one, and the current ratio of Segmore Corporation is seven to one. Evaluate the following statement: the current position of the Segmore Corporation may be considered the sounder of the two.
13. How is the accounts receivable turnover calculated? What would a rising accounts receivable turnover indicate? In what other manner can the collectibility of receivables be evaluated?

14. How is the price-earnings ratio calculated? What effect do dividends have on a company's price-earnings ratio?

15. How is the working capital turnover calculated? What would cause an increase in this ratio?

Problem 12-1

Comparative data for the Heavyload Corporation appear below:

HEAVYLOAD CORPORATION
Comparative Income Statement
For the Years Ended December 31, 1970 and December 31, 1971

	1971	1970
Gross sales	$978,500	$894,200
Sales returns and allowances	6,300	5,700
Net sales	$972,200	$888,500
Cost of goods sold	681,850	623,300
Gross margin	$290,350	$265,200
Operating expenses	175,300	163,550
Operating income	$115,050	$101,650
Nonoperating charges	240	570
Net income before income taxes	$114,810	$101,080
Income taxes	57,500	50,700
Net income	$ 57,310	$ 50,380

Required:

a. Prepare a "common-size" income statement for the Heavyload Corporation for each of the two years.

b. Prepare a comparative income statement in which the net change is shown in dollar and percentage terms for each item in the income statement.

Problem 12-2

Comparative statements for the Hangthere Electric Company are shown as follows:

HANGTHERE ELECTRIC COMPANY
Comparative Balance Sheet

ASSETS

	($000) DECEMBER 31	
	1971	1970
Current Assets:		
Cash	5,850	6,080
Short-term marketable securities at cost (approximate market value)	3,960	9,950

	($000) DECEMBER 31	
	1971	1970
Notes and accounts receivable..........	21,980	19,100
Inventories	16,680	12,620
Total current assets	48,470	47,750
Fixed Assets:		
Buildings (net)	870	640
Machinery and equipment (net)	2,840	1,860
Land	440	370
Total fixed assets	4,150	2,870
Total assets	52,620	50,620

LIABILITIES AND STOCKHOLDERS' EQUITY

Current Liabilities:		
Notes and drafts payable..............	6,330	5,480
Accounts payable	16,090	14,140
Accrued taxes	3,850	4,110
Total current liabilities	26,270	23,730
Long-term Debt:		
Bonds payable	4,760	4,280
Mortgages payable	2,510	2,900
Total long-term debt	7,270	7,180
Stockholders' Equity:		
Common stock, $100 par..............	2,970	2,950
Capital surplus	3,540	3,540
Retained earnings	12,570	13,220
Total stockholders' equity	19,080	19,710
Total liabilities and stockholders' equity	52,620	50,620

HANGTHERE ELECTRIC COMPANY
Comparative Condensed Income Statement
For the Years Ended December 31

	($000)	
	1971	1970
Sales	155,920	161,690
Cost of goods sold	144,700	142,560
Gross margin	11,220	19,130
Operating expenses	11,410	11,640
Net operating income (loss)	(190)	7,490
Federal income tax	105[a]	3,880
Net income (loss)	(85)	3,610

[a]Tax refund arising from loss carryback.

Required:

Prepare a comparative balance sheet and income statement using horizontal analysis and showing changes in dollar and percentage terms.

Problem 12-3

Using the comparative data for Hangthere Electric Company presented in problem 12-2, prepare a common-size balance sheet and an income statement comparing financial structure percentages for 1971 with those of 1970. Comment on the significance of common-size statements.

Problem 12-4

Using the data for the Hangthere Electric Company as given in problem 12-2, calculate the following financial ratios and explain what they should mean to the management:

a. Current ratio[a]
b. Acid-test ratio[a]
c. Inventory turnover[b]
d. Receivables turnover[b]
e. Average day's sales uncollected[b]
f. Inventory to net working capital[a]
g. Working capital turnover[b]
h. Debt-to-equity ratio[a]
i. Current debt to net worth[a]
j. Fixed assets to net worth[a]

---

[a]As of December 31, 1970, and as of December 31, 1971.
[b]For the year ended December 31, 1971.

Problem 12-5

Using the data for the Hangthere Electric Company given in problem 12-2, calculate the following comparative operating measurements for 1970 and explain what they should mean to the management:

a. Net profits on net sales
b. Net profits on net working capital
c. Sales to net plant
d. Return on total capital
e. Return on owners' equity
f. Earnings per share on common stock
g. Times interest charges earned

The company has included interest charges in the operating expenses. The interest charges during the year 1970 amounted to 4 percent of the total long-term debt at December 31, 1970.

Problem 12-6

The following are condensed data prepared for the Midtown Department Store for the year ending March 31, 1971.

MIDTOWN DEPARTMENT STORE
Condensed Income Statement
For the Year Ending March 31, 1971

Net sales	$999,400
Cost of goods sold	708,900
Gross margin	$290,500
Operating expenses	137,200
Operating income	$153,300
Federal income tax	74,060
Net income	$ 79,240

MIDTOWN DEPARTMENT STORE
Condensed Balance Sheet
March 31, 1971

ASSETS

Current liabilities	$118,500
Fixed assets (net)	464,200
Total assets	$695,800

LIABILITIES AND STOCKHOLDERS' EQUITY

Current liabilities	118,500
Other liabilities	46,800
Stockholders' equity	530,500
Total liabilities and stockholders' equity	$695,800

During the year ended March 31, 1971, the company had an average of 8,659 shares of common stock (par $10) outstanding and an average of 1,438 shares of 6 percent, preferred stock (par $50) outstanding. As of March 31, 1971, the common stock was selling in the market for $74.25, and the preferred was selling at $68.75. Dividends of $1.89 per share were declared during 1971 on the common stock. No interest was paid during the year.

Required:

Compute the following ratios indicative of profitability for the Midtown Department Store:

a. Return on total capital
b. Return on owners' equity
c. Earnings per share (for preferred and common)
d. Price-earnings ratio (for preferred and common)
e. Yield (for preferred and common)

Problem 12-7

Referring to the data given in problem 12-6 for the Midtown Department
Store and the following additional information, calculate the following
ratios to determine the productivity of the company's working capital:

a. Inventory turnover
b. Receivable turnover
c. Collection period
d. Inventory to net working capital
e. Net sales to net working capital
f. Debt to equity
g. Debt to total capital
h. Current debt to net worth
i. Fixed assets to net worth

The current assets on March 31, 1970, and March 31, 1971, were made up
of the following items:

	MARCH 31	
	1971	1970
Cash	$ 23,500	$ 21,800
Notes receivable	19,400	19,300
Accounts receivable	56,200	58,700
Inventories	117,800	106,400
Prepaid expenses	14,700	10,900
Total Current Assets	$231,600	$217,100

Case 12
Century Industries

Century Industries is a conglomerate which owns a number of small-
and medium-sized firms. The company has a very alert and aggressive
management which is always anxious to explore new opportunities for
expansion. Century Industries has just begun negotiations with Pollution
Engineering, Inc., with the idea of possible merger. Pollution Engineering
designs and manufactures antipollution devices and, although somewhat
unknown in the industry at present, is considered in some quarters to be
a real comer. If merger plans work out, the stockholders of Pollution Engineering would be given shares of stock in Century Industries. Pollution
Engineering's most recent financial statements and other relevant data are
shown in Exhibits 12-1, 12-2, 12-3, and 12-4.

As a member of Century's investment research department you are asked to prepare a detailed analysis of Pollution Engineering's financial statements, including the calculation of ratios which you feel would assist in answering the following questions:

1. How profitable is Pollution Engineering?
2. How effectively is the working capital being managed? What additional data would be helpful in appraising working capital management?
3. How well balanced is the equity structure of Pollution Engineering? Would a bank which is considering granting a large loan to Pollution Engineering use the same standard for judging the balance of equity structure as might be used by Century Industries?
4. What is Pollution Engineering's current debt-paying ability?
5. Assume that Pollution Engineering has developed a number of patents which have been valued by industry experts in excess of two million dollars. How does this fact change your analysis?

Exhibit 12-1
POLLUTION ENGINEERING
Balance Sheet

ASSETS

	DECEMBER 31 1970	DECEMBER 31 1969
Current Assets:		
Cash	$ 15,183	$ 22,825
Marketable securities, at cost which approximates market value	1,308	12,054
Accounts receivable	133,094	130,070
Inventories, at the lower of cost or market	143,799	125,471
Prepaid expenses	3,806	3,671
Total current assets	$297,190	$294,091
Investments, at cost	$ 45,192	$ 4,127
Property, plant, and equipment:		
Land and buildings	$100,330	$ 88,621
Machinery and equipment	153,700	133,509
	$254,030	$222,130
Less: Accumulated depreciation	110,515	101,886
	$143,515	$120,244
Other assets:		
Patents and other product development costs, less amortization	$ 5,585	$ 5,940
Goodwill	7,237	7,236
Deferred charges	2,623	2,065
	$501,342	$433,703

LIABILITIES

	DECEMBER 31	
	1970	1969
Current Liabilities:		
Notes payable	$ 22,289	$ 8,604
Accounts payable	28,249	31,211
Accrued liabilities	53,946	54,661
Federal, state, and foreign income taxes	4,914	11,445
Advance payments on contracts	68,826	57,296
Dividends payable	2,698	2,475
Total current liabilities	$180,922	$165,622
Deferred income taxes	$ 10,402	$ 6,402
Long-term Debt:		
5⅞% sinking fund debentures due 1992	$ 50,000	$ 46,150
3⅜% sinking fund debentures due 1979, less debentures held in treasury of $711,000 in 1968 and $1,276,000 in 1967	7,500	7,724
3⅜% convertible subordinated debentures due 1981, less $125,000 of debentures held in treasury ...	1,308	2,106
Notes payable to banks	34,000	—
Other term payables	4,276	2,919
	$ 97,084	$ 58,899
Shareholders' Equity:		
Preferred stock, no par value		
Authorized, 1,000 shares; issued, 425 shares of series A convertible preferred stock (liquidating value $19,133), stated at	$ 4,562	$ 4,562
Common stock, $1 par value		
Authorized, 15,000 shares; issued, 4,659 shares in 1970 and 4,856 shares in 1969, stated at.......	30,303	30,124
Retained earnings (see accompanying statement)...	181,991	171,255
	$216,856	$205,941
Deduct: Common stock held in treasury, at cost, 121 shares in 1970 and 346 shares in 1969........	3,922	3,231
	$212,934	$202,710
	$501,342	$433,703

Exhibit 12-2
POLLUTION ENGINEERING
Income Statement

	FOR THE YEARS ENDED DECEMBER 31	
	1970	1969
Net sales	$664,891	$761,234

	FOR THE YEARS ENDED DECEMBER 31	
	1970	1969
Costs and expenses:		
Cost of sales	$556,984	$659,374
Selling, general, and administrative expenses.......	59,131	53,427
	$616,115	$712,801
Operating profit	$ 48,776	$ 48,433
Other income and deductions:		
Interest earned	$ 2,055	$ 2,066
Dividends received	496	558
Interest expense	(6,662) (	3,069)
Gain on sale of investments	1,267	230
Miscellaneous, net	128	164
	($ 2,972) ($	51)
Profit before taxes	45,804	48,382
Federal, state, and foreign taxes on income	$ 23,700	$ 23,320
Net income for the year	$ 22,104	$ 25,062

Exhibit 12-3
POLLUTION ENGINEERING
Statement of Retained Earnings

	FOR THE YEARS ENDED DECEMBER 31	
	1970	1969
Balance at beginning of year	$171,255	$155,920
Net income for the year	22,104	25,063
	$193,359	$180,983
Deduct: Cash dividends:		
Preferred stock	457	—
Common stock	10,911	9,728
Balance at end of year	$181,991	$171,255

Exhibit 12-4
POLLUTION ENGINEERING
Selected Data

Market Price of Common Stock at December 31

1968	....	$70 per share
1969	....	$58 per share
1970	....	$95 per share

Market Price of Preferred Stock at December 31

1968	....	None
1969	....	$12 per share
1970	....	$17 per share

13

Funds Flow

In chapter 5 we were concerned with two major financial statements:
the balance sheet, which indicated the firm's financial position at an instant
of time; and the income statement, which disclosed the results of the firm's
operations for a specified period. In measuring profits and losses, the income statement reflected the flow of assets in and out of the business, as
measured by revenues and expenses. The revenues were shown in the
period *earned*, but not necessarily in the period in which the cash was
actually received. The expenses were matched with the revenues and
shown in the period of *use*, which was likewise often not the period of
payment. Our objective with the income statement was to measure the
flow of *assets*, not the flow of funds nor the flow of cash. While the income
statement answers some important questions regarding the activities of
the accounting period, it does not tell the reader all he might like to know.

In this chapter we will discuss three other statements that shed additional light on the accounting period. The *schedule of changes in working*

capital summarizes changes which have taken place in specific components of working capital. The *statement of source and application of funds* (sometimes called the *funds statement*) analyzes changes in working capital, and the *cash flow statement* analyzes changes in the firm's cash position.

SOURCE AND APPLICATION OF FUNDS

As it is used in this section, the term "funds" may be defined as the working capital, i.e., current assets minus current liabilities. The statement of source and application of funds attempts to analyze the activities of an accounting period to determine what caused changes in the working capital position. It has sometimes been nicknamed the "where-go, where-gone" statement.

Management watches the working capital of a firm with particular interest because these net assets are the heart of the revenue-producing activity of the business. Profits are determined in part by the effectiveness with which the working capital is controlled. For this reason, management is interested in knowing what changes have taken place in the composition of the working capital, as well as what caused these changes to occur. A *schedule of changes in working capital* answers the first need, while a *statement of source and application of funds* answers the second. The former statement shows the changes that have taken place in the specific components of working capital, i.e., how much each current asset and current liability has changed. The latter statement, on the other hand, shows what *caused* these changes to take place.

Sources of Funds

All sources of funds may be classified in three broad categories: decreases in noncurrent assets, increases in noncurrent liabilities, and increases in owners' equity. This may be seen more easily by referring to our accounting equation and doing a little reconstruction. The accounting equation, as stated in chapter 2, follows:

$$\text{ASSETS} = \text{LIABILITIES} + \text{OWNERS' EQUITY}$$

For the purpose of analysis this may be broken down as follows:

$$CA + NCA = CL + NCL + OE$$

where   CA = Current assets
      NCA = All noncurrent assets
      CL = Current liabilities
      NCL = All noncurrent liabilities
      OE = Total owners' equity

Now, collecting the funds or working capital, the equation appears:

$$CA - CL = NCL + OE - NCA$$

Since our equation must remain in balance, an increase in net working capital or funds (the left side of the equation) must be accompanied by an increase in noncurrent liabilities, or an increase in owners' equity, or a decrease in noncurrent assets (the right side of the equation). To summarize, increases in working capital are the result of one of the following:

Sources of Funds

1. +NCL (an increase in noncurrent liabilities, such as issuing bonds)
2. +OE (an increase in owners' equity, such as issuing capital stock or earning a profit)
3. −NCA (a decrease in noncurrent assets, such as the sale of a building)

Application of Funds

Similarly, all applications or uses of funds may be classified in three categories. These are obtained by just reversing the signs in our accounting equation:

$$-CA + CL = -NCL - OE + NCA$$

Decreases in working capital, then, come about by one or more of the following:

Application of Funds

1. +NCA (an increase in a noncurrent asset, such as the purchase of a machine)
2. −NCL (a decrease in a noncurrent liability, such as the retirement of a bond)
3. −OE (a decrease in owners' equity, such as the declaration of a dividend)

Nonapplicable Transactions

In preparing a statement of source and application of funds we are concerned only with those transactions that have affected both sides of our revised equation. There are many transactions where both debit and credit involve fund, or working capital, accounts. For example, the collection of an account receivable requires a debit to Cash and a credit to the Accounts Receivable. We are not concerned with these transactions because, while they reflect a change in the composition of the funds, they do not increase or decrease the funds. Again, the entry recording the transaction must involve at least one account from each side of the revised equation or it will not appear on the statement of source and application of funds.

Sometimes transactions occur where none of the accounts used to record the transactions is a fund account. Such transactions involve only the right side of our equation and, again, have no effect on the funds statement. For example, a company may have some bondholders convert their bonds into stock. Such a transaction would not involve the funds statement, since both the debit to Bonds Payable and the credit to Capital Stock are on the right side of the equation. To summarize:

When a transaction involves *only* fund accounts
or
When a transaction involves *no* fund accounts

No effect on funds statement

When a transaction involves both a fund account and a nonfund account

It does affect the funds statement

Funds Provided by Operations

A funds statement which would itemize all sources and applications for operating purposes could be prepared. This would mean that nearly every item on the income statement would also appear on the funds statement, since most revenues provide funds and most expenses use funds. Such a statement would be extremely involved, and other major sources and applications would be lost in a mass of figures. For this reason, the funds statement is generally prepared with the net funds provided by operations summarized in one figure.

Computing the funds provided by operations is often a difficult task for the student, since it is customary to work backwards. It might be easier to understand if we prepared a supplementary schedule itemizing all income statement items that did use or provide funds. For example, given the following income statement, the student can easily calculate the funds provided by operations.

Sales		$1,000
Less: Cost of goods sold		600
Gross profit		$ 400
Selling expense[a]	$100	
Administrative expense[a]	100	
Depreciation expense	50	250
Net profit		$ 150

[a]Excluding depreciation

Going through this statement item by item, we find that all components except depreciation provide or use funds. Sales, whether for cash or on account, provide funds, since both cash and accounts receivable are current assets. Cost of goods sold uses funds, regardless of whether the goods were taken from inventory, purchased for cash, or purchased on account. Selling and administrative expenses (except for depreciation, which is shown separately) use funds, whether they represent cash payments, accruals, or expiration of prepayments. The funds provided by operations may be itemized as follows:

Sources:		
Sales of merchandise		$1,000
Applications:		
For merchandise sold	$600	
For selling expenses	100	
For administrative expenses	100	800
Funds provided by operations		$ 200

While the foregoing method of calculating funds provided by operations is easy to follow, it would be rather time-consuming with a more detailed income statement. A faster method of calculating the same figure is to work backwards. Inasmuch as most items in the income statement *do* provide or use funds, why not start out with the net income and merely adjust for the relatively few items that *do not* affect funds? In the previous example, the only item appearing in the income statement that did not involve funds was depreciation. The funds provided by operations can be calculated quickly as follows:

Net income (per income statement) $150.00
Add back depreciation 50.00
   Funds provided by operations $200.00

Note that in this shortcut approach the depreciation was added back, not because it is a source of funds, but because it was deducted in the income statement and did not use funds. It was added back to offset the previous deduction. There are a number of other items that should be similarly treated to arrive at funds provided by operations:

ADDITIONS

1. Depreciation of fixed assets
2. Depletion of wasting assets
3. Amortization of patents
4. Amortization of bond discount
5. Losses on sale of fixed assets (charged to income)

DEDUCTIONS

1. Amortization of bond premium
2. Gains on sale of fixed assets (credited to income)

Preparation of Funds Statement

A source and application of funds statement can be prepared by analyzing changes that have taken place in a firm's balance sheet during a period of time. Two balance sheets as of different dates are compared, and the net change in each account is calculated. The sum of the changes in current assets and current liabilities constitutes the net increase or decrease in working capital that occurred during the period. This change is sometimes itemized on a separate *schedule of changes in working capital*. The changes in all other accounts are then analyzed, together with supplementary data, to construct a *statement of source and application of funds*. Such a statement will show just what caused the increase or decrease in funds. Of course, the net change in working capital shown in the source and application of funds statement must agree with the net change in working capital shown by the schedule of changes in working capital.

There are many different approaches to the preparation of a funds statement. The two approaches discussed in this chapter are the *worksheet method* and the *T-account method*.

The Worksheet Method. To study the preparation of a source and application of funds statement with the aid of a worksheet, refer to the statements of the Computograph Corporation shown in Figures 13-1 and 13-2.

Figure 13-1

COMPUTOGRAPH CORPORATION
Balance Sheet
July 31

	1971	1970
Cash	$ 17,992	$ 20,443
Accounts receivable	56,130	49,299
Allowance for doubtful accounts	(1,291)ᵃ	(1,060)
Inventories	64,592	59,287
Prepaid insurance	1,824	1,599
Machinery and equipment	45,475	48,146
Allowance for depreciation, machinery and equipment	(28,914)	(25,200)
Building	40,000	40,000
Allowance for depreciation, building	(18,500)	(17,300)
Land	2,391	1,091
Goodwill	0	1,000
	$179,699	$177,305
Accounts payable	14,061	10,933
Notes payable	9,013	7,902
Accrued taxes	12,772	13,879
Bonds payable	1,910	2,559
Common stock	49,980	48,980
Retained earnings	91,963	93,052
	$179,699	$177,305

ᵃParentheses denote deduction.

Figure 13-2

COMPUTOGRAPH CORPORATION
Statement of Income and Retained Earnings
For Year Ended July 31, 1971

Sales		$269,086
Cost of goods sold		127,851
Gross margin		$141,235
Selling expense	$49,322	
Administrative expense	80,631	
Income taxes	6,200	136,153
Net operating income		$ 5,082
Loss on sale of machine		171
Net income		$ 4,911
Retained earnings, July 31, 1970		93,052
Earnings available for dividend		$ 97,963
Less dividend	$ 5,000	
Less write-off of goodwill	1,000	6,000
Retained earnings, July 31, 1971		$ 91,963

ADDITIONAL DATA FOR FIGURE 13-2

Equipment which cost $5,171 and had accumulated depreciation of
$1,000 was sold at a loss of $171. Selling expense includes depreciation on building of $600. Administrative expense includes de-
preciation on building of $600, plus depreciation on machinery of
$4,714.

A worksheet prepared from the information contained in these two statements is presented in Figure 13-3. The worksheet was prepared as follows:

1. The balance sheets as of July 31, 1970, and July 31, 1971, were
   entered in the first pair of columns.
2. The net change in each balance sheet account was calculated
   and extended to the appropriate column.
3. The adjustments were next entered in the appropriate columns.
   The objective of these adjustments was to account for every
   dollar of change in each noncurrent account by itemizing each
   source or application separately, or reversing out amounts which
   had no effect on the funds. Note that the adjustments "wash out"
   all changes affecting noncurrent accounts. Where an account balance had changed for more than one reason, separate adjustments
   were made to itemize each source or application separately. An
   explanation of each of the adjustments made in the worksheet
   follows:
   a. Retained earnings increased by the amount of profit ($4,911).
      This represents a source of funds.
   b. Machinery that cost $5,171 and that had accumulated depre-
      ciation of $1,000 was sold at a loss of $171, thereby providing
      $4,000 of funds. Note that the $171 loss was added to profits
      because this amount had previously been deducted in the
      income statement, but had not used any funds. The only funds
      provided or used were the $4,000 that has been itemized
      separately.
   c. The balance of the change in the machinery account
      ($2,500) must represent machinery acquired during the period,
      which has been itemized as an application of funds.
   d. The depreciation of machinery in the amount of $4,714 is
      added to profits because the same amount was deducted as
      an expense, but had not used any funds.
   e. The depreciation on the building in the amount of $1,200 has
      also been added to profits to offset the prior deduction.
   f. The increase in the Land account apparently represents an
      application of $1,300 in funds for land acquisition.
   g. The entry writing off goodwill is simply reversed in the work-
      sheet, since it had no effect on funds. The reversal thereby
      accounts for the entire change in goodwill and a portion of
      the change in retained earnings.

Figure 13-3

COMPUTOGRAPH CORPORATION
Worksheet for Statement of Source and Application of Funds
For the Year Ended July 31, 1971

	Balance Sheet July 31 1971	1970	Net Change DR	CR	Adjustments DR	CR	Working Capital Increase	Decrease	Fund Statement Applications	Sources
Cash	17992	20443		2451				2451		
Accounts Receivable	56130	49299	6831				6831			
Allowance for Doubtful Accounts	1291*	1060*		231				231		
Inventories	64592	59287	5305				5305			
Prepaid Insurance	1824	1599	225				225			
Machinery & Equipment	45475	48146		2471	5171(a)	2500(c)				
Allowance for Depr. – M&E	28914*	25200*		3714	4914(a)	1000(c)				
Building	40000	40000								
Allowance for Depr. – Building	12391*	1091*	1300		1200(c)					
Land	1000	1000	1000		1000(e)					
Goodwill										
	179699	173305								
Accounts Payable	14061	10933		3128				3128		
Notes Payable	9013	7902		1111				1111		
Accrued Taxes	12772	13879	1107				1107			
Bonds Payable	1910	2559		649		649(d)				
Common Stock	49980	48980		1000		1000(f)				
Retained Earnings	91963	93052	1089		4911(a)	1000(b) / 5000(g)				
	179699	173305	16506	16506						
Funds Provided by:										
Operations:										
Net Income						4911(a)				
Loss on sale of machine						4714(a)				
Depreciation M&E						1200(c)				
Depreciation Building						4500(c)				
Sale of Machinery						1000(b)				1096
Issuance of Common Stock										4000
										1000
Funds Applied to:										
Purchase of Machinery						2500(c)			2500	
Purchase of Land						1300(e)			1300	
Retirement of Bonds						649(d)			649	
Payment of Dividends						5000(g)			5000	
					27445	27445			9449	9449
Net Increase in Funds									6547	1599
							13468	13468	15996	15996

*Deductions

h. The decrease in bonds payable apparently came about by the retirement of $649 of bonds.

i. The increase in common stock represent funds provided by issuance of common stock.

j. The balance of the change in retained earnings can be accounted for only by assuming the company paid dividends in the amount of $5,000.

4. All amounts which were not washed out in the adjustments columns were extended to the appropriate columns. Changes in all current assets and current liabilities were extended to the working capital pair of columns. All other amounts were extended to the funds statement pair of columns. The funds provided by operations, consisting of net income and adjustments thereto, were extended as a single amount.

5. The working capital columns were footed and a balancing figure entered. This forced figure, which represents the net increase or decrease in funds, was also entered in the funds statement pair of columns to balance out the worksheet.

A formal statement of source and application of funds is presented in Figure 13-4. The schedule of changes in working capital is shown in Figure 13-5.

Figure 13-4

COMPUTOGRAPH CORPORATION
Statement of Source and Application of Funds
For the Year Ended July 31, 1971

Sources:
 Operations:
  Net profit $4,911
  +Depreciation of machinery 4,714
  +Depreciation of building 1,200
  +Loss on sale of machinery 171 $10,996

 Proceeds from sale of machine 4,000
 Proceeds from issuance of common stock ... 1,000
  Total funds provided $15,996

Applications:
 Retirement of bonds .... $ 649
 Purchase of land 1,300
 Purchase of machinery 2,500
 Payment of dividends 5,000
  Total funds applied 9,449

Net increase in working capital .... $ 6,547

Figure 13-5

COMPUTOGRAPH CORPORATION
Schedule of Changes in Working Capital
For the Year Ended July 31, 1971

Increases:
Accounts receivable (net) increase		$ 6,600
Inventories increase		5,305
Prepaid insurance increase		225
Accrued taxes decrease		1,107
		$13,237

Decreases:
Cash decrease	$2,451	
Accounts payable increase	3,128	
Notes payable increase	1,111	6,690
Net increase in working capital		$ 6,547

The T-Account Method. In many cases the student will find it faster to use T-accounts than to construct a worksheet. With this method, the T-accounts are used to reconstruct the various entries that have provided or used funds. As with the worksheet method, it is necessary to wash out the items that had no effect on funds and to consider those items that were charged against income but did not reduce funds.

The first step is to enter in a T-account the net change that has taken place in each balance sheet account. The entry, however, must be made on what would seem to be the *opposite* side. That is, if an account had a net *debit* change during the period, this would be shown in the T-account as a *credit*. The reason for this reversing procedure is to provide a check that all amounts are accounted for. If we properly record the transactions in the T-accounts, every account will balance to zero. Reversing the beginning balances is the technique used to provide a check figure in each account.

To speed up the process, one T-account can be used for the net change in working capital, but separate accounts should be prepared for each noncurrent item. Two additional T-accounts are also prepared to reflect funds provided by operations and to summarize the sources and applications of funds. This latter account can then be used to prepare a formal funds statement.

To illustrate the T-account method, refer to the comparative financial statements of the Computograph Corporation, Figures 13-1 and 13-2. The net changes may be entered in the T-accounts, as shown below. Note that all changes in funds accounts are summarized in the working capital account. Also, the debits and credits are *reversed:* the debit changes are entered in the T-accounts as credits and the credit changes are shown in the T-accounts as debits.

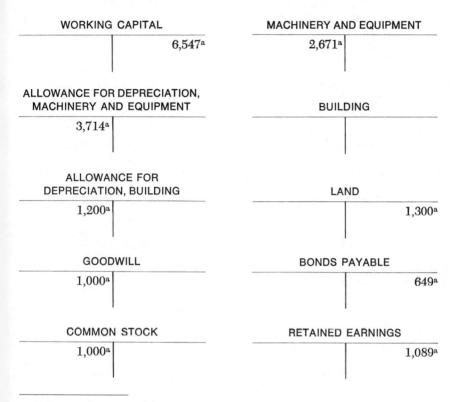

WORKING CAPITAL			MACHINERY AND EQUIPMENT		
	6,547[a]		2,671[a]		

ALLOWANCE FOR DEPRECIATION, MACHINERY AND EQUIPMENT		BUILDING	
3,714[a]			

ALLOWANCE FOR DEPRECIATION, BUILDING		LAND	
1,200[a]			1,300[a]

GOODWILL		BONDS PAYABLE	
1,000[a]			649[a]

COMMON STOCK		RETAINED EARNINGS	
1,000[a]			1,089[a]

---

[a]Balancing figure. Net debit changes in accounts during the period have been entered in T-accounts as credits, and credit changes have been entered as debits.

The student can now reconstruct the various entries that provided or used funds by making entries in the T-accounts. After all entries have been entered in the accounts, each account should balance to zero. The Funds Provided by Operations T-account and the Source and Application of Funds T-account can be used to construct the formal statement.

The completed T-accounts for the Computograph Corporation would appear as follows:

WORKING CAPITAL			MACHINERY AND EQUIPMENT			
(12) 6,547	6,547[a]			2,671[a]		
			(3) 2,500		(2) 5,171	
			5,171		5,171	

ALLOWANCE FOR DEPRECIATION,
MACHINERY AND EQUIPMENT

	3,714ᵃ		
(2)	1,000	(4)	4,714
	4,714		4,714

BUILDING

ALLOWANCE FOR DEPRECIATION,
BUILDING

1,200ᵃ	(5)	1,200

LAND

(6)	1,300		1,300ᵃ

GOODWILL

1,000ᵃ	(7)	1,000

BONDS PAYABLE

(8)	649		649ᵃ

COMMON STOCK

1,000ᵃ	(9)	1,000

RETAINED EARNINGS

(7)	1,000		1,089ᵃ
(10)	5,000	(1)	4,911
	6,000		6,000

ᵃBalancing figure.

FUNDS PROVIDED BY OPERATIONS

(1) Net income	4,911	(11)
(2) Loss on machine	171	
(4) Depreciation on machinery	4,714	
(5) Depreciation on building	1,200	
	10,996	

(11) 10,996

10,996   10,996

SOURCE AND APPLICATION OF FUNDS

(2) Sale of Machinery	4,000	(3) Purchase of Machine	2,500
(9) Issuance of Stock	1,000	(6) Purchase of Land	1,300
(11) Funds from Operations ...	10,996	(8) Retirement of Bonds	649
		(10) Payment of Dividends	5,000
		(12) Increase in Working Capital ...	6,547
	15,996		15,996

Numbers in the T-account entries refer to the following events:

1. The profit for the period was closed to the Retained Earnings account.

2. Equipment which cost $5,171 and on which depreciation of $1,000 had been accumulated was sold for $4,000. Note that the $171 loss was entered in the Funds Provided by Operations T-account, since this amount was charged to the income of the period.

3. Equipment was purchased for $2,500.

4. Depreciation on machinery and equipment for the period was $4,714.

5. Depreciation on building for the period was $1,200.

6. Land was purchased for $1,300.

7. Goodwill was written off against Retained Earnings.

8. Bonds payable in the amount of $649 were retired during the period.

9. Common stock was issued for $1,000.

10. Dividends of $5,000 were paid.

11. The balance in the Funds Provided by Operations account ($10,996) represents the total funds provided by operations during the period and should be transferred to the Source and Application of Funds T-account.

12. The balance in the Source and Application of Funds account ($6,547) represents the net increase (or decrease) in working capital during the period. This amount should always agree with the balance in the Working Capital T-account and a single entry (12) closes the last two T-accounts.

Note that in each case the transactions were recorded in the T-accounts just as they were recorded in the company's accounts. In those instances where an amount would have been charged or credited to the profit or loss of the period the same amount has been entered in the Funds Provided by Operations T-account. For example, the loss on the sale of the machine and the depreciation recorded during the period would both have been charged against the profits for the period and therefore these same amounts appear in the Funds Provided by Operations T-account. After all entries have been entered in the T-accounts, each account should balance to zero.

The student should keep in mind that both the worksheet and the T-accounts are merely tools to aid in the preparation of the formal statements. None of the entries recreated here are formally entered in the accounting records, since they have all been recorded in the normal manner during the accounting period.

THE CASH FLOW STATEMENT

In the previous section the term *funds* was defined as working capital: the current assets minus the current liabilities. Funds might just as appropriately be defined as cash only. An analysis of source and application of funds using this narrower defintion is called a *cash flow statement*. Such a statement indicates the sources, uses, and the net change in the Cash account during the period. The analysis required to prepare a cash flow statement is very similar to that followed in preparing the statement of source and application of funds. If we rewrite the accounting equation to fit this more restrictive definition, it would appear as follows:

$$C = L + OE - NCaA$$

where C = Cash
L = All liabilities
OE = Owners' equity
$NCaA$ = All noncash assets

With such a revision, the left side of the equation is narrowed down to consist of cash only, and the right side expanded to include all items other than cash. The number of possible sources and uses of cash is accordingly much greater than under the broad definition.

The Worksheet

A cash flow statement can be prepared by either of the techniques described earlier in this chapter. If the worksheet is used, the working capital pair of columns should be eliminated and a change in the cash balance extended to the last pair of columns as the balancing figure. The net change in the cash account should, of course, agree with the net increase or decrease shown on the cash flow statement. The only other change in the worksheet would be to expand the section on the funds provided by operations.

This would be necessary because changes in the current asset and current liability balances necessitate adjustments to cash provided by operations. The column headings for a cash flow worksheet might appear as follows:

BALANCE SHEET JULY 31		NET CHANGE		ADJUSTMENTS		CASH	
1971	1970	DEBIT	CREDIT	DEBIT	CREDIT	OUTFLOW	INFLOW

The T-Account

If the T-account analysis method is followed, it would be necessary to set up a separate T-account for each current asset and each current liability to replace the single Working Capital account. The changes in these accounts will generally be accounted for by adjustments to the Cash Provided by Operations account.

The Abbreviated Worksheet

Because working capital is so directly related to operations, most of the changes in these account balances have an effect on the cash provided by operations. This means that the major difference between the statement of source and application of funds and a cash flow statement is in the net cash or funds provided by operations. While there are only a few items on an income statement that do not provide or use funds, there are numerous income statement items that do not provide cash. In fact, in order to arrive at cash provided by operations, so many adjustments to net income must be made that it may be desirable to prepare a separate worksheet for this purpose. Such a worksheet starts out with the revenue and expenses and, through adjustments, converts these figures to cash receipts and disbursements. Once the cash provided by operations is obtained, it is a relatively simple matter to prepare a cash flow statement, since most other items correspond to those appearing on a statement of source and application of funds. A worksheet for calculating cash provided from operations appears in Figure 13-6. Since all other sources of funds and all applications of funds in the Computograph Corporation were for cash, a cash flow statement such as the one shown in Figure 13-7 can be prepared.

Figure 13-6

COMPUTOGRAPH CORPORATION

Worksheet to Determine Cash Provided by Operations

For the Year Ended January 31, 1968

	Income statement		Adjustments		Cash	
	Revenue	Expense	Add	Deduct	Provided	Applied
Sales	269086					
Add: Increase in Allow. for Doubtful Accounts			231			
Deduct: Increase in Accounts Receivable				6831	262486	
Cost of Goods Sold		127851				
Add: Increase in Inventory			5305			
Deduct: Increase in Accounts Payable				3128		
Deduct: Increase in Notes Payable				1111		128917
Selling Expense		49322				
Administrative Expense		80631				
Add: Increase in Prepaid Insurance			225			
Deduct: Depreciation of Machinery & Equip				4714		
Deduct: Depreciation of Building				1200		124264
Income Taxes		6200				
Add: Decrease in Accrued Taxes			1107			7307
Loss on sale of Machine		171				
Deduct: Loss on sale of Machine				171		
Net Profit		264175				
		4911				
	269086	269086				
Cash Provided By Operations					262486	260488
						1998
					262486	262486

276

Figure 13-7

COMPUTOGRAPH CORPORATION
Cash Flow Statement
For the Year Ended July 31, 1971

Sources of cash:
Operations (per worksheet)	$1,998
Sale of machine	4,000
Issuance of common stock	1,000
	$6,998

Uses of cash:
Purchase of machine	$2,500	
Purchase of land	1,300	
Retirement of bonds	649	
Payment of dividends	5,000	9,449
Decrease in Cash		$2,451

PROJECTED CASH FLOW

Probably the most useful application of cash flow analysis is the use of the techniques described here to project the cash flows for some future period. This type of information can be very useful in the management of cash. By projecting cash inflows and outflows, management can make plans to invest excess sums when they are available and arrange for borrowing in periods of cash deficiency. Projected cash flow is discussed in chapter 15 as part of the broader problem of budgeting.

SUMMARY

Three statements which relate to the activities of an accounting period have been discussed in this chapter: the schedule of changes in working capital, the statement of source and application of funds, and the cash flow statement. The first two of these deal with the funds, or the working capital, of the enterprise. The *schedule of changes in working capital* itemizes the changes that have occurred during the period in specific fund items, i.e., it specifies the amount and direction of change in each current asset and current liability account. The *source and application of funds*, on the other hand, analyzes the changes that have taken place and discloses the *reasons* the changes have occurred. This statement, as the name implies, indicates where the increases in working capital came from and where the decreases in working capital went. These two statements explain what has happened to the firm's working capital position and why changes occurred.

Funds statements may be prepared by either the worksheet or T-account method. Both methods attempt to itemize the specific sources and applications by accounting for the changes that have occurred in various non-current accounts.

The third statement introduced in this chapter was the *cash flow statement*, which attempts to account for the changes which have occurred in the company's cash position during a specified period of time. It is similar to a statement of source and application of funds except in the area of funds (or cash) provided by the operations. Many items which are shown as income under the accrual system do not provide cash. Likewise, many of the expenses shown in the income statement do not use cash. A worksheet is generally used to calculate the "cash effect" of the various transactions on the income statement in order to arrive at cash provided by operations. Most other sources or uses of cash correspond to those shown on the funds statement.

QUESTIONS

1. What is the definition of the term *funds* as used in the statement of source and application of funds?
2. How do a schedule of changes of working capital and a statement of source and application of funds differ in content? How is the information supplied by each useful to management?
3. Summarize the three major sources of funds as derived from changes in the accounting equation. List several examples of each type of change.
4. List the three major applications of funds which may be derived from changes in the accounting equation. Give an example of each.
5. Is depreciation a source of funds? How does depreciation affect the funds flow? How is depreciation shown in a statement of source and application of funds? Why is it so shown?
6. If the schedule of changes in working capital shows an increase in current assets of $22,000 and an increase in current liabilities of $10,000, what will the statement of source and application of funds show?
7. What is the difference in content of a statement of source and application of funds and a cash flow statement? What do the two statements have in common?
8. How does a stock dividend affect the statement of source and application of funds? How would such a transaction affect a cash flow statement?
9. If sales were $22,930 during a given period and the accounts receivable decrease $2,110 during the same period, what would be the net cash effect?
10. During the last year the Towner Company's Inventory account decreased by $4,291; Accounts Payable increased by $950; and the Cost of Goods Sold was $27,870. How much was the net cash outflow for goods?

11. The Income Tax Payable account had balances of $59,000 on December 31, 19X1, and $75,000 on December 31, 19X2. The income statement shows $59,000 as the income tax charges for the year. How much was the company's cash outflow for taxes?

12. If a company sold equipment which cost $17,000 and had a book value of $5,000 for $3,000 cash, how would it record this transaction on a statement of source and application of funds? (Assume that the company uses the current operating concept in preparing its income statement.)

13. How would the transaction referred to in question 12 be shown in the "funds" statement, assuming that the company used an all-inclusive income statement?

14. Does depreciation have the same effect on a company's cash flow that it does on its "funds" flow? Explain.

PROBLEMS

Problem 13-1

State how each of the following transactions will affect the statement of source and application of funds. Assume that the company prepares an all-inclusive income statement.

a. Write-off of an obsolete machine which had cost $250,000 and had accumulated depreciation of $237,500.
b. Purchase of land for $100,000.
c. Sale of same land for $130,000.
d. Issue of fifty shares of common stock (par $50) in payment of attorney's fees associated with organizing the company. The fair market value of the attorney's services was $3,200.
e. Payment of $11,000 cash dividend.
f. Write-off of goodwill carried at $230.
g. Issue of $1,350,000 of 6 percent second mortgage bonds at 98.
h. Amortization of one-twentieth of the second mortgage bond discount.
i. Five percent stock dividend declared on 82,620 shares of outstanding common stock. The stock has a par of $50 and had a market value at date of declaration of $155 per share.
j. Purchase of a building for $115,000, the company paying $45,000 cash and signing a mortgage note payable in three years for the balance of the purchase price.
k. Write-off of uncollectible accounts amounting to $1,632.

Problem 13-2

Data relating to the Longview Corporation are presented below:

	DECEMBER 31	
	1971	1970
Current assets	$219,300	$175,000
Plant and equipment	235,400	183,600

Delivery equipment	42,800	47,000
Land	19,900	24,200
Goodwill		460
	$517,400	$430,260
Accumulated depreciation,		
plant and machinery	102,800	97,300
Accumulated depreciation,		
delivery equipment	15,260	13,800
Current liabilities	102,700	86,400
Bonds payable	105,000	75,000
Bond premium	1,100	500
Capital stock	115,000	100,000
Paid-in caiptal in excess of par,		
common stock	17,800	13,500
Retained earnings	57,740	43,760
	$517,400	$430,260

During the calendar year 1971 the company sold for $25,000 machinery that had originally cost $75,000 and that had accumulated depreciation at the time of sale of $47,000. The company includes gains and losses on the sale of equipment in reporting net income. Goodwill was written off against Retained Earnings. Net income for the year was $14,440. Depreciation on the delivery equipment was $5,400 for the year, and an old delivery truck was sold at book value.

Required:

Prepare a statement of sources and applications of funds and a schedule of changes in working capital for the year 1971.

Problem 13-3

A comparative balance sheet of Davis Company at October 31, 1969, and October 31, 1970, carried the following information:

DEBITS

	OCTOBER 31	
	1970	1969
Cash	$ 45,641	$ 32,951
Equipment	69,253	63,673
Accounts receivable (net)	70,806	52,926
Patent	21,140	22,650
Inventory	71,810	75,270
Land	50,865	62,865
Building	130,000	130,000
	$459,515	$440,335

CREDITS

Accumulated depreciation, equipment	$ 26,683	$ 23,573
Accounts payable.....................	48,275	52,870
Accrued payables (selling)	2,595	4,620

Accrued payables (administrative)	2,400	2,102
Accumulated depreciation, building	45,500	39,000
Common stock, $100 par value...........	168,000	162,000
Premium on common stock	4,935	4,575
Retained earnings	61,127	51,595
Mortgage payable	100,000	100,000
	$459,515	$440,335

DAVIS COMPANY
Income Statement
For the Year Ended October 31, 1970

Sales		$446,510
Cost of goods sold		377,936
Gross profit		$ 68,574
Selling expenses^a	$ 23,604	
Administrative expense^a	12,863	
Depreciation, equipment.............	4,010	
Depreciation, building	6,500	
Amortization of patent	1,510	48,487
Net profits from operation		$ 20,087
Income taxes		7,435
Net profits before nonrecurring charges		$ 12,652
Add: Nonrecurring charges:		
Gain on sale of land	320	
Loss on sale of equipment	200	120
Net income		$ 12,772

^aExcluding depreciation and patent amortization.

Examination of the records for 1970 showed that cash dividends of $3,240 were paid, and equipment costing $1,600 with accumulated depreciation of $900 was sold at a loss of $200.

Required:

Prepare a source and application of funds statement and a schedule of changes in working capital.

Problem 13-4

Using the information given in problem 13-3, prepare a cash flow statement and a worksheet to show cash provided by operations for the Davis Company.

Problem 13-5

The 19X1 and 19X2 balance sheet for International Company showed the following amounts:

DEBITS

	DECEMBER 31	
	19X2	19X1
Cash	$ 31,500	$ 20,100
Accounts receivable (net)	33,400	35,500
Inventories	35,563	25,432
Prepaid insurance	1,400	1,200
Office equipment	35,445	32,750
Land	26,365	15,190
Building	85,300	85,300
Delivery trucks	33,020	26,430
	$281,993	$241,902

CREDITS

Accumulated depreciation, office equipment	$ 18,210	$ 16,150
Accumulated depreciation, trucks	13,126	10,940
Accounts payable	47,104	56,520
Current accrued payables (selling)	1,875	2,910
Common stock, $25 par value	125,000	100,000
Premium on common stock	8,200	6,200
Retained earnings	42,888	27,857
Accumulated depreciation, building	25,590	21,325
	$281,993	$241,902

1. Two delivery trucks costing $5,415 each were purchased. A delivery truck which originally cost $4,240 was sold at a loss of $625. The loss was charged directly to the Retained Earnings account.
2. Fully depreciated office equipment that cost $1,395 was discarded, and its cost was taken from the accounts.
3. Depreciation expense charged on office equipment, $3,455; on the building, $4,265; and on the delivery trucks, $5,286.
4. A cash dividend of $5,000 was paid.

Required:

Prepare a source and application of funds statement and a schedule of changes in working capital.

Problem 13-6

INTERNATIONAL COMPANY
Income Statement
For the Year Ended December 31, 19X2

Sales		$559,967
Cost of goods sold		469,315
Gross profit		$ 90,652
Administrative expenses[a]	$12,300	

Selling expenses[a]	25,000		
Insurance expense	5,100		
Depreciation, office equipment	3,455		
Depreciation, building	4,265		
Depreciation, delivery trucks	5,286	55,406	
Net operating income		$ 35,246	
Income taxes		14,590	
Net profit		$ 20,656	

---

[a]Excluding depreciation.

Required:

Using the above information together with that given in problem 13-5, prepare a cash flow statement and a worksheet to show cash provided by operations.

Problem 13-7

The financial statements of Frank Manufacturing Corporation for 1969 and 1970 follow. The corporation was formed on January 1, 1967.

FRANK MANUFACTURING CORPORATION
Comparative Balance Sheet
December 31

ASSETS

	1970	1969	INCREASE (DECREASE)
Current Assets:			
Cash	$ 33,500	$ 27,000	$ 6,500
Accounts receivable (net of allowance for bad debts of $1,900 and $2,000)	89,900	79,700	10,200
Inventories (at lower of cost or market)	136,300	133,200	3,100
Prepaid expenses	4,600	12,900	(8,300)
Total	264,300	252,800	11,500
Investments:			
Land held for future plant site	35,000	–	35,000
Fixed Assets:			
Land	47,000	47,000	–
Buildings and equipment (net of accumulated depreciation of $155,600 and $117,000)	551,900	425,000	126,900
Total	598,900	472,000	126,900
Other Assets:			
Organization expense	1,500	3,000	(1,500)
Total	$899,700	$727,800	$171,900

LIABILITIES AND STOCKHOLDERS' EQUITY

Current Liabilities:

Accounts payable	$ 3,000	$ 7,800	$ (4,800)
Notes payable	8,000	5,000	3,000
Mortgage payable	3,600	3,600	–
Accrued liabilities	6,200	4,800	1,400
Income taxes payable	87,500	77,900	9,600
Total........................	108,300	99,100	9,200

Long-term Liabilities:

Notes payable	–	18,000	(18,000)
Mortgage payable	70,200	73,800	(3,600)
Total	70,200	91,800	(21,600)
Deferred income, investment credit	16,800	18,900	(2,100)

Stockholders' Equity:

Capital stock; $1 par value; shares authorized, 300,000 in 1970 and 20,000 in 1969; shares issued and outstanding, 162,000 in 1970 and 120,000 in 1969	162,000	120,000	42,000
Capital contributed in excess of par value	306,900	197,900	109,000
Reserve for contingencies	25,000	–	25,000
Retained earnings	210,500	200,100	10,400
Total........................	704,400	518,000	186,400
Total.......................	$899,700	$727,800	$171,900

FRANK MANUFACTURING COMPANY
Statement of Income and Retained Earnings
For the Years Ended December 31

	1970	1969	INCREASE (DECREASE)
Sales	$980,000	$900,000	$ 80,000
Cost of goods sold	540,000	490,000	50,000
Gross profit	440,000	410,000	30,000
Selling and administrative expenses	262,000	248,500	13,500
Net income from operations	178,000	161,500	16,500
Other income and (deductions), net	(3,000)	(1,500)	1,500
Net income before income taxes	175,000	160,000	15,000
Provision for income taxes	85,400	77,900	7,500
Net income after income taxes	89,600	82,100	7,500
Retained earnings, Jan. 1	200,100	118,000	82,100
Ten percent stock dividend distributed....	(36,000)	–	(36,000)
Cash dividends paid	(18,200)	–	(18,200)
Appropriation for contingent loss	(25,000)	–	(25,000)
Retained earnings, Dec. 31	$210,500	$200,100	$ 10,400

The following information was given effect in the preparation of the foregoing financial statements:

1. The 10 percent stock dividend was distributed on August 1. The investment in land for a future plant site was obtained by the issuance of 10,000 shares of the corporation's common stock on October 1. On December 1, 20,000 shares of common stock were sold to obtain additional working capital. There were no other 1970 transactions affecting contributed capital.
2. During 1970 depreciable assets with a total cost of $17,500 were retired and sold as scrap for a nominal amount. These assets were fully depreciated at December 31, 1969. The only depreciable asset acquired in 1970 was a new building which was completed in December; no depreciation was taken on its cost.
3. When new equipment, with an estimated life of ten years, was purchased on January 2, 1969, for $300,000, the decision was made to record the resulting investment credit in a deferred income account with the benefit of the investment credit being allocated over the useful life of the machine by a reduction of the provision for income taxes. The income tax rate for 1969 and 1970 was 50 percent.
4. In 1970, $10,000 was paid in advance on long-term notes payable. The balance of the long-term notes is due in 1971.
5. A reserve for a contingent loss of $25,000 arising from a lawsuit was established in 1970 by debiting the Retained Earnings account.

Required:

Prepare a formal statement of source and application of funds for the Frank Manufacturing Company for the year ended December 31, 1970. The formal statement should include the financial aspects of all significant transactions. Supplementary schedules, such as the schedule of changes in working capital accounts, should be presented in good form.

AICPA Adapted

Case 13
WOOLLEY BLANKET COMPANY

Increasing sales have brought the Woolley Blanket Company to full-capacity production. In order to meet future demand, the board of directors has decided to expand the existing facilities. Financing of the addition will be funded through a long-term bank loan.

Prior to the meeting with the bank, the president of the company has requested that the usual financial statements and analysis reports be completed. The chief accountant assigns his subordinates the task of collecting the supplementary data and preparing the documents.

While the formal financial statements have not yet been prepared, all adjustments except recording of the income tax expense have been entered in the accounts. An adjusted trial balance at December 31, 1970, is shown in Exhibit 13-1. The company estimates that income tax expense for the year will amount to 40 percent of the net income before taxes.

In addition to the data contained in Exhibits 13-1 and 13-2, you are provided with the following facts. Early in January of 1970 the company sold one of the factory buildings, including the equipment contained therein. At date of sale, the building had accumulated depreciation amounting to $1,245,000 and the equipment, accumulated depreciation amounting to $500,000. The building had originally cost $4,000,000. Proceeds from the sale of the equipment amounted to $1,530,000. Bond discount amortization for 1970 is included in the interest expense.

With the above information the accounting department can now prepare the needed statements. Form and clarity are important in the presentation. As a staff accountant, answer the following questions:

1. What was the Woolley Blanket Company net income for the year 1970?
2. How much did the company's working capital change during the year? What changes occurred in the specific elements of the company's working capital?
3. Prepare a statement of source and application of funds. Of what value would this statement be to the bank?
4. Comment on the present financial position of the Woolley Blanket Company as compared with last year. Do you feel the bank should grant the loan?

Exhibit 13-1

WOOLLEY BLANKET COMPANY
Adjusted Trial Balance
December 31, 1970

Cash	5,835	
Marketable securities	10,000	
Notes receivable	2,690	
Accounts receivable	20,335	
Allowance for bad debts		410
Accrued interest receivable	800	
Inventories	32,900	
Prepaid expenses	2,725	
Land	4,800	
Buildings	36,000	
Accumulated depreciation, building		8,220
Equipment	16,830	
Accumulated depreciation, equipment		4,850
Deferred charges, bond discount	160	

Notes payable		1,560
Accounts payable		6,840
Accrued payables		1,630
Mortgage payable		3,000
Bonds payable		10,000
Preferred stock		23,000
Capital in excess of par, preferred stock		1,700
Common stock		33,000
Retained earnings, Dec. 31, 1969		16,780
Dividends	1,380	
Sales		153,000
Interest earned		560
Cost of goods sold	82,000	
Rent expense	6,000	
Repairs and maintenance	8,000	
Depreciation expense	1,495	
Interest expense	685	
Selling and administrative expense	28,665	
Loss on sale of building	2,000	
Loss on sale of equipment	1,250	
	264,550	264,550

(all figures in thousands of dollars)

Exhibit 13-2

WOOLLEY BLANKET COMPANY
Balance Sheet
December 31, 1969

CURRENT ASSETS

Cash...		$ 6,565
Marketable securities		7,500
Notes receivable, trade		1,240
Accounts receivable	$ 12,710	
Less: allowance for bad debts	375	12,335
Accrued interest receivable		720
Inventories		24,875
Prepaid expenses................................		1,365
Total current assets		$ 54,600

FIXED ASSETS

Land		$ 4,000
Buildings	$ 32,000	
Less: accumulated depreciation	8,640	23,360
Equipment	$ 13,550	
Less: accumulated depreciation..................	4,680	8,870
Total fixed assets		$ 36,320
Deferred charges, bond discounts		$ 180
Total assets		$ 91,010

CURRENT LIABILITIES

Notes payable	$ 2,010
Accounts payable	5,650
Accrued payables	1,870
Total current liabilities	$ 9,530

LONG-TERM LIABILITIES

Mortgage payable	$ 3,500
Bonds payable	10,000
Total long-term liabilities	$ 13,500
Total liabilities	$ 23,030

STOCKHOLDERS' EQUITY

Preferred stock, $100 par	$ 18,000
Capital in excess of par	1,200
Common stock	32,000
Retained earnings	16,780
Total stockholders' equity	$ 67,980
Total equities	$ 91,010

(all figures in thousands of dollars)

14

Planning
and
Control

One of the major purposes of an accounting system is to assist management in formulating plans and to aid them in controlling operations so that these plans are met. In order to plan for the future properly, management must clearly understand the firm's present position and the results of past operations. Detailed balance sheets, income statements, funds statements, cash flow statements, and other internal reports are prepared for this purpose. These reports serve as the basis for future plans and assist management in establishing realistic objectives.

Once the objectives have been established for an enterprise, controls must be set up to assure that prescribed management objectives are met. The chief financial officer of the company is usually charged with this responsibility and accordingly is sometimes called the controller. Thus, the chief financial officer becomes an important part of the management team and generally holds the rank of vice president in the company's organization structure.

When an accountant speaks of control as it relates to the overall business enterprise, he usually uses the expression *internal control*. Internal control has been defined as comprising

> ... a plan of organization and all the coordinate methods and measures adopted within a business to safeguard its assets, check the accuracy and reliability of its accounting data, promote operational efficiency, and encourage adherence to prescribed managerial policies.[1]

OBJECTIVES OF INTERNAL CONTROL

The definition lists four distinct objectives of a system of internal control:

1. Safeguard assets,
2. Check the accuracy and the reliability of accounting data,
3. Promote operational efficiency,
4. Encourage adherence to prescribed managerial policies.

Internal control includes everything from the basic organizational structure on down to routine documents and procedures that are aimed at accomplishing the above objectives.

One important aspect of an internal control system is to assure balance between the objectives. These objectives do not always move in the same direction, and a procedure adopted to reach one objective may tear down another. For example, some controls instituted to safeguard assets tend to become nothing more than red tape stifling operational efficiency. In an attempt to escape this red tape, personnel sometimes find a loophole which enables them to circumvent a prescribed managerial policy. A well-balanced system of internal control will preclude this by giving attention to all objectives simultaneously, rather than trying to accomplish them one at a time.

A good system of internal control is constantly being changed to keep it working in a dynamic business world. This means not only adding new controls as changing conditions warrant, but also dropping those that have outlived their usefulness. Sometimes controls tend to become like taxes: once they are instituted, they are difficult to do away with. Such should not be the case. Management should constantly review the adequacy of internal control to be sure that each control is contributing to the objectives of the system.

Another important aspect of internal control is cost. As with other areas

---

[1]*Statements on Auditing Procedure Number 33* (New York: American Institute of Certified Public Accountants, 1963), p. 27.

of operation, the managers should be interested in getting maximum results for every dollar expended. Each control instituted should be weighed to be sure that the benefits derived exceed the cost of implementation. Consideration should be given to finding the least costly method of accomplishing the objective. For example, in safeguarding assets, a company should institute controls to assure employee honesty. Yet, setting up a system to guarantee that the company's assets were not misappropriated would be prohibitively expensive. A more economical way of meeting the objectives would be to supplement some simple controls with a fidelity bond. Such a plan would not guarantee the safeguard of the assets, but would compensate the company for a loss, should it occur. Similarly, detailed stock record cards and hand receipts for small office equipment, such as rulers and pens (and even paper clips!) would probably reduce the theft of those items by employees. The cost of maintaining such a system, on the other hand, would likely be many times greater than the savings enjoyed. Is it worth spending one dollar to preclude a ten-cent loss? The benefits of any system of internal control should be carefully weighed against the cost.

PRINCIPLES OF INTERNAL CONTROL

There are a number of principles that management should incorporate into the internal control system to be sure that the firm's objectives are met. A list of principles may include:

1. Sound organizational structure
2. Competent personnel
3. Separation of duties
4. Forms and procedures
5. Mechanical devices
6. Review and appraisal
7. Spreading risk

Sound Organizational Structure

The definition of internal control cited at the beginning of this chapter indicated that a plan of organization is an essential part of such a system. An organizational chart which clearly defines the lines of authority and the span of control within the company is the starting point for such a system. A good organizational chart should follow the rules of a good outline. For example, any given level on an organizational chart implies a degree of equality. If a company has four vice presidents, one may assume that the firm has four major functions and that all are of approximately equal significance. Each level in the organizational structure should be a subdivision of the next higher level. The word subdivision implies that there must be at least two parts. If there is need for two levels in the organization, then the second level should have at least two parts. Each unit in the organization should report to one boss, thus clearly fixing the responsibility. Insofar as practicable, communications within the firm should follow the organizational structure.

Competent Personnel

Some firms have rightly claimed that their greatest asset, loyal and well-qualified personnel, does not even appear on the balance sheet. Certainly the adequacy of the personnel is a major factor in determining the extent to which internal control is effective. The competency of the personnel is determined by the recruiting, screening, interviewing, training, retention, promotion, and compensation policies of the company. Part of the employee's training must give him an understanding of the internal control system insofar as it relates to his particular function. Lack of understanding may be listed as one of the primary causes of failure of internal control.

Separation of Duties

Whenever practicable, duties should be arranged so that no one person in the organization has complete control over a particular transaction. In order to accomplish this, the responsibility for record keeping, custodianship, and the operating functions should be separated. For example, whereever possible the bookkeeper, the cashier, and the salesman should be three separate persons. One employee should not be permitted access to others' functions. Assignments should be delegated so that the work of one employee or department will serve as a check on the work of others. Although small firms may be handicapped in their ability to employ this principle, they can, nevertheless, make some segregation of duties.

Mechanical Devices

Mechanical devices such as cash registers, corporate seals, and time clocks have long been used as a form of control. The technological revolution of this century, however, has developed control devices to a point where almost no business is without some form of mechanical control. The potential of devices such as radio transmitters the size of a coin or a hidden closed-circuit television camera is astounding. A company could use these devices as a deterrent, as well as a means of detecting shoplifting, and save countless dollars in assets that otherwise might be lost. Likewise, these devices could be used to detect breakdowns in automated assembly lines and thereby promote operational efficiency. The control inherent in a company-wide telephone or teletype system can hardly be comprehended unless one reflects on the chaos that would result if such a system were removed.

In addition to the devices mentioned above, a list of commonly used mechanical devices includes checkwriters, burglar alarms, fire alarms, automatic sprinklers, door locks, time-controlled vaults, adding machines, calculators, electronic data-processing equipment, computers, etc. Although we have just scratched the surface, the student can see the vast potential of mechanical devices in helping control a firm's operations.

Procedures

The procedures adopted within a business are an integral part of the internal control system. Procedures should be established to incorporate extensively other principles of internal control, such as the use of mechanical devices and the separation of duties. For example, a cash register is a mechanical device that can provide control over cash if it is used in conjunction with proper operating procedures. The machine alone provides little control. If only one person at a time is given access to the cash register, the cash register's tape is read by someone other than the cashier, a cash register receipt is required on all sales, etc., then the register can be a useful control. On the other hand, if several employees have access to the same cash drawer or the cash drawer is left open, the control is greatly weakened.

Procedures can control how and by whom duties are to be performed, how and to whom the documents and goods flow, how and when the employees are trained, what mechanical devices are to be employed, and so on. Dual signatures on checks, authorizing signatures, and checking mathematical accuracy are some of the procedures commonly followed to strengthen internal control.

Spreading Risk

Risk, one of the inherent characteristics of a business enterprise, is one thing from which we cannot escape. There are means, however, of spreading many of the risks to limit the loss of any given business. The most common means of accomplishing this is through insurance. In exchange for a specified premium, the insurance company agrees to compensate the company for losses covered by the policy. Insurance thereby becomes an important means of achieving internal control.

It has been said that if you are willing to pay the premiums, anything can be insured. It is novel to read some of the risks against which Lloyd's of London has insured. As with other forms of control, the cost of the control (the insurance premium) must be weighed carefully against the potential loss. Most companies self-insure or coinsure to a degree, because they do not feel a particular coverage is worth the cost.

Some of the more important types of business insurance are life insurance, fire insurance (including extended coverage), fidelity bonds, and public liability insurance.

Life Insurance.   Companies often insure the lives of key officers or owners. Such insurance may be taken out for either of two possible reasons: first, to compensate the company for the actual economic loss sustained by the loss of service from this employee. Such might be the case with an accounting or law firm. If one of the partners in many such firms were to die, there would be serious economic loss to the firm. The second reason for business life insurance is to provide the funds necessary to buy out the interest of the deceased owner. In this manner, the business can continue to operate without causing a serious working capital shortage.

Fire Insurance.   Buildings, equipment, and inventory generally are insured against loss from fire. Companies often add extended coverage clauses to the basic fire insurance contract to insure against losses such as wind, hail, floods, snow, explosion, sprinkler leakage, and similar perils. The assets are generally insured for their appraised value rather than for the historical cost.

Most fire insurance policies contain a coinsurance clause which requires that the company carry insurance equal to a certain percentage of the asset's current insurable value. For example, an 80 percent coinsurance clause on a building which has an insurable value of $500,000 at date of fire would require that the company have insurance in force of at least $400,000. If the company has less than this amount of insurance, the insurance company is only obligated to pay that fraction of the loss represented by the ratio of insurance actually carried to the total insurance required by the coinsurance clause. Suppose the company carried only $300,000 insurance and that its building was 50 percent destroyed by fire. In that event the insurance company would only pay $187,500, or 75 percent of the loss, since the company carried only 75 percent of the insurance required by the coinsurance clause.

Because property values tend to change over time, many companies find themselves to be involuntary coinsurers. When the insurance policy is taken out they carry sufficient insurance to meet the coinsurance requirement, but several years later they find that the property value has increased, causing them to fall below the required coverage. For this reason it is important that management review insurance coverage at regular intervals and update the insurance coverage to be sure that the assets are adequately protected.

Another clause found in most fire insurance policies is called the contribution clause. This provision states how claims will be paid in the event several policies are carried on one asset, e.g., whether the companies will share the loss on a prorata basis or whether one company will serve as primary insurer while the others serve as secondary insurers. A contribution clause discourages arson by preventing companies from overinsuring their property.

Fidelity Bonds. Fidelity bonds are taken out to insure a company against losses resulting from the dishonesty of employees. Such bonds may be either *position* or *name* bonds. The position bond covers anyone holding a position detailed in the bond, such as the cashier or treasurer. The company is automatically protected with such policies, regardless of the turnover in these positions. The name bond, on the other hand, covers only the person cited in the bond. Should the company appoint a new treasurer, for example, it would be necessary to obtain a new bond.

Liability Insurance. Most companies carry insurance to protect them against loss or damage suffered through negligence of the company or its employees. For example, a restaurant would carry insurance to protect them should a customer suffer from food poisoning. Likewise, an amusement park would carry insurance to protect them should the rollercoaster collapse with a carload of accounting students.

Workmen's compensation insurance is required by most states to enable employees to recover damages suffered in connection with their employment. The insurance company contracts to assume all liabilities which result from the workmen's compensation laws of the particular state. Workmen's compensation insurance is an example of a typical liability insurance carried by most concerns.

Review and Appraisal

Possibly the capstone of an internal control system is the review and appraisal. There are two aspects to this principle: first, the built-in review and appraisal within the system, which provides for the work of one employee to check automatically on the work of another; second, and possibly most important, the independent review of the system as a whole. Such a review can be performed by a management team, by internal auditors who report high enough in the organization to permit some degree of independence, or by independent certified public accountants.

The review and appraisal should not be as concerned with the extent to which the system exists as with whether or not the system is, in fact, operating. A system can look good on paper, but break down in practice. For example, a control procedure may require dual signatures on all checks so that two persons will check to see that the disbursement is proper. In reviewing the actual operation, the appraiser may find that one of the parties signed a number of blank checks in advance, thus causing a breakdown in the system. The review of the internal control should include sufficient tests of the controls to insure that the desired objectives are being met.

INTERNAL CONTROL ILLUSTRATION

We have already noted that internal control is a very broad subject covering all aspects of the business. Because the control system must be custom-made for the individual concern, it is not possible to make a model for an ideal system, nor will space permit discussing all applications of internal control. It may, on the other hand, be useful to examine one aspect of a company's operation to see how the principles of internal control might be incorporated into this specific case. Because of its importance to most firms, the procurement function has been selected for discussion.

In order to gain effective control over the procurement function, many companies have a centralized purchasing department. Only this arm of the company has authority to procure goods or services in behalf of the business enterprise; employee procurement (hiring) is usually handled by a separate personnel department. The accounting department in such companies will make payment only in those instances where they are furnished proper documentation from purchasing to indicate that the order was placed in accordance with company policy.

Figure 14-1 diagrams the flow of documents related to a purchase in a typical company. In this instance a *purchase requisition* has been prepared by the requesting organization to communicate its needs to the central purchasing department. Upon receipt of the purchase requisition, the purchasing department would proceed to locate possible suppliers and obtain the best possible terms. Variations in quality, price, and shipping terms among the potential suppliers would be evaluated in order to obtain the best possible combination. Requests from various departments would be consolidated, insofar as practicable, to take advantage of quantity discounts and to reduce the paper work involved. Where the order is significant in amount, the company policy often requires that several bids be obtained and that the low bid be accepted, unless accepting another bid is justified on technical grounds (such as proven superior quality). The size of the order placed will be determined by the quantity discounts available and the various inventory carrying costs involved. When the purchasing agent arrives at the best possible terms, the order is placed. Normally, the order is communicated to the vendor (supplier) in a written *purchase order*.

At the time the vendor ships the goods, a *vendor's invoice* is normally prepared. This document is usually mailed directly to the buyer's accounting department. Upon receipt, the goods are counted and inspected by the personnel of the receiving department and a *receiving report* is prepared. Inasmuch as the quantities received sometimes are not the same as the quantities ordered, it is preferable that the persons in the receiving department not be aware of the quantities ordered or shipped. Although copies of the purchase order and vendor's invoices (packing slips) are often sent to such persons, these documents should not disclose quantities or prices. Documents which do not reflect prices or quantities are described as "blind copies." This control is essential in order to assure that the goods are actually counted. In those instances where the quantities are known, it would be too easy for the receiving clerk to merely copy the same quantities without making a careful count of the goods actually received. Also, an overage of small, expensive items might be a temptation to receiving personnel. When the goods have been counted, the receiving report is prepared to notify various parties that the goods have arrived.

Note that copies of the purchase order, receiving report, and vendor's invoice go to the accounting department. Various checks are made at this point to assure that the goods for which the company has been billed are the same as those that were ordered and received. Invoices are checked for mathematical accuracy regarding prices, extensions, footings, etc. When the accountant is assured by examination of the various documents that the invoice is correct and valid, a *voucher* is prepared to record the purchase and authorize the payment.

Vouchers are normally filed by due date to assure prompt payment. Where discounts are available, the due date is generally considered as the last date the discount can be taken. As payment is made, the voucher with supporting documents (purchase order, receiving report, and vendor's invoice) is cancelled and placed in the paid file in numerical order.

The foregoing discussion has centered around the procedures related to the procurement function. Of course, there would be many mechanical devices and other features of internal control incorporated into this or any other system. The procurement illustration demonstrates controls which one might find in a typical company. Each company must, of course, design

Figure 14-1

PROCUREMENT FUNCTION
Document Flow Chart

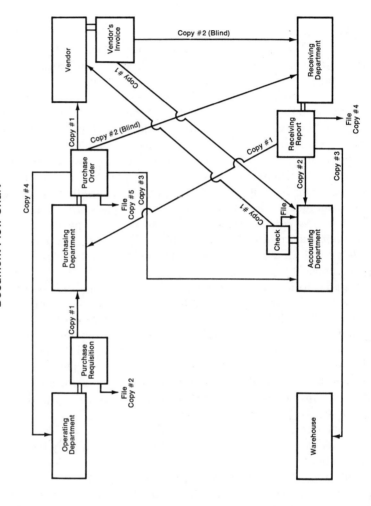

Summary of Purchasing Documents

A. Purchase Requisition

1. Copy 1 to purchasing department to communicate need for goods or services.
2. Copy 2 file for future reference.

B. Purchase Order

1. Copy 1 to vendor to communicate request for merchandise or services.
2. Copy 2 (blind) to receiving department to alert them that the goods will be arriving.
3. Copy 3 to accounting department for future·comparison with vendor's invoice and receiving report.
4. Copy 4 to operating department to notify them that their request has been processed.
5. Copy 5 file for future reference.

C. Vendor's Invoice

1. Copy 1 to the accounting department to request payment for the goods or services.
2. Copy 2 (packing slip) to the receiving department accompanying the shipment of goods. Other copies as required for the vendor's own use.

D. Receiving Report

1. Copy 1 to the purchasing department to notify them the goods have been received.
2. Copy 2 to the accounting department for future comparison with the vendor's invoice and the purchase order.
3. Copy 3 accompanies the goods to the warehouse so the custodian can account for the goods received.
4. Copy 4 file for future reference.

its own control system, tailoring it to its individual needs. In designing the system, the four objectives of internal control should be kept in mind:

1. Safeguarding assets
2. Checking the accuracy and reliability of accounting data
3. Promoting operational efficiency
4. Encouraging adherence to prescribed managerial policies.

Proper balance must be maintained between these four objectives.

SUMMARY

Internal control comprises a broad program of procedures and other devices adopted by a business enterprise to safeguard the assets, check the accounting data, promote efficiency, and encourage adherence to company policies. A good internal control system will maintain proper balance between these objectives and in each case will give proper consideration to both the benefits to be derived and the costs of implementation. Some of the principles upon which a good system of internal control is based are a sound organizational structure, competent personnel, separation of duties, the use of forms and procedures, the use of mechanical devices, periodic review and appraisal, and the spreading of risk. Each business enterprise must tailor-make a control system to fit its own needs within the broad framework of these principles.

QUESTIONS

1. What is internal control? What are the four major objectives of a system of internal control?
2. Why is it important to maintain balance in an internal control system? Illustrate how the objectives of internal control could conflict if proper balance were not maintained.
3. What are some programs that a company might adopt to assure the competency of personnel?
4. Why might a business be interested in life insurance on key personnel? What control is provided by such policies?
5. Why is it important for a company to separate the duties of various employees? Would you expect a company with two employees or one with two hundred employees to have better internal control? Why?
6. What is a fidelity bond? What are the two major types of fidelity bonds? Explain the difference between the two.
7. What are some mechanical devices that might be found in a large department store? Indicate how each might provide control and what procedures might be necessary to insure that the control actually works.
8. How is the audit function related to internal control? Why is independence important in auditing? Contrast the control values of an internal audit and an independent audit.
9. Why is a firm's organizational structure considered a part of the system of internal control? How are other principles of internal control related to the organizational structure?
10. What are some of the risks from which a company might protect itself through insurance? What should determine the amount of insurance carried?
11. What is the difference between a purchase order and a purchase requisition? What purpose is served by each? Who should receive copies of each of these documents? Why?
12. What documents should be compared and checked for accuracy before payment for goods is made? What are some of the calculations and comparisons that should be made?

PROBLEMS

Problem 14-1

Thrift Center is a locally owned discount department store with only one outlet. The company has seventeen departments and one hundred employees, and during the past year it had gross sales of over $5,000,000. The company owns a building of 50,000 square feet which houses the company offices, store, and warehouse. None of the owners of the company is employed by the firm, nor do any of them actively participate in the management.

Required:

List ten specific controls which you would recommend that Thrift Center adopt, and explain how each might contribute to the control of the firm. What might occur if each of these controls was omitted?

Problem 14-2

Following is a partial list of embezzlement methods. In each case cite a specific internal control procedure that you feel might assist in preventing or detecting the embezzlement, and explain how the control would work.

a. "Selling" the combination to the company's safe
b. Failing to record a sale of merchandise and then pocketing the cash
c. Carrying fictitious employees on payroll and then cashing the checks
d. Collecting an account receivable which had previously been written off as bad and then pocketing the cash
e. Removing small amounts of cash from the cash register (by cashier)
f. Paying false invoices which have been submitted through collusion with vendors
g. Issuing credits or refunds for false claims for goods returned by customers
h. Stealing merchandise from the warehouse
i. Selling scrap materials and then pocketing proceeds
j. Using copies of previously used documents to support a cash disbursement
k. Destroying sales ticket and pocketing the money
l. Having merchandise ordered in company name delivered to one's home

Problem 14-3

Holladay Wholesale Supply has four operating divisions that sell goods to customers. In order to take advantage of quantity discounts and to provide additional internal control, the company has a central purchasing department. All requests for goods or services must be channeled through this department and receive the approval of Mr. Frank Alden, the purchasing agent. Mr. Alden consolidates the requests from the various divisions and prepares numbered purchase orders, which are sent directly to vendors. As goods are received, they are counted by a clerk in the receiving department and a receiving report is prepared. A copy of the receiving report is sent to the purchasing agent, and vendors' invoices, as received, are also routed directly to the purchasing department. Mr. Alden promptly compares the purchase order, the receiving report, and the vendors' invoices as to prices, quantities, extensions, footings, etc. If he finds everything in order he prepares a voucher authorizing the accounting department to make payment.

Although Holladay Wholesale pays Mr. Alden a salary of only $7,500 he has recently built a new house in Country Club Acres, an exclusive east bench subdivision. He dresses exceptionally well and drives an expensive foreign auto to work. The profits of Holladay Wholesale have slipped drastically in recent years, and the company manager suspects fraud.

Required:

Review the company's internal control, list any weaknesses noted therein, describe how fraud may have occurred, and suggest improvements in the internal control system.

Problem 14-4

The Y Company, a client of your firm, has come to you with a problem. It has three clerical employees who must perform the following functions:

1. Maintain general ledger
2. Maintain accounts payable ledger
3. Maintain accounts receivable ledger
4. Prepare checks for signature
5. Maintain disbursements journal
6. Issue credits on returns and allowances
7. Reconcile the bank accounts
8. Handle and deposit cash receipts

Assuming that there is no doubt as to the ability of any of the employees, the company requests that you assign the above functions to the three employees in such a manner as to achieve the highest degree of internal control. It may be assumed that these employees will perform no other accounting functions than the ones listed and that any accounting functions not listed will be performed by persons other than these three employees.

Required:

a. State how you would distribute the above functions among the three employees. Assume that, with the exception of the nominal jobs of the bank reconciliation and the issuances of credits on returns and allowances, all functions require an equal amount of time.
b. List four possible unsatisfactory combinations of the above listed functions.

AICPA Adapted

Problem 14-5

The Patricia Company had poor internal control over its cash transactions. Facts about its cash position on November 30, 1969, were as follows:

The cash books showed a balance of $18,901.62, which included cash on hand. A credit of $100 on the bank's records did not appear on the books of the company. The balance per the bank statement was $15,550, and outstanding checks included numbers 62 for $116.25, 183 for $150, 284 for $253.25, 8621 for $190.71, 8623 for $206.80 and 8632 for $145.28.

The cashier removed all of the cash on hand in excess of $3,794.41 and then prepared the following reconciliation:

Balance per Books, November 30, 1969		$18,901.62
Add: Outstanding checks		
No. 8621	$190.71	
No. 8623	206.80	
No. 8632	145.28	442.79
		$19,344.41
Add: Cash on hand		3,794.41
Balance per bank, November 30, 1969		$15,550.00
Deduct: Unrecorded credit		100.00
True cash, November 30, 1969		$15,450.00

Required:

a. How much did the cashier remove, and how did he attempt to conceal his theft?

b. Taking only the information given, name two specific features of internal control which were apparently missing.

c. If the cashier's October 31 reconciliation is known to be in order and you start your audit on December 5, 1969, for the year ended November 30, 1969, what specific auditing procedures would uncover the fraud?

AICPA Adapted

Problem 14-6

An internal control questionnaire includes the following items. For each item, explain what is accomplished by the existence of the controls involved.

a. Are each day's cash receipts deposited intact and without delay?

b. If an imprest (special) fund is represented by a bank account, has the bank been notified that no checks payable to the company should be accepted for deposit?

c. Are write-offs of bad debts approved by an officer?

d. Are payroll disbursements made from an imprest (special) bank account restricted to that purpose?

e. Are cash register tapes read and controlled by someone other than the cashier?

f. Are dual signatures required on all checks? If so, are blank checks signed before they are filled in?

g. Are vouchers, original vendors' invoices, and other supporting documents cancelled or mutilated after payment is made?

AICPA Adapted

Problem 14-7

The accounting and internal control procedures relating to purchases of materials by the Branden Company, a medium-sized concern manufacturing special machinery to order, have been described by your junior accountant in the following terms:

"After approval by manufacturing department foremen, material purchase requisitions are forwarded to the purchasing department supervisor, who distributes such requisitions to the several employees under his control. The latter employees prepare prenumbered purchase orders in triplicate, account for all numbers, and send the original purchase order to the vendor. One copy of the purchase order is sent to the receiving department, where it is used as a receiving report. The other copy is filed in the purchasing department.

"When the materials are received, they are moved directly to the storeroom and issued to the foremen on informal requests. The receiving department sends a receiving report (with its copy of the purchase order attached) to the purchasing department and sends copies of the receiving report to the storeroom and to the accounting department.

"Vendors' invoices for material purchases, received in duplicate in the mail room, are sent to the purchasing department and directed to the employee who placed the related order. The employee then compares the invoice with the copy of the purchase order on file in the purchasing department for price and terms and compares the invoice quantity with the quantity received as reported by the shipping and receiving department on its copy of the purchase order. The purchasing department employee also checks discounts, footings, and extensions, and initials the invoice to indicate approval for payment. The invoice is then sent to the voucher section of the accounting department, where it is coded for account distribution, assigned a voucher number, entered in the voucher register, and filed according to payment due date.

"On payment dates, prenumbered checks are requisitioned by the voucher section from the cashier and prepared except for signature. After the checks are prepared they are returned to the cashier, who puts them through a check signing machine, accounts for the sequence of numbers, and passes them to the cash disbursement bookkeeper for entry in the cash disbursements book. The cash disbursements bookkeeper then returns the checks to the voucher section, which notes payment dates in the voucher register, places the checks in envelopes, and sends them to the mail room. The vouchers are then filed in numerical sequence. At the end of each month, one of the voucher clerks prepares an adding machine tape of unpaid items in the voucher register, compares the total thereof with the general ledger balance, and investigates any difference disclosed by such comparison."

Required:

Discuss the weaknesses, if any, in the internal control of Branden's purchasing and subsequent procedures and suggest supplementary or revised procedures for remedying each weakness with regard to

a. Requisition of materials.
b. Receipt and storage of materials.
c. Functions of the purchasing department.
d. Functions of accounting department.   AICPA Adapted

Case 14
CECIL'S DIESELS

Recently Cecil Hunt, president and general manager of Cecil's Diesels, a medium-sized manufacturing company, became concerned with the increase in the cost of hand tools used in the manufacturing process. Within the past nine months, orders had been placed for more than $30,000 worth of hand tools. Normally, expenditures for hand tools have not exceeded $20,000 per year.

The company's control over hand tools is similar to that used for raw materials and supplies. Large orders must be requisitioned through the company's central purchasing department. However, if the total purchase amounts to $200 or less, the operating department is permitted to place the order directly with the vendor. When shipments are received, the goods and the invoices are sent directly to the factory where they are inventoried and stored by the storeroom clerk. The factory superintendent is required to initial all invoices before he forwards them to the accounting department, where payment is made. Mr. Hunt estimates that 75 percent of all hand tool orders amount to less than $200.

While making a tour through the factory, Mr. Hunt decided to stop by the office of the factory superintendent, Ralph Robinson, to discuss hand tool purchasing and control procedures. "Ralph, it looks like we're losing control of our hand tools. Expenditures are nearly double what they were a year ago. What do you think we ought to do about the problem?" questioned Mr. Hunt.

Mr. Robinson was surprised, as he felt his factory control was second to none. He explained that production was up substantially from a year ago, so some increase in expenditure was to be expected. Also, he noted, "They just don't make tools like they used to! The price keeps going up while the quality goes down."

The discussion continued and finally came around to the issue of purchasing procedures. Mr. Robinson felt the present system was very effective and that it saved the purchasing department time by relieving them of processing many small orders. Also, he felt that the personnel in the factory were better able to judge what type of hand tools to order. In certain cases in the past, when orders had been placed by the purchasing department the wrong tools showed up. Also, many of the suppliers' salesmen were good friends of Mr. Robinson, and he was concerned that they would not receive the same personal treatment if the purchasing were centralized. Mr. Hunt concluded the discussion and returned to his office.

On the way to his office Mr. Hunt passed the storeroom, which he noticed was unattended. Late that afternoon he called Mr. Alter, the storeroom clerk, to his office. Mr. Alter had been with the firm for fifteen years and was considered a loyal and devoted employee. Last year he was awarded the Outstanding Employee Plaque for having his inventory records within 1 percent of the physical count for the last five years.

Mr. Alter explained that he had complete charge of the storeroom. When an order was received from a vendor he personally verified the quantities received with the vendor's invoice. He also maintained the perpetual inventory records for all goods stored in the warehouse and prided himself on their accuracy. He did not allow anyone else to make entries on the stock record cards. Mr. Alter was relieved at lunch time by Joe Finney, a maintenance worker.

When questioned about the vacant storeroom earlier that afternoon, Mr. Alter explained that he was on his coffee break. Occasionally it is necessary for him to leave the stockroom unattended. When this is necessary, he has found the factory personnel to be very helpful. If they take something from the storeroom during his absence they leave a note on his desk so he can make the proper entries on the records as soon as he returns.

The purchasing and storage procedures continue to concern Mr. Hunt in spite of the explanation provided by his employees. He calls you, a management consultant, to review the procedures and to recommend changes where you feel they are appropriate.

QUESTIONS

1. Is Mr. Robinson's defense of the present system justified?
2. What weaknesses, if any, are apparent in the purchasing procedures for hand tools?
3. What weaknesses are apparent in the stockroom?
4. What change in procedures would you suggest?

15

Budgeting

A budget is a financial plan. It is a guide to all levels of management to indicate how resources should be and have been utilized in order to maximize the goals of the business enterprise. Budgets, like other plans, can vary greatly in detail. Their scope and complexity should be designed to fit the particular business and the needs of management. Generally, greater detail results in increased usefulness, but it is also accompanied by a larger cost. As in all areas of internal control, the scope of the budget should be set by carefully weighing the relative cost and benefits.

BUDGET APPROACH

Budgets may be prepared from either of two points of orientation. Both follow the organization chart, but one starts at the bottom and works up, while the other starts with the top management and works down. The first of these, the bottom-up, seems to concentrate on needs. The lowest manager in the organization prepares an estimate of his needs and then forwards it up the organizational lines to his superior. The superior consolidates this request with others in his organization, makes any changes of his own, and then passes the request up the channel. Under this system, the company budget is merely a composite of the budgets of all company components. As soon as the total budget is arrived at, top management's attention turns to the task of how the necessary funds will be raised.

The top-down approach is just the opposite. The basic assumption under this form of budgeting is that since resources are limited, the organizational requirements must be adjusted to live within these available resources. Top management establishes the total company budget, allocating resources to the various divisions of the company along organizational lines. At each management level the available budget is merely sliced into smaller pieces and the funds alloted to the various components of that organization. Each project is assigned a priority, and low-priority items are cut in order to live within the budget.

Probably the best budgets utilize to some degree principles encountered in both of these budgeting concepts. The bottom-up budget introduces the concept that *need* must be an important consideration in the budgeting process. This approach also recognizes that lower levels of management, those most familiar with actual operations, are often best equipped to determine critical needs.

On the other hand, the top-down approach recognizes that often all needs cannot be satisfied from the limited resources that may be available to the company. The best result, then, is often obtained by preparing a budget with both these concepts in mind. Such a budget will recognize that the needs of management at all levels in the organization should be considered in the budgeting process, and that these needs should be evaluated in order to live within the available resources.

BEHAVIORAL SCIENCE CONSIDERATIONS

The preceding discussion has focussed attention on the budget-making process: should it start at the top and work down through the organizational structure, or the reverse? Let us now turn our attention to a more important consideration—the *people* involved in the budgeting process. What impact will the various features of a budget have on the managers and workers who are to be judged and controlled by the budget? A management consultant recently observed:

The use of budgetary control techniques has spread throughout all kinds of industries and companies, both large and small, so that their employment in some form is now the rule rather than the exception. Inevitably, the application and operation of these techniques have been subject to misuse. Two major abuses are:

1. The indiscriminate introduction of a textbook system which is not tailored to the peculiar characteristics of the company, thus causing inefficiencies to be built into the system.
2. The operation of a budgetary control system without taking into account the peculiar characteristics of the people involved, thus tending to generate forces which in the long run decrease efficiency and negate many of the system's advantages.

There is a tendency for companies to expect results from the technique alone, failing to recognize that effective use and application of budgeting depend upon the actions of responsible individuals and an appreciation of the importance of sound interpersonal relations.[1]

Research conducted under the auspices of the Controllership Foundation disclosed at least four behavioral problems related to budgets:

1. Budget pressure tends to unite employees against management and tends to place the factory supervisor under tension. . . .
2 The budget staff can obtain feelings of success only by finding fault with factory people.
3. The use of "needlers" by top management tends to make the factory supervisors see only the problems of their own department.
4. Supervisors use budgets as a way of expressing their own patterns of leadership.[2]

Behavioral scientists have raised many important questions related to the behavior of people in response to various budgeting techniques.[3] Does a budget actually assist management in achieving company goals? What impact does the budget have on morale and productivity of the workers? Does a budget decrease the firm's long-run efficiency by introducing forces

---

[1]Michael E. Wallis, "Behavioral Consideration in Budgeting," *Management Accounting* 47 (Aug. 1966): 3.

[2]Chris Argyris, *The Impact of Budgets on People* (New York: The Controllership Foundation, Inc., 1952), p. 25, as quoted by Don T. DeCoster and John T. Ferkatis in "Budget Induced Pressure and Its Relationship to Supervisory Behavior," *Journal of Accounting Research* 6 (Autumn 1968): 237.

[3]See, for example, Selwyn W. Becker and David Green, Jr., "Budgeting and Employee Behavior," *The Journal of Business* 35 (Oct. 1962): 392-402; Andrew C. Stedry, "Budgeting and Employee Behavior: A Reply," *The Journal of Business* 37 (Apr. 1964): 195-202; Selwyn W. Becker and David Green, Jr., "Budgeting and Employee Behavior: A Rejoinder to a 'Reply,'" *The Journal of Business* 37 (Apr. 1964): 203-5; Wallis, op. cit.; Argyris, op. cit.

that work counter to the budget's stated objectives? While the answers to these questions are not yet clear, sufficient evidence has been accumulated to make it apparent that the behavioral science implications of budgeting cannot be taken lightly.

PREPARING THE BUDGET

The company-wide budget, sometimes referred to as a master budget, is prepared from a number of separate forecasts, including:

1. The sales forecast
2. The cost of sales forecast
3. The selling expense forecast
4. The administrative expense forecast
5. The capital expenditure forecast
6. The cash forecast

The above forecasts will provide most of the figures necessary to project an income statement for the budget period and a balance sheet for the end of the budget year.

The Sales Forecast

The key to the usefulness of the master budget lies in the accuracy of the sales forecast. Great care must be taken in its preparation because each of the other component forecasts is based upon figures arrived at from the forecasted sales. The master budget will reflect amost geometrically an error made in the sales forecast because of the close relationship of this forecast to each of the other components.

Preparation of a sales forecast will vary greatly, depending upon the size and geographical territory covered by the company. There are certain basic factors, however, that should be considered in all cases. The importance of and difficulty in appraising each of these will, of course, differ from company to company.

Economic Climate. An appraisal of the general economic outlook in all areas served by the company is an essential first step. Generally, there are published economic forecasts for most major sectors. These must be carefully evaluated in terms of the specific locations of the company's sales outlets. For example, the economic outlook for a given state may be very favorable, while the outlook for a certain community in that state might be very dim. Local strikes, drought conditions, or any number of other factors could adversely affect what might otherwise be a cheerful economic picture.

Industry Outlook.   Once the economic outlook is settled, it is necessary to forecast, in general terms at least, the outlook for a particular industry. Not all industries share equally in prosperity. Trade associations and government estimates often are helpful in forecasting industry sales. Each year the presidents of the major automobile companies, for example, predict the industry's sales. It is interesting to note that the three big automobile producers generally come up with relatively close forecasts as to what their industry will do.

Market Shares.   The company must next estimate what it can reasonably expect to capture as its share of the industry output. What is its competitive position? How has it changed from previous years? This forecast must be very detailed by product line and sales territory. It is not sufficient for Chevrolet to forecast that it will sell one million automobiles in a given year. It must also predict how many of each model it will sell and which dealers will sell them. Nothing can produce more havoc with a budget than to gear to produce Camaros, for example, and have the orders flood in for Impalas instead.

Trend in Buyer Tastes.   At each level of sales forecasting, management must realistically appraise the change in trends in buyer tastes. Too often we tend to look at last year as a firm guide for the coming year. Buyers are fickle. Their tastes change, and the budget must attempt to forecast the direction and degree of these changes.

Changes in Product Line.   If possible, the company should try to pretest new products in carefully controlled market studies. These studies, not mere guesswork, should serve as the basis for estimating the sales of the new product. Consideration should also be given to other contemplated changes in sales factors, such as increasing the sales force or expanding into new territories.

The Cost of Sales Forecast

Because costs vary greatly according to the level of production, the cost of sales can be forecast only after projected sales have been forecast. The quantities to be produced (or purchased) are arrived at by considering the quantities that are expected to be sold, together with the desired inventory levels. The purchases (or production) will be equal to the change in inventory levels. Thus, the problem of forecasting the cost of sales is a function of the projected inventory levels. These two figures must be forecast simultaneously.

Establishing the cost of sales forecast for a nonmanufacturing firm is generally accomplished by merely extending the quantities forecast in the sales budget (plus or minus the projected inventory change) by their estimated prices. Reference is usually made to current catalog prices, with consideration given to any expected price changes.

Forecasting the cost of sales for a manufacturing enterprise is much more complex because estimates must be made of all manufacturing costs. Generally, this can best be accomplished by preparing separate material, manpower, and overhead forecasts. These forecasts should be extended at prices expected to prevail in the budget period for the particular level of production forecast. Special attention should be paid to possible price changes, pending labor negotiations, and expected level of production.

In regard to the expected level of production, two possible approaches might be followed. The first would be to project the most likely level of operation and then forecast costs at that level. This would be known as a *static budget,* and the figures so developed would be utilized as the budget, regardless of the actual level of production achieved. A second approach would be to prepare several different budgets, each based upon costs that might be expected at a different level of production. This series of budgets is known as a *flexible budget.* The company would select from the flexible budget those figures that corresponded to the actual level of production. A flexible budget is illustrated later in the chapter.

Selling Expense Forecast

Many selling expenses vary directly with sales volume and can be most accurately forecast by reference to sales figures already computed. For example, salesmen are often at least partially compensated on a commission basis. Salesmen's commissions, then, could easily be calculated by multiplying the fixed contractual rate by the dollar sales volume. Other selling expenses can be forecast by referring to prior periods and revising these costs to reflect expected conditions. Adequate attention should be given to forecasting the expense of any special promotional cost for new products and new territories. Product expansion often does not come cheap in terms of advertising and promotional costs, and realistic estimates must be made at the same time that the increase in volume is calculated. Optimistic sales personnel sometimes do not give sufficient thought to the cost of promotion in their enthusiasm for the product.

Administrative Expense Forecast

The administrative forecast is probably the most fixed of all forecasts made in the budgeting process. For this reason, most administrative costs may be estimated from the prior period costs with consideration being given, of course, to any contemplated changes. The problem with relying on past costs as guides to future costs is the danger of assuming that, because these are accomplished facts, they are proper. Administrative costs should be subject to careful scrutiny each period, even though they do not vary as much as other costs. A recent article in the Wall Street Journal noted the increased tendency of companies to spend large sums on exotic decor and lavish office facilities for executives. Once these special services are acquired, they tend to remain in many companies without review or question. The Wall Street Journal noted that "since the mid-1930's, David Sarnoff, chairman of Radio Corporation of America, has been getting his usual 10:00 a.m. shave in the private one-chair barber shop adjacent to his office."[4] Sound internal control requires that every material item in a budget be reviewed as to need and propriety. It seems that special care should be exercised in the area of administrative expenses.

The Capital Expenditure Forecast

A capital expenditure represents an outlay for a fixed asset. Such expenditures are expected to provide benefits that will last beyond the current period. Capital expenditures represent outlays (usually in the form of cash) made during the budget period that do not represent expenses in that period and, therefore, have not been included in other forecasts.

Inasmuch as capital expenditures affect numerous accounting periods, it is necessary to make longer term forecasts in this area. Capital budgets are often made for five-, ten-, and twenty-year periods. The detail found in the budget for the coming year, of course, should greatly exceed that found for the fifth or tenth year. As the particular budget period draws near, the forecast is revised to reflect this increased detail.

Most companies face a never-ending array of requests for capital assets. Effective budgeting requires that management have some method of ranking and evaluating these requests. Some of the major techniques that have been used for this purpose are discussed in chapter 20.

Once a request has been approved, it becomes a part of the capital expenditure forecast for that specific budget period, subject, of course, to future consideration and evaluation before the expenditure is actually made. Approved projects at estimated costs constitute the current capital expenditure budget. It should be noted that cost estimates must be continually reviewed because of inflation and other factors. In many instances, fixed assets are not constructed or purchased until several years after the original cost estimates have been made. These figures should not be incorporated into the budget until consideration has been given to the price level changes that have occurred in the interim.

---

[4]*Wall Street Journal*, July 16, 1965, p. 1.

The Cash Forecast

The cash forecast attempts to predict cash receipts and expenditures for a given period of time. In a cash forecast, the intervals are generally rather short because of the necessity of maintaining a debit balance in the cash account at all times. It is not sufficient to know that total cash receipts will exceed the total cash disbursement for the coming year. It is important to know when these cash flows occur, in order to assure that sufficient funds will be on deposit in the bank to cover each check issued. Generally, cash forecasts are prepared for a one-year period, but are broken down to show expected receipts and disbursements by month, or at least by quarter.

For most concerns there are at least three major sources of cash: *collection on account and/or cash sales, contributions of owners*, and *borrowing*. Collections on account are forecast by applying the company's collection experience to the sales forecast previously developed. The average collection period experienced in recent accounting periods can usually be used for this purpose. For example, if experience indicates that 50 percent of the sales on account are collected during the month following the sale and 25 percent in each of the two succeeding months, then we can recognize this delay in preparing a cash forecast. Thus, if sales of $100,000 are forecast for January, cash flows from these sales of $50,000 in February, $25,000 in March, and $25,000 in April would be forecast. Projected cash sales would be added to these figures to arrive at forecasted operating receipts. Investments by owners and borrowing would generally be used only to supplement this operating inflow to the extent necessary to assure proper cash balances are maintained.

Cash outflows are similarly projected from figures arrived at in other forecasts. Major classes of expenditures likely would include payment for

1. Accounts payable,
2. Payrolls,
3. Other out-of-pocket factory costs,[5]
4. Administrative expenses,[5]
5. Selling expenses,[5]
6. Capital expenditures, and
7. Dividends.

Payments on account are estimated by referring to the purchase forecast as well as to the discount and credit terms offered by suppliers. It is

---

[5]In the cash budget, the expense figures should only include items which will require cash expenditure. Expenses such as depreciation are excluded because we are trying to forcast cash flows rather than income.

generally sound business to plan to make all payments within the discount period.[6] Payments other than on account can be estimated by referring to other forecasts previously mentioned.

The final step in preparing the cash budget is to compute the cash shortage or excess. Cash shortages are generally covered by additional investment by the owners, or through borrowing. Excess funds are normally invested.

Illustration of Cash Forecast

In preparing the cash forecast for the One-Stop Department Store for the first half of the coming year, the controller assembled the following data (in thousands of dollars):

	NOV.	DEC.	JAN.	FEB.	MAR.	APR.	MAY	JUNE
Sales	$720	$960	$240	$360	$600	$360	$480	$240
Merchandise Purchases	300	400	100	500	400	100	100	600
Equipment Purchases				400				
Quarterly Tax Payments			15			15		

Past experience has shown that about one-sixth of the company's sales and one-tenth of its purchases are for cash, and the balance is on account. The terms with most suppliers are net thirty days. The receivables have been collected at the rate of 25 percent in the month of the sale, 60 percent in the next month, 13 percent in the next month, and 2 percent have proved uncollectible. The equipment purchase will require a 25 percent down payment and twelve monthly payments of $25,000. The company has $200,000 outstanding from a fall working-capital loan which it plans to repay in January. Expenditures for selling expenses have been $20,000 per month, plus 10 percent of the month's sales, while payments for administrative expenses have been $30,000 per month.

A cash forecast based upon the foregoing data appears as Figure 15-1.

The amount and timing of loans, repayments, investments in securities, and liquidation of securities are forced into the cash budget after all other figures have been forecast. These might be designated as the balancing figures. Generally a company temporarily invests any excess cash in short-term securities and then liquidates these investments as the funds are needed. When additional cash is required, it is usually borrowed for a short term and is repaid in periods of net cash gain.

---

[6]It has already been noted that terms 2/10; n/30 (2 percent discount if paid within ten days, the total amount due within thirty days) amounts to earning interest at the rate of 36 percent per annum.

Figure 15-1

ONE-STOP DEPARTMENT STORE
Cash Forecast Summary
For the Six Months Ended June 30, 19XX

	JAN.	FEB.	MAR.	APR.	MAY	JUNE
Receipts (see Schedule A)	$648	$359	$431	$474	$445	$369
Payments (see Schedule B)	459	326	625	496	223	249
NET CASH GAIN (LOSS)	$189	$ 33	($194)	($ 22)	$222	$120
Cash balance, beginning of month ..	$ 35	$ 22	$ 55	$ 36	$ 13	$ 9
Net cash gain (loss)	189	33	(194)	(22)	222	120
Borrowing (repayment)	(200)	..	175	..	(175)	..
Security liquidation (investment)	..	..	..	..	(50)	(120)
Interest earned (paid)	(2)	..	..	(1)	(1)	1
CASH BALANCE, end of month...	$ 22	$ 55	$ 36	$ 13	$ 9	$ 10

Schedule A
Projected Cash Receipts
For the Six Months Ended June 30, 19XX

	JAN.	FEB.	MAR.	APR.	MAY	JUNE
Cash sales (one-sixth)	$ 40	$ 60	$100	$ 60	$ 80	$ 40
Collections on account						
25 percent month of sale	50	75	125	75	100	50
60 percent next month	480	120	180	300	180	240
13 percent next month	78	104	26	39	85	39
	$648	$359	$431	$474	$445	$369

Schedule B
Projected Cash Disbursements
For the Six Months Ended June 30, 19XX

	JAN.	FEB.	MAR.	APR.	MAY	JUNE
Merchandise						
Cash purchase (10 percent)	$ 10	$ 50	$ 40	$ 10	$ 10	$ 60
Payment on account (30 day) ...	360	90	450	360	90	90
Administrative expense	30	30	30	30	30	30
Selling expenses:						
Fixed	20	20	20	20	20	20
Variable (10 percent of sales) ...	24	36	60	36	48	24
Equipment						
Down payment (25 percent)		100				
Installments (12 equal)			25	25	25	25
Tax payments	15			15		
	$459	$326	$625	$496	$223	$249

THE MASTER BUDGET

Pulling all the parts together into a master budget which will really be a useful management tool is not an easy task. To begin with, many of the factors discussed separately in this chapter are really mutually determined. For example, the sales forecast cannot be prepared without considering capital expenditures that may be needed to provide necessary production. Capital expenditure budgets, by the same token, cannot be prepared without regard to available funds as reflected in the cash budget. There are so many variables that the real art lies in pulling the interrelated pieces together into a master budget.

Most companies rely on a budget committee to prepare the master budget. This committee generally consists of the controller (or other chief financial officer) and the heads of the major divisions. It is customary for the controller to serve as chairman of the budget committee, the group charged with the responsibility of compiling, implementing, and reviewing the budget.

Periodic comparisons of actual and budgeted figures on a regular basis are essential if the budget is going to serve as an effective management guide. Most budgets are broken down by quarter or even by month. During these periods, regular comparisons are made to see how actual operating conditions coincide with those predicted in the budget. When expended amounts are over or under budgeted amounts, an explanation is required. Major deviations should be carefully examined by the budget committee and, where warranted, supplemental appropriations approved.

THE FLEXIBLE BUDGET

The flexible budget is really just a series of budgets, each one designed for a different level of production. Management simply selects the one most appropriate, as determined by the percent of capacity at which the company actually operates. Flexible budgets are prepared under the theory that all costs can be classified as either fixed or variable. Fixed costs are those that are fixed in total dollar amount but vary per unit of production. Variable costs, on the other hand, vary directly with production (or sales) in total, but remain constant per unit. Many costs, of course, are neither fixed nor variable. These, sometimes called semi-variable costs, must be broken into their fixed and variable components.

A flexible budget for the assembly department of the Balmer Banjo Company is shown in Figure 15-2. The first step in constructing this type of budget is to project the costs at the standard, or ideal, attainable level of production. These costs are then classified as fixed or variable or, where

Figure 15-2

BALMER BANJO COMPANY
Assembly Department
Flexible Monthly Manufacturing Overhead Budget

	TYPE CF COST	BUDGETED AT							
		110 PERCENT		100 PERCENT		90 PERCENT		80 PERCENT	
		COMPONENT	TOTAL	COMPONENT	TOTAL	COMPONENT	TOTAL	COMPONENT	TOTAL
Foreman	F		$16,500		$16,500		$16,500		$16,500
Building repairs	F		900		900		900		900
Machine repairs	F	$ 400		$ 400		$ 400		$ 400	
	V	880	1,280	800	1,200	720	1,120	640	1,040
Depreciation, building	F		12,500		12,500		12,500		12,500
Depreciation, machinery	V		2,200		2,000		1,800		1,600
Factory supplies	F	800		800		800		800	
	V	1,870	2,670	1,700	2,500	1,530	2,330	1,360	2,160
Fire insurance	F		2,100		2,100		2,100		2,100
Property tax	F		3,300		3,300		3,300		3,300
Heat	F		1,600		1,600		1,600		1,600
Light and power	F	700		700		700		700	
	V	2,640	3,340	2,400	3,100	2,160	2,860	1,920	2,620
Payroll taxes	F	950		950		950		950	
	V	4,730	5,680	4,300	5,250	3,870	4,820	3,440	4,390
Custodial labor	F	8,400		8,400		8,400		8,400	
	V	1,100	9,500	1,000	9,400	900	9,300	800	9,200
Other indirect labor	F	12,100		12,100		12,100		12,100	
	V	4,400	16,500	4,000	16,100	3,600	15,700	3,200	15,300
Total budgeted overhead			$78,070		$76,450		$74,830		$73,210
Projected direct labor hours			27,500		25,000		22,500		20,000
Budgeted overhead rate per hour			$2.84		$3.06		$3.66		$3.33

necessary, broken into their fixed and variable components. The fixed costs are carried at the same figure into the budget at each level of production. The variable costs are assumed to vary directly with production, and are calculated in each case as a percent of the standard costs, the percentage used being the same as the percent of standard at which the company would be operating. For example, the variable machine repairs for banjos are projected at $800 at standard volume and at 110 percent of this figure ($880) at 110 percent of standard volume. As soon as all costs have been projected, the budget for each level can be totaled and the various overhead rates calculated.

In preparing a flexible budget, management is really admitting the uncertainty of the future and preparing a budget for any eventuality. When the actual volume of output is known, the proper budget can be selected to help control the costs at that particular level of production.

It should be noted that the flexible budgeting concept has application in many areas besides overhead and even manufacturing operations. A flexible budget might similarly be used by a department store, for example, except that in this case the variable costs would be assumed to vary with sales rather than with production. In all instances where volume is difficult to project, the flexible budget can be a useful control device.

SUMMARY

Budgets are financial plans designed to increase efficiency by providing control over the costs of an enterprise. They may be prepared from either of two points of orientation. Bottom-up budgets start with the requests of the lowest budget division of a company and work up through the organization. At each level the requests are reviewed, then consolidated and passed to the next higher level in the organization. Top-down budgets start with the establishment of a company-wide budget that is successively sliced into smaller and smaller segments as budgeted amounts are assigned to the various divisions. There are numerous human behavior problems that must be considered in establishing and implementing the budget.

The preparation of a master, or company-wide, budget is an extremely complex task. Forecasts must be made of sales, cost of sales, production levels, material purchases, manpower requirements, overhead costs, inventory levels, selling and administrative expenses, cash position, and expected capital equipment expenditures. Each of these forecasts is related to others, but the most critical relationship is with the sales forecast. The accuracy of each of the other forecasts is directly tied to the reliability of the sales forecast.

Budgets are useful as control devices only to the extent that periodic comparisons are made between budgeted and actual figures. Variances from budgeted amounts should be closely investigated and adequately justified before revisions are made.

QUESTIONS

1. Why might the sales forecast be called the key to successful budgeting? How is the sales forecast related to other forecasts which are necessary in the budgeting process?
2. Why is it desirable to make periodic comparisons between budgeted and actual costs? What action should be taken when sizeable differences exist?
3. What are the two "points of orientation" from which a budget can be prepared? What are the relative advantages and disadvantages of each?
4. What are some of the important considerations in preparing a sales forecast? How is some of this essential information obtained?
5. What is a flexible budget? What is a static budget? When would each be useful? What advantages and disadvantages do you see in a flexible budget?
6. What are capital expenditures? How does the period for capital budgeting differ from that required for cash budgeting?
7. Why do capital expenditures often exceed the original estimates?
8. Why is cash forecasting of major importance to a business enterprise? Can a company have too much cash?
9. Define fixed and variable costs. Can all costs be so classified? Explain.
10. In preparing a cash budget, when and how should the collections on customers' accounts be shown?
11. What causes the overhead rate in a flexible budget to differ at various levels of production? Does the overhead rate increase or decrease as the company approaches plant capacity?
12. What group is generally responsible for preparation of the master budget? Of whom does this group usually consist?

PROBLEMS

Problem 15-1

On April 1, 1971, the Sigma Sales Company applied to the Mid-State Bank for a short-term inventory loan. It is the firm's intention to borrow sufficient cash to acquire needed inventory during the peak season and to repay the loan from cash collected from the sales. The vice president of the Mid-State Bank is familiar with this type of loan and asks Sigma Sales to present a detailed cash forecast for the next six months, indicating how the cash will be used and how the loan will be repaid. Sigma purchases all goods on terms of 2/10; n/30 and follows the practice of taking all available discounts. Merchandise is sold to Sigma customers on ninety-day, interest-free contracts. The contracts require one-fourth down and the balance in three equal, thirty-day installments. The sales and purchase forecasts appear below (in thousands of dollars):

	JAN.	FEB.	MAR.	APR.	MAY	JUNE	JULY	AUG.	SEPT.
Sales[a]	400	500	500	1,100	2,000	1,500	800	500	500
Purchases (gross)[a] .	300	400	800	1,000	500	400	200	200	200

[a]Assume that all purchases and sales occur on the last day of the month.

Salesmen's commissions are 10 percent of sales and are paid in the month following sale. Other selling expenses are paid in the month of sale and are usually about 15 percent of the sales of that month. Administrative expenses are $50,000 per month regardless of sales volume. The depreciation expense is $20,000 per month, and no new equipment purchases are anticipated during this budget period.

The bank officials indicate that if they are satisfied with Sigma's projected cash flows, a loan sufficient to meet the maximum cash requirements can be granted within two or three days. The entire loan would be deposited in the company's checking account at that time. In the event a loan is granted, payments will be accepted by the bank in any amount in excess of $50,000. Interest will be charged at the rate of 6 percent on the unpaid balance, but a full month's interest will be charged for any fraction of a month during which a balance is outstanding. Sigma's cash balance on April 1, 1971, is $28,000, and the company requires a minimum operating balance of $25,000.

Required:

a. Prepare a cash forecast for the Sigma Sales Company for the six months ended September 30.

b. What is the maximum amount of loan required? When could the loan be repaid?

Problem 15-2

The sales forecast for the next eight months for a model F37 ball-point pen manufacturer by Easyrite Manufacturing Company is shown below:

	SALES BUDGET (IN 000 UNITS)
July	10,000
August	15,000
September	8,000
October	7,000
November	9,000
December	10,000
January	5,000
February	4,000

The company attempts to maintain an inventory of finished goods on hand at the beginning of each month of 80 percent of the sales anticipated during that month. The balance of the goods required for sale is manufactured during the month of sale. Inasmuch as the manufacturing process is very short, the company never has any goods in process at the end of a day. Each ball-point pen requires the following parts:

Plastic	3 units
Cartridge	1 unit

The company has several sources from which the plastic can be purchased and accordingly attempts to have an inventory on hand at the beginning of each month sufficient to satisfy one-half of that month's production. Cartridges, on the other hand, are purchased from a single source. In order to avoid production delays that might be caused by a strike of the supplier, a two-months' supply of cartridges should be on hand at the beginning of each month. The inventories on hand at July 1 are as follows:

Finished pens	7,990 units
Plastic (raw material)	15,100 units
Cartridges (raw material) ....:....	29,000 units

Required:

Prepare a budget showing the quantities of plastic and cartridges that should be purchased during the months of July, August, September, October, and November.

Problem 15-3

The ball-point pens referred to in problem 15-2 are manufactured on an assembly line. Three types of employees are used in the production process: assemblers, testers, and packagers. The assemblers are paid $1.75 per hour, testers are paid $4.00 per hour, and packagers are paid $2.25 per hour. The company has experienced no difficulty in the past in finding a sufficient number of employees. In fact, a waiting list is maintained from which the personnel department can call in new employees as needed. None of the jobs requires any extensive training since the tasks performed are relatively simple.

The manufacture of a model F37 ball-point pen requires direct labor as follows (these standard times allow for rest periods, set-up time, etc.):

Assembler	16 minutes
Tester	4 minutes
Packager	2 minutes

Employees may be dismissed without any notice, but once they are called to work they are entitled to a full eight-hours' pay. The company operates eight hours per day, twenty-two days per month.

Required:

Prepare a budget showing the man-hours and labor costs for each class of labor for each of the six months remaining in the current year. Refer to problem 15-2 for sales forecast.

Problem 15-4

Gregory Products Company manufactures an office desk that is marketed on a national basis. About 40 percent of the units sold during the past several years have been on government contract; the balance was sold through retail office supply dealers. Gregory has accounted for 7 percent of the industry desk sales and expects to maintain its share of the market. A reliable industry trade magazine has forecast total industry desk sales of 2,000,000 units for the coming year. Gregory's desks have been sold to dealers at $122 each and to the government at $104 each.

The company estimates fixed manufacturing costs of $1,500,000 and fixed administrative expenses of $1,000,000. Variable costs associated with production of each desk are estimated as follows:

Variable manufacturing	$75.00
Advertising expense[a]	0.50
Selling expense[a]	1.00

[a]Only applies to desks sold to dealers.

Federal and state income taxes are expected to be 50 percent of net income before taxes. The company now has an inventory of 10,000 desks (cost $830,000) and plans a year-end inventory of 10 percent of the current year's sales.

Required:

a. How many desks should Gregory Products plan to produce next year?

b. Prepare an estimated income statement for the year.

Problem 15-5

The Hopsing Laundry Company has compiled the following information from budgets pertaining to the first quarter of its fiscal year:

	JULY	AUGUST	SEPTEMBER
Purchases of merchandise	$79,000	$ 85,500	$103,000
Purchase of equipment		9,200	
Payment of quarterly dividend ..		15,000	
Payroll	10,000	11,000	12,000
Payment for cash expense	5,600	4,700	6,200
Sales	89,000	122,000	185,000

The company estimates that 80 percent of the sales is made on account. Past experience indicates that 10 percent is collected in the month of sale,

75 percent in the next month, 14 percent in the third month, and 1 percent proves uncollectible.

All merchandise is purchased on account and paid for in the month following purchase. The equipment will be purchased on a C.O.D. basis.

The employees are paid on the tenth of the month for the last half of the preceding month and on the twenty-fifth of the month for the first half of the current month. Each payroll represents one-half of the total monthly payroll.

The company had the following account balances at July 1 of the current year:

Cash	$16,300
Accounts Receivable	43,400
Accounts Payable	71,000
Payroll Payable	5,000

An aging of the July 1 Accounts Receivable balance indicates that $29,000 should be collected in July, $11,500 in August, and $2,800 in September.

Required:

Prepare cash budgets for the months of July, August, and September.

Problem 15-6

Data pertaining to the operation of Twin Peak Sales Company have been forecast for the year 1970 as follows:

1. Net sales for the year are estimated at $5,400,000, with 10 percent of the sales coming in the month of December. The salesmen are paid an 8 percent commission, payment being made in the month following the sale. Commissions accrued at the end of 1969 were $51,000.
2. In addition to their commissions, the forty salesmen are each paid a base salary of $200 per month, payment being made on the tenth of the following month.
3. Administrative salaries have totalled $12,000 per month during the past year. A 5 percent across-the-board pay increase for all administrative personnel will become effective April 1, 1970. Administrative salaries are paid on the tenth of the following month.
4. The building rent is $17,500 per month and is payable the first day of each month. Thirty percent of the building space is used for administrative purposes, and the balance is the sales floor.
5. The annual fire insurance premium (assessed on a square-footage basis) in the amount of $4,400 was paid on November 1, 1969. The state insurance commission has just approved a 6 percent rate increase for fire insurance companies insuring in the company area. This increase is effective on July 1, 1970, on all premiums due after that date.
6. The office equipment is recorded on the company books at a cost of $125,000 and the sales furniture and fixtures at $640,000. All equipment is depreciated on a straight-line basis at a 10 percent per annum rate.

7. Office supplies on hand at January 1, 1970, were $5,950. It is estimated that $50,000 of office supplies will be used during the year and that $7,000 in office supplies will be on hand at the end of the year.
8. The company has prepaid advertising pertaining to the year 1970 in the amount of $15,400. Contracts for advertising will require payments of $122,850 during the year. It is estimated that prepaid advertising will amount to $10,000 at December 31, 1970.
9. Salesmen's travel expenses are budgeted at $8,000 per month, and executive travel (other than sales) expenses are budgeted at $3,000 per month. The Travel Advances account had a balance of $4,350 ($2,000 sales advances) at January 1, 1970 and is expected to have a zero balance at the end of the year.
10. Other cash administrative expenses are budgeted at $45,200 and other cash selling expenses at $73,150.

Required:
a. Prepare a budget for selling expenses for the year 1970.
b. Prepare a budget for administrative expenses for the year 1970.
c. Prepare a budget of cash payments pertaining to selling expenses for the year 1970 (to be incorporated in a cash budget).
d. Prepare a budget of cash payments pertaining to administrative expenses for the year 1970 (to be incorporated in a cash budget).

Problem 15-7

The Standard Mercantile Corporation is a wholesaler which ends its fiscal year on December 31. As the company's CPA you have been requested in early January 1971 to assist in the preparation of a cash forecast. The following information is available regarding the company's operations:

1. Management believes the 1970 sales pattern is a reasonable estimate of 1971 sales. Sales in 1970 were as follows:

January	$ 360,000
February	420,000
March	600,000
April	540,000
May	480,000
June	400,000
July	350,000
August	550,000
September	500,000
October	400,000
November	600,000
December	800,000
Total	$6,000,000

2. The accounts receivable at December 31 total $380,000. Sales collections are generally made as follows:

During month of sale	60 percent
In first subsequent month	30 percent
In second subsequent month	9 percent
Uncollectible	1 percent

3. The purchase cost of goods averages 60 percent of selling price. The cost of the inventory on hand at December 31 is $840,000, of which $30,000 is obsolete. Arrangements have been made to sell the obsolete inventory in January at half of the normal selling price on a C.O.D. basis.

   The company wishes to maintain the inventory as of the first of each month at the level of predicted sales for the next three months as determined by the sales forecast. All purchases are paid for on the tenth of the following month. Accounts payable for purchases at December 31 total $370,000.

4. Recurring fixed expenses amount to $120,000 per month, including depreciation of $20,000. For accounting purposes the company apportions the recurring fixed expenses to the various months in the same proportion as the ratio of that month's estimated sales to the estimated total annual sales. Variable expenses amount to 10 percent of sales. Payments for expenses are made as follows:

	DURING MONTH INCURRED	FOLLOWING MONTH
Fixed expenses	55%	45%
Variable expenses	70%	30%

5. Annual property taxes amount to $50,000 and are paid in equal installments on December 31 and March 31. The property taxes are in addition to the expenses in item 4 above.
6. It is anticipated that cash dividends of $20,000 will be paid each quarter on the fifteenth day of the third month.
7. During the winter, unusual advertising costs requiring cash payments of $10,000 in February and $15,000 in March will be incurred. The advertising costs are in addition to the expenses in item 4 above.
8. Equipment replacements are made at the rate of $3,000 per month. The equipment has an average estimated life of six years.
9. The company has filed a declaration of estimated income taxes which will require payment of $60,000 on March 31, 1971.
10. At December 31, 1970, the company had a bank loan with an unpaid balance of $280,000. The loan requires a principal payment of $20,000 on the last day of each month, plus interest at ½ percent per month on the unpaid balance at the first of the month. The entire balance is due on March 31, 1971.
11. The cash balance at December 31, 1970, is $100,000.

Required:

Prepare a month-by-month cash forecast statement for the first three months of 1971 for the Standard Mercantile Corporation. The statement should show the amount of cash on hand (or deficiency of cash) at the end of each month. All computations and supporting schedules should be presented in good form.

AICPA Adapted

Case 15
GREEN THUMB PRODUCTS, INC.

Mr. J. P. Wagner founded Green Thumb Products, Inc. in 1960. Green Thumb produces gardening tools that are distributed on a regional basis by wholesalers. In 1969 the company tripled its sales through an agreement to supply a regional retail chain with gardening tools, and Mr. Wagner expects sales to continue growing over the next few years.

In order to meet the increasing demand for the company's products, Mr. Wagner has ordered a new machine for a total contract price of $5,000. The machine is scheduled to arrive in February, at which time it will be necessary to pay 50 percent of the purchase price. The balance will be paid in five equal monthly installments beginning in March.

Mr. Wagner is concerned about the possible strain this purchase will place on the company's cash position. He would like to arrange a loan with the local bank, but is not sure how much he will need or just when the company would be able to repay the loan. Since he is sure the bank will raise these same questions he asks you, as a junior accountant, to prepare a report which he can present to the bank to support his loan application. After considerable research, you locate the following information.

Green Thumb's sales are seasonal, but constant production is maintained throughout the year. The company's gross margin has remained rather constant in recent years. Production costs are all cash expenditures except for depreciation of plant and equipment, which has amounted to $1,000 per year. All operating expenses except bad-debt expense represent cash expenditures. These operating expenditures are expected to amount to $500 per month during the coming year. The present policy of paying dividends semiannually on June 1 and December 1 is expected to be maintained with no change in the dividend rate. Mortgage payments are due December 31 of each year. The company's estimated tax liability for the coming year is $2,000, to be paid in four quarterly installments in January, April, July, and October.

The company has decided to engage in a vigorous advertising program during the coming year. Brochures have already been ordered and are to be delivered in February, at which time the entire $1,000 cost is to be paid. The brochures will be distributed in February and November to wholesale and retail outlets to introduce them to Green Thumb products. Mailing costs are expected to be $250 per mailing.

Green Thumb products are sold on terms of 2/10; n/30. Unfortunately, the company has not been too successful in collecting its receivables. Experience has shown that 20 percent of the sales are collected in the month of sale and within the discount period; 10 percent of the sales are collected in the month following the sale but still within the discount period; 15 percent of the sales are collected in the month following the sale and no discount is taken on them; 50 percent of the sales are collected in the second month following the sale and no discount is taken; and 5 percent of the sales are never collected.

The company has followed a policy of maintaining a minimum cash balance of $1,000 at all times. Mr. Wagner estimates any excess cash can be invested at the rate of 5 percent per annum and that borrowed funds will cost the company 8 percent per annum.

QUESTIONS

1. Prepare a cash forecast summary with all the necessary back-up schedules.
2. Prepare a projected income statement for 1970.
3. When will it be necessary for Mr. Wagner to borrow money?
4. How much should he borrow?
5. Should Mr. Wagner apply for a short-term or a long-term loan?
6. When can Mr. Wagner begin to repay the loan?

Exhibit 15-1

GREEN THUMB PRODUCTS, INC.
Balance Sheet
December 31, 1969

Current Assets:		
Cash		$ 1,020
Accounts receivable (net)		3,360
Inventories		5,920
Fixed Assets:		
Plant and equipment	$29,810	
Accumulated depreciation	10,940	18,870
Other assets		740
Total		$29,910
Current Liabilities:		
Accounts payable		$ 3,110
Miscellaneous accruals		500
Mortgage current		500
Long-term Liabilities:		
Mortgage payable		6,500

Stockholders' Equity:

Common stock ($20 par)	10,000
Capital in excess	2,000
Retained earnings	7,600
	$29,910

Exhibit 15-2

GREEN THUMB PRODUCTS, INC.
Income Statement
For the Year Ending December 31, 1969

Sales	$77,450
Cost of goods sold	64,980
Gross profit	$12,470
Operating expenses	5,470
Earnings before taxes	$ 7,000
Federal income tax	1,400
Net income	$ 5,600
Dividends	1,000
Addition to retained earnings	$ 4,600

Exhibit 15-3

GREEN THUMB PRODUCTS, INC.

	ESTIMATED SALES, 1970	ACTUAL SALES, 1969
January	$ 5,700	$ 6,400
February	7,875	7,500
March	11,000	9,000
April	11,450	11,500
May	12,800	12,000
June	7,250	7,060
July	6,000	6,200
August	5,050	5,000
September	2,880	2,790
October	2,700	2,600
November	2,840	2,900
December	5,400	4,500
	$80,945	$77,450

16

Income Taxes
and
Business Decisions

Since the United States Constitution was amended to authorize an income tax in 1913, these taxes have continued to grow in importance. Today, income taxes are the major source of revenue for the federal government and are an increasingly important source for many state and local governments. In fiscal year 1968, the federal receipts from personal income tax were nearly 68 billion dollars and from corporate income taxes approximately 32 billion dollars.[1] Total federal government receipts for the same year were approximately 156 billion dollars. Thus, income tax accounted for nearly two-thirds of the federal government's receipts in fiscal year 1968. As income tax receipts have grown to be the major source of federal revenue, the tax laws have become an increasingly important factor in the management decision-making process. It has now become commonplace for the businessman to call on his CPA and attorney for advice regarding the tax consequences of a particular proposal.

---

[1]The Annual Report of the Council of Economic Advisors, p. 281.

The effect of income taxes on business decisions is much too comprehensive a subject to be covered in the scope of this course. In fact, the subject is so complex and ever changing that even those who devote full time to tax problems find themselves in need of constant updating. Nevertheless, the modern business executive must be familiar with those major provisions of the tax law which provide for special choices. These provisions allow the taxpayer to choose among alternate tax methods which often have a significant impact on the amount of the tax liability, or at least on the timing of tax payments. While the businessman cannot be expected to master all of the provisions of the tax law, he should be sufficiently familiar with the various alternatives so that he can seek the advice of a professional tax advisor when the need arises.

THE TAX UNIT

Even before a business unit is formed, consideration must be given to income taxes inasmuch as the tax liability itself is affected by the legal form the business takes. If the business enterprise is organized as an individual proprietorship or partnership it is not subject to any form of income tax. On the other hand, if the firm is organized as a corporation, it is considered as a separate taxable unit and is subject to the corporate income tax; one exception to this is the "Subchapter S" Corporation, discussed below. This is one of the prices a corporation pays for the special status it enjoys as a legal entity—separate and apart from its owners. Although the corporation has always enjoyed special legal status as a "person created by law," it seems strange that Congress has singled out this form of business as the only business unit subject to tax. William Paton, one of the great names in accounting history, observed:

> A review [of the history of federal income taxation] shows clearly that most members of Congress 50 years ago understood that the corporation was not an entity appropriately subject to this type of taxation; they were interested in the corporation primarily as possible agent for withholding and remitting taxes levied on stockholders and employees as individuals. But if these legislators were to sit in on the tax hearings and discussions going on in Washington these days they would be startled to learn that through the invention of "Mr. Corporation" a taxable person has been found ostensibly capable of shouldering a large part of the burden that would otherwise fall on the individual citizens—the "people".[2]

---

[2]William A. Paton, *Corporate Profits* (Homewood, Ill.: Richard D. Irwin, Inc., 1965), p. viii.

The student should recognize, of course, that the entire tax load must, of necessity, be borne by the people—the citizens. The corporate tax must be passed on to the individual members of society through lower wages, higher consumer prices, or lower dividends. Where the corporation is used as a device to funnel these taxes to the citizens, it is difficult to measure just how this load is distributed. Congress, of course, continues to justify the practice because most voters appear to be fooled by this hidden tax, whereas they would likely resist any attempt to raise the same revenue by means of a direct tax.

Regardless of the merit or "justice" of the corporate tax, it must be recognized as an important factor to be considered in the decision-making process. The corporation is subject to two federal income taxes: the normal tax and the surtax. The current rates are as follows:

Normal Tax .... 22 percent
Surtax .... 26 percent

The normal tax is levied against the corporation's entire taxable income while the surtax is levied only on taxable income in excess of $25,000 per year.

Corporate dividends are included in the taxable income of the individual stockholders, and in this sense corporate income is subject to double taxation: it is taxed to the corporation and, when paid out to the stockholders, is subject to individual income tax. In order to partially offset this double taxation, each taxpayer may exclude the first one hundred dollars of dividends received from qualifying corporations during the taxable year. This dividend exclusion is two hundred dollars for persons filing joint returns where both husband and wife received dividends or if the stock was jointly owned. All amounts in excess of the exclusion are treated as ordinary income and taxed according to the individual's tax bracket. Current individual income tax rates vary from 14 to 70 percent, and are summarized in Figure 16-1.

Partnerships are not subject to income tax, but are required to file an information return (form 1065). This return reports the business profit and, more important, shows how the income was distributed to the individual partners. Each partner then includes his share of the partnership income in his individual income tax return. That portion of the partnership income representing ordinary income is then taxed according to the individual taxpayer's tax bracket.

Proprietorships are likewise not subject to income taxes. The individual proprietor merely reports his business income on a supporting schedule which accompanies his individual income tax return. All such earnings are taxed at individual rates, according to the owner's tax bracket.

Subchapter S of the tax code allows the stockholders of certain corporations with ten or fewer stockholders to elect to be taxed as a partnership. These corporations are commonly referred to as "Subchapter S" corporations. This election provides for special treatment of these businesses in that those that qualify under this provision avoid the double taxation described above. Each stockholder is subject to individual tax rates on his share of the corporation's earnings, but the corporation is not also subject to the corporate taxes. Most corporations, of course, do not qualify for this special treatment.

Certain other corporations, including banks, trust companies, insurance companies, public utilities, regulated investment companies, nonresident foreign corporations, and nonprofit enterprises are given special tax treatment.

NET INCOME VERSUS TAXABLE INCOME

Income taxes are levied on the *taxable income* as defined by the tax law. This tax base is not to be confused with *net income*, which is arrived at by careful application of generally accepted accounting principles. Taxable income is not computed by application of accounting principles, but by following the provisions laid down in the tax code. Taxable income is what Congress, the Tax Court and other courts, the Internal Revenue Service and others (often with no accounting background at all) say it is. The tax code is a complex piece of legislation which has been influenced by sound public policy, lobbyists of all political shades, court decisions, and, to a lesser degree, accounting principles. For this reason it would be mere coincidence if net income and taxable income were to agree.

There are two primary reasons why taxable income, as shown on the tax return, may not agree with net income, as shown on the same company's income statement: definitional differences and timing differences.

Definitional Differences

There are some items which the accountant regards as revenue or expense permanently excluded by definition from taxable income. For example, the interest earned on municipal bonds is not part of taxable income, although the amount should be included in net income. Penalty for late payments of taxes and fines for violation of the law are similarly not deductible for tax purposes but would be properly deducted to arrive at

Figure 16-1

1971 INDIVIDUAL INCOME TAX RATE SCHEDULES

Schedule I
Single Taxpayers

TAXABLE INCOME		TAX	
OVER	BUT NOT OVER	14% of taxable income	OF EXCESS OVER
Not over $500			
$ 500	$ 1,000	$ 70+15%	$ 500
1,000	1,500	145+16%	1,000
1,500	2,000	225+17%	1,500
2,000	4,000	310+19%	2,000
4,000	6,000	690+21%	4,000
6,000	8,000	1,110+24%	6,000
8,000	10,000	1,590+25%	8,000
10,000	12,000	2,090+27%	10,000
12,000	14,000	2,630+29%	12,000
14,000	16,000	3,210+31%	14,000
16,000	18,000	3,830+34%	16,000
18,000	20,000	4,510+36%	18,000
20,000	22,000	5,230+38%	20,000
22,000	26,000	5,990+40%	22,000
26,000	32,000	7,590+45%	26,000
32,000	38,000	10,290+50%	32,000
38,000	44,000	13,290+55%	38,000
44,000	50,000	16,590+60%	44,000
50,000	60,000	20,190+62%	50,000
60,000	70,000	26,390+64%	60,000
70,000	80,000	32,790+66%	70,000
80,000	90,000	39,390+68%	80,000
90,000	100,000	46,190+69%	90,000
Over 100,000		53,090+70%	100,000

Schedule II
Married Taxpayers Filing Joint Returns

TAXABLE INCOME		TAX	
OVER	BUT NOT OVER	14% of taxable income	OF EXCESS OVER
Not over $1,000			
$ 1,000	$ 2,000	$ 140+15%	$ 1,000
2,000	3,000	290+16%	2,000
3,000	4,000	450+17%	3,000
4,000	8,000	620+19%	4,000
8,000	12,000	1,380+22%	8,000
12,000	16,000	2,260+25%	12,000
16,000	20,000	3,260+28%	16,000
20,000	24,000	4,380+32%	20,000
24,000	28,000	5,660+36%	24,000
28,000	32,000	7,100+39%	28,000
32,000	36,000	8,660+42%	32,000
36,000	40,000	10,340+45%	36,000
40,000	44,000	12,140+48%	40,000
44,000	52,000	14,060+50%	44,000
52,000	64,000	18,060+53%	52,000
64,000	76,000	24,420+55%	64,000
76,000	88,000	31,020+58%	76,000
88,000	100,000	37,980+60%	88,000
100,000	120,000	45,180+62%	100,000
120,000	140,000	57,580+64%	120,000
140,000	160,000	70,380+66%	140,000
160,000	180,000	83,580+68%	160,000
180,000	200,000	97,180+69%	180,000
Over 200,000		110,980+70%	200,000

Unmarried Taxpayers; Heads of Household

TAXABLE INCOME		TAX	
Not over $1,000		14% of taxable income	
OVER	BUT NOT OVER		OF EXCESS OVER
$ 1,000	$ 2,000	$ 140 + 16%	$ 1,000
2,000	4,000	300 + 18%	2,000
4,000	6,000	660 + 19%	4,000
6,000	8,000	1,040 + 22%	6,000
8,000	10,000	1,480 + 23%	8,000
10,000	12,000	1,940 + 25%	10,000
12,000	14,000	2,440 + 27%	12,000
14,000	16,000	2,980 + 28%	14,000
16,000	18,000	3,540 + 31%	16,000
18,000	20,000	4,160 + 32%	18,000
20,000	22,000	4,800 + 35%	20,000
22,000	24,000	5,500 + 36%	22,000
24,000	26,000	6,220 + 38%	24,000
26,000	28,000	6,980 + 41%	26,000
28,000	32,000	7,800 + 42%	28,000
32,000	36,000	9,480 + 45%	32,000
36,000	38,000	11,280 + 48%	36,000
38,000	40,000	12,240 + 51%	38,000
40,000	44,000	13,260 + 52%	40,000
44,000	50,000	15,340 + 55%	44,000
50,000	52,000	18,640 + 56%	50,000
52,000	64,000	19,760 + 58%	52,000
64,000	70,000	26,720 + 59%	64,000
70,000	76,000	30,260 + 61%	70,000
76,000	80,000	33,920 + 62%	76,000
80,000	88,000	36,400 + 63%	80,000
88,000	100,000	41,440 + 64%	88,000
100,000	120,000	49,120 + 66%	100,000
120,000	140,000	62,320 + 67%	120,000
140,000	160,000	75,720 + 68%	140,000
160,000	180,000	89,320 + 69%	160,000
Over 180,000		103,120 + 70%	180,000

net income. Items such as these are permanently excluded from taxable income calculations, and although the public policy behind these exclusions might be regarded as sound, it would not be good accounting to disregard the items in deriving the firm's net income.

Timing Differences

Most differences are not permanent in nature, but merely represent differences in timing. These items of revenue and expense are utilized in both computations of income and are simply recognized in different accounting periods. In other words, both accountants and tax officials agree the items should be considered, but these same parties disagree as to *when* the items in question should be recognized. For example, a dance studio may receive one hundred dollars today in payment for a fifty-two-week dance course to be offered over the next twelve months. The accountant would say the one hundred dollars is revenue, and the amount should be apportioned between accounting periods in proportion to the number of lessons provided. The tax officials, on the other hand, would agree the sum is revenue, but would require immediate recognition of the entire amount on the income tax return regardless of when it may be earned and without regard to when the services are to be rendered.

INCOME TAX ALLOCATION

Inasmuch as income tax charges themselves are a business expense, the timing differences discussed above will result in showing the tax expense in the wrong period unless proper tax allocation procedures are followed. To illustrate, assume the Miller Company earns $25,000 in net income per year before deducting depreciation and taxes. The company uses straight-line depreciation to calculate net income, but uses the sum-of-the-years'-digits depreciation for tax purposes. In all other respects net income and taxable income are in agreement. The company's only depreciable asset is a machine which was purchased January 1, 1970, at a cost of $18,000. The company estimated the machine would last five years and have a salvage value of $3,000. Depreciation on the machine would be as follows:

	1970	1971	1972	1973	1974
Per books	$3,000	$3,000	$3,000	$3,000	$3,000
Per tax return	5,000	4,000	3,000	2,000	1,000
Extra tax deduction ...	+ $2,000	+ $1,000	$ –0–	– $1,000	– $2,000

Note that the extra depreciation the company is allowed in the first two years is exactly offset by reduced depreciation in the last two years. The difference is merely one of timing, as discussed in the previous section. The effect of accelerated depreciation is to postpone the payment of some of the income taxes until later years.[3] If the matching concept is to be properly employed, the tax should be charged to expense in the period the income is recognized, regardless of when the tax is actually paid. This means that the current year's tax expense should be calculated on net income before tax, the current tax liability should be calculated according to taxable income, and the difference charged (or credited) to the deferred tax liability account. Such a practice would more accurately match revenue and expense as illustrated below:

	1970	1971	1972	1973	1974
Net income before depreciation and tax ...	$25,000	$25,000	$25,000	$25,000	$25,000
Depreciation per books...	3,000	3,000	3,000	3,000	3,000
Net before tax	$22,000	$22,000	$22,000	$22,000	$22,000
Income tax expense[a]	4,840	4,840	4,840	4,840	4,840
Net income	$17,160	$17,160	$17,160	$17,160	$17,160

[a]Assume a 22% tax rate.

The amount charged or credited to the deferred tax liability account would be calculated as follows:

	1970	1971	1972	1973	1974
Income tax expense	$4,840	$4,840	$4,840	$4,840	$4,840
Current tax liability[a]	4,400	4,620	4,840	5,060	5,280
Charge (credit) deferred tax liability	$(440)	$(220)	$ –0–	$ 220	$ 440

[a]The current tax liability would be 22 percent of taxable income:
    1970: 22% of $20,000 = $4,400
    1971: 22% of $21,000 = $4,620
    1972: 22% of $22,000 = $4,840
    1973: 22% of $23,000 = $5,060
    1974: 22% of $24,000 = $5,280

The journal entries to record the annual income tax liability are summarized below:

```
1970
Dec. 31   Income Tax Expense ...................   4,840
              Current Income Tax Liability ........        4,400
              Deferred Income Tax Liability .......          440
```

[3]To be able to postpone taxes represents a decided tax advantage since money has a time value. The company can put to work the funds that otherwise would be used to pay taxes, to increase earnings. Later, the taxes must be paid, but the income received from using the funds during the interim period represents extra earnings. The concept of time value of money is described in detail in chapter 19.

```
1971
Dec. 31  Income Tax Expense ...................   4,840
              Current Income Tax Liability ........          4,620
              Deferred Income Tax Liability .......            220

1972
Dec. 31  Income Tax Expense ...................   4,840
              Current Income Tax Liability ........          4,840

1973
Dec. 31  Income Tax Expense ...................   4,840
         Deferred Income Tax Liability ...........    220
              Current Income Tax Liability ........          5,060

1974
Dec. 31  Income Tax Expense ...................   4,840
         Deferred Income Tax Liability ...........    440
              Current Income Tax Liability ........          5,280
```

At the end of the machine's life the timing differences would be offset, leaving a zero balance in the Deferred Income Tax Liability account.

ACCOUNTING METHODS

The tax law recognizes two primary methods of accounting: the cash basis and the accrual basis. For the most part, the accrual basis used for tax purposes is similar to that followed in the earlier chapters of this book. Revenue is generally recognized as earned when the goods are delivered or the services rendered, and applicable expenses then matched with the revenue. There are instances where the Internal Revenue Service requires the taxpayer to modify the accrual method as with revenue received in advance, discussed above.

A taxpayer on the cash basis, on the other hand, recognizes revenue when the cash or its equivalent is received, without regard to when the goods or services are delivered. Expenses are similarly deducted when paid in cash, to the extent that they are authorized. There are certain exceptions which cannot be expensed in the period of cash payment. A taxpayer on the cash basis would be required to depreciate a fixed asset, for example, even though it is paid for in cash.

Many businesses use the cash basis to account for an installment sale. Where an item is sold on an installment contract and payment is received over an extended period of time, the installment sales basis of accounting enables the taxpayer to realize the revenue over the period of collection and thereby defer the payment of taxes.

The installment sales method may be illustrated by reference to the following assumed facts regarding a television set sold on an eighteen-month installment contract on October 1, 1970:

Selling price	$500
Cost	290
Down payment	50
Monthly installments	25

With a cost of $290 and the selling price of $500, the television set will afford the company a gross profit of $210, or 42 percent. Under the installment sales method this gross profit is recognized as the cash is collected rather than in the period of sale, as would be customary under the accrual basis of accounting. The tax effect of this method is to defer the payment of taxes, which normally would be paid in the period of sale, until the period the cash is collected. Journal entries for the year 1970 to account for the above installment sale are as follows:

1970				
Oct.	1	Installment Accounts Receivable	500	
		Inventory (Cost of Installment Sales)[a]		290
		Deferred Gross Profit on Installment Sales..		210
Oct.	1	Cash	50	
		Installment Accounts Receivable........		50
Nov.	1	Cash	25	
		Installment Accounts Receivable.........		25
Dec.	1	Cash	25	
		Installment Accounts Receivable.........		25
Dec. 31		Deferred Gross Profit on Installment Sales.....	42	
		Realized Gross Profit on Installment Sales..		42
		To record realized gross profit of 42 percent of collections during year		

[a]The Merchandise Inventory account would be credited if the perpetual inventory method were used, or the Cost of Installment Sales account would be credited if the periodic inventory method were used. The Cost of Installment Sales account would in turn be closed to the Cost of Goods Sold account to reduce the cost of goods sold other than on the installment sales basis.

If the buyer failed to make his January and February installments, and the set was repossessed on February 15, 1971, with a fair market value of $250, the following entry would be made:

1971			
Feb. 15	Repossessed Merchandise Inventory	250	
	Deferred Gross Profit on Installment Sales.....	168	
	Installment Accounts Receivable		400
	Gain on Repossession		18

THE INVESTMENT CREDIT

The investment credit was originally enacted as a temporary device to induce businesses to invest in new capital equipment. Since it was devised as a means of stimulating the private investment sector of the economy, it has been suspended and reinstated from time to time as economic conditions have warranted. It was most recently repealed by the Tax Reform Act of 1969 and so is not presently in effect.

The investment credit worked as a subsidy from the federal government to those businesses that made qualified investments. The amount calculated as an investment credit was deducted from the income tax liability and thereby directly reduced the amount of taxes paid. It was allowed in addition to depreciation deductions and did not reduce the tax basis of the property. The credit was 7 percent of the cost of the qualified property if the asset acquired had an estimated useful life of eight or more years; 4 ⅔ percent if the estimated useful life was six or seven years; 2 ⅓ percent if the useful life was four or five years; and no credit was allowed on assets which had a useful life of less than four years. There were certain limits on the amount of investment credit allowed in any one year, as well as on the nature of the assets which qualified. While the investment credit is not currently a part of the tax law, it may very well be reinstated in the event of an economic downturn.

ACCELERATED DEPRECIATION

The two types of accelerated depreciation discussed in chapter 9, the sum-of-the-years'-digits and the declining balance, are acceptable (within certain limitations) for tax purposes. As previously illustrated, either of these methods will accelerate the depreciation deduction so that more is allowed in early years and less deductible in later years. It is important to note that accelerated depreciation does not increase the total tax deduction nor decrease taxes. Instead, it changes the allocation of the total depreciation so that a larger proportion is deductible in earlier years, thereby postponing the payment of applicable taxes until later years.[4]

Taxpayers can also elect to take an additional first-year depreciation deduction of 20 percent of the cost of taxable property. This election is in addition to the regular first-year depreciation, but is limited to a maximum of $2,000 ($4,000 on a joint return). The extra depreciation taken during the first year reduces the tax basis of the property so that the regular de-

---

[4]Again the student should note that postponement of taxes is a tax advantage. See chapter 19.

preciation is figured on the reduced amount. Thus, extra first-year depreciation, like accelerated depreciation, does not increase total depreciation deduction, but merely increases the proportion taken during the first year.

PERCENTAGE DEPLETION

In chapter 9 we noted that wasting assets such as mineral deposits, timberlands, and similar properties are subject to depletion. Two methods of depletion are allowable for tax purposes: the cost method and the percentage method. The cost method is similar to that used in good accounting. The depletion for any period is calculated by multiplying the asset cost times the ratio of units sold during the period to the total estimated number of units which the property will produce (similar to units of production depreciation).

The percentage depletion method, on the other hand, has no counterpart in accounting theory. The authorized percentage is applied to the gross income from the property without regard to cost. Under percentage depletion the owner of the property (and/or the lessee) can obtain a tax deduction in excess of the cost of the asset. To the extent this is done, the percentage depletion allowance amounts to a subsidy to the particular industry in the form of tax-free income. The percentage allowed varies according to the type of mineral, where the deposits are located, and the purpose for which the mineral or wasting asset is used. The allowable percentages for some of the common wasting assets are:

Oil and gas wells . . . . 22 percent
Sulphur, uranium, lead, mercury, manganese, nickel, platinum,
    tin, and zinc . . . . 22 percent
China clay, rock asphalt, granite, limestone, marble, and potash . . . 15 percent
Coal, sodium chloride . . . . 10 percent
Building clay, peat moss, pumice and sand . . . . 5 percent

INVENTORY METHODS

The tax law permits taxpayers to use either FIFO (first-in, first-out) or LIFO (last-in, first-out) to price goods in inventory. The method selected for tax purposes need not correspond to the actual physical flow of the goods. The LIFO inventory method is often favored during periods of rising prices and has been adopted by an increasing number of taxpayers during the "creeping inflation" which we have experienced for the last quarter of a century. LIFO matches the most recent costs with revenue which, during periods of rising costs, reduces the firm's taxable income and in turn reduces the tax liability. Firms which carry large inventories would normally find LIFO inventory pricing an especially profitable tax election.

The tax advantage of LIFO inventory method may be seen in the following illustrations. Assume Theide Corporation has five hundred units of product AWOL on hand at the end of the fiscal year and that purchases during the period were as follows:

$$
\begin{array}{rl}
400 \text{ units @ } \$50 \text{ each} = & \$\ 20{,}000 \\
800 \text{ units @ } \$55 \text{ each} = & 44{,}000 \\
200 \text{ units @ } \$57 \text{ each} = & 11{,}400 \\
300 \text{ units @ } \$60 \text{ each} = & 18{,}000 \\
250 \text{ units @ } \$65 \text{ each} = & 16{,}250 \\
\hline
& \$109{,}650
\end{array}
$$

If the LIFO inventory method were used, the goods on hand would be valued at $25,500 (400 units @ $50, plus 100 units @ $55), and the goods sold would be priced at $84,150, ($109,650 – $25,500). If the FIFO method were used, the ending inventory would be valued at $31,250 (250 @ $65, plus 250 @ $60), and the cost of goods sold would be shown at $78,400 ($109,650 – $31,250). Thus, the taxable income would be $5,750 less under the LIFO method than under the FIFO method.

The difference in tax liability under the LIFO method as compared with other methods is sometimes rather substantial, especially for companies whose operations require carrying large inventories and where prices are subject to wide fluctuation. The following quotation from the 1958 annual report of R. J. Reynolds Tobacco Company illustrates the possible magnitude.

> During the second year of the company's use of the LIFO method of inventory valuation, first adopted in 1957, acquisitions of both flu-cured and Burley tobaccos were made at prices higher than were paid in the previous year. The resulting LIFO adjustment enabled the company to effect a further saving in income taxes estimated at $8,500,000. Thus, during the two years under LIFO, the company was able to conserve about $23,000,000 that otherwise would have been required for taxes.[5]

INVOLUNTARY CONVERSIONS

When property is stolen or destroyed by accident, the act may be termed an involuntary conversion. If the property is insured and the

---

[5]Quoted by Robert N. Anthony in *Management Accounting Text and Cases*, rev. ed. (Homewood, Ill.: Richard D. Irwin, Inc., 1960), p. 218.

proceeds from the insurance exceed the book value of the stolen or destroyed property, the transaction gives rise to an accounting or book gain. Such a gain is not taxable, provided the insurance proceeds are reinvested in similar property within a specified period of time, because the tax law recognizes that there has been no economic change. If only a portion of the insurance proceeds are reinvested, the gain is taxable to the extent of the uninvested portion. Losses on involuntary conversions are generally deductible in full.

While the gain on the involuntary conversion may not be taxable, the tax basis of the property must be reduced by the amount of any untaxed gain. This requirement reduces the amount of depreciation which will be allowed on the new asset. Thus, the effect of the law is to postpone the payment of taxes until the periods over which the new asset will be used.

To illustrate the tax effect of an involuntary conversion, assume the Lund Corporation has a building which originally cost $250,000 and which is 50 percent depreciated. The building, which is fully insured at its current market value of $400,000, is completely destroyed by fire. This involuntary conversion would result in a book gain of $275,000 [$400,000 − ($250,000 − $125,000)]. Compare the tax consequences of four different assumptions regarding use of the insurance proceeds:

1. The entire proceeds are reinvested (within the required time limit) in a similar building which has an estimated life of twenty years.
   Taxable gain: zero
   Tax basis of new building: $125,000 ($400,000 − $275,000)
   Annual straight-line depreciation $6,250 ($125,000 ÷ 20)
2. Three hundred thousand dollars of the proceeds is reinvested (within the required time limit) in a similar building which has an estimated life of twenty years.
   Taxable gain: $100,000
   Tax basis of new building: $125,000 ($300,000 − $175,000)
   Annual straight-line depreciation: $6,250 ($125,000 ÷ 20)
3. Five hundred thousand dollars is invested (within the required time limit) in a similar building which has an estimated life of twenty years.
   Taxable gain: zero
   Tax basis of new building: $225,000 ($500,000 − $275,000)
   Annual straight-line depreciation: $11,250 ($225,000 ÷ 20)
4. None of the proceeds is reinvested within the required time limit.
   Taxable gain: $275,000

NONTAXABLE EXCHANGES

Gains and losses from certain exchanges are not recognized at the time of the exchange; instead, recognition is postponed until the disposal of the property received in such an exchange. In such cases the tax basis in the old property is carried forward to the new property without regard to fair market values. When additional cash or other assets ("boot") are given in the exchange, the basis in the property is increased by the amount of the "boot." The party receiving the "boot" is required to pay tax on the gain to the extent of any "boot" he receives. Exchanges which may be treated as nontaxable under certain circumstances include:

1. Securities exchanged for securities of the same corporation.
2. Property held for investment (or productive use) for similar property.
3. Property transferred to a corporation controlled by the transferer.
4. Insurance policies exchanged for other insurance policies.
5. Government bonds exchanged for substantially identical bonds.
6. Stock and property exchanged in corporate reorganizations.

The tax treatment of a nontaxable exchange might be illustrated by assuming that a farmer in Idaho exchanged a five-hundred-acre dry farm with a tax basis of $25,000 for a cattle ranch in Utah which had an appraised value of $150,000. No gain would be recognized on the exchange, but the tax basis in the cattle ranch (new property) would be $25,000 (same as the basis in the old property). If the Idaho farmer paid "boot" of $5,000 in addition to trading his dry farm, the gain would still not be taxable insofar as the Idaho farmer is concerned. His tax basis, in this case, would be $30,000: the basis in the old property ($25,000), plus the "boot" ($5,000). If the Utah rancher also recognized a gain on the exchange, this gain would be taxable up to the amount of "boot" received.

In chapter 9, the tax method of recording "trade-ins" was discussed. Note that these trades were treated as nontaxable exchanges, no gain or loss was recognized, but the basis in the new equipment was the same as the basis in the old plus the "boot."

CAPITAL GAINS AND LOSSES

Gains and losses realized on the sale of certain assets may be subject to a lower tax rate than would be the case if these items were treated as ordinary income. The most important factors affecting the tax treatment are the nature and use to which the asset is put, and the time period over which the asset is held by the taxpayer. To qualify for the lower tax rate the asset must be defined as a *capital asset,* which is any property held by the taxpayer *except:*

1. Real or depreciable property used in a trade or business.
2. Copyrights and literary, musical, or artistic compositions created by the personal efforts of the taxpayer.
3. Accounts or notes receivable, generated through sale of merchandise or rendering services.
4. Certain discounted short-term government obligations.

Under special circumstances, property other than capital assets such as depreciable business property may also be given capital gains treatment.

The period of time over which the asset is held is also important. If the property is held *more* than six months, the gain or loss may be referred to as *long term*, and if held six months or less, as *short term*. The distinction is an important one inasmuch as short-term gains are treated as ordinary income. Net long-term capital gains, on the other hand, to the extent they exceed short-term capital losses, are taxed at not more than 50 percent of the rate applicable to ordinary income.

Assume that Phillip Woolston sold the following securities during the taxable year 1970:

NUMBER OF SHARES	SECURITY	DATE OF PURCHASE	COST	DATE OF SALE	PRO-CEEDS	GAIN OR <LOSS>
100	General Motors	2-15-69	$8,000	11-19-70	$9,010	$1,010
50	Union Carbide	4-19-70	2,300	6-20-70	2,100	<200>
100	Piper Aircraft	9-3-69	4,900	4-25-70	4,275	<625>
75	Combustion Engineering	8-30-70	5,115	12-10-70	5,225	110
200	Russ Toggs	5-23-68	4,600	10-14-70	9,440	4,840

Inasmuch as the stocks of Union Carbide and Combustion Engineering were held less than six months, the loss and gain are short-term. The net short-term loss is $90 ($200 − $110). The other transactions are all long-term since the securities were held more than the required six months. Woolston has a net long-term capital gain of $5,225 ($4,800 + $1,010 − $625). The net gain from sale of capital assets is $5,135 (the $5,225 net long-term capital gain, less the $90 net short-term capital loss). Mr. Woolston would be allowed a long-term capital gain deduction of $2,567.50, representing 50 percent of the net gain from sale of capital assets. The balance of $2,567.50 would be taxed as ordinary income, but the tax is limited to 25 percent of the net gain of $5,115.00.[6] Thus, the net effect is that Mr. Woolston may pay less than 25 percent tax on long-term capital gains if he is in a relatively low tax bracket, but is not required to pay more than 25 percent regardless of his tax bracket.

The reason behind special treatment for long-term capital gains is that to some degree, at least, they do not represent real economic gains, since

---

[6] If net long-term gains exceed $50,000, higher rates may apply.

they arise largely from changes in price levels. The theory behind this treatment is similar to that followed with involuntary conversions: the taxpayer may be no better off after the gain transactions than before because the buying power of the money he receives in the exchange has decreased.

Had Mr. Woolston sustained a net loss on capital asset transactions the loss could be partially offset against his ordinary income. Prior to the Tax Reform Act of 1969, there was no distinction made between short-term and long-term losses, both were fully deductible up to a limit of $1,000 per year. Two changes were made in the Act of 1969. First the amount of the loss deduction was reduced to $500 per year ($1,000 in a joint return if the capital assets were jointly owned). Second, while short-term losses are still deductible in full up to the $500 limit, only 50 percent of a long-term loss may be taken into account for the purpose of calculating the deductions. Thus, a $1,000 long-term loss would only produce a $500 deduction whereas a $500 short-term loss would produce a full $500 deduction.

OPERATING LOSS CARRYOVER

If a taxpayer sustains a loss from operating his trade or business, or from theft or casualty, this may ordinarily be fully offset by ordinary income from other sources. To the extent the loss exceeds other income, the amount may be offset against income of other years. The loss may be applied backward to the three preceding years (carryback) and then, if any remains, forward (carryover) to the following five years. It must be applied to the oldest year first and then, to the extent any remains, forward to each succeeding year. This provision requires the taxpayer to recompute the tax liability for prior years to which the loss is applied, and thereby enables him to receive a tax refund for any excess payments.

Assume that Wilford Hanks sustains a net operating loss of $30,000 in 1970 and that his taxable incomes for the three preceding years and the five subsequent years were as follows:

1967	$10,000
1968	3,000
1969	1,000
1971	5,000
1972	8,000
1973	2,000
1974	10,000
1975	6,000

The loss would be carried back first to 1967 ($10,000) then to 1968 ($3,000), then to 1969 ($1,000) leaving a $16,000 carryover. This would be carried forward, first to 1971 ($5,000), then to 1972 ($8,000) and 1973 ($2,000), with the remaining $1,000 carried forward to 1974. The tax liability for the years 1967–69 would need to be recalculated so that tax refunds could be obtained.

SUMMARY

Income tax laws have become an increasingly important consideration in the management decision-making process. Of particular significance are those provisions in the laws which permit taxpayers to choose among alternative tax treatments or otherwise provide special tax advantages. Some of the important topics in the federal tax laws with which the businessman should familiarize himself are what constitutes a taxable unit, how taxable income differs from the accounting net income, alternate acceptable accounting methods, the investment credit, accelerated depreciation, percentage depletion, alternate inventory methods, involuntary conversions, nontaxable exchanges, treatment of capital gains and losses, and the carryover of operating losses.

Only the corporate form of business is subject to income tax. While proprietorships and partnerships are exempt from income tax, the owners of these enterprises are required to pay tax on their share of the earnings. The owners of corporations also pay tax on their share of distributed earnings (dividends).

Net income is arrived at by application of generally accepted accounting principles and often does not agree with taxable income as defined by law. The differences between net income and taxable income might be classified as definitional (permanent) or timing (temporary). The matching concept requires that the accountant allocate the tax expense to the proper period in those instances where the differences arise through timing. The law permits business units to calculate taxable income on an accrual basis or cash basis.

The investment credit has been used from time to time as a means of stimulating businessmen to invest in capital equipment. Under this method, currently not part of the law, businesses were given a subsidy or discount on new equipment purchased and the maximum investment credit was 7 percent of the new asset cost.

Accelerated depreciation permits the taxpayer to write proportionately more of the asset cost off during the early years of the asset's life, thereby postponing the payment of taxes. Percentage depletion represents a special subsidy to industries engaged in extraction of "wasting assets."

Businesses may elect to use either LIFO or FIFO inventory methods for tax purposes; the most popular method during periods of rising prices is LIFO, because it minimizes the current tax liability.

Destruction of property by accident (such as fire) is known as an involuntary conversion. Gains on such transactions are normally not taxed at the time of conversion, but the taxpayer's basis in the new property is reduced. Certain exchanges of "similar property" are likewise not taxed at the time of the transaction, but the basis in the old property is carried over into the new.

Gains realized on the sale of capital assets may be subject to lower tax rates than those applied to ordinary income. Legitimate operating losses may be carried back and, if applicable, carried forward to profitable years and offset against the income of those years to reduce the tax liability.

The tax laws are complex and ever changing. The typical businessman cannot hope to become an expert in tax matters and also attend to the other matters of the business. He must, however, be alert to changes in the laws and particularly to election of alternative tax concessions which affect business decisions. His knowledge in these areas must be sufficient to enable him to know when to seek the advice of his tax counselors.

QUESTIONS

1. Distinguish between "taxable income" and "net income." What is the basis for calculating each of these figures? Who determines what should be utilized in the calculations?
2. What difference does it make in regard to income tax treatment whether a firm is a proprietorship, partnership, or corporation? Does size of the firm in terms of the number of stockholders have anything to do with the possible tax treatment?
3. What is a "Subchapter S" corporation? What tax option is available to corporations that qualify under this provision of the tax law?
4. Define "boot." What effect does "boot" have on the treatment of a nontaxable exchange?
5. What types of differences between net income and taxable income require tax allocation procedures? Give an example of such a difference.
6. How may operating loss carryovers be used to reduce the tax liability over a period of years? To what years may operating losses be carried?
7. Comment on the statement: "Accelerated depreciation is a tax loophole which provides certain large businesses with extra tax deductions. This provision should be eliminated from the tax law because it is tantamount to a subsidy to these companies."
8. Define a "capital" asset. Distinguish between the treatment of a long-term and short-term capital gain.
9. What is percentage depletion? How does this differ from cost depletion as used in good accounting?
10. What revenues and costs are deferred under the installment sales method of accounting? Do you feel this method does an adequate job of matching revenues and expenses?

11. What inventory method is most popular for tax purposes during periods of rising prices? Why?
12. What is an "involuntary conversion"? How are gains and losses on involuntary conversions treated for tax purposes?
13. Why is it sometimes said that corporate income is subject to double taxation? To what extent are individual stockholders freed from this double taxation?

PROBLEMS

Problem 16-1

A branch office of the Coutla Corporation was destroyed by fire on August 2, 1970. The building had been constructed by the company in the early fifties at a cost of $242,000. It was first occupied on January 1, 1953; at that time the company estimated it would have a useful life of forty years, after which it could be sold for $50,000. The company has used straight-line depreciation for both tax and book purposes.

Perform the calculations listed below for each of the four following situations (in each case the new building was purchased or constructed within the time period required for involuntary conversions):

1. The company carried no insurance on the building, and it completed construction of a new branch office building at a cost of $496,000;
2. The building was fully insured for its current appraised value of $329,000, and the entire proceeds were reinvested in a new branch office building;
3. The building was fully insured for its current appraised value of $329,000, and a new branch office building was purchased at a cost of $496,000;
4. The building was fully insured for its current appraised value of $250,000 and a new branch office building was purchased at a cost of $202,000.

Required:

a. Calculate the accounting gain or loss.
b. Calculate the taxable gain or loss.
c. Calculate the tax basis on the new property.

Problem 16-2

The Compton Storage and Transfer Company has a number of large semi-trailers used to transport customers' goods across the country. It has been the company's practice to depreciate this particular equipment on a straight-line basis over a six-year period because it is felt this method of depreciation best matches the depreciation cost with the revenue earned by using the trailers. Several years ago the company's CPA firm pointed out the advantages of sum-of-the-years'-digits depreciation for tax purposes. They said this technique would enable the company to accelerate the depreciation deductions and thereby reduce the company's current tax liability. The company controller still felt the straight-line method enabled the company to more accurately measure income than would be the case under accelerated depreciation. The CPA firm indicated it would be acceptable to use sum-of-the-years'-digits for tax purposes and straight-line for book purposes, provided the company used proper tax allocation procedures. Ten trailers were purchased January 3, 1969, at a cost of $35,000 each. It was estimated that each trailer would have a salvage value of $3,500 at the end of its useful life.

Required:

Prepare General Journal entries to record the company's tax liability each December 31 using straight-line depreciation for book purposes and sum-of-the-years'-digits depreciation for tax purposes. Assume a constant tax rate of 52 percent and that prior to any deduction for depreciation the taxable income and net income are $250,000 per year.

Problem 16-3

The Foremost Appliance Center uses the installment sales method of accounting for all major appliances which are sold on contract. On December 24, 1969, the company sold a home entertainment center (stereo and color TV combination) to John Rutherford. Rutherford traded in his old TV set which had a fair market value of $50, as the down payment and agreed to pay $100 per month for twelve months as the balance on the interest-free contract. The home entertainment center cost Foremost Appliance $712.50 and carried a manufacturer's suggested selling price of $1295. Because the company was anxious to reduce year-end inventories, the unit was sold to Mr. Rutherford for a total contract price of only $1,250. The salesman's commission of $65.00 was paid on December 31, 1969, and there were no other expenses directly related to the sale.

Mr. Rutherford made no cash payments, and after numerous reminders the set was repossessed on February 28, 1970. Because the Rutherford children had seriously damaged the set it had a fair market value at the time of repossession of only $600. Foremost did not feel legal action against Mr. Rutherford would prove fruitful.

Required:

a. Prepare journal entries to record the above data (including any necessary year-end adjustments), assuming the company uses the installment sales method of accounting.
b. What would be the net effect of these transactions on the taxable income of Foremost Appliance Center for the tax years 1969 and 1970 (assume December 31 closing)?
c. What would the net tax effect have been in each of these years had the company used regular accrual accounting rather than the installment sales method?

Problem 16-4

During the taxable year 1970, Mr. Irvin Thompson completed the following stock transactions:

TRANSACTION DATE	TYPE OF TRANS-ACTION	NUMBER OF SHARES	NAME OF COMPANY	TRANSACTION AMOUNT
January 8	Purchased	200	Delta Air Lines	$ 6,665
January 29	Sold	100	Cities Service	6,442
March 18	Sold	50	Allied Electric	2,894
March 24	Purchased	500	Deseret Pharmaceutical	26,500
April 30	Sold	200	Delta Air Lines	7,180
August 26	Purchased	1,000	Cannon Construction	1,215
September 30	Sold	250	Deseret Pharmaceutical	12,888

All sales relate to stocks purchased during the same year except for the Cities Service stock, which was acquired on November 13, 1962, at a cost of $4,521, and the Allied Electric stock, which was acquired October 19, 1969, at a cost of $3,420.

Required:
    a. Calculate the gain or loss on each sale.
    b. Calculate the net long-term gain or loss.
    c. Calculate the net short-term gain or loss.
    d. What amount would Mr. Thompson include in his tax return as ordinary income, assuming he is in a 30 percent tax bracket?

Problem 16-5

Leisure Time, Incorporated was formed several years ago by a group of sports enthusiasts with the idea of capitalizing on the rapidly expanding recreation industry. The company reported taxable income of $10,000 in 1966; $17,000 in 1967; $22,000 in 1968; and $33,000 in 1969. Because profit trends had been favorable in recent years the management decided to greatly expand operations during 1970 and engaged in the following transactions:

    1. On February 12, 1970, purchased a site for $49,000 on which the company planned to construct a miniature golf course. Several months later the state highway department announced construction of a freeway with an exit near this site. On December 10, 1970, the company accepted an offer from a national motel chain which wanted to build a motel on the site, selling the undeveloped property for $170,000.

    2. On April 8, 1970, the company traded a bowling alley with a tax basis of $112,000 and a current appraised value of $325,000 for a larger bowling alley with an appraised value of $400,000. The difference in appraised values was paid in cash.

    3. On April 25, 1970, the company purchased 1,000 shares of Winter Sports, Inc. at a total cost of $29,400. On September 1, 1970, Winter Sports announced sharply reduced earnings, and the stock price began to fall. On December 15, 1970, Leisure Time decided to "bail out" and sold the entire 1,000 shares for only $10,220.

    4. On July 9, 1970, a boat-sale firm was purchased at a cost of $100,000.

   5. On September 1, 1970, General Motors stock was sold for $39,990. This stock had been acquired on December 20, 1969, at a cost of $38,810. The funds provided by this sale were used to buy a trampoline recreation center.

   6. Operating profits (excluding gains and losses from the foregoing transactions) for the year 1970 were $14,400.

   7. In early February of the following year it became apparent that the firm's president had been spending far too much time "playing the stock market" and not enough time on company operations. On March 1, 1971, the president was fired, and the new president decided to freeze all investments and concentrate his efforts on the firm's deteriorating operating position. In spite of his efforts, the company sustained an operating loss during 1971 in the amount of $92,000.

Required:

Assuming current tax rates applied to all years, calculate the company's adjusted tax liabilities for the years 1966 through 1971, inclusive. Show your calculations in good form.

Problem 16-6

Aaron, Barney, and Clyde are joint owners of an insulation business which operates under the name ABCO. Each of the owners is married and each owner files a joint tax return with his wife. During the year 1971 the partners' taxable income (after personal deductions and exemptions) from sources other than ABCO was Aaron, $2,000, Barney, $25,000, and Clyde, $18,000.

Part A:

Assume that ABCO is a partnership and that the partners have agreed to share profits by allowing a salary of $10,000 to Aaron (the managing partner) with the balance of the profits to be shared in the ratio 1:2:3 by Aaron, Barney, and Clyde, respectively. During the year, the partners withdrew the following sums: Aaron, $10,000 (the agreed salary); Barney, $1,000; and Clyde, $2,000. The net income of the firm (prior to any deduction for salary or other compensations to partners) was $85,000. What is the tax liability of the firm ABCO? What is the tax liability of each of the partners?

Part B:

Suppose ABCO were a corporation (instead of a partnership) not qualifying under Subchapter S. Aaron is allowed an $8,000 salary as manager, and this amount is paid to him during the year. Dividends declared and paid during the year amount to $5,000: $2,000 to Aaron, $1,000 to Barney, and $2,000 to Clyde. The net income of the firm (prior to any deductions for salary or other compensation to partners) was $85,000. Aaron and Clyde owned their stock jointly with their wives, but Barney holds his stock in his own name. What is the tax liability of the firm ABCO? What is the tax liability of each of the partners?

Part C:

How would your answer in part B differ if ABCO had qualified under Subchapter S?

Part D:

Which form of business would you prefer for ABCO if you were a partner? Would this method be equally desirable to all owners?

Problem 16-7

In each of the independent situations described below, answer the questions after considering the facts given. In most instances there would be other items to be included in taxable income as well as certain exemptions, deductions, and credits. Ignore these unknown items, calculating the tax liability and answering other questions based upon the information given. Support your answers with calculations in good form.

Part A:

Mr. Jim Murdock completed the following transactions in his stock market account:

January 22, purchased 100 shares of NITCO common stock for $3,292
January 30, sold 50 shares of Stuart Sales, Inc. common stock for $2,555
March 13, sold the 100 shares NITCO for $4,820
May 22, purchased 500 shares of Lightning Uranium Mines common stock for $500
July 24, sold 200 shares of Mountain Motors common stock for $3,920
October 15, sold 250 shares of Lightning Uranium Mines for $1,800
December 2, sold 100 shares of Lightning Uranium Mines for $975.

The Stuart Sales, Inc. stock was acquired March 18 of the prior year for $3,200, and the Mountain Motors stock was acquired the previous April 29 at a cost of $2,340. Calculate the tax liability associated with Mr. Murdock's stock transactions under the assumption he is in a 22 percent tax bracket.

Part B:

Jack and Jill Johnson are married and file a joint return. Dividends received during the year were as follows:

General Electric (j) $25
Eastern Airlines (h) $10
Litton Industries (h) $18
RCA (j) $44
Ford Motor (h) $32
Sun Oil (j) $14
J. C. Penney (w) $20
Honeywell (j) $52
Bethlehem Steel (h) $30

What amount of dividends will be taxed as ordinary income on the Johnsons' tax return? (h = husband owns stock; w = wife owns stock; j = husband and wife jointly own stock)

Part C:

Southland Manufacturing constructed a factory building which was first occupied on July 1, 1960, at a cost of $2,400,000. The building was expected to last forty years and have a salvage value of $400,000. The company uses straight-line depreciation on all assets and records fractional year depreciation to the closest full month. On February 27, 1970, the building was completely destroyed by fire. The building had an appraised value at date of fire of $3,000,000, but was only insured for $2,500,000. The company constructed a new factory at a total cost of $3,120,000 and moved into the new building on December 1, 1970. The new factory has an estimated life of forty years and a $500,000 salvage value. How much was the gain or loss? How much of the gain or loss is taxable in 1970? How much of the gain or loss is taxable in 1971? What is the tax basis of the new building?

Part D:

Jerry Hendrekson is in the excavating business and has four eight-yard-capacity dump trucks. On many occasions he has had need of a larger truck and so accepts an offer from a truck rental company to trade two of his eight-yard-capacity trucks for one twelve-yard-capacity truck. Jerry's trucks had a book value (tax basis) of $2,000 each, but had a current market value of $3,000 each. The larger truck was of similar age and condition as Jerry's smaller trucks, and it had a current market value of $5,500. What, if any, is the recognized gain or loss to Jerry on the transaction? What is his tax basis in the new truck?

Case 16
QUALITY SALES, INC.

Quality Sales, Inc. was formed in the early 1960s as a firm specializing in the sale of washing machines. For many years the company operated as a discount outlet selling below retail prices, but only on a C.O.D. basis. In 1971 to conform to the modern trend toward installment selling, the company changed its marketing strategy. Where all sales had previously been made for cash only, during 1971 all sales were made on installment contract. The company decided, therefore, to adopt the installment sales method of accounting. The books disclosed the following at December 31, 1971 (the end of the taxable year):

QUALITY SALES, INC.
Trial Balance
December 31, 1971

Cash	100,000	
Installment Accounts Receivable	900,000	
Merchandise Inventory (Jan. 1, 1971)	180,000	
Equipment	360,000	
Accumulated Depreciation, Equipment		135,000
Equipment	360,000	
Other Assets	200,000	
Current Liabilities		250,000
Deferred Tax Liability		36,000

Capital Stock		400,000
Retained Earnings		760,000
Purchases	1,040,000	
Cost of Installment Sales.....................		1,010,000
Deferred Gross Profit on Installment Sales........		790,000
Rent Expense	85,000	
Salaries Expense	185,000	
Other Expenses ...:.........................	30,000	
Gain on Sale of Capital Assets		9,000
	3,390,000	3,390,000

Adjustments have not been made to record depreciation for the year 1971. All new equipment was purchased January 3, 1968, at a cost of $360,000. The company assumes the equipment will have no salvage value and uses straight-line depreciation for book purposes. However, the company uses sum-of-the-years'-digits depreciation for tax purposes. Except for this difference in depreciation methods and the resulting effect on the company's current tax liability, the firm's net income and taxable income are in agreement.

The gain on sale of capital assets is the net result of three separate stock transactions. Stock of Motyke Corporation, purchased September 27, 1968, for $44,414, was sold on April 30, 1971, for $85,390. Stock of American Products Company was sold February 22, 1971, for $8,320. This stock was acquired on November 9, 1970, for $6,170. On November 23, 1971, the company sold Allgone Company stock for $27,074. This stock had been acquired in early 1967 at a cost of $61,200.

The directors of quality sales are considering a cash dividend, and they are anxious to know the results of 1971 operations and to have a statement of financial position on that date. The profits earned during 1970 amounted to $221,000. Preliminary figures furnished by the sales manager indicate the number of units sold in 1971 (5,000 units) was 25 percent higher than in the previous year. With this encouraging news the directors are looking forward to record profits this year. The president has been asked to report at the next director's meeting, and he asks you to prepare financial statements and other data that might assist him in making his report.

QUESTIONS

1. Were profits up or down in 1971? Why? How can the president explain this?
2. Do you think it is desirable to use different methods of depreciation for book and tax purposes? Why?
3. Do you support the installment sales method as a good system for measuring income? What is the tax effect of this method?
4. Prepare the journal entry to record the year's income tax expense and income tax liabilities. Show supporting calculations.

17

Costs
for
Control

Costs may be accumulated in various ways to serve different purposes. From the standpoint of product costing, inventory valuation, profit determination, and similar problems, the costs must be identified with products manufactured. The job order and process cost accounting systems discussed previously were set up to accumulate costs by product primarily for financial reporting purposes. From the standpoint of control, however, this type of cost accumulation is not very useful.

To control costs, we must know first what the costs *should* be; second, what the actual costs are; third, who is responsible for the control of each cost. This means that the costs must be preplanned, budgeted, and accumulated by *responsibility centers*. In this type of accumulation we are concerned with assigning each cost to the individual responsible for its control, rather than with assigning it to a particular product. This means that cost accounting really has a dual function: to measure profit accurately by assignment of costs to specific products, and to control costs by assigning them to a particular responsibility center. This dual purpose of costing may be seen in Figure 17-1.

Figure 17-1

DUAL PURPOSE OF COSTING

PRODUCT	RESPONSIBILITY CENTER				TOTAL PRODUCT COSTa
	A	B	C	D	
1	$10	$15	$5	$8	$38
2	50	40	90	20	200
3	8	7	21	9	45
4	16	22	19	10	67
5	31	70	40	60	201
TOTAL COST BY RESPONSIBILITY CENTERb	$115	$154	$175	$107	$551

aCosts are accumulated horizontally by *product* (numbers 1–5).

bCosts are accumulated vertically by responsibility center (A–D). The costs total $551 either way. They are merely accumulated differently to serve different purposes.

Note that the costs are the same in both cases and are merely accumulated in two different ways. The horizontal accumulation is by product, while the vertical accumulation is by responsibility center. In the case of product accumulation we would expect to see considerable allocation of costs, while for control purposes we would find almost no allocation. The method of accumulation in each case is established to accomplish a specific objective. Proper accounting practices for the purpose of measuring a product's cost may not apply from a standpoint of control.

STANDARD COST ACCOUNTING

The cost accounting systems discussed to date have accumulated *actual* costs, either by job or by process. Accounting systems might also be set up to accumulate *standard* costs. The primary purpose of such systems is to provide cost control, although a standard cost system might also be used for financial accounting purposes as noted in the following:

> Standard costs are acceptable [for financial accounting purposes] if adjusted at reasonable intervals to reflect current conditions so that at the balance sheet date standard costs reasonably approximate the cost computed under one of the recognized bases.[1]

Under a standard cost system the emphasis is placed upon what it *should* cost to produce a given product, rather than upon what it does cost. Standards are established specifying what it will cost to produce the product if operations are highly efficient. These standards are set at a sufficiently high level so that they are attainable only under the best production conditions. Periodic comparisons are then made between the actual costs and the standard costs to evaluate efficiency. Differences between actual costs and standard costs are called *variances*. These variances serve as flags to management, indicating the general areas requiring special attention. Variances may occur in material, labor, or overhead costs.

Material Variances

The actual material costs may vary from the established standard because of fluctuations in either the price paid or the quantity used. Where both the actual quantity and price vary from standard, there is a combination variance. Thus, three material variances are possible: material price variance, material usage (or quantity variance), and a combination price-quantity variance. This can be seen in Figure 17-2, in which the variances are diagrammed based upon the following facts:

> Standard price of materials: $2 per pound
> Standard quantity of material: 40 pounds
> Actual price paid for materials: $2.05 per pound
> Actual quantity of materials used: 42 pounds

The material price variance in this instance is $2.00 ($0.05 × 40 pounds), the material quantity variance is $4.00 (2 pounds × $2.00), and the combination price-quantity variance is $0.10 ($0.05 × 2 pounds). As a matter of convenience, accountants generally treat the combination variance as part of the price variance. This is done because the former variance is generally very insignificant in relation to the other two. Also, since the combination variance is the result of two factors, its calculation adds nothing to control. Where this combination variance is treated as part of the price variance, the formulas for material variances would be

---

[1] *Accounting Research and Terminology Bulletins,* fin. ed. (New York: American Institute of Certified Public Accountants, 1961), p. 30.

$$\text{MPV} = (\text{SP} - \text{AP}) \times \text{AQ} = (\$2.00 - \$2.05) \times 42 = -\$2.10$$

$$\text{MQV} = (\text{SQ} - \text{AQ}) \times \text{SP} = (40 - 42) \times \$2.00 = -\$4.00$$

where

MPV = Material price variance
MQV = Material quantity variance
SP = Standard price per unit of material
AP = Actual price per unit of material
SQ = Standard quantity of materials (actual output × standard quantity per unit of output)
AQ = Actual quantity of materials used to produce actual output

A positive sign signifies a favorable variance (better than standard performance), while a negative sign signifies an unfavorable variance (worse than standard performance).

Figure 17-2

VARIANCE ANALYSIS

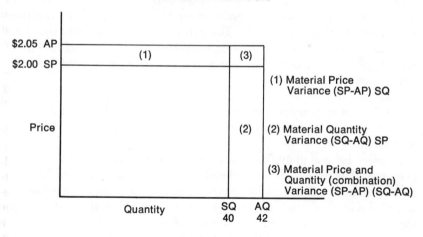

Labor Variance

Labor costs may be analyzed in a manner similar to that just used for materials, except that the terminology is different. Inasmuch as the price of labor is usually stated as an hourly rate, the price variance is known as the *labor rate variance*. Likewise, since the quantity of labor used is generally measured in terms of the actual hours worked by employees, this is generally referred to as the *labor efficiency variance*. The combination rate-efficiency variance is normally combined with the labor rate variance as shown by the following formulas:

$$LRV = (SR - AR) \times AH$$
$$LEV = (SH - AH) \times SR$$

where

  LRV = Labor rate variance
  LEV = Labor efficiency variance
  SR   = Standard rate of labor per hour
  AR   = Actual rate of labor per hour
  SH   = Standard hours of labor (actual output × standard hours per unit of output)
  AH   = Actual hours of labor worked to produce actual output

Overhead Variances

There are many ways of analyzing the difference between actual and standard overhead. The simplest way, of course, is to have a single overhead variance. In a sense, this is what we did in chapter 7 when we utilized a predetermined overhead rate. The entire difference between the actual overhead incurred and that applied to production was treated as over- or underapplied overhead. This difference could have been termed an *overhead variance*.

The single overhead analysis just described has limited usefulness because it does not provide management with any information regarding *why* the variances occurred and, therefore, provides no real means of control.

In order for one to analyze the overhead in a meaningful manner, it is necessary that the standard overhead rate be divided into fixed and variable components. The variable overhead rate will remain constant regardless of the level of plant activity because, by definition, the variable costs vary directly with production. The fixed overhead, on the other hand, remains constant in *total*. As the level of production varies, so also does the fixed overhead rate change, as this constant sum must be spread over a greater or smaller number of units. The higher the level of production, the lower the fixed overhead rate.

With the overhead rate broken into fixed and variable components, three overhead variances can be calculated: a budget variance, a capacity variance, and an efficiency variance.

The *overhead budget variance* is the difference between the costs budgeted for the period (at a specified level of production) and the cost actually incurred. This variance arises from paying more or less than was anticipated for items of overhead. The formula for the overhead budget variance is

$$OBV = BOH - AOH$$

where

OBV = Overhead budget variance
BOH = Budgeted overhead costs or [budgeted fixed costs plus (actual hours worked × standard variable overhead rate)]
AOH = Actual overhead costs

The *overhead capacity variance* arises from operating at a higher or lower level of activity than that provided for in the budget. The variance may be calculated by the following formula:

$$OCV = (AH \times SOR) - BOH$$

where

OCV = Overhead capacity variance
BOH = Budgeted overhead costs (the same figure as used in the budget variance)
AH = Actual hours direct labor worked
SOR = Standard overhead rate total (at budgeted level of production)

The *overhead efficiency variance* is the difference between the standard and the actual hours at the standard overhead rate. The standard hours represent the time that it *should* have taken to produce the actual output. This variance is really the result of labor efficiency and reflects the fact that overhead costs are saved or wasted according to how effectively the employees work. The formula for the overhead efficiency variance is

$$OEV = (SH - AH) \times SOR$$

where

OEV = Overhead efficiency variance
SH = Standard hours (the hours it should have taken to produce the actual output)
AH = Actual hours direct labor worked
SOR = Standard overhead rate

The three overhead variance analyses may be illustrated by assuming the following facts. During the month of June, the Hawking Manufacturing Company budgeted overhead costs of $240,000 and production of 100,000 units of output. The overhead budget is composed of

		RATE PER HOUR
Fixed costs	$ 80,000	$0.10
Variable costs	160,000	0.20
	$240,000	$0.30

The standard cost system specified eight hours of direct labor per unit of output. Production records for the month revealed actual hours worked as 790,000 hours, output of 100,000 units, and actual overhead costs of $245,000. The overhead variances may be calculated as follows[a]:

1. Overhead Budget Variance

[$80,000 + (790,000 hours × $0.20)] – $245,000 =
$238,000 – $245,000 = –$7,000

2. Overhead Capacity Variance

(790,000 hours × $0.30) – [$80,000 + (790,000 hours ×
$0.20)] = $237,000 – $238,000 = –$1,000

3. Overhead Efficiency Variance

(800,000 hours – 790,000 hours) × $0.30 = +$3,000

4. Net Overhead Variance

(–$7,000 – $1,000 + $3,000) = –$5,000

---

[a]Plus (+) signifies favorable (credit); minus (−) signifies unfavorable (debit).

Establishing Standards

Standards are established by carefully analyzing what it would cost to produce a given product under *attainable, efficient* production conditions. Engineering studies may be necessary to establish the best combination of ingredients. Careful analysis of materials, dimensions, and prices may be necessary to arrive at the best value. Layout men may assist in deciding just how the necessary parts must be cut or assembled to assure minimum waste. Time and motion studies may be made to determine the time required to perform a given task at maximum efficiency. In short, all management resources are brought to bear on the question of *what it should cost* to produce a given product when everyone performs effectively.

Advantages of Standards

One of the major advantages of a standard cost system is the fact that it enables management to operate under the *management-by-exception* principle by causing it to focus its attention on inefficiencies. The variances generated under such a system make management aware of the problem areas. It is then able to spend its time in, and to direct its efforts toward, the areas that appear to be most fruitful. In establishing standards, management must carefully scrutinize the entire business operation to arrive at the best methods of production.

Record keeping is simplified with the standard cost system and, accordingly, cost data are readily available and easily calculated. Under a standard cost accounting system most of the cost flows are recorded at standard figures. This means that the various inventory accounts are carried at standard rather than at cost. Such a practice greatly simplifies the perpetual inventory records, because no record need be maintained for unit costs. The records reflect quantities only, because it is obvious that quantities received or issued are at standard cost.

Limitations of Standards

It is neither easy nor cheap to establish accurate standards, and once set, they are subject to change. When major changes occur in the product, in any of its components, or in the method of manufacture, the once-valid standard becomes obsolete. Standards have limited usefulness and little application where items are produced on a one-time basis or where the items produced differ greatly from period to perioid.

Variances generated under a standard cost system often do not tell all that is desired. A price variance, for example, might have a multitude of causes: quantities sufficient to take advantage of quantity discount may not have been ordered; a strike may have required the use of a more expensive form of shipping; substantial price increases may have been posted by suppliers. Thus, we see that variances can easily be misinterpreted; rather than enabling management to pinpoint the problem easily, variances merely call attention to the general problem area.

Standard cost systems sometimes create serious problems in labor relations. The minute someone shows up with a stop watch to start timing an operation, the typical worker feels a threat to his security. The fear of not being able to meet standards and therefore possibly losing one's job is always present. The fear that management may misinterpret the variance and, without giving the workers any chance for explanation, use it as a whipping post could cause the foremen to "shake in their boots." Any attempt to check on efficiency usually receives little enthusiasm from the employees.

Standard Cost System Illustrated

Journal entries for a standard cost system may be illustrated based upon the following assumed facts:

STANDARD COST TO PRODUCE ONE UNIT OF OUTPUT

Materials, 40 pounds @ $2.00 per pound	=	$ 80.00
Labor, 27 hours @ $3.00 per hour	=	81.00
Overhead, 100 percent of direct labor cost	=	81.00
		$242.00

BUDGETED OVERHEAD	AMOUNT	RATE PER HOUR
Fixed overhead	$ 5,400	$1.00
Variable overhead	10,800	2.00
TOTAL	$16,200	$3.00

1. Ten thousand pounds of material are purchased on account at a cost of $20,500.

Journal entry: Raw Materials 20,000
                 Raw Material Price Variance 500
                 Accounts Payable 20,500

The materials are entered in the Raw Materials account at $20,000. This represents the actual quantity purchased (10,000 pounds) at the standard price ($2.00 per pound). The accounts payable, of course, must be recorded at the actual cost of the material ($20,500), the difference representing the material price variance. Inasmuch as the variance is unfavorable, it appears as a debit. One may confirm the amount of the material price variance by utilizing the formula previously cited:

$$MPV = (SP - AP) \times AQ$$
$$MPV = (\$2.00 - \$2.05) \times 10,000 \text{ lbs.} = -\$500$$

2. The factory payroll, amounting to $15,325, is computed as fol-

lows: 4,800 direct labor hours at $3.10 per hour and 178 indirect labor hours at $2.50 per hour.

Journal entry: Direct Labor 14,400
               Direct Labor Rate Variance 480
               Manufacturing Overhead 445
               Payroll Payable 15,325

The Direct Labor account is charged with $14,400, which represents the actual direct labor hours worked (4,800 hours) times the standard direct labor rate ($3.00 per hour). The Manufacturing Overhead account is charged with the actual indirect labor cost of $445 (178 hours at $2.50 per hour), while the Payroll Payable account is credited for the actual total payroll cost of $15,325. The balancing figure is $480, the direct labor rate variance, and may be calculated as follows:

$$\text{LRV} = (\text{SR} - \text{AR}) \times \text{AH}$$
$$\text{LRV} = (\$3.00 - \$3.10) \times 4{,}800 \text{ hrs.} = -\$480$$

3. Overhead costs incurred during the month (in addition to the $445 indirect labor recorded above) are as follows:

a. Paid factory power bill $2,300
b. Factory insurance expired during the month amounted to $1,450. The insurance has previously been recorded as prepaid.
c. Rent for the factory building for the month is due but unpaid in the amount of $6,000.
d. Machinery and equipment (factory) depreciation amounts to $5,000 for the month.

Journal entry: Manufacturing Overhead 14,750
               Cash 2,300
               Prepaid Insurance 1,450
               Rent Payable 6,000
               Accumulated Depreciation,
                 Machinery and Equipment 5,000

No variances for overhead are recorded until the figures regarding production for the period are available.

4. Production is issued 6,825 pounds of material to produce 175 equivalent units.

Journal entry: Work in Process 14,000
               Raw Materials 13,650
               Raw Material Quantity Variance .. 350

The Work in Process account should be charged only for the amount of material that *should* have been used, i.e., the equivalent production (175 units) times the standard quantity per unit (40 pounds) times the standard price ($2.00 per pound), or $14,000. The Raw Materials account must be credited for the actual quantity used (6,825 pounds) times the standard price ($2.00 per pound). The difference is a favorable (credit) variance of $350, calculated as follows:

$$MVQ = (SQ - AQ) \times SP$$
$$MVQ = (7{,}000 \text{ lbs.} - 6{,}825 \text{ lbs.}) \times \$2.00 = +\$350$$

5. Forty-eight hundred hours of direct labor were worked to produce 175 equivalent units.

Journal entry: Work in Process 14,175
Direct Labor Efficiency Variance 225
Direct Labor   14,400

As was done with material, the Work in Process account should be charged only with the labor cost that *should* have been incurred to produce 175 units. According to a preestablished standard, we should have used $14,175 of labor (175 units × 27 hours per unit × $3.00 per hour). The Direct Labor account should be credited for the actual direct labor hours worked (4,800 hours) at the standard labor rate ($3.00 per hour), or $14,400. The difference of $225 represents an unfavorable labor efficiency variance. The amount of this variance may be checked by utilizing the formula as follows:

$$LEV = (SH - AH) \times SR$$
$$LEV = (4{,}725 \text{ hrs.} - 4{,}800 \text{ hrs.}) \times \$3.00 = -\$225$$

6. Overhead is applied to production at a rate of 100 percent of direct labor costs.

Journal entry:

Work in Process 14,175
Overhead Budget Variance 195
Overhead Capacity Variance 600
Overhead Efficiency Variance 225
Manufacturing Overhead   15,195

Now that the production for the period is known (175 equivalent units), we can apply overhead to work in process and calculate the three overhead variances. The charge to work in process is again determined by what should be *charged* according to standard (175 units × $81 overhead per unit). The credit to overhead is for the amount of the actual overhead costs recorded during the period (journal entry (2), above, $445, + journal entry (3), $14,750 = $15,195). The difference of $1,020 represents the total overhead variance which may be broken down by formula as follows:

OVERHEAD BUDGET VARIANCE

OBV = BOH − AOH
OBV = [$5,400 + (4,800 hrs. × $2.00)] − $15,195
OBV = $15,000 − $15,195 = −$195

OVERHEAD CAPACITY VARIANCE

OCV = (AH × SOR) − BOH
OCV = (4,800 hrs. × $3.00) − [$5,400 + (4,800 hrs. × $2.00)]
OCV = $14,400 − $15,000 = −$600

OVERHEAD EFFICIENCY VARIANCE

OEV = (SH − AH) × SOR
OEV = (4,725 hrs. − 4,800 hrs.) × $3.00 = −$225

7. One hundred sixty units are completed during the period and transferred to the warehouse:

Journal entry: Finished Goods 38,720
             Work in Process 38,720

In the previous entries the Work in Process account was charged only with standard costs. This means that as units are completed they are placed in the finished goods inventory at standard costs of $242 per unit. Likewise, as goods are sold, they are removed from the finished goods inventory at standard.

8. One hundred fifty units are sold on account for $400 per unit.

Journal entry: Accounts Receivable 60,000
             Sales 60,000
             Cost of Goods Sold 36,300
             Finished Goods 36,300

9. The variance accounts generally are carried on the books as deferred charges (asset caption) or deferred credits (liability caption) from month to month. Normally they are closed to the Cost of Goods Sold account at the end of the year. The following entry would close the variance accounts:

Journal entry: Cost of Goods Sold 1,875
             Raw Material Quantity Variance 350
             Raw Material Price Variance 500
             Direct Labor Rate Variance 480
             Direct Labor Efficiency Variance 225
             Overhead Budget Variance 195
             Overhead Efficiency Variance 225
             Overhead Capacity Variance 600

SUMMARY

Costs may be accumulated for two major purposes: to value inventory and cost of goods sold and, in turn, to measure profits; or to increase efficiency by controlling costs. Conventional cost accounting systems are designed primarily to accomplish the first objective. The second may be achieved by preplanning, budgeting, and accumulating costs by responsibility center. Costs can be controlled only to the extent that variances between actual and predetermined standards can be calculated and responsibility for such variances fixed.

Standard cost systems are often employed by manufacturing enterprises primarily as a means of control. Where this is done, standards are carefully established to show what costs *should be* under ideal, attainable circumstances. Variances are generated to point out areas where standard costs vary from actual costs. These variances indicate problem areas to which management should devote its attention. The standard cost system illustrated in this chapter generated seven variances: material price, material quantity, labor rate, labor efficiency, overhead budget, overhead capacity, and overhead efficiency.

QUESTIONS

1. What is a responsibility center? Can the same costs be accumulated by job and also by a responsibility center? Explain.
2. What is the purpose of a standard cost accounting system?
3. What are standards? How are standards established? Can standard costs be utilized for valuing inventories and similar financial accounting purposes?
4. What the three variances that might arise with respect to materials? Why are only two variances generally recorded? What happens to the third variance where only two are actually recorded?
5. List the variances that generally are recorded with respect to materials and labor, and in each case indicate who would be responsible for such a variance.
6. List the three types of overhead variances cited in this chapter and indicate how each is calculated. What might cause an unfavorable variance in each case?
7. List some of the advantages and limitations of a standard cost system. What conditions are essential if a standard cost system is to work?
8. Given the following facts, calculate the material price variance: standard price per pound, $0.75; standard quantity used to produce one unit of output, fifteen pounds; actual quantity purchased, one thousand pounds; actual price paid, $0.73 per pound. Is the variance favorable or unfavorable?
9. Given a production of 35 equivalent units and material usage of 500 pounds (assuming the same facts as in the preceding question), what is the material usage variance? Is this variance favorable or unfavorable?

10. If you were given a trial balance of a manufacturing enterprise which utilized a standard cost accounting system, how would you recognize which variances were favorable and which were unfavorable?

11. Calculate the overhead variances of the Ness Manufacturing Company from the following facts: budgeted overhead costs, $197,500 (of which $100,000 are fixed costs); actual overhead costs, $189,000; standard overhead rate per direct labor hour, $3.95; actual direct labor hours worked, 47,500 hours; standard direct labor hours, 47,000 hours.

PROBLEMS

Problem 17-1

The unit standard cost of product J of the Jones Production Company is $84.35, divided as follows:

Material 16 units at $3.10/unit	$49.60
Labor 8½ hours at $2.50/hour	21.25
Overhead	13.50

During October, 18,000 units of material were purchased at an average price of $3.18 per unit, and 17,500 units of material were used. The total number of direct labor hours worked, at an average rate of $2.65 per hour, was 9,075. Actual overhead costs for the month were $14,995. The number of units of product J started and completed during October was 1,100.

Required:

Prepare journal entries for the above information.

Problem 17-2

The Ajax Chemical Company uses standard costs in its cost accounting system. The unit standard cost of chemical W is $11.20, computed as follows:

Raw Materials, 2 pounds @ $0.95/pound	$ 1.90
Labor, 3 hours @ $2.85/hour	8.55
Overhead	0.75
	$11.20

The following were the inventory balances on April 1, 1975:

Raw Materials (500 lbs.)	$ 475
Work in Process (150 units, one-third complete)	560
Finished Goods (200 units)	2,240

Material, labor, and overhead are applied at the same rate in the production process, so that if the work in process inventory is one-half complete, it will have been charged with one-half of each type of cost.

The following activities took place during April:

1. Purchases of 1,600 pounds of raw material were made at an average price of $0.98 per pound.
2. A total of 2,540 direct labor hours were worked at an average rate of $2.90 per hour.
3. Actual overhead costs for the period totalled $625 (credit "Various Accounts").
4. The company started 850 units during the period. At the end of the period 200 were still in process and were on the average one-half complete. The April 30 inventory of raw material shows 240 pounds on hand.
5. The company sold 860 units during the period at an average price of $18.75. The company records the cost of goods sold at the time sales are made. Two-thirds of the sales were for cash.

Required:

    a. Prepare journal entries to record the transactions that occurred in April.

    b. Assume that the company closes its books each month. Prepare the closing entries for April.

Problem 17-3

The unit standard cost of Model H of the Howe Long Corporation is $63.75 as follows:

Material, 18 units @ $1.25/unit $22.50
Labor, 6 hours @ $2.75/hour 16.50
Overhead 24.75

During the month of June the company purchased 11,150 units of material at an average cost of $1.35 per unit, and 9,610 units of material were used. A total of 2,945 direct labor hours were worked at an average rate of $2.70 per hour. Actual overhead costs were $12,640. The number of units of Model H started and completed during the month was 500.

Required:

    a. List the variances that can be calculated from the above information.

    b. Calculate the amount of the variances.

    c. Indicate whether the variances are favorable or unfavorable.

Problem 17-4

During the first quarter of 1968, the Kat Manufacturing Company estimated that it would produce 50,000 Kiddie Kats. At normal operating capacity, the fixed overhead costs are expected to amount to $62,500, and the variable overhead should run to $0.75 per direct labor hour. The company's standard cost system provides for the use of $4.00 of material and two hours of labor in the production of each finished unit.

The production records of the Kat Manufacturing Company disclosed that 62,000 Kiddie Kats were produced during the period. The company incurred actual overhead costs of $172,000, and the employees worked 125,000 direct labor hours.

Required:
Prepare a three-variance overhead analysis.

Problem 17-5
The Vowles Company showed the following quarterly production of product W for the year ended June 30, 1971.

QUARTER	UNITS PRODUCED	MATERIAL USED (IN POUNDS)	DIRECT LABOR HOURS
1	600	1,795	910
2	500	1,505	740
3	500	1,495	755
4	400	1,205	595

QUARTER	MATERIAL PURCHASED (IN POUNDS)	COST OF MATERIAL	DIRECT LABOR COSTS
1	2,000	$960	$1,638
2	1,600	784	1,332
3	1,500	750	1,359
4	1,200	600	1,071

The contract with the United Rainc Labor Union is about to expire, and negotiations are already underway for a new contract. Union leaders have indicated that the employees want several of their fringe benefits increased. The union has also asked for a 10 percent increase in wages. The company has decided to meet all of the union's demands, inasmuch as a strike at this time would be disastrous to the company's competitive position. A new contract will probably be signed at the end of August for a three-year period.

Material prices have been climbing for several periods, but it now appears that they have stabilized. A systems engineer has made a study of the company's manufacturing process. His report stated that by using a better grade of material, material usage could be cut by one-sixth. However, the better grade of material would cost about one-tenth more per pound than the most recent price paid for material.

If the company uses the better grade of material, the plant employees would have to be more careful during production to keep spoilage down. On the average it would probably take one-third longer to produce the same amount of output.

Required:
a. Develop new standards for the Vowles Company, assuming that the company makes the changes suggested by the systems engineer.

    b. Should the company make the suggested changes? Show support-
ing computations.

Problem 17-6

Product Manufacturing Company uses a standard cost accounting system.

Production of one unit of product A has the following standards:

Material, 15 pounds @ $1.10/pound	$16.50
Labor, 12 hours @ $2.50/hour	30.00
Overhead, $3.75 per direct labor hour	45.00
	$91.50

    During the month of December, the company budgeted overhead costs
of $31,500 for the production of 700 units of product A. The fixed over-
head is expected to be $16,800 for the month, and the variable overhead
will be applied at the rate of $1.75 per direct labor hour.
    Production records for the month revealed that 650 units were pro-
duced during the month. A total of 9,725 pounds of material was used.
The employees were paid $19,928.25 for 7,815 direct labor hours.
    During the month the company purchased 10,000 pounds of material
for $11,200. Actual overhead charges incurred during the month were
$32,600.

Required:
List and calculate seven variances from the above information.

Case 17
INSOLUBLE SOAP COMPANY

    The Insoluble Soap Company, an established firm in the detergent
industry, has experienced declining profits in recent years despite the
fact that sales have shown a steady increase. Stockholders and other
interested parties have voiced concern over the poor earnings performance. Frank Lee, the company president, has decided the unfavorable
earnings trend must be stopped and accordingly calls in T. M. Hymm,
the controller, for an explanation. Somewhat defensively, Hymm suggests
possible trouble areas, but can't really provide the president with any
answers. Wisely, Hymm asks for time to further investigate the probable
problem, and Lee gives him two days to come up with some concrete
evidence to support his explanations.
    Back in his office, Hymm sets out to rectify a situation he was well
aware of, but elected not to disclose. Insoluble Soap had established a
standard cost system ten years ago, but in the last two years had failed
to update or even use it.
    Hastily, the controller puts several other accountants to work revamping

standards and calculating current variances. In their search, the accountants uncover the following information:

1. The raw materials mix has changed since the last standards were set, thereby increasing the quality of detergent. This change in mix has, however, caused a 50 percent increase in the cost of raw materials. Quantity requirements per case have remained constant.
2. Labor costs have increased 18 percent due to a new three-year union contract negotiated last year. Because new machinery was acquired last year, the hours of direct labor required to produce a product have decreased by 10 percent.
3. The company allocates overhead on the basis of direct labor hours. The estimated number of direct labor hours has increased by 80,000 since the standard was last revised. Mr. Hymm feels this increased volume, when added to the previous standard volume, represents a fair standard.
4. The estimated overhead costs at normal or standard volume have increased by $968,000, of which $584,000 constitutes fixed costs.

   As a staff accountant, you are assigned the task of preparing the data for the controller to answer the following questions:

1. What new standards would you recommend for the company, assuming they plan to reestablish a standard cost system?
2. Based upon the new standards, what variances resulted from operations this past year?
3. Having calculated the appropriate variances, suggest several possible causes for each.
4. What might be done to remedy the existing problems?

EXHIBIT 17-1

INSOLUBLE SOAP COMPANY
Selected Data

Year 1967 (Standard)

Standard cost per case:
Raw material, 20 pounds @ $0.04/pound	$0.80
Direct labor, 0.20 hours @ $3.00/hour	.60
Overhead	1.50
Total standard cost per case	$2.90

Standard annual volume: 1,760,000 hours
Total fixed costs at standard volume: $8,800,000

Year 1970 (Actual)

Raw materials used	200,490,000 pounds
Cost of raw materials used	$13,031,850
Direct labor hours worked	1,700,200 hours
Direct labor costs	$6,120,720
Actual overhead costs	$14,840,000
Actual output	9,780,000 cases

18

Costs
for
Decision Making

The cost accounting systems discussed in previous chapters have pertained solely to manufacturing concerns. These systems were designed primarily to determine the unit cost of manufactured products and thereby arrive at inventory values. In these systems, all costs that were associated with the factory operation were designated as *product* costs; that is, they were charged to the products produced, thus becoming inventory costs. On the other hand, costs not associated with the factory, such as administrative and selling expenses, were designated as *period* costs and were expensed in the period in which they occurred. This classification of costs was useful in determining inventory values and in assuring the proper matching of revenues and expenses.

Cost accounting has application far beyond the manufacturing enterprise. Cost data may be used to determine the profitability of various departments in a department store, to select the least cost method of distribution for a wholesaler, to determine service charges in the various departments of a bank, or to aid the management of any enterprise in making countless decisions.

COST CONCEPTS

Unfortunately, neither one definition of cost nor one classification of the cost data will satisfy all needs. The careful classification of costs into product and period costs made to determine the inventory value may be useless when utilized to determine the price at which those very units of output are to be sold. All costs are not relevant in every situation, and, therefore, some additional cost concepts are essential. Particular attention will be given here to those concepts that are important in making decisions regarding future courses of action.

Differential Costs

Probably the most important concept of cost related to the decision-making process is that of differential costs. These are the additional costs which will be incurred if management chooses one course of action as opposed to another. Differential costs are the extra, or incremental, costs resulting from a particular decision. In choosing between alternatives it is the differential costs that are relevant in making the best choice.

Sunk Costs

Sunk costs are costs which have already been incurred and which will not be affected by a future decision. They may be defined as the difference between the net book value and the current market value of an asset. To illustrate, assume a company has a machine that it bought one year ago at a cost of $10,000. Depreciation to date has been only $1,000; but because of technological change, the machine has become obsolete and, therefore, can be sold for only $5,000. The sunk cost in this instance is $4,000 ($9,000–$5,000).

In choosing between alternatives, the sunk costs can virtually be ignored. Management's attitude toward sunk costs may be summarized by the expression "don't cry over spilt milk." While the benefit of hindsight often gives us reason to question the wisdom of some of our past decisions, the losses resulting from these faulty choices should not cause us to make a compounding mistake. We can proceed to select the best course of action by disregarding the sunk costs and considering only those future costs that are pertinent.

Opportunity Costs

When we choose to follow one alternative we are also choosing *not* to follow another. By making a choice we automatically elect to give up all the benefits that would have accrued had we chosen some other alternative. These foregone benefits are lost opportunities and, to the extent that they can be quantified, they should be considered as part of the cost of the decision. The relevant opportunity costs in a particular case would be the benefits that would accrue under the next best alternative.

To illustrate the concept of opportunity costs, assume that the Mantle Company decides to buy a new delivery truck with a list price of $4,500. The company's old delivery truck has a book value of $1,000; it may be disposed of by trading it in on the new truck with a $1,200 allowance, selling it in the secondhand market for $900, or using it for a garbage truck and, thereby, saving the purchase of a $700 used truck for that purpose. If the company elects to trade the truck in, it is foregoing the $900 cash that it would receive under the second alternative and the saving of $700 it would enjoy under the third alternative. The relevant opportunity cost in this instance is the $900, since it represents the benefits foregone by not selecting *the next best alternative*. The $900 should be considered as much a cost of the new truck as the payment of $3,300 in cash.

Imputed Costs

In order to make a fair comparison of alternatives, it is sometimes necessary to impute certain costs. Imputed costs are costs that have not been recorded in the accounting records and, in many cases, never will be recorded. They are theoretical costs that must be assigned if the correct decision is to be made. The most common imputed cost is probably interest. Whenever we make a decision that will tie up large sums of capital, the interest on these amounts must be considered. If the company plans to borrow the necessary funds, the actual interest that will be paid under the various alternatives should be calculated. On the other hand, if the owners' funds are to be used, then the estimated cost of this capital must also be figured.

Out-of-Pocket Costs

The term "out-of-pocket costs" is sometimes used to designate those costs that will actually require cash expenditures. Sometimes these costs are more important than total costs, especially where available funds are extremely limited. In certain instances, management may actually make a choice based upon which alternative will require the least cash outlay instead of on which will generate the most revenue. In these instances, the out-of-pocket costs are most significant.

Replacement Costs

The replacement cost of an asset is the cost required to replace an existing asset with a comparable one in the current market. Although accountants steadfastly stick to historical cost as the basis for recording assets, these accounting costs are not meaningful in many decisions. The pricing decision, for example, is one that must consider the replacement cost of assets. Suppose, for example, that we have on our shelves an item of inventory that cost us $500, but because of a manufacturer's price increase would cost us $750 to replace. Which price (the $500 historical cost or the $750 replacement cost) is most relevant in setting the sales price? If we ignored the replacement price, selling the item for $700 and replacing it for $750, we would actually sustain a loss of $50 (although the books would reflect the $200 profit). Replacement costs cannot be ignored in the decision-making process.

APPLICATION OF COST CONCEPTS TO DECISION MAKING

In the preceding paragraphs we have discussed some of the concepts that are important in making management decisions. Let us now turn to some actual cases which require utilization of these principles.

Replacing Fixed Assets

Almost from the moment a fixed asset is purchased, management is faced with the question of when it should be replaced. This is particularly true in areas that experience rapid technological change. A company may purchase a machine, planning to use it for five years. Shortly after purchase a new machine is developed making the existing machine obsolete, and economic conditions dictate replacing an almost new machine.

In deciding whether or not to replace the existing machine, management must calculate the differential costs and revenues and select the alternative that will make the maximum contribution to overall profits. The difficult task in making these decisions is to decide which costs are relevant. Often the issue is clouded with misleading cost figures presented by machine manufacturers in an attempt to make management unhappy with what they already have. Often the machine representatives present total cost comparisons which make replacement appear more attractive than it actually is.

To illustrate an asset replacement problem, let us consider the case of the Pearson Publishing Company. The company currently owns a gasoline-powered forklift, purchased two and one-half years ago at a cost of $5,000. At the time of the purchase it was estimated that the lift would last ten years and would have a $500 salvage value.

The Speedlift Company has just introduced a new electric model forklift that lists for $6,000. Although the old lift could be sold today for only $2,000, a salesman offers the Pearson Publishing Company a $2,200 trade-in allowance as an incentive to make the trade. He says the new lift will also last ten years, and the company could expect a $1,000 salvage at the end of that time. In addition, the salesman presents the following figures in support of his proposal:

Annual Cost of Operation

	OLD LIFT	SPEED LIFT
Gasoline	$ 175	$ 0
Batteries and charges	0	125
Maintenance	150	100
Operator's wages	6,000	6,000
Insurance	30	20
Depreciation	450	480
	$6,805	$6,725

To support the cost differences, the salesman presents satisfactory statistics and testimonials, such as reduced maintenance and insurance cost. Based upon his presentation, it would appear that the company could save $80 per year by making the trade.

The above analysis is based on total operating costs as they would be recorded in the company's books of account. We have previously noted, however, that these costs are not always meaningful in decision making. The sunk costs on the old machine are not relevant, and certain imputed costs have been ignored. A more meaningful cost comparison follows:

Annual Cost of Operation

	OLD LIFT	SPEED LIFT
Gasoline	$ 175	$ 0
Batteries and charges	0	125
Maintenance	150	100
Operator's wages	6,000	6,000
Insurance	30	20
Depreciation	200[a]	480[b]
Imputed interest	81[c]	218[d]
	$6,636	$6,943

[a] Depreciation on the old lift should be based upon the present fair market value, since anything in excess of this is a sunk cost. The fair market value today ($2,000), less estimated salvage value ($500), leaves $1,500 to be depreciated over the 7½ years remaining life, or $200 annual depreciation.

[b] Depreciation of the new lift should be the same as under the salesman's figures, since none of the costs of the new lift are sunk costs at this point. The cost of the new lift would be $5,800 ($3,800 cash paid plus the $2,000 fair market value of the trade-in). The annual depreciation on the new machine would be $480 ($5,800 minus $1,000 divided by 10).

[c] Interest on the old lift may be imputed by computing the average amount that will be invested under this alternative. The investment today would be $2,000 (the fair market value today). The investment at the beginning of the last year of its life (6½ years hence) will be $700 ($500 salvage value, plus the last year's depreciation of $200). The average investment under this alternative would be $1,350 ($2,000 plus $700 divided by 2) and the average imputed interest $81 ($1,350 × 0.06).

[d] Interest on the new machine may be imputed by figuring the average investment under this alternative. The investment at the beginning of the first year would be $5,800 (cost of the new machine), and the investment at the beginning of the last year would be $1,480 ($1,000 salvage value, plus the last year's depreciation of $480). The average investment under this alternative will be $3,640 ($5,800 plus $1,480 divided by 2) and the average interest, $218 ($3,640 × 0.06).

This analysis presents quite a different picture. Instead of saving it $80 per year, the trade would cost the firm $307 per year. The difference, of course, is the result of ignoring the sunk cost in the old machine and recognizing that the new lift will cause the company to tie up more capital—something that is not without cost.

Accepting Additional Volume

Manufacturing firms are often faced with the opportunity of taking on additional volume at a price that on the surface would appear to be unprofitable. For example, a large department store chain may negotiate a contract with one of the major tire producers to manufacture tires to be marketed under the department store brand name. The agreed contract price may actually be below the price at which the same manufacturer sells similar quality tires to its own distributors, and, in fact, may even be below the manufacturer's total average unit cost. Such a practice would seem foolish, but careful analysis of the pertinent costs would show that such action may indeed serve to maximize the profits of the firm.

In this type of problem the differential or incremental costs, rather than the total cost, are pertinent. Also important, of course, are the incremental revenues. If the incremental revenues will exceed the incremental costs, then such a contract should normally be accepted, regardless of what the total average unit cost may be.

In calculating the incremental revenue, it is important to give consideration to the impact of the proposed contract on the company's regular sales. Will the goods purchased under the contract be sold in a foreign market,[1] or will they be sold in direct competition to the manufacturer's regular output? Any decrease in revenue anticipated from regular sales should be subtracted from the contract price in arriving at incremental revenue.

Another important consideration in this type of contract is the alternate uses to which the facilities could be placed. If a company has excess capacity and no other immediate prospects for utilizing these facilities, then accepting additional volume could prove advantageous. If production is near full capacity, on the other hand, the additional volume could create bottlenecks and inefficiencies that could cause regular costs to rise sharply. For example, a certain operation may require overtime with the resulting 50 percent premium pay.

The application of these principles may be seen in a simple illustration. Peacock Electronics is a manufacturer of color television sets. Several years ago, Peacock invested substantially in a new plant to keep up with the skyrocketing demand for color sets. Recently the demand has leveled off, creating considerable excess capacity at the Peacock factory. The company's own sets are distributed through factory-authorized dealers, primarily in the eastern and midwestern sections of the country.

The Sunshine Department Store would like to introduce its own name-brand color TV set and offers Peacock $210 per set to produce it. The Sunshine set would be identical to the Peacock model NB-2525, except for minor trim and identification modifications. The Sunshine set will be distributed in 165 department stores located in five western states, and no direct competition is expected. Without the contract, Peacock is expected to operate at only 75 percent of capacity.

---

[1]The term *foreign market* is used to denote any market in which the company does not sell its own product. For example, a manufacturer may be organized to sell his own product in only the western portion of the United States. A contract with a firm selling only in the eastern portion of the country, then, would be considered as pertaining to a foreign market.

Peacock has a modern cost accounting system, and the controller reports that the average unit cost of a model NB-2525 during the coming year should be $245 per set. This model is sold to Peacock dealers at a price of $299 per set. Other pertinent cost data are summarized below:

Model NB-2525

Fixed overhead allocated	$2,100,000
Variable manufacturing costs	$193 per set
Expected production during the coming year	50,000 units
Variable selling costs	$10 per set

Sunshine Model

Additional fixed overhead	$ 50,000
Contract price	$210 per set
Units contracted	8,000 units
Variable manufacturing costs	same as NB-2525
Variable selling costs[a]	none

---

[a]No additional selling costs are anticipated with the Sunshine model since they will be sold on a contract basis, F.O.B. Peacock factory.

The above data may be summarized as follows to reveal the pertinent facts regarding the proposed contract:

DIFFERENTIAL REVENUE

8,000 sets at $210 each	$1,680,000

DIFFERENTIAL COSTS

Fixed overhead increase	$ 50,000	
Variable costs (8,000 units × $193)	$1,544,000	$1,594,000
NET DIFFERENTIAL REVENUE		$ 86,000
Differential revenue per set (86,000 divided by 8,000 sets)		$ 10.75

Although the contract specifies a price considerably below the company's total cost, the proposal should be accepted because it will add $86,000 to Peacock's total profit. This decision is reached because of consideration of differential costs and revenues.

Make or Buy

Most manufacturing firms are constantly faced with make-or-buy decisions. This is especially true for products that are assembled from many component parts. With each part, the manufacturer must decide whether it will be in the firm's best interest to produce the component or to purchase it from an outside supplier. There are many factors that must be considered in reaching such a decision. Does the firm have the facilities to produce the part? Does it have the trained personnel and adequate experience with the product? Does it have sufficient volume to attain economies of scale? Can it maintain adequate control of quality if it purchases? What would be its position if the supplier were to suffer a strike? Will purchase make it overly dependent on its suppliers? These are just a few of the important questions that must be answered in reaching the proper decision. Some of these questions are hard to quantify, while others readily lend themselves to incremental analysis.

A manufacturer of color television sets would encounter many make-or-buy problems. For some time Peacock Electronics has considered manufacturing its own picture tubes. At present, the company is purchasing twenty-five-inch tubes from a major color TV producer for $108 each. Peacock has ample space in the factory to produce its own tubes (even after accepting the Sunshine Department Store volume) and sufficient experience so that no major technical problems are anticipated. Manufacturing the tubes will require purchasing special equipment at a cost of $750,000. This equipment should be capable of producing 250,000 tubes, but is expected to have no salvage value. Because of excess capacity, production is currently being charged overhead at the rate of 200 percent of direct labor. The cost of manufacturing the tubes may be summarized below:

Direct materials	$ 20.00
Direct labor	40.00
Patent royalties	5.00
Depreciation on new equipment	3.00
Factory overhead (200% of direct labor)	80.00
TOTAL	$148.00

The above figures make the present practice of buying seem very attractive. The unit cost to produce will be $148, as opposed to only $108 to buy. Careful analysis, however, might reveal the following pertinent facts: if the new equipment is acquired, the company will borrow the necessary funds at 6 percent interest, and variable overhead applicable to the tubes is expected to run at only 75 percent of direct labor (the balance of the overhead rate representing an allocation of fixed overhead).

The expected tube production costs may properly be summarized in incremental terms as follows:

Direct materials	$20.00
Direct labor	40.00
Patent royalties	5.00
Depreciation on new equipment	3.00

Variable factory overhead[a]	30.00
Imputed interest[b]	.54
TOTAL	$98.54

[a]75 percent of direct labor.

[b]At present output of 50,000 TV sets per year, the equipment should have about a five-year life. Investment at the beginning of the first year will be $750,000 and at the beginning of the last year $150,000, or an average investment of $450,000. The average annual interest would be $27,000 ($450,000 × 0.06), or $0.54 per unit.

The above figures reverse the decision in favor of producing, since the incremental cost to make is expected to be only $99 as opposed to the current purchase price of $108.

The marginal analysis followed in the preceding illustration is a *short-run* solution to the problem of idle plant capacity. The solution points out how a company can temporarily put to work space and facilities that would otherwise go unused. It should be noted that in the long run *all* costs must be covered, and a company cannot continue indefinitely to make decisions based on this type of analysis. What are the long-run implications of a decision by Peacock to produce its own tubes? To begin with, it will be tying up space for at least a five-year period. Could this space be put to better use? These and other long-run factors should influence Peacock's final decision.

Dropping a Department

Income statements are often prepared by product line or department so that management can evaluate the profitability of various operations. Where this type of analysis is performed it is not uncommon to find that one or more of the departments shows a loss. Consideration must then be given to the question of whether or not this unprofitable operation should be eliminated. In making a decision, consideration should be given to the following:

1. The cross relationship between various products or departments
2. The nonquantitative factors, such as prestige
3. The costs and revenues that will be eliminated.

It is extremely difficult to measure the impact of the sales of one product on those of another. Yet it is common practice for a firm to continue to produce an item at a loss in order to carry a complete line. A grocery store, for example, may continue to operate an unprofitable produce department because customers may cease to patronize the store entirely if they cannot do all of their grocery shopping in one stop. Careful consideration should be given to the interrelationship of the revenues of all products before any are eliminated.

Sometimes companies retain unprofitable departments or products as a device to create goodwill. An automobile manufacturer may introduce a high-performance sports car, on which the company never expects to break even, strictly to create or maintain a progressive image. Similarly, a shoe store may continue to carry some exclusive Italian imports at a loss in order to establish its name. It is hoped, of course, that these products will contribute to long-term profit maximization, but their value in the short run may be difficult to establish.

Probably the most important consideration in eliminating a department or product is the effect that such a decision will have on the company's overall profits. Some of the costs which are properly chargeable to a particular product or department will continue to be incurred even after that operation has been eliminated. For this reason, the elimination of an unprofitable department may actually tend to reduce the company's overall profit.

Consider the Waltham Clothing Stores. The company started business five years ago and, although operations as a whole have earned a profit in each of these years, the children's department has yet to show a profit in a single year. A departmentalized income statement for the most recent fiscal year is shown in Figure 18-1.

Upon receiving this statement, management's attention was focused upon the continued unfavorable record of the children's department. The following data were assembled to assist in deciding whether or not to eliminate this department:

1. Elimination of the children's department is expected to decrease sales of the men's and women's departments by 5 percent because of the interrelationship of departments. A portion of these departments' sales may be attributed to customers who come in to buy from the children's department.
2. The following costs, which are chargeable to the children's department, are expected to be eliminated, or reduced as indicated. All other costs are expected to remain the same, even though the children's department is eliminated:

EXPENSE	ANTICIPATED REDUCTION
Advertising	$ 500
Sales Salaries	20,000
Other Selling Expenses	1,000
Office Salaries	1,000
Insurance	200
Other Administrative Expenses	100
TOTAL	$22,800

Figure 18-1

WALTHAM DEPARTMENT STORE

Departmentalized Income Statement
For the Year Ended January 31, 1968

	MEN'S CLOTHING	WOMEN'S CLOTHING	CHILDREN'S CLOTHING	COMBINED TOTAL
Sales	$251,000	$363,500	$75,000	$689,500
Cost of Goods Sold	149,200	222,300	43,000	414,500
Gross Margin	$101,800	$141,200	$32,000	$275,000
Expenses:				
Selling Expenses:				
Advertising	$ 2,000	$2,000	$ 1,000	$ 5,000
Delivery	8,000	9,000	8,000	25,000
Rent	18,000	20,000	12,000	50,000
Sales Salaries	25,000	30,000	20,000	75,000
Other	5,000	7,000	5,000	17,000
Total Selling Expenses	$58,000	$68,000	$46,000	$172,000
Administrative Expenses:				
Office Salaries	$ 9,000	$ 9,000	$ 7,000	$ 25,000
Insurance	900	900	700	2,500
Heat & Light	7,500	8,000	4,500	20,000
Other	1,000	1,000	500	2,500
Total Administrative Expense	$18,400	$18,900	$12,700	$ 50,000
Total Expenses	76,400	86,900	58,700	222,000
Operating Profit <Loss>	$ 25,400	$ 54,300	<$26,700>	$ 53,000
Income Taxes	12,700	27,150	13,350	26,500
Net Profit <Loss>	$ 12,700	$ 27,150	<$13,350>	$ 26,500

A combined income statement can now be recast to show how the company's total net profit would be affected by the proposed elimination. Such a statement is shown in Figure 18-2.

Figure 18-2

WALTHAM'S CLOTHING STORE
Recast Income Statement with Elimination of Children's Department
For the Year Ended January 31, 1968

Sales[a]			$583,585
Cost of goods sold			352,925
Gross profit			$230,660
Selling expenses:			
Advertising	$ 4,500		
Delivery	25,000		
Rent	50,000		
Salaries	55,000		
Other	16,000	$150,500	
Administrative expense:			
Office salaries	24,000		
Insurance	2,300		
Heat and lights	20,000		
Other	2,400	$ 48,700	
Total expenses			199,200
Operating profit			$ 31,460
Income taxes			15,730
Net profit			$ 15,730

[a]Sales and Cost of Goods Sold are calculated as 95 percent of the combined sales of men's and women's departments because of interrelationship of department sales.

The elimination of the children's department would reduce the company's profit by $10,800. Even though the department operates at a loss, it makes a contribution to profits by partially covering the company's fixed costs. Unless another department that will make a larger contribution to the fixed cost can be added to replace the children's department, the department should be retained.

Other Applications

In this chapter we have illustrated four instances where total cost as determined by the accounting records would be inadequate for decision-making purposes. Incremental costs, sunk costs, opportunity costs, out-of-pocket costs, and imputed costs were introduced as concepts that are important in the decision-making process. The cost concepts introduced can be applied similarly to many other decisions, including plant shutdown or abandonment, selling a product as it is or processing it further prior to sale, or selecting the best method of manufacture. The illustrations were simplified in that each decision involved only two alternatives. In practice, of course, there may be many alternatives. Where this is true, the alternatives can be paired off and successively eliminated until the best alternative is selected.

Breakeven Analysis

The cost-volume-profit relationship of a company is of utmost importance to management. By analyzing this relationship, one may calculate the volume at which the company will break even on the potential profit or loss at any given level of sales activity, or evaluate the impact that various proposals may have on the company's profits.

In order to make such an analysis, the company must classify the costs which it incurs according to their behavior in relationship to volume. Some costs, known as *variable costs*, vary directly in relationship to the sales volume. As more units are sold these costs increase proportionately. Other costs remain constant within certain limits; no measurable increase is experienced with such costs as volume is increased. These may be termed *fixed costs*. There are, of course, other patterns of behavior which might cause a cost to be classified as *semifixed* or *semivariable*. For purposes of breakeven analysis, these latter costs must be classified as either fixed or variable, or at least broken into their fixed and variable components.

Calculation of Breakeven Point

The breakeven point may be defined as the point at which sales revenue will exactly equal the total costs. Profit is realized at any attainable volume beyond this point and a loss sustained at any volume below this point. Knowledge of where the breakeven point lies is a factor profoundly affecting many management decisions. The breakeven volume in terms of *units of output* may be expressed as follows:

$$USP \times X = FC + (UVC \times X)$$

where

USP = Selling price per unit of output
X = Number of units that must be sold to break even
FC = Total fixed costs
UVC = Variable costs per unit of output

The breakeven point in terms of *dollar volume* may be calculated as follows:

$$Y = FC + \frac{UVC}{USP} Y$$

where

$\quad$ Y $\ =\ $ Dollar sales volume necessary to break even
$\quad$ FC $\ =\ $ Total fixed costs
UVC $\ =\ $ Variable costs per unit of output
USP $\ =\ $ Selling price per unit of output

To illustrate the calculation of a breakeven point, let us assume the following facts. The Beehive Products Company produces a beehive which sells for $45 per unit. The variable costs of production and sales are $20 per unit, and the company has fixed costs of $300,000 per year. The unit breakeven point for the company would be 12,000 units per year, calculated as follows:

$$USP \times X = FC + (UVC \times X)$$
$$\$45X = \$300,000 + \$20X$$
$$\$45X - \$20X = \$300,000$$
$$\$25X = \$300,000$$
$$X = 12,000 \text{ units}$$

The breakeven point in terms of necessary sales volume may be found by multiplying the unit sales price ($45) by the number of units required to break even (12,000), or by direct calculation as follows:

$$Y = FC + \frac{UVC}{USP} Y$$

$$Y = \$300,000 + \frac{\$20}{\$45} Y$$

$$Y = \$300,000 + \frac{4}{9} Y$$

$$Y - \frac{4}{9} Y = \$300,000$$

$$\frac{5}{9} Y = \$300,000$$

$$Y = \$540,000$$

The Contribution Margin

The amount by which the selling price per unit exceeds the variable cost per unit may be described as the *marginal contribution per unit*. This marginal contribution represents the amount contributed by each unit sold toward the company's fixed costs and to the firm's profits after these fixed costs are covered. The marginal contribution may be utilized to calculate the breakeven point in units as follows:

$$\text{Unit breakeven point} = \frac{\text{Total fixed costs}}{\text{Marginal contribution per unit}}$$

$$= \frac{\$300,000}{\$25 \text{ per unit}}$$

$$= 12,000 \text{ units}$$

The *marginal contribution rate* expresses the marginal contribution as a percent of sales. The marginal contribution rate of Beehive Products is 55.5 percent ($25/$45). The breakeven point in dollars may be calculated by utilizing the marginal contribution rate as follows:

$$\text{Dollar breakeven point} = \frac{\text{Total fixed costs}}{\text{Marginal contribution rate}}$$

$$= \frac{\$300,000}{.555}$$

$$= \$540,000$$

Multiproduct Breakeven

It is also possible to calculate the breakeven point of a firm that produces and markets any number of products, provided the *sales mix remains constant*. To illustrate, assume the following facts relative to the output of Barker Bakery:

	PER UNIT			
	VARIABLE COST (IN CENTS)	SELLING PRICE (IN CENTS)	MARGINAL CONTRIBUTIONS (IN CENTS)	PERCENT OF TOTAL SALES VOLUME
Bread	18	30	12	50
Cakes	40	80	40	35
Cookies (dozen)	28	70	42	15

If the sales mix remains constant, we can assume that all products are sold in packages which include .5 loaves of bread, .35 cakes, and .15 cookies. The total marginal contribution of each such package would be $0.263 calculated as follows:

$$.5 (\$0.12) + .35 (\$0.40) + .15 (\$0.42) = \$0.263$$

If the company had fixed costs of $5,000, the breakeven point would be calculated as follows:

$$\text{Unit breakeven point} = \frac{\text{Total fixed costs}}{\text{Marginal contribution per unit}}$$

$$= \frac{\$5,000}{\$0.263}$$

$$= 19,011 \text{ units}$$

This company's breakeven point would consist of 9,506 loaves of bread (50 percent of 19,011), 6,654 cakes (35 percent of 19,011), and 2,852 dozen cookies (15 percent of 19,011).

The Breakeven Chart

The revenues and costs at various sales volumes may be plotted on a breakeven chart. Such a chart is useful in that it reveals not only the breakeven point, but also the expected profit or loss at any attainable volume. The chart may be prepared by first plotting the variable cost curve. Where costs vary directly with volume, this curve represents a straight line that intersects the point of origin. It is drawn by marking the total variable costs at any volume (other than zero) and drawing a straight line that intersects this point and the point of origin. The fixed costs may next be added on top of the variable costs to arrive at a total cost curve. This curve will originate on the Y axis at that point which corresponds with the total fixed costs and will then run parallel to the variable cost curve.

Finally the total revenue curve is plotted. This curve also intersects the point of origin, and where all goods are sold at a single price is a straight line. It is plotted by fixing a point representing the dollar sales revenue at any volume (other than zero) and by drawing a line that intersects that point and the point of origin. The point at which the total revenue and the total cost curves intersect represents the volume at which the firm will break even. Inasmuch as many of the costs for a manufacturing company are inventory costs, this type of breakeven analysis assumes that production and sales will both be at the same level. A breakeven chart for the Beehive Products Company is shown in Figure 18-3.

Figure 18-3

BEEHIVE PRODUCTS COMPANY
Breakeven Chart

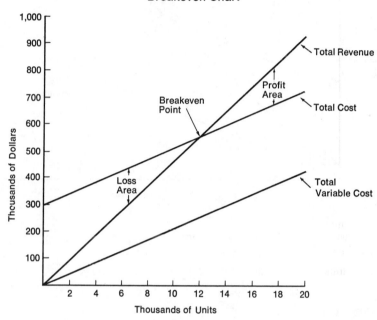

The profit or loss at a particular volume can easily be calculated from the chart by drawing a vertical line through the total cost and revenue curves and then extending two horizontal lines to the Y axis. The differences between the amounts so indicated is the profit (if the volume is above the breakeven point) or the loss (if the volume is below the breakeven point). In Figure 18-4, the profit at n volume is $125,000 ($a$-$b$, or $765,000 −$640,000). The loss at m volume is $125,000 ($d$-$c$, or $315,000–$440,000).

Breakeven Charts for Planning

The breakeven chart can be used to appraise various cost-volume-profit alternatives which a company may face. By plotting these relationships

Figure 18-4

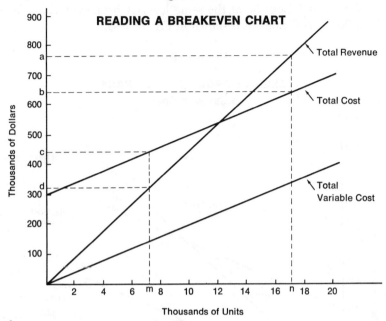

READING A BREAKEVEN CHART

Thousands of Units

Proof:

17,000 units × \$20 = \$340,000	7,000 units × \$20 = \$140,000
Fixed cost 300,000	Fixed cost 300,000
Total cost \$640,000	Total cost \$440,000
17,000 units × \$45 = 765,000	7,000 units × \$45 = 315,000
Profit \$125,000	Loss \$125,000

under the various alternatives, management can make important comparisons. For example, a proposed plant expansion may be evaluated if the impact of the expansion on the breakeven point and rate of profits can be seen; or comparisons can be made to predict the results of an existing plant's automation, with fixed costs substituted for variable costs.

To illustrate the use of breakeven charts for business planning, let us assume that the Pogo Manufacturing Company is contemplating automating its assembly line. Automation of the plant will require an outlay of \$500,000 in new equipment and should reduce variable costs, primarily labor, by 30 percent. The outlay will increase the plant capacity by 25 percent. Data related to present operations (prior to automation) may be summarized as follows:

Fixed costs \$1,000,000
Selling price per unit \$18

Variable costs per unit $8
Plant capacity .... 200,000 units

Figure 18-5 compares the existing cost-profit-volume relationship with
that predicted after the proposed automation. Note that the breakeven
point is increased from 100,000 units to 120,968 units, but that the angle
between the total cost curve and the total revenue curve is also increased.
This means that the rate of profit or loss would be increased by the proposed change. If the company can operate well beyond the new breakeven point, profits will be improved by the proposed change. Increasing
the breakeven point, on the other hand, increases the risk of loss if adequate volume cannot be sold.

Figure 18-5

BREAKEVEN CHART
Production Change

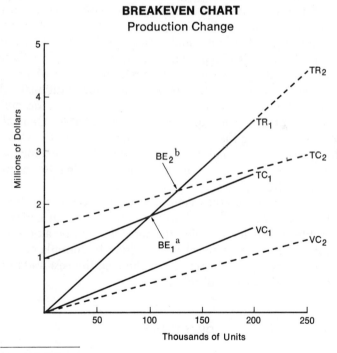

[a]BE[1] = 100,000 units
[b]BE[2] = 120,968 units

Other Modifications

Countless alternatives can be compared and evaluated by breakeven
analysis such as the above. Various price alternatives can be compared,

plant expansion proposals can be evaluated, the best product mix can be selected, the impact of price changes can be appraised, and so on. The charts can also be modified to incorporate other than straight-line relationships. The revenue curve can be drawn to reflect a lower price per unit as sales are increased. The total cost curve can be redrawn with steps to reflect the fact that fixed costs cannot logically be expected to remain constant throughout the entire range of volume. Variable cost curves might also be drawn to reflect economies and diseconomies of scale.

SUMMARY

All costs which are relevant for financial reporting purposes are not equally applicable to decision making. In order to properly choose between alternative courses of action, it is necessary to classify costs according to their function in the decision-making process. Some concepts helpful in this respect are differential costs, sunk costs, opportunity costs, imputed costs, out-of-pocket costs, and replacement costs. Understanding these concepts can aid in making decisions concerning the timing of fixed asset replacement, accepting or rejecting opportunities for additional volume, determining whether to make or buy a desired product, or dropping an existing department that may appear to be unprofitable. Generally, in short-run decision making the sunk costs are ignored, and the alternative having the lowest incremental cost is accepted. The incremental cost should include the value of lost opportunities including those, such as interest, that must be imputed.

Breakeven analysis is a useful means of evaluating a firm's cost-volume-profit relationship. This involves classifying all costs of an enterprise as fixed or variable. The point at which the company will break even under specified cost conditions may be calculated either by formula or by chart. The breakeven chart has the advantage of showing the cost and profit relationship under a whole range of volumes.

QUESTIONS

1. Distinguish between product and period costs. In what period is each of these costs recognized as an expense?
2. Define opportunity costs. What applications do opportunity costs have to the decision-making process?
3. Are any costs other than those actually recorded on the books ever considered in decision making? Explain.

4. What are "sunk" costs? What attitude should the decisionmaker have toward "sunk" costs?

5. What costs are probably most important in decisions regarding the replacement of existing machinery? What nonquantitative factors might also be relevant?

6. What long-run factors should be considered in deciding whether to make or buy a required component for a manufactured product?

7. Will profit be maximized in all cases by eliminating unprofitable departments? Explain.

8. If a company has fixed costs of $75,000, sells its product for $0.98, and has variable costs of $0.64 per unit, how many units must it sell to break even?

9. In what way might a breakeven chart be useful for more than the mere calculation of the breakeven point by formula? Illustrate.

10. What effect would automating a plant have on a firm's breakeven point if the fixed costs increased while the variable costs decreased?

11. Would it be feasible for a company to have a single cost accumulation system which would fill all needs? Explain.

PROBLEMS

Problem 18-1

The Craigmont Production Company owns a four-year-old machine which cost $12,000. At the time of purchase, it was estimated that the machine would last fifteen years and have a salvage value of $1,950.

A new machine has been developed that could reduce some of the operating costs. The new machine would cost $14,800 and is estimated to last eighteen years with a salvage value of $2,200. A trade-in allowance of $7,395 would be given for the old machine. Assume an interest rate of 6 percent.

Annual Cost of Operation

	OLD	NEW
Operators' wages	$4,500	$3,900
Insurance	25	15
Maintenance	340	260
Part replacement	260	210
Depreciation	670	700
	$5,795	$5,085

Required:

Determine whether the new machine should be purchased. Show your analysis.

Problem 18-2

The Lucky Manufacturing Company makes refrigerators in a plant with a capacity of 100,000 units per year. The Manitoba Distributing Company would like to add refrigerators under the name Manitoba to its line. It has offered to pay $270 apiece for 10,000 refrigerators.

Lucky Manufacturing Company sells its refrigerators to its dealers for $350 and has an average cost of $295, as follows:

Fixed overhead allocated	$3,150,000
Variable manufacturing costs	$235 per set
Expected production during the coming year .	75,000 units
Variable selling costs.	$18 per unit

If it were to produce the Manitoba model, the Lucky Manufacturing Company would have additional fixed overhead costs of $180,000. Because of slight changes to the door design, the variable manufacturing costs would be $243 per set. Since Lucky Company would have a contract, there would be no variable selling costs involved.

Lucky Manufacturing Company and Manitoba Distributing Company operate in different markets.

Required:

Prepare a schedule to show the profit or loss (total and per unit) that would result from the contract.

Problem 18-3

The Plotter Manufacturing Company is presently purchasing part CS 108 from an outside firm for $273.10. A study of plant activity indicates that part CS 108 could be manufactured in the plant if a machine costing $630,000 were purchased. The machine could produce 105,000 parts. Direct materials needed to produce the part would cost $82.65 per unit. Twenty-two hours of direct labor at $3.78 per hour are estimated as necessary to complete each part. Overhead is presently charged at a rate of 150 percent of direct labor; the company needs 15,000 parts per year.

Required:

a. Prepare a schedule to show the cost to manufacture the part, based upon the above facts. Should the company continue to purchase part CS 108 or should it manufacture the part?
b. After careful analysis it has been determined that variable overhead applicable to the part will be only 110 percent of direct labor. With this additional information, should Plotter Company continue to purchase the part or start manufacturing it? Show calculations.

Problem 18-4

The income statement for the Blue Sky Department Store follows:

BLUE SKY DEPARTMENT STORE
Income Statement
For the Year Ended June 30

DEPARTMENT

	A	B	C	TOTAL
Sales	$550,407	$151,275	$552,945	$1,254,627
Cost of goods sold	396,430	96,354	418,703	911,487
Gross margin	$153,977	$ 54,921	$134,242	$ 343,140

Expenses:
Selling expenses:

	A	B	C	TOTAL
Store rent	$ 35,000	$ 15,000	$ 25,000	$ 75,000
Advertising	4,000	3,000	3,000	10,000
Salesmen's salaries	45,000	25,000	30,000	100,000
Delivery	12,000	8,000	23,000	43,000
Total selling expenses	$96,000	$ 51,000	$ 81,000	$ 228,000

Administrative expenses:

	A	B	C	TOTAL
Office salaries	$ 10,000	$ 10,000	$ 10,000	$ 30,000
Insurance	842	655	793	2,290
Heat and light	8,450	6,742	7,480	22,672
Telephone	4,000	4,000	4,000	12,000
Other	2,000	1,000	2,000	5,000
Total administrative expenses	$ 25,292	$ 22,397	$ 24,273	$ 71,962
Total expenses	$121,292	$ 73,397	$105,273	$ 299,962
Operating profit (loss)	$ 32,685	($ 18,476)	$ 28,969	$ 43,178

Inasmuch as this is the fifth consecutive year that department B has shown a net operating loss, the Blue Sky management has considered eliminating the department. It is estimated that 50 percent of the advertising costs charged to department B could be eliminated, but that the balance represents an allocation of the company-wide advertising costs. Likewise, $5,000 of Salesmen's Salaries charged to department B represents that department's share of the company's sales manager's salary. The sales manager's salary will not be cut if department B is eliminated. Management does not feel that the sales of either of the remaining departments will be adversely affected if department B is eliminated. The controller estimates that the only other potential cost reductions caused by the proposed elimination would be as follows:

EXPENSE	ANTICIPATED REDUCTION
Delivery	$2,965
Insurance	246
Other administrative	358

Required:

Prepare an income statement showing the effect of discontinuing department B, assuming only the variables described above. Should the department be eliminated?

Problem 18-5

An examination of Door Corporation's records revealed the following information:

Fixed costs $485,000
Variable costs per unit 12
Selling price per unit 46

Required:

a. Compute the breakeven point in units and in terms of dollar volume.
b. If Door Corporation wants a profit of $162,000 after a 50 percent income tax, how many units must be sold?
c. If variable costs increase to $18 per unit, what is the breakeven point?
d. If fixed costs increase by $132,000 and variable costs decrease by $2 per unit, what will be the breakeven point? (Disregard assumption (c) above.)

Problem 18-6

The Lever Corporation has $385,000 in fixed costs. The product it produces is sold at $450 per unit. Variable costs on the product are $380 per unit.

Required:

a. Determine the breakeven point.
b. Prepare a breakeven chart.

Problem 18-7

The Bahama Department Store has expanded during the past few years. Because of this expansion, its present delivery truck is unable to make all of the firm's deliveries.

The present delivery truck cost $6,850 when it was purchased three years ago. The store had planned to use it for six years, after which it was expected the salvage value would be $850. The costs to operate the present truck for a year are as follows:

Gasoline.......................... $1,790
Maintenance 375
Operator's wages 3,780
Insurance 650
Depreciation 1,000
                                   $7,595

The Quick Delivery Company contracts to deliver for firms. For $6,022 per year the company will make 40 percent of the Bahama Department Store's deliveries. The rest of the deliveries would be made using the Bahama Department Store's present delivery truck.

If the Bahama Department Store wants to stop making deliveries, the Quick Delivery Company will make all of the store's deliveries for only $13,325 per year. In this event, the old truck would be sold for its fair market value of $2,480.

The Bahama Department Store could purchase a new delivery truck large enough to make all of its deliveries. The new truck would have a list price of $12,960 and could be used for six years, at the end of which time expected salvage value would be $1,900. The trade-in value of the old truck would be $2,480. The annual cost to operate the new truck would be:

Gasoline	$3,425
Maintenance	565
Operator's wages	3,780
Helper's wages (part-time)	2,300
Insurance	890
Depreciation	1,843
Total cost	$12,803

Required:

Which of the three plans should the Bahama Department Store adopt? Use a 6 percent interest rate and show computations.

Case 18
EDDIE'S BAND INSTRUMENTS

Eddie's is a small musical shop specializing in the sale and repair of band instruments. When the company was first formed its main business was in the area of repair, and consequently it made a sizeable investment in equipment necessary to repair both woodwind and brass instruments. As the company grew, sales became an increasingly larger proportion of the overall business, and the owners found themselves hard-pressed to keep up with both sales and repairs. Eddie's current revenue is based on approximately 50 percent sales and 50 percent repairs, with half of these repairs on woodwind instruments and the other half on brass instruments.

The company has developed the skill to generate revenue of $12 an hour when repairing the woodwind instruments, but finds that the average revenue on the repair of brass instruments fluctuates greatly, ranging from $5 to $10 an hour. This inferior earning rate is due in part to the high turnover in repair personnel and consequent cost of adequately training new men. In addition, even a well-trained man is hard pushed to produce at a rate sufficient to cover his hourly wages plus the overhead costs related to the brass instrument repair facilities. Mr. Arndt, the general manager, is attempting to determine how he can increase the profit margin from brass musical instrument repair without seriously affecting the present sales volume.

Mr. Arndt has asked his accountant to prepare an estimate of the average repair costs for brass instruments. The accountant, Miss Theide, reviewed last year's costs and came up with the following figures:

Average labor cost @ $4/hour		$25.45
Materials		
Shop materials	$4.00	
Repair parts	6.00	10.00
Department overhead		
Rent	$4.41	
Depreciation	1.14	
Maintenance	.10	
Other direct expenses	1.00	6.65
Proportion of general administrative overhead		2.50
Total Average Cost		$44.60

Mr. Arndt was extremely alarmed by these figures; the average charge for repairing brass instruments had been only $35 and he therefore felt that they were losing $9.60 per repair. Since their business depended on being able to provide complete repair coverage, he knew he could not just refuse to take on the brass instrument repair work, but somehow had to reduce these losses.

Following his discussion with his accountant, Mr. Arndt started looking around to see how he could change the company's loss on repairs of brass instruments into a profit. He first approached a large musical instrument repair company located in the East. After looking at the quality of Eddie's repairs the company reported that it was somewhere between that of their general repair, a $48 retail value for a factory charge of $28.80, and their complete overhaul and reconditioning or like-new quality, a $60 retail value for a factory charge of $36. Mr. Arndt determined that an additional expense of approximately $6 per instrument would be required to cover the packing, freight and insurance charges to and from the eastern factory.

Mr. Arndt then approached his repair shop and sales manager for an opinion on the effect of raising the repair charges from $48 to $60. Mr. Schmitt, the sales manager, indicated that while increasing the charges might decrease total unit volume, it probably wouldn't decrease total dollar volume of instrument repairs. He also felt they would have no trouble keeping one full-time man busy on brass instrument repairs. In order to make the $60 charge, the company would need to spend approximately $1,000 for additional equipment. It could then add the baked epoxy finish to its current repair quality and thereby justify the higher price. He felt that by doing this, the company could approximate the favorable earning rates currently enjoyed on woodwinds and would have a better profit margin than if they sent the brass instruments out for repairs. Schmitt justified his conclusions by working out a comparison of the cost of repairs. His figures are as follows:

Retain Repairs			Send Out for Repairs	
Average labor		$25.45	Contract price	$36.00
Materials			Shipping, packing charges	6.00
Shop material	$4.00		Total	$42.00
Repair parts	6.00	10.00		
Total		$35.45		
Repair price		$60.00	Repair price	$60.00
Cost of repair		35.45	Cost of repair	42.00
Gross profit		$24.55	Gross profit	$18.00

Noting that Schmitt's cost of repairs didn't agree with the accountant's, Mr. Arndt asked his accountant to review her figures with them.

Miss Theide said, "Schmitt's figures look pretty attractive, all right, but they don't tell the whole story. The truth of the matter is that it presently costs us nearly $45 to repair a brass instrument. Now you are talking about raising prices and lowering unit volume. Do you know what that will do to per unit overhead costs? If you raise the price of repairs to an average of 54 percent above present prices and hold dollar volume constant, the unit volume will go down by a corresponding amount, leaving fewer units to bear the overhead costs. Also, the depreciation on the new machine you propose acquiring would add $1.30 per unit to overhead based upon this reduced unit volume. It would, therefore, cost us nearly $46 to make these repairs as compared to only $42 for sending them out."

Schmitt said, "What about the machinery? We still need to keep it for minor repair work. Besides, a lot is homemade and, therefore, its true worth to us is much greater than its book value. We probably couldn't even get one-half of its book value if we tried to sell it."

Mr. Arndt, seeing that this heated argument wasn't going to help him solve the problem, said, "I agree. We will need to keep the machinery for minor repair work, but we have to do something because our work is already six months behind. Since our last repairman left we have had our best salesman back in the shop trying to help catch up on the work. Even though he is a good repairman, I know he can make considerably more for us by selling than he can by repairing. Besides, there is more profit in sales than in repairs. In addition, even if we hire a new repairman, someone would have to train him, and this would cost us time and reduced output."

Mr. Arndt then told his accountant and sales manager that he would study the figures some more and would let them know his decision before he took any action.

QUESTIONS

1. Assuming no additional information can be readily obtained, what action should be taken?
2. What nonquantitative factors should be considered before making the decision?

19

Fundamentals
of
Compound Interest

Money has a time value. This means that we are concerned not only with the amount of money we pay or receive, but also with *when* the payment or receipt takes place. If we were informed that we had just won $10,000 in a contest, most of us would be delighted. On the other hand, if this notice were followed by a second notice which read "payable in full January 1, 2000," our joy would turn to despair. We all have a time preference for money that possibly best can be summarized by the expression "The sooner, the better." The sooner we receive money, the more valuable it is to us.

This concept is extremely important in the decision-making process. If we purchase a new machine, we are concerned not only with how much this investment will return, but also with *when* the amounts will be forthcoming. Suppose a company with a choice of investing in one of two machines expected the following cash flows to accrue as a result of the respective investments:

YEAR	MACHINE A	MACHINE B
1	$ 1,000	$ 5,000
2	2,000	4,000
3	3,000	3,000
4	4,000	2,000
5	5,000	1,000
	$15,000	$15,000

Although the two machines will return an identical sum ($15,000), it is obvious that machine B represents a preferable investment, strictly because it will provide the return sooner.

While the above example provides an obvious solution, the exact effect of cash-flow timing in most instances cannot be evaluated properly by superficial analysis. We need some tool which will enable us to place on a comparable basis amounts receivable or payable at different points of time. This can be done by utilizing the fundamentals of compound interest.

FUTURE WORTH OF A SUM

Interest is the factor which causes amounts to have different values at different points of time. A dollar, invested at 7 percent interest compounded annually, will amount to $1.40 at the end of five years. The $0.40, the compounded interest, accounts for the growth. This may be seen from the following calculations:

Initial investment	$1.000
Interest earned during first year (7 percent $\times$ $1)	0.070
Accumulation at end of first year	1.070
Interest earned during second year (7 percent $\times$ $1.07)	0.075
Accumulation at end of second year	1.145
Interest earned during third year (7 percent $\times$ $1.145)	0.080
Accumulation at end of third year	1.225
Interest earned during fourth year (7 percent $\times$ $1.225)	0.086
Accumulation at end of fourth year	1.311
Interest earned during fifth year (7 percent $\times$ $1.311)	0.092
Accumulation at end of fifth year	1.403

The fund increases by earning interest not only on the initial investment (principal), but also on the interest accumulated in prior years.

The formula for computing the future worth of a dollar is

$$(1 + i)^n$$

where

i = the interest rate
n = the number of interest periods

Table A in the appendix has been prepared by utilizing this formula. The various rates of interest are shown along the top, and the number of interest periods are shown down the left-hand margin. We can read from the table what a dollar will be worth at any given rate and after any given period of time. We can see how Table A was constructed by referring back to the above calculations. The amount accumulated at the end of the respective years may be summarized as follows:

END OF YEAR	AMOUNT
1	1.070
2	1.145
3	1.225
4	1.311
5	1.403

Since the above figures correspond to those shown in the 7 percent column of Table A, we could have determined the future amount much faster by merely referring to the table in the first place.

Table A has been prepared to show what one dollar will amount to at some future point in time at specified interest rates. If we want to know what a sum other than one dollar will amount to, we merely multiply the sum by the appropriate factor in the table.[1] For example, $75 will amount to $179.78 at the end of fifteen years if invested at 6 percent, compounded annually ($75 $\times$ 2.397).

PRESENT VALUE OF A SUM

In the above instance we determined the future worth of a sum where the present worth was known. Suppose we know the future worth but want to know the present worth. In this instance we must "pull out" the interest (properly called compound discount) to arrive at the present value. The formula for calculating the present value of one dollar is shown below.

$$\frac{1}{(1 + i)^n}$$

---

[1]Fortunately, we do not need to make these calculations. Prepared interest tables are readily available.

Table C in the appendix reflects the application of the above formula to a variety of rates and interest periods. To find the present value of one dollar we merely read from the table the facts corresponding to the specified rate and interest period. Assume that we want to know how much we need to invest now (present value) in order to accumulate $179.78 in fifteen years at 6 percent interest, compounded annually. The table indicates that for each one dollar we want in the future, we must invest about forty-two cents now. That means we will need to invest seventy-five dollars now to accumulate the desired sum fifteen years hence ($179.78 × $0.417). The three-cent difference is a result of rounding.

Note the complementary nature of Tables A and C. Table A gives the future worth in those instances where the present worth is known. Table C gives the present worth where the future worth is known. In our first example, we saw that $75 would amount to $179.78 at the end of fifteen years. In the second instance, we found that $179.78 due at the end of fifteen years has a present value of only $75. The tables are, indeed, complementary.

ANNUITIES

An annuity is a series of equal cash flows occurring at equal time intervals. The cash flows are usually referred to as rents. Of course an annuity problem can be solved by utilizing only Table A or Table C, taking each cash flow separately and then summing the results. Since this practice is rather time-consuming, separate tables are normally utilized to solve annuity problems.

Amount Annuity

When we desire to know what a series of rents will amount to on the date the last rent is paid, we must calculate the *amount of an ordinary annuity*. Table B, which reflects the amounts of given ordinary annuities, was prepared from the following formula:

$$\frac{(1 + i)^n - 1}{i}$$

To illustrate the use of Table B, let us assume that Mr. Burton plans to set aside $750 per year, the first payment to be paid on June 1, 1967, and the last payment on June 1, 1971. How much will he have accumulated on the date of the last payment if the interest rate is 4 percent, compounded annually? The problem may be diagrammed as follows:

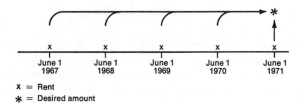

x = Rent
* = Desired amount

By referring to Table B, we note that the fund will accumulate to $4,062 ($750 × 5.416). Two factors cause the fund to grow through the passage of time: the periodic payments and the compound interest. This may be seen in the diagram and the accumulation table shown in Figure 19-1.

Figure 19-1

ACCUMULATION TABLE AND CHART
The Amount of an Ordinary Annuity

YEAR ENDED JUNE 1	RENT	INTEREST EARNED	TOTAL FUND
1967	$750	$ 0	$ 750
1968	750	30	1,530
1969	750	61	2,341
1970	750	94	3,185
1971	750	127	4,062

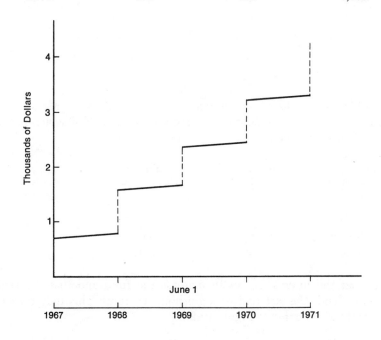

Present Value Annuity

In the above case, the interest and the rents *both* cause the total fund to increase. In a present value problem the two work in opposite directions. The periodic rents decrease the fund, and the interest increases the fund.

The present value of an annuity indicates the sum that must be deposited to provide for a series of equal withdrawals. An ordinary annuity provides for the first withdrawal to come one period after the deposit. The formula for the present value of an ordinary annuity is shown below.

$$\frac{1 - \dfrac{1}{(1 + i)^n}}{i}$$

Table D in the appendix is a present value table for ordinary annuities. To illustrate its use, let us assume that Mr. Watch wants to deposit a sum on October 1, 1967, which will provide the tuition for his oldest son to begin college October 1, 1968. He plans to invest the money at 5 percent interest and would like to provide for four annual tuition payments in the amount of $800 to be made from the fund each October 1. How much must Mr. Watch invest? The problem is to determine the present value of an ordinary annuity of four rents of $800; it may be diagrammed as follows:

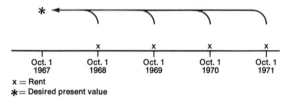

x = Rent
* = Desired present value

Table D indicates that an investment of $2,863.80 will satisfy Mr. Watch's condition ($800 × 3.546 = $2,836.80). The following table of accumulation proves this answer to be correct.

YEAR ENDED OCTOBER 1	INTEREST INCREASE	RENT <DECREASE>	FUND BALANCE
1967	$ 0	$ 0	$2,837
1968	142	<800>	2,179
1969	109	<800>	1,488
1970	74	<800>	762
1971	38	<800>	0

Note that the interest serves to increase the fund and that the rents reduce the fund, the last rent extinguishing the fund. This may be seen more clearly by referring to Figure 19-2.

Figure 19-2

TABLE OF PRESENT VALUE OF ORDINARY ANNUITY

(Withdrawal of Equal Amounts from Preestablished Fund)

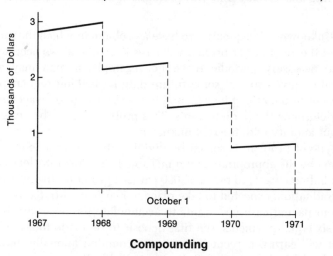

Compounding

In each of the preceding illustrations we have assumed an annual compounding period. The interest rate i used in each calculation was the annual rate specified in the problem, and the number of periods n corresponded to the number of years. When compounding is not on an annual basis, it is necessary to express the interest rate on the basis of the compounding period. This is done by dividing the annual rate of interest by the number of compounding periods per year. This concept may be illustrated by the following examples:

ANNUAL RATE	NUMBER OF YEARS	COMPOUNDING PERIOD	INTEREST RATE	NUMBER OF PERIODS
6 percent	10	Annual	6 percent	10
6 percent	10	Semiannual	3 percent	20
6 percent	10	Quarterly	1½ percent	40
6 percent	10	Monthly	½ percent	120

Types of Annuity Problems

Typically, annuity problems seek one of three unknowns: the periodic rent, the rate of interest, or either the present value or future amount (depending on the nature of the problem). We can solve for any one of these factors, given the other two.

Amount or Present Value Unknown.   In the preceding illustrations we were always seeking the third factor, i.e., the present value or future amount. Tables B and D in the appendix were set up so that we could find this answer by merely multiplying the factor from the table, at the given interest rate and given number of periods by the periodic rent.

Rent Unknown.   Frequently we have a problem in which the rate of interest and the amount (or present value) is known, and we need to determine the necessary periodic rents. For example, a man may wish to accumulate a given sum at some future date by making regular periodic deposits. Given the rate of interest and the desired sum to be accumulated, we can determine the periodic rents. This problem would be described as an amount annuity with the rent unknown.

This type of problem is solved by dividing the future amount (the desired sum) by the appropriate factor in Table B. To illustrate, let us assume that Mr. Salmon wants to buy a $3,000 car as a gift honoring his son's high school graduation, expected to take place in five years. Mr. Salmon always believes in paying cash and wants to accumulate the necessary funds by making six equal payments, the first deposit to be made today. If his investment will earn 6 percent interest, compounded annually, how much must each of his deposits be? Referring to Table B, we locate the factor 6.975, an amount of ordinary annuity of six rents at 6 percent. If we divide the desired future sum ($3,000) by the factor (6.975), we find that an annual deposit of $430.11 will meet Mr. Salmon's needs.

Or suppose a man wishes to deposit a given sum today, making a number of regular, equal future withdrawals on it. Given the amount of the deposit and the rate of interest, we can tell him the amount each withdrawal (rent) must equal. This problem would be described as finding the rent of a present value annuity. The solution to such a problem is found by dividing the present value (the initial deposit) by the appropriate factor from Table D.

Rate Unknown.   In some instances the present value (or amount) and the periodic rents are given, but the rate of interest is unknown. For example, suppose we know the amount of a loan and the monthly payments required, but the lender has failed to disclose the true rate of interest. In this instance we have the present value of an annuity with all factors known except the rate.

Although the tables are crude, they do enable us to approximate the true rate of interest in such a problem. The exact rate, of course, can be calculated mathematically by using the formula previously cited. For most purposes, however, it is sufficient to know the range in which the true rate lies, and the tables are sufficient for this purpose.

The true rate of interest is that rate which will exactly equate the sum of the periodic rents with the present value (or amount). To illustrate, assume that Mr. Jones purchases an automobile which he could have bought for $3,500 cash. He elects instead to pay $1,500 down and the balance in twenty-four monthly installments of $94 each. The sum of the monthly payments will be $2,256 ($94 × 24 months), while the balance due is only $2,000 ($3,500 – $1,500). This difference ($256) represents the amount of interest he will pay for the privilege of deferring the payments. But what is the rate of interest? If we divide the $2,000 (the present value of the monthly rents) by the $94 (the rent), we get a factor of 21.277. Turn to Table D and attempt to find 21.277 where $n = 24$. The factor closest to 21.277 is 21.243. Reading up this column, we note the rate of interest to be 1 percent per period, or, in this case, 1 percent per month (an annual rate of about 12 percent). Usually it is necessary to interpolate or merely to note that the factor is somewhere between two figures given in the table. In those instances, we would merely say the rate lies in the range indicated by the column headings.

Variations in Annuity Problems

The annuity problems discussed in the preceding section relate to ordinary annuities. Let us now discuss two other types of annuities: the annuity due and the deferred annuity.

Annuities Due. Annuity tables are prepared under the assumption that the rent always comes at the end of the interest period. This means that the last rent occurs the same day as the fund is accumulated in the amount of an ordinary annuity. Since we are moving in the opposite direction with the present value problem, there is a lapse of one period between the deposit and the first withdrawal under an ordinary annuity. Thus, the time line for the amount of an ordinary annuity is

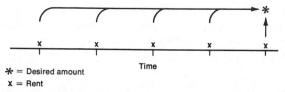

＊ = Desired amount
x = Rent

The time line for the present value of an ordinary annuity, on the other hand, would appear as follows:

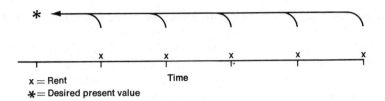

x = Rent
*= Desired present value

In both instances the rent occurred at the *end* of the period, but, since the flows move in opposite directions, there is a one-period difference. The appendix tables we have used (Tables B and D) have taken this into consideration. They automatically provide the solutions to ordinary annuity problems.

With an annuity due, the rent occurs at the beginning of the period. Thus, the time line for the amount of an annuity due is

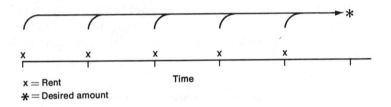

x = Rent
* = Desired amount

The time line for the present value of an annuity due is

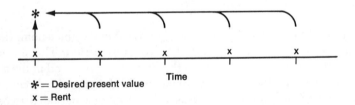

*= Desired present value
x = Rent

Because the annuity due and the ordinary annuity are so similar (the same number of rents, but one interest period difference), it is not necessary to prepare separate interest tables. We can use Table B (the amount of an ordinary annuity) to solve an annuity-due problem by reading off the table for $(n + 1)$ and then *subtracting* 1.000 from the factor. Similarly, for the present value of an annuity due we examine Table D for $(n - 1)$ and then add 1.000.

Deferred Annuities. Sometimes annuity problems have a number of interest periods in which there are no rents. For example, assume Mr. Huffaker wants to provide for his newborn son's education by depositing on the date of his son's birth a sum sufficient to provide for four annual with-drawals of $1,000 beginning on the boy's eighteenth birthday. Such a fund is expected to earn 4 percent interest. The time line would appear as follows:

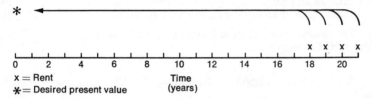

x = Rent
∗ = Desired present value

This may be described as the present value of an ordinary annuity of four rents, deferred seventeen periods. It can be solved by breaking the problem into two parts, as follows:

1. The present value of an ordinary annuity of four rents of $1,000 each:

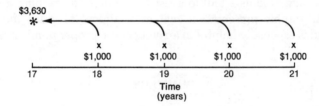

2. The present value of $3,630, due seventeen periods hence:

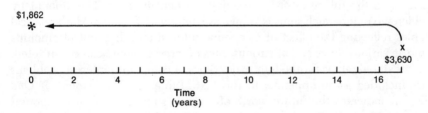

Mr. Huffaker will need to deposit $1,862 at his son's birth to provide the four withdrawals of $1,000 each, beginning with his son's eighteenth birth-day.

Deferred annuity problems can also be solved by utilizing only factors taken from Table D. Under this method the present value of an ordinary annuity for the deferred period is subtracted from the present value of an ordinary annuity for the entire period. The difference between these two factors represents the present value of the deferred annuity. The technique may be illustrated by referring to the facts in the preceding problem and solving as follows:

Present value of an ordinary annuity of 21 rents. 14.029
Less: Present value of an ordinary annuity of 17 rents. 12.166

   Net: The present value of an ordinary annuity of 4 rents
     deferred 17 periods 1.863

$$1.863 \times \$1,000 = \$1,863$$

This is the amount which Huffaker must deposit today in order to provide for the desired withdrawals (the one-dollar difference from the prior solution is due to rounding).

Complex or multiple-part problems, such as the deferred annuity just illustrated, can often be solved best by breaking the problem into parts and solving a step at a time. The use of time lines such as those used in this chapter is suggested as a tool to assist the student in reaching a solution. Often this graphic presentation enables a student to grasp the concept sooner and is especially helpful in arriving at the proper number of interest periods.

SUMMARY

Each of us has a time preference for money. If we forego the privilege of using our money now, we demand compensation known as *compound interest.* By the same token, we are willing to discount sums which may be due us in the future in order to enjoy the benefits now. The amount by which we reduce such sums is known as *compound discount.* Mathematical tables reflecting the effect of compound interest and discount of amounts due at various times and at various rates of interest have been constructed. Abbreviated tables for the four major types of compound interest problems are included as an appendix to this text. Table A, *The Amount of One Dollar,* indicates the future worth of a single sum invested at compound interest. Table B, *The Amount of an Annuity of One Dollar,* indicates the future worth of a series of rents, each rent of equal amount and each occurring at equal time intervals. Table C, *The Present Value of One Dollar,* indicates the value a single sum due in the future has today. Table D, *The Present Value of an Annuity of One Dollar,* indicates the present worth of a series of rents due in future periods, each rent of equal amount and each time interval equal. These tables may easily be modified to solve special problems such as those related to annuities due and deferred annuities.

The fact that money has a time value is of utmost importance in the decision-making process. Management cannot simply add up the future costs or benefits of various alternatives without regard to when these costs or benefits will occur. Cash flows occurring at different points of time must be time adjusted to make comparisons meaningful. In chapter 20 some of the managerial and accounting applications of compound interest will be discussed.

QUESTIONS

1. What do we mean when we say money has a time value? Why does money have a time value? Would money have a time value even without inflation?
2. What does the difference in the values of a given sum of money at two points in time represent?
3. Which of the following flows of money would you prefer, and why? Flow A: $8, year one; $5, year two; $4, year three. Flow B: $3, year one; $6, year two; $8, year three.
4. Define an annuity. Distinguish between an ordinary annuity, an annuity due, and a deferred annuity.
5. When both the rents and the interest cause a fund to increase through passage of time, the situation may be described as the _____ of an annuity.
6. When the interest causes a preestablished fund to increase, but the periodic rents cause the fund to decrease, the situation may be described as the _____ of an annuity.
7. What interest rate and number of periods are applicable on a 6 percent, four-year contract where interest is compounded semiannually? Where interest is compounded quarterly? Where interest is compounded monthly?
8. What are the three unknowns commonly sought in annuity problems? In each case list what is known as well as what is unknown. How can annuity tables be used to solve each type of problem?
9. How can Table B, the amount of an ordinary annuity, be converted to reflect the amount of an annuity due?
10. How can Table D, the present value of an ordinary annuity, be converted to reflect the present value of an annuity due?
11. Assuming that interest is compounded annually at a rate of 8 percent, what is the present value on January 1, 1971, of five rents of $100 each, payable at the end of each of the next five years beginning December 31, 1971?
12. If $10 is deposited each quarter for four years at 8 percent interest, compounded quarterly, what sum will have accumulated as of the date of the last deposit?
13. What will $500, deposited January 1, 1967, at 4 percent interest, compounded annually, amount to on January 1, 1975? What would the same sum amount to if the interest rate were 4 percent, compounded semiannually? Explain the difference.

PROBLEMS

Problem 19-1

The XYZ Corporation is considering installing a new billing machine. Two new machines, both resulting in the same amount of savings over the five-year life of the machines, are being considered. The yearly savings for each machine are as follows:

	MACHINE A	MACHINE B
Year 1	$ 1,000	$ 3,000
Year 2	2,000	3,000
Year 3	3,000	3,000
Year 4	4,000	3,000
Year 5	5,000	3,000
	$15,000	$15,000

Required:

If the cost of capital required to purchase either one of these machines is 6 percent, which machine should be purchased? Why? (Assume that all savings come at the end of the year.)

Problem 19-2

If you deposit $500 in a savings account at your bank, how much will you have at the end of five years if the bank pays 6 percent interest

a. annually?
b. semiannually?
c. quarterly?
d. monthly?

Problem 19-3

Mr. Smith wants to buy a $4,000 piece of land in seven years.

Required:

How much must he deposit in his savings account today in order to have the $4,000 when he needs it, assuming that he can earn 4 percent annual interest on his account?

Problem 19-4

Required:

Prepare an accumulation table showing the date, the rents, the interest earned, and the fund balance for the following annuity: rents of $800 each are deposited each January 1, at 5 percent, for six years beginning January 1, 1968. Show the accumulation through January 1, 1974.

Problem 19-5

Which would you rather have: $700 today or $830 five years from now, if you can invest this money at the annual rate of 3 percent?

Required:
   a. Solve, using Table A.
   b. Solve, using Table C.

Problem 19-6

Mr. Johnson has just sold his old car to Mr. Wright. Mr. Wright signed a note promising to pay Mr. Johnson $10 a month for twenty-four months. Mr. Johnson promptly deposits each of these receipts in his savings account, which pays 6 percent interest, compounded monthly.

Required:
   Determine how much Mr. Johnson will have in his account immediately after the last payment is deposited. Assume each deposit is made on the last day of each month and earns no interest for that one day of the month.

Problem 19-7

Mr. Jones wants to make a deposit now to pay for his son's college education. His son will start college in seven years and will require $2,000 a year for four years.

Required:
   If Mr. Jones earns 4 percent on his deposit, determine how much he should now invest to provide for his son's education. Assume that $2,000 is to be withdrawn from the fund at the beginning of each school year.

Problem 19-8

David Smith's banker promises David that if he will invest $20 per quarter for eight years, he will have $749.88 at the time he makes his last deposit.

Required:
   Determine the rate of interest David will be earning.

Problem 19-9

John Nelson has just signed a note for a home improvement loan in the amount of $2,400. He has promised to repay the loan in quarterly installments of $120 each.

Required:
   If the time-adjusted rate of interest is 2 percent per quarter, determine how long it will take to repay the loan.

Problem 19-10

On Jerry's tenth birthday, his grandfather opened a savings account in Jerry's name with a $20 deposit, promising to make deposits of equal amounts on each future birthday.

Required:
   If Jerry leaves this money in the bank at 4 percent interest, determine how much will be in the bank on his twenty-first birthday after the deposit on that date.

Problem 19-11

Mr. and Mrs. Smith have decided to take a trip around the world when Mr. Smith retires. They plan to place $1,000 in the bank on January 1 of each of the next fifteen years. The bank will probably pay 6 percent interest, compounded annually. The last deposit will be made on January 1, 1985, the date Mr. Smith will retire. They plan to start their trip on January 1, 1986, by making the first withdrawal. Their trip will take three years.

Required:

Calculate the amount that the Smiths can withdraw at the beginning of each of the three years if the fund is to be completely exhausted.

Problem 19-12

Mr. Jones is going to place $500 in the bank on December 31 of each of the next ten years. The bank will pay 4 percent interest annually for the first four years and 6 percent interest during the remaining period.

Required:

Compute the amount Mr. Jones will have in his account after he has made the final deposit.

Case 19

NIEBUHR CORPORATION

Niebuhr Corporation is beginning its first capital budgeting program. You have been retained to assist the budget committee in the evaluation of a project, designated as Proposed Expansion Project number 12 (PEP 12), to expand operations.

1. The following capital expenditures are under consideration:

Fire sprinkler system	$ 300,000
Landscaping	100,000
Replacement of old machines..........................	600,000
Projects to expand operations (including PEP 12)	800,000
Total	$1,800,000

2. The corporation requires no minimum return on the sprinkler system or the landscaping. However, it expects a minimum return of 6 percent on all investments to replace old machinery. It also expects investments in expansion projects to yield a return that will exceed the average cost of the capital required to finance the sprinkler system and the landscaping in addition to the expansion projects.

3. Under Proposed Expansion Project number 12 a cash investment of $75,000 will be made one year before operations begin. The investment will be depreciated by the sum-of-the-years'-digits method over a three-year period and is expected to have a salvage value of $15,000. Additional financial data for PEP 12 follow:

TIME PERIOD	REVENUE	VARIABLE COSTS	MAINTENANCE, PROPERTY TAXES, AND INSURANCE
0-1	$80,000	$35,000	$ 8,000
1-2	95,000	41,000	11,000
2-3	60,000	25,000	12,000

The amount of the investment recovered during each of the three years can be reinvested at a rate of return approximating 15 percent. Assume that all cash flows relative to operating PEP 12 come at the end of the respective time periods.

4. The capital structure of Niebuhr Corporation follows:

	AMOUNT	PERCENTAGE OF TOTAL CAPITAL
Short-term notes at 5 percent interest	$ 3,500,000	10
4 percent cumulative preferred stock, $100 par	1,750,000	5
Common stock	12,250,000	35
Retained earnings	17,500,000	50
Total Capital	$35,000,000	100

Assume that the cost of retained earnings is 4.8 percent. The cost of other funds should be calculated.

5. Additional data available to you are summarized below:

	CURRENT MARKET PRICE	EXPECTED EARNINGS PER SHARE	EXPECTED DIVIDENDS PER SHARE
Preferred stock, noncallable..	$120	–	$4.00
Common stock	50	$3.20	1.60

Assume that the corporate income tax rate is 50 percent.

Required:

a. Assume that the cutoff rate for considering expansion projects is 15 percent. Prepare a schedule calculating the annual cash flows for operations for PEP 12; the present value of the net cash flows for PEP 12.

b. The budget committee has asked you to check the reasonableness of the cutoff rate. You realize that one of the factors to be considered is an estimate of the average cost of capital to this firm.

Prepare a schedule, supported by computations in good form, to compute the average cost of capital weighted by the percentage of the capital structure which each element represents.

c. Assume that the average cost of capital computed in (b) is 9 percent. Prepare a schedule to compute the minimum return (in dollars) required on expansion projects to cover the average cost of capital for financing the sprinkler system and the landscaping in addition to expansion projects. Assume that it is necessary to replace the old machines.

d. Assume that the minimum return computed above is $150,000 Calculate the cutoff rate on expansion projects.

AICPA Adapted

20

Investment
and
Financing Decisions

Two of the most significant problems faced by management are discussed in this chapter: how can the best investment opportunities be selected from the wide array of possibilities, and how should these investments be financed?

INVESTMENT DECISIONS

Most companies are faced with a wide variety of investment opportunities. The list of requests generally is much longer than the available funds will cover. Management needs some tools to help in selecting those investment alternatives that will prove most profitable. In this chapter, we will discuss four techniques that can be used to select profitable investment opportunities: the *payback period,* the *average rate of return,* the *time-adjusted rate of return,* and the *profitability index.*

The Payback Period

In capital equipment investments, management is generally very concerned with how long it will be before the investment is repaid. A payback period may be calculated to reflect the number of years it will take to recover the investment. This is done by dividing the investment by the annual incremental cash flow. An investment of $50,000 expected to have a cash flow of $10,000 per year has an estimated payback period of five years.

In figuring the annual return, we are concerned with the total cash flow, not merely with the profit. We are interested in how long it will take to get our money back. The total cash flow in a particular period consists of the profits after taxes, plus the depreciation of the same period.

The payback period may be effective in evaluating investments expected to provide relatively uniform returns over the life of the asset. This concept is also useful in those instances where risks are very high and, in turn, returns are very uncertain beyond the short run. Forecasting the future is a difficult task at its best, and the further we attempt to probe into the future, the more uncertain it becomes. Thus, if we were considering investing in a machine to produce hula hoops we would likely require a very short payback period, since the useful life of such a machine is very uncertain.

Where the expected returns on an investment are not evenly distributed over the asset's life, two methods might be employed to calculate the payback period. First, the average return can be calculated and the payback figured on this basis. Second, the annual return can be accumulated until the sum is equal to the total investment. To illustrate these two techniques, let us assume that an investment of $75,000 is expected to produce the following annual cash flow:

YEAR	CASH FLOW
1	$ 15,000
2	20,000
3	25,000
4	30,000
5	20,000
6	10,000
7	5,000
8	5,000
Total	$130,000

The average payback period would be 4.6 years, calculated as follows:

$$\frac{\text{Investment}}{\text{Average cash flow}} = \frac{\$75,000}{(130,000 \div 8 \text{ years})} = 4.6 \text{ years}$$

The payback may be more accurately estimated by accumulating the cash flows as follows:

YEAR	CASH FLOW	CUMULATIVE CASH FLOW
1	$15,000	$15,000
2	20,000	35,000
3	25,000	60,000 ←—75,000
4	35,000	95,000

Accumulating the cash flows in this manner, we note that the payback will come in slightly less than 3½ years.

The payback period concept has two serious limitations: it ignores the time value of money, and it fails to account for any return after the initial payback period.

The Average Rate of Return

The average rate of return does take into consideration all returns throughout the entire life of the investment, thereby overcoming the second objection raised against the payback period. Like the payback period, however, the average rate of return fails to account for the time value of money.

The average rate of return on an investment is calculated by dividing the average return (profits after taxes) by the average investment. Since we are calculating the return *on* investment, we are not concerned with depreciation, which represents a return *of* investment. The average investment is usually calculated by adding the asset's book value as of the beginning of the first and last year of the asset's life and dividing the total by two.

The average rate of return is meaningful only when profits are evenly distributed over the asset's life, since large variations in profits would make the average meaningless. Inasmuch as this method ignores the time value of money, the longer the investment's life, the less accurate is the average return.

To illustrate the calculation of the average rate of return, let us assume the Kameron Manufacturing Company is contemplating buying a new machine at a cost of $10,000. It is expected that the machine will last seven years, after which it will have a $900 salvage value. Straight-line depreciation is used to apportion the cost of all assets. The company expects $1,500 per year to be added to after-tax profits if it invests in the machine. The average rate return may be figured as follows:

Cost of machine	$10,000
Less salvage	900
Net cost	$ 9,100
Annual depreciation ($9,100 ÷ 7 years)	$ 1,300
Book value at the end of asset's life (salvage)	$ 900
Add: back depreciation of last year	1,300
Book value at the beginning of last year	$ 2,200
Book value at the beginning of first year	10,000
Sum of book values	$12,200

Average investment ($12,200 ÷ 2) = $6,100

$$\text{Average rate of return of investment} = \frac{\text{Average return}}{\text{Average investment}} = \frac{\$1,500}{\$6,100} = 25\%$$

The Time-adjusted Rate of Return

We have previously noted that money does have a time value and that management is just as concerned with *when* the return will come as it is with *how much* the return will be. The time-adjusted rate of return on an investment can be calculated by utilizing the fundamentals of compound interest discussed in chapter 19. Such a calculation does give proper consideration to the timing of the cash flows. The time-adjusted rate of return on an investment is calculated by equating the present value of the cash inflows with the present value of the cash outflows at an unknown interest rate.

To illustrate, let us assume that Motors Manufacturing Company is considering introducing a new Mini-Cycle which it plans to market at $500 per unit. Production of the Mini-Cycle will require installing special equipment at a cost of $500,000. The special equipment is expected to have a useful life of only five years, at the end of which time it will be sold for an estimated $50,000. Variable costs of producing the Mini-Cycle (excluding depreciation) are expected to run about $300 per unit, and sales are forecast as follows: first year, 200 units; second year, 1,000 units; third year, 2,500 units; fourth year, 1,500 units; fifth year, 800 units.

The cash inflows may be calculated as follows:

Selling price per unit		$500
Less: Cost per unit:		
Depreciation ($450,000 ÷ 6,000 units)	$ 75	
Other variable costs	300	375
Pretax profit per unit		$125
Tax (assume 40 percent rate)		50
Aftertax profit per unit		75
Add back: Depreciation[a]		75
Cash flow per unit		$150

Annual Cash Flows

First year	200 × $150	=	$ 30,000	
Second year	1,000 × $150	=	150,000	
Third year	2,500 × $150	=	375,000	
Fourth year	1,500 × $150	=	225,000	
Fifth year	800 × $150	=	120,000 + 50,000 (salvage value of equipment) = $170,000	

[a]Depreciation has been added back because it was deducted as an expense (line 2) to arrive at profit, but did not affect cash flows. The depreciation has no effect on cash flows except insofar as the tax deduction reduces the outflow for taxes.

The total cash flows may be diagramed as follows:

Outflow today = Present value of future inflows

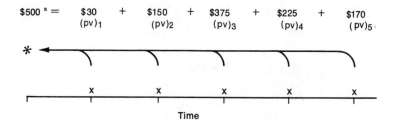

$500 [a] = $30   + $150   + $375   + $225   + $170
               (pv)₁   (pv)₂   (pv)₃   (pv)₄   (pv)₅

Time

[a]All figures represent thousands of dollars.

We can now equate the present value of the cash inflows and determine the effective rate of return. With a computer the exact rate could be calculated easily. Without one, however, the rate can be approximated by utilizing appendix Table C on a trial and error basis. As a starting point we might arbitrarily try 10 percent. The present value of the cash inflows from operating the machine would amount to $692,040, if discounted at 10 percent (see Figure 20-1). This figure indicates that the rate used was too low.

Figure 20-1

CALCULATION OF TIME-ADJUSTED RATE OF RETURN
Mini-Cycle Machine

YEAR	ANNUAL CASH FLOW	10 PERCENT FACTOR	PRESENT VALUE	40 PERCENT FACTOR	PRESENT VALUE
1	$ 30,000	.909	$ 27,270	.714	$ 21,420
2	150,000	.826	123,900	.510	76,500
3	375,000	.751	281,625	.364	136,500
4	225,000	.683	153,675	.260	58,500
5	170,000	.621	105,570	.186	31,620
	Total		$692,040		$324,540

YEAR	ANNUAL CASH FLOW	25 PERCENT FACTOR	PRESENT VALUE	22 PERCENT FACTOR	PRESENT VALUE
1	$ 30,000	.800	$ 24,000	.820	$ 24,600
2	150,000	.640	96,000	.672	100,800
3	375,000	.512	192,000	.551	206,625
4	225,000	.410	92,250	.451	101,475
5	170,000	.328	55,760	.370	62,900
	Total		$460,000		$496,400

YEAR	ANNUAL CASH FLOW	20 PERCENT FACTOR	PRESENT VALUE
1	$ 30,000	.833	$ 24,990
2	150,000	.694	104,100
3	375,000	.579	217,125
4	225,000	.482	108,450
5	170,000	.402	68,340
	Total		$523,005

If we next tried 40 percent we would get a present value of $324,540; now the rate is too high. Thus, by trial and error we can proceed to discount the cash flows until we find the rate that will give us a present value of

$500,000. Continuing, we find that at 25 percent, the present value is $460,000; at 22 percent, $496,400; and at 20 percent, the present value is $523,005. The calculations for all of these figures are summarized in Figure 20-1. From these calculations we learn that the time-adjusted rate of return that can be expected from the investment is nearly 22 percent (actually between 20 percent and 22 percent).

Profitability Index

Where a company has a preestablished cutoff rate for investments, the calculation of a profitability index may be useful. This js done by discounting the cash inflows at the company's cutoff rate, and the discounted cash flow is then divided by the cost of the investment to get the profitability index. An index figure of 1 or greater than 1 indicates that potential investment is desirable, and of less than 1, undesirable.

Suppose that Motors Manufacturing had established an investment cutoff rate of 15 percent, i.e., the company is only interested in investments that will return at least 15 percent. The cash flows can be discounted at this cutoff rate as follows:

YEAR	ANNUAL CASH FLOW	15 PERCENT FACTOR	PRESENT VALUE
1	$ 30,000	0.870	$ 26,100
2	150,000	0.756	113,400
3	375,000	0.658	246,750
4	225,000	0.572	128,700
5	170,000	0.497	84,490
			$599,440

The profitability index for the new Mini-Cycle equipment can be calculated as follows:

$$\frac{\text{Present value of cash inflows}}{\text{Cost of investment}} = \frac{\$599,400}{\$500,000} = 1.2$$

Since the profitability index is 1.2 (greater than 1), the company should invest in the new equipment if even more profitable investments are not available. One of the desirable features of the profitability index is that it enables management to rank several investment opportunities by the magnitude of the index.

Limitations of Quantitative Tools

It should be noted that many investment decisions do not lend themselves to quantitative analysis. For example, some investments are made for aesthetic reasons, e.g., the landscaping of a factory building. How does one measure the rate of return on a lawn? Also, some capital expenditures are of an emergency nature, and the investment must be made without regard to the possible cost or potential return; such might be the case if the boiler in an office building were to explode. A capital expenditure would be necessary to replace the boiler, but it is quite doubtful that management would sit down and compute the payback period before ordering the boiler replaced. It seems, however, that most capital expenditures relate to expansion of operations, upgrading of equipment, ventures into new fields, and similar activities which do lend themselves to some kind of quantitative analysis. In such instances, the techniques just discussed are extremely useful.

FINANCING ASSET ACQUISITION

We have just discussed some of the methods that might be used to select profitable investments. Now let us turn to the problem of how to finance these investments. There basically are two sources from which a company can obtain the funds necessary to finance new capital expenditures: inside financing, which utilizes funds provided by stockholders; and outside financing, which uses funds furnished by creditors. The decision regarding which source to use is an involved one, as it is related to the risks inherent in trading on the equity.[1] Generally, such a decision should not be made for each separate asset acquisition, but rather on the basis of the overall debt-to-equity structure desired. It is not within the scope of this discussion to provide a formula for obtaining the proper balance. In fact, such a task still confounds the great theorists in the field of corporate finance.[2]

On the other hand, we can discuss some useful techniques for choosing the best method of debt financing using outside funds. Generally speaking, we select the method of debt financing that results in the lowest effective interest rate. In many instances, such as with a commercial bank loan, the effective interest rate is given by the lender. Often, however, the true rate is hidden.[3] In these instances we can utilize the principles of compound interest discussed in chapter 19 to place different forms of borrowing on a comparable basis and select the lowest cost.

---

[1]See chapter 12 for a discussion of the principle.

[2]See articles by Modigliani and Miller and rejoinder by Durand in Ezra Solomon, ed., *The Management of Corporate Capital* (Chicago: Free Press of Glencoe, 1959).

[3]Even under the Truth in Lending Act all interest rates are not disclosed.

Effective Bond Yield

Although bonds bear a coupon rate or face rate, this rarely reflects the effective rate of interest. Most bonds are sold at a premium or a discount in order to adjust the yield on the bonds to correspond with the current market conditions. The premium or discount, then, is really just an adjustment of interest. If a company were to issue a $1,000 bond at the price of 103 (percent), it would receive $1,030 and be required to repay only $1,000. This extra $30, paid at the time the bonds are issued, compensates the company for the extra interest which it will pay over the life of the bond. Similarly, if a $1,000 bond were sold at a price of 94, the $60 discount would represent an adjustment of interest. In this case, the company would receive only $940, but would be required to repay $1,000. The extra $60 it would be required to repay the bondholder at maturity would compensate for the failure to make sufficient interest payments over the life of the bond.

Thus, a company must calculate the yield, or effective interest rate, on a bond issue if it is to know the cost of borrowing. Because the extra interest (the premium or discount) is paid at the date of issue or maturity and all other payments of interest come at regular intervals between, it is necessary to recognize the time difference in the payments in order to calculate the effective interest rate. In other words, it would not be accurate merely to apportion the extra interest to the various periods on a stright-line basis, since this method would not recognize the time value of money.[4] We must utilize the principles of compound interest to determine the effective yield. To illustrate, let us assume that the Carbo Company issues $100,000 face value of 6 percent, five-year bonds on January 1, 1971, at a price of 104. The bonds pay interest semiannually on June 30 and December 31 each year. The cash flows would be diagramed as follows:

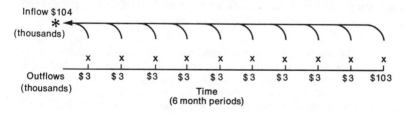

Inflow $104 (thousands)

Outflows (thousands) $3 $3 $3 $3 $3 $3 $3 $3 $3 $103

Time
(6 month periods)

---

[4]In chapter 10 the straight-line method was used to amortize the bond premium or discount. That technique was sufficient to illustrate the concept of amortization. The student can see, however, that the straight-line amortization does not reflect the true interest cost. For this reason, accountants sometimes use the "effective yield" method of amortization, which does consider the time value of money. In this chapter we are concerned primarily with the problem of determining the true interest rate and not with the techniques of accounting for the bond.

With a premium, the effective yield will always be less than the coupon rate, and with a discount, the reverse will be true. The interest rate that will equate the cash inflow of $104,000 with the present value of the cash outflows is the true rate of interest inherent in the obligation. By referring to present value tables, we learn that the appropriate rate is 5 percent per annum (or 2½ percent per interest period).[5] This is seen in the following calculations:

PV of interest @ 2½ percent per period for ten periods $3,000 × 8.752)	$ 26,256
PV of $100,000 principle repayment ($100,000 × 0.781)	78,100
	$104,356
PV of above at effective interest rate	$104,000

In order to determine the true rate of interest in such a problem, it would be necessary to have more detailed tables than those presented in the appendix. Tables with sufficient detail are readily obtainable at most book stores and are not presented here because of space limitations. Because bond yield problems are so common, tables can also be obtained which reflect the effective yield directly. An example of a bond yield table is shown in Figure 20-2. Such a table, of course, was prepared from present value tables similar to those in the appendix.

Lease or Borrow

Leasing is often nothing more than a form of financing. The lease is simply the tool by which the funds necessary to acquire the use of the asset are obtained. A lease of this type may be defined as a *financial lease* and usually contains the following features:

1. The decision to lease is based primarily on financial considerations rather than on strictly operational reasons; i.e., leasing is considered a source of capital by management. This method is selected after considering other forms of financing such as issuing capital stock, retaining earnings, or borrowing through bank term loans or mortgage bonds.
2. The lease is normally noncancellable, or it is cancellable only under heavy penalty during the initial term of the lease.

---

[5]The present value tables in the appendix are not detailed enough to show fractional rates. A book of mathematical tables (available in most libraries) will show the following factors: The present value of an ordinary annuity of one dollar for ten periods at 2½ percent = $8.752; the present value of one dollar due ten years hence, at 2½ percent = $0.781.

3. Rentals payable under the lease agreement are designed to return to the lessor the total cost of the asset involved, plus the return on the investment of funds during the initial term of the lease.
4. The lessor, the legal owner of the asset, retains title to the property involved at the expiration of the initial lease term. However, provision is often made for the lessee to obtain use of the property after this date by the lessor's granting to the lessee either an option to renew the lease at reduced rates or an option to buy the property. In either case, the lessee must make additional payments, above and beyond the asset cost, plus a return thereon, in order to have continued use of the property.
5. Financial leases often contain what is usually termed a "rejectable offer" clause. Under this provision the lessee may offer to purchase the leased asset at any time, according to a schedule of predetermined prices. If the lessor rejects the offer of the lessee, the agreement is automatically canceled.
6. Financial leases normally employ the *net lease* principle, which requires the lessee to pay all maintenance costs, repairs, insurance, taxes, alterations, and all other costs (other than initial cost) normally associated with ownership. The purpose of this clause is to make the rental payments clear, or net, to the lessor, so that the return he receives during the initial term of the lease is certain and determinable in advance.
7. The primary security behind a financial lease is normally the general credit of the lessee rather than the value of the leased property.

Actually, the financial lease is a relatively new concept which has come into wide usage since World War II. Other forms of leasing, on the other hand, date back for hundreds of years before Christ.[6] The fact that this old device has been used for an entirely different purpose has caused much confusion in the financial community.[7] The advertising done by leasing companies has added to the confusion because they have tried to convey the idea that leasing is a substitute for buying, when, in fact, financial leasing is a substitute for borrowing. Whether a company leases or buys, it has presumably decided it needs the asset. The important question then should be that of the best way to obtain the necessary financing. The choice is between leasing and borrowing, not between leasing and buying.

As with other forms of debt financing, the best choice is the form with the lowest cost. The difficulty arises from the fact that leases do not state

---

[6] For centuries, the lease was used almost exclusively in connection with agricultural land. It was a tool which enabled the ruling class to retain control of vast estates, benefit from the land's production, and yet be freed from the problems associated with the actual farming operations. With the coming of the Industrial Revolution and the urbanization which accompanied it, the lease was extended beyond its initial bounds. Today it is difficult to find a capital good which is not available through leasing should the customer desire it.

[7] See, for example, Donald R. Gant, "Illusions in Lease Financing," *Harvard Business Review* 37 (Mar.-Apr. 1959): 121-42.

Figure 20-2

SAMPLE BOND TABLE
$100, 4 Percent Bond

YEARS AND MONTHS

YIELD	18-9	18-10	18-11	19	19-1	19-2	19-3	19-4
3.00	114.26	114.31	114.35	114.40	114.45	114.49	114.54	114.59
3.05	113.49	113.53	113.58	113.62	113.66	113.71	113.75	113.80
3.10	112.72	112.76	112.81	112.85	112.89	112.93	112.97	113.01
3.15	111.96	112.00	112.04	112.08	112.12	112.16	112.20	112.23
3.20	111.21	111.25	111.28	111.32	111.36	111.39	111.43	111.46
3.25	110.46	110.50	110.53	110.57	110.60	110.63	110.67	110.70
3.30	109.72	109.76	109.79	109.82	109.85	109.88	109.91	109.94
3.35	108.99	109.02	109.05	109.08	109.11	109.14	109.16	109.19
3.40	108.26	108.29	108.32	108.35	108.37	108.40	108.42	108.45
3.45	107.54	107.57	107.59	107.62	107.64	107.66	107.69	107.71
3.50	106.83	106.85	106.87	106.90	106.92	106.94	106.96	106.98
3.55	106.12	106.14	106.16	106.18	106.20	106.21	106.23	106.25
3.60	105.42	105.43	105.45	105.47	105.48	105.50	105.52	105.53
3.65	104.72	104.73	104.75	104.77	104.78	104.79	104.81	104.82
3.70	104.03	104.04	104.05	104.07	104.08	104.09	104.10	104.11
3.75	103.34	103.35	103.36	103.38	103.38	103.39	103.40	103.41
3.80	102.66	102.67	102.68	102.69	102.69	102.70	102.71	102.72
3.85	101.99	101.99	102.00	102.01	102.01	102.02	102.02	102.03
3.90	101.32	101.32	101.33	101.33	101.33	101.34	101.34	101.34
3.95	100.65	100.66	100.66	100.66	100.66	100.66	100.66	100.67
4.00	100.00	100.00	100.00	100.00	100.00	100.00	100.00	100.00
4.05	99.34	99.34	99.34	99.34	99.34	99.33	99.33	99.33
4.10	98.70	98.69	98.69	98.69	98.68	98.68	98.67	98.67
4.15	98.05	98.05	98.04	98.04	98.03	98.03	98.02	98.01
4.20	97.42	97.41	97.40	97.40	97.39	97.38	97.37	97.37
4.25	96.79	96.78	96.77	96.76	96.75	96.74	96.73	96.72
4.30	96.16	96.15	96.14	96.13	96.12	96.11	96.09	96.08
4.35	95.54	95.53	95.52	95.51	95.49	95.48	95.46	95.45
4.40	94.92	94.91	94.90	94.89	94.87	94.85	94.84	94.82
4.45	94.31	94.30	94.28	94.27	94.25	94.23	94.22	94.20
4.50	93.71	93.69	93.67	93.66	93.64	93.62	93.60	93.58
4.55	93.11	93.09	93.07	93.05	93.03	93.01	92.99	92.97
4.60	92.51	92.49	92.47	92.45	92.43	92.41	92.39	92.37
4.65	91.92	91.90	91.88	91.86	91.83	91.81	91.79	91.76
4.70	91.33	91.31	91.29	91.27	91.24	91.21	91.19	91.17
4.75	90.75	90.73	90.70	90.68	90.65	90.63	90.60	90.58
4.80	90.18	90.15	90.12	90.10	90.07	90.04	90.02	89.99
4.85	89.60	89.58	89.55	89.53	89.49	89.46	89.44	89.41
4.90	89.04	89.01	88.98	88.95	88.92	88.89	88.86	88.83
4.95	88.47	88.44	88.42	88.39	88.35	88.32	88.29	88.26

YIELD	18-9	18-10	18-11	19	19-1	19-2	19-3	19-4
5.00	87.92	87.88	87.85	87.83	87.79	87.76	87.72	87.69
5.05	87.36	87.33	87.30	87.27	87.23	87.20	87.16	87.13
5.10	86.81	86.78	86.75	86.72	86.68	86.64	86.61	86.57
5.15	86.27	86.23	86.20	86.17	86.13	86.09	86.05	86.02
5.20	85.73	85.69	85.66	85.62	85.58	85.54	85.51	85.47
5.25	85.19	85.16	85.12	85.09	85.04	85.00	84.96	84.93
5.30	84.66	84.62	84.59	84.55	84.51	84.47	84.43	84.39
5.35	84.14	84.10	84.06	84.02	83.98	83.93	83.89	83.85
5.40	83.61	83.57	83.53	83.49	83.45	83.40	83.36	83.32
5.45	83.10	83.05	83.01	82.97	82.93	82.88	82.84	82.80
5.50	82.58	82.54	82.50	82.46	82.41	82.36	82.32	82.27
5.55	82.07	82.03	81.98	81.94	81.89	81.85	81.80	81.76
5.60	81.57	81.52	81.48	81.43	81.38	81.34	81.29	81.24
5.65	81.06	81.02	80.97	80.93	80.88	80.83	80.78	80.74
5.70	80.57	80.52	80.47	80.43	80.38	80.33	80.28	80.23
5.75	80.07	80.02	79.98	79.93	79.88	79.83	79.78	79.73
5.80	79.58	79.53	79.48	79.44	79.38	79.33	79.28	79.23
5.85	79.10	79.05	79.00	78.95	78.89	78.84	78.79	78.74
5.90	78.61	78.56	78.51	78.47	78.41	78.36	78.30	78.25
5.95	78.14	78.08	78.03	77.98	77.93	77.87	77.82	77.77

Source: *Executives Bond Values Tables* (Boston: Financial Publishing Company, 1966). Reprinted by permission.

[a]This table shows the price you would pay for a $100 bond with a 4 percent coupon rate, maturities varying from 18 years 9 months to 19 years 4 months. For example, if you purchased a $100, 4 percent bond maturing in 18 years 9 months to yield 5 percent, you would pay $87.92.

the rate of interest; instead, they hide the interest charges in the rent.[8] Again, we can utilize the principles of compound interest to calculate the effective rate of interest in the lease. This may be done by comparing the relative cash flows under the two proposals.

Illustration without the Tax Effect. The Modern Company has decided it needs a new automatic "pill-popping" machine, but cannot decide how to finance the investment. The production manager argues that the machine should be leased, while the controller feels that the machine should be purchased and the necessary funds borrowed from the bank. Facts related to the alternatives may be summarized as follows:

Lease: Five-year, noncancellable, "net" lease. Annual rentals of $1,500 per year payable at the beginning of each year.

[8]Most leasing companies do not admit the leasing is a form of debt financing and therefore will not even admit interest is a factor, let alone tell the prospective lessee what the rate is. They prefer to have businessmen regard the lease as some magic "cureall" which has not cost.

Borrow: The company can borrow the necessary funds from its local bank at 6 percent interest. If this were done, the loan would be repaid in five equal, annual installments, payable at the end of each year. The machine can be purchased for $7,500 and is expected to last five years, at which time it should have a salvage value of $2,000. The company uses sum-of-the-years'-digits depreciation and is subject to a 50 percent income tax rate.

The cash flows under the two alternatives may be summarized as follows:

BEGINNING OF YEAR[a]	CASH OUTFLOWS	
	LEASE	BORROW
1	$1,500	$ 0[b]
2	1,500	1,781
3	1,500	1,781
4	1,500	1,781
5	1,500	1,781
6	2,000[c]	1,781

[a]The beginning of one year is considered the same as the end of the previous year (actually one day different).

[b]The $1,781 payments under the loan constitute the amount necessary to repay the loan in five equal installments (the present value of an ordinary annuity of five rents). Actually, the terms of repayment of the loan are of no concern since the effective interest rate is already given in this instance. We are, on the other hand, concerned with the timing of the payments under the lease because no interest rate has been given, and this we must calculate.

[c]If the company leases the machine, then it must give up the machine at the end of the five years; whereas if it borrows, it gets to keep the machine. The salvage value must, therefore, be considered as a cash outflow under leasing.

In the case of borrowing, all relevant facts for making the decision were given (the interest rate of 6 percent and the present value of $7,500). With the lease, however, the interest rate is hidden. If we equate the present value of the cash flows under leasing with the cash price ($7,500), we will have the effective rate of interest implicit in the lease. Thus, by trial and error, we find the rate of interest in the Modern Company lease to be 10 percent per annum.

Present value of first rent	$1,500
Present value of other 4 rents ($1,500 × 3.170)	4,755
Present value of salvage ($2,000 × .621)	1,242
Total present value	$7,497
Desired present value	$7,500

Interest rate = 10 percent per annum

Illustration with the Tax Effect. The previous example ignored the tax difference between leasing and buying. If Modern Company leases the machine, the rentals will be tax deductible. If it owns the machine, the depreciation plus interest will be tax deductible. If the tax deductions are not the same, the amount of taxes paid under the various alternatives will be different and the cash flows will be affected to that extent. This can easily be accounted for by calculating the *tax shield*, the advantage (or disadvantage) because of the difference in timing of tax payments that may arise by leasing as opposed to borrowing, and adding this to or deducting it from the lease rentals. This is shown in Figure 20-3.

Note that the net effect of the tax shield in this case is only $64. This means that the interest rate in the lease is actually slightly less than the early calculations show. (The present value with the tax shield is only $7,433, whereas it was $7,497 without the tax shield. Since the correct interest rate will give us a present value of $7,500, we know that the 10 percent rate is slightly too high.)

Although the effect of the tax shield in this problem was not significant, it could be in certain cases. Where the tax deduction is materially different under the various alternatives, the tax shield should be added (or deducted) from the lease rental in order to get the effective interest rate the company will pay if it leases.

Nonquantitative Factors

That the true rate of interest is the most important factor influencing the choice between debt alternatives can hardly be questioned. It is not, however, the only factor that should be considered. Often there are important restrictions such as specific required ratios, limited payment of dividends, and imposed penalties for early repayment placed upon the borrower. These, of course, must also receive attention, and, in those instances where the interest rates are competitive, they may be the factors upon which the decision will hinge.

Leasing has one particular nonquantitative advantage that warrants special mention. It is the fact that accountants give leasing a competitive treatment in the financial statements. When an asset is purchased and the funds are obtained through debt financing, both the asset and the liability are shown on the balance sheet. When the asset is acquired through a financial lease, on the other hand, *neither* the asset nor the liability is shown in the balance sheet. The only disclosure given is in a casual footnote specifying the approximate annual rental, but not mentioning the amount of liability.

Figure 20-3

CALCULATION OF TAX SHIELD
LEASE OR BORROW

Total Tax Deductions

DEDUCTION IF BORROW			DEDUCTION IF LEASE	EXTRA DEDUCTION VIA BORROW	TAX SHIELDᶜ
DEPRª	INTERESTᵇ	TOTAL			
$1,833	$ 450	$2,283	$1,500	+$ 783	+$391
1,467	370	1,837	1,500	+ 337	+ 168
1,100	285	1,385	1,500	− 115	− 57
733	196	929	1,500	− 571	− 285
367	101	468	1,500	− 1,032	− 516
$5,500	$1,402	$6,902	$7,500	−$ 598	−$299

Calculation of Interest
under 6 Percent Loan

PAYMENTᵈ	INTEREST	PRINCIPAL	REMAINING BALANCE
$1,781	$450	$1,331	$6,169
1,781	370	1,411	4,758
1,781	285	1,496	3,262
1,781	196	1,585	1,677
1,781	101	1,680	0

Calculation of PV of Tax Shield at 10 Percent

TAX SHIELD	FACTORS (TABLE C)	PRESENT VALUE
+$391	.909	+$355
+ 168	.826	+ 139
− 57	.751	− 43
− 285	.683	− 195
− 516	.621	− 320
		−$ 64

Present Value of Lease Rentals $7,497
Less: Tax Shield . . . .   − 64
     Net Present Value $7,433

ªSum-of-the-year's-digits depreciation used.

ᵇInterest calculations are shown in table below.

ᶜTax shield assumes 50 percent tax rate. This column indicates the extra amount of taxes that will be paid (positive) or saved (negative) under the lease.

ᵈLoan repaid in five equal installments of $1,781 ($7,500 ÷ 4.212).

A typical such footnote reads:

> At January 31, 1961, the total minimum annual rentals payable
> under leases expiring after five years was approximately $11,700,000.
> Leases covering about 79% of this amount will expire on various
> dates during the next 20 years.[9]

The failure of accountants to disclose these asset and liability figures
properly presents a very real advantage of leasing over borrowing. By
leasing, a company can grossly misstate its financial position and, thereby,
probably have access to many more dollars in assets than would be the case
with borrowing. One large grocery chain, for example, reported in 1960
long-term liabilities of only $35,000,000. Had the same company disclosed
its leases as liabilities, the total would have been $431,000,000! Yes, there
is a real advantage to leasing where accountants give such biased reporting.

The apparent reason for this preferential treatment is the ignorance of
businessmen regarding the true nature of the financial lease. When accountants and others recognize the financial lease for what it is, a means
of financing, one can expect this artificial advantage to disappear.

SUMMARY

Two important management problems have been discussed in this
chapter: how to select the most profitable investments, and how to finance
these investments. Four techniques were introduced as tools for helping
management select the most profitable investments. The *payback period*
may be used to indicate the time required to recover the amount invested.
The *average rate of return* may be calculated to reflect the rate of profit
that might be expected from a particular investment. Both of these tools,
however, ignore the fact that money has a time value. The *time-adjusted
rate of return* overcomes this weakness by calculating the effective (time-
adjusted) rate that the company can expect to earn from an investment.
The *profitability index* also recognizes the time value of money, but ranks
investments according to a predetermined cutoff rate.

The funds to acquire new assets may come from either owners or creditors. In those instances where debt financing is used, that form of debt
having the least cost as expressed by the effective interest rate should normally be selected. Often, the effective interest rate is hidden and must be
calculated. This is particularly true with bonds and financial leases. Bonds
generally have a coupon interest which must be coupled with a premium
or a discount in order to calculate the *yield*. Financial leases have the
interest buried in the rentals, and this must be extracted using compound
interest tables if one is to find the effective rate implied in the lease.

---

[9]J.C. Penney Company, *Annual Report*, Jan. 31, 1961.

QUESTIONS

1. How can the payback period be useful in evaluating investment alternatives? What are the limitations of this method?
2. Fungic Company is contemplating buying a machine which will cost $960 and last six years with no salvage value. The machine should generate $200 in profits per year. What is the expected payback period on the machine?
3. Referring to the facts in the preceding question, calculate the average rate of return anticipated from the machine. What are the advantages of this method of evaluating investment opportunities?
4. What is the major advantage of the time-adjusted rate of return method over the payback and average rate of return methods? What is the time-adjusted rate of return on the Fungic Company machine, referred to in question 2?
5. What is a profitability index? How is the profitability index calculated? Why is this method easier than the time-adjusted rate of return method? Assuming that the Fungic Company has a preestablished cutoff rate of 20 percent (see question 2), calculate and interpret the profitability index.
6. What is the "effective yield" on a bond? Why is the coupon rate generally different from the effective yield?
7. What is a financial lease? What are the major features that distinguish a financial lease from a service lease?
8. Why is it more appropriate to say "lease versus borrow" than to say "lease versus buy"?
9. In figuring the cash outflows under leasing, why is it necessary to treat the salvage value (fair market value) of an asset as a cost of leasing?
10. How do accountants show leases in the financial statements? Do you agree with this treatment? Does the method give leasing or borrowing a special advantage?

PROBLEMS

Problem 20-1

The Jones Bakery is trying to decide whether to keep its old mixer or to replace it with a new model. The old machine is valued at $50 on the books and probably could be sold for that amount. It costs $960 a year to operate. The new mixer, while operating at the same speed as the old mixer, will cost only $600 a year to operate; it will cost $2,500 to purchase. Both machines are expected to operate for ten years, after which the old machine will have a $5 scrap value and the new machine a $15 scrap value.

Required:

Determine whether the Jones Bakery should buy a new machine. Show supporting computations. (You may assume that all operating costs are paid at the end of the year. Disregard the effect of taxes.)

Problem 20-2

The Castro Construction Company is considering investing in two machines, A and B, which will give the yearly profits listed below. Both machines have a cost of $2,500, an estimated life of five years, and expected salvage value of $500. The company uses straight-line depreciation on all machinery.

	A	B
Year 1	$ 300	-0-
Year 2	700	$1,000
Year 3	1,000	1,500
Year 4	1,000	1,000
Year 5	800	100
	$3,800	$3,600

Required:

Determine which provides the fastest payback, the best average rate of return, and the best time-adjusted rate of return. Show all supporting computations.

Problem 20-3

The Smith Paper Company is considering the purchase of a new rolling machine. It is considering three available machines: machine A, which costs $1,000 and is expected to return profits of $228 a year for five years; machine B, which costs $2,500 and is expected to return $600 a year in profits for nine years; and machine C, which costs $5,000 and is expected to return $600 in profits per year for twenty-five years. The company has a policy of not making any investment which will not yield a 10 percent pretax return.

Required:

Calculate a profitability index for each of these three investment alternatives, and from this index determine which of the three is the best investment. (Assume the company uses straight-line depreciation.)

Problem 20-4

The Youngstown Electric Company has decided upon a $200,000 expansion for its plant; it plans to finance this expansion program with 50 percent equity and 50 percent debt financing.

The Youngstown Bank has offered to lend the funds to Youngstown Electric on an installment loan with the following provisions:

"The Youngstown Electric Company is to pay yearly installments of $10,000 per year, starting five years after the date of the loan, and these payments are to be made for a period of fifteen years, at the end of which the balance of the loan will be due. The interest rate will be 5¾ percent on the declining loan balance. All yearly payments will apply first to the amount of accrued interest and the remainder to the principal."

A local brokerage firm has also offered to aid the Youngstown Electric Company in obtaining the needed $100,000 through the issuance of ten-year bonds with a coupon rate of 5½ percent. Interest on the bonds would be paid semiannually. An underwriting group has guaranteed Youngstown a net price of $96,211.75.

Required:

Compute the true interest costs of these two alternatives. Which would be best? Show all computations.

Problem 20-5

The Tiger Tank Company has decided to acquire a new model 3040 automatic lathe. The list price on such a lathe is $31,430 F.O.B. Tiger's factory. A $500 cash discount is available if Tiger purchases the lathe directly from the manufacturer. The factory superintendent estimates that a model 3040 lathe will have a useful life of eight years, after which it should have a salvage of $3,000. For a number of years the firm has been in a critical cash position, as funds generated from operations have continually been invested in plant, equipment, and inventories. Because of the tight cash position, no company funds are available for the new machine. The controller has investigated many possible sources of funds and has narrowed the choice down to two possibilities.

1. A local leasing company has offered a model 3040 lathe under a "net" lease which requires Tiger Tank Company to pay all maintenance and operating costs. The eight-year lease requires annual rentals of $5,000 for each of the first four years and annual rentals of $4,000 for each of the remaining years. All lease payments are due at the beginning of the year. The lease has a purchase option which would allow Tiger Tank Company to purchase the lathe at the end of the lease for $3,000.
2. A big loan company has agreed to advance the necessary cash on an 8 percent installment loan. The loan would be repaid in eight equal year-end installments. Each installment on the note would be applied first to interest (8 percent of the unpaid balance) and the remainder to principal. The controller feels that the 8 percent interest rate is too high, but the company's bank has refused to extend more credit to Tiger Tank Company.

Required:

Determine whether Tiger Tank Company should lease or borrow, and present calculations to support your recommendation. Ignore the tax shield.

Problem 20-6

The Schroeder Blanket Mills have four operating divisions. In November of each year the division managers submit a list of estimated capital equipment requirements for the coming year. This year the funds for capital expenditures are extremely limited, and the company controller has insisted that all requests be carefully scrutinized so that the available funds will be put to the best possible use. The baby-blanket division has requested an automatic sewing machine and submitted the following data to support the request.

Machine cost	$15,800
Machine life	10 years
Machine salvage value	$ 1,800
Annual additional revenue	$ 6,000
Annual additional out-of-pocket costs	$ 1,000
Depreciation method	Straight-line
Income tax rate	50 percent

Required:

    a. Calculate the expected payback period.
    b. Calculate the expected average rate of return.
    c. Calculate the expected time-adjusted rate of return.
    d. Calculate the profitability index, assuming an after-tax cutoff rate of 20 percent.

Problem 20-7

Olympus Real Estate Company furnishes each of its ten salesmen with a new car every two years. This year the company management has decided to acquire ten Chevrolet Impalas which list for $2,990 F.O.B. destination. The local Chevrolet dealer has agreed to allow a $1,500 trade-in allowance on each of the old cars that the company must dispose of. The new Impalas should have an average salvage value of $1,600 at the end of the two-year period. If the cars are purchased, the Olympus Real Estate Company will borrow the necessary funds from a local bank under a "line of credit" agreement. The company is currently being charged interest at the rate of 6 percent per annum on bank loans (calculated on the unpaid balance of the loan).

One of the salesmen has suggested that the company lease the cars. He says that most of his friends drive leased cars because it's cheaper. Investigation reveals that identical Chevrolet Impalas can be leased for only $66 per month per car, payable at the beginning of each month. The lease would be noncancellable for the two-year period and would require the lessee to assume all costs normally associated with ownership (taxes, maintenance, gas, oil, insurance, etc.). A deposit of $100 per car is required when the lease is signed, but the entire deposit will be refunded at the end of the lease. If the Impalas are leased, the old cars will be sold on the local auto auction. It is estimated that Olympus Real Estate Company will net $1,200 per car if this is done.

Required:

Should the company lease the cars or should they purchase the cars and borrow the necessary funds from the bank? What is the interest rate implied in the lease? Show all supporting computations.

Case 20

EAST COAST INSULATION SUPPLY COMPANY

East Coast Insulation Supply was formed in February 1970 by Cliff Hatch, Dick Flowers, and Frank Davis. All three owners had several years' experience in various phases of the insulation business. Dick and Frank were to work as salesmen, with Dick taking the northern territory and Frank the southern territory. Cliff was to work as office manager and would handle all counter sales.

It is customary for firms in this industry to furnish cars for the salesmen. This presented a real problem to the owners because they were grossly undercapitalized and needed to invest as much as possible of the company funds in inventory. Cliff had recently picked up a leasing company's brochure that made leasing cars sound very attractive. Cliff was especially impressed by the following feature:

> Leasing releases cash tied up in equipment or in reserves for replacement. The cash you realize in disposing of equipment you own is freed for you to put to more desirable uses. Leasing permits you to operate further on your own capital. Because your lease is not considered a loan, it protects your borrowing capacity.

The partners discussed the merits of leasing versus buying at great length. Frank agreed to contact Atlantic Leasing Company and see what he could arrange. The company was very cooperative and quickly drew up a draft copy of a lease agreement. It allowed the lessee to pick the exact car he wanted, including color and optional equipment desired. Although the company was talking in terms of leasing three identical cars, the draft lease was drawn up for only one, a Pontiac Catalina. The leasing company said identical lease documents could be drawn up for the other vehicles. Pertinent paragraphs of the proposed lease agreement are contained in Exhibit 20-1.

Dick checked with the local Pontiac dealer to see what sort of "deal" he could work out with him. A Pontiac Catalina, identical to the one specified in the lease, had a window price including destination charges of $3,662. After considerable negotiation, the salesman agreed to a $150 per car discount. The discounted amount would be subject to state sales tax of 4½ percent, and license and registration fees would amount to $9 per car. The Pontiac dealer would finance each car purchased by requiring a down payment of $493 and twenty-four monthly installments of $150, the first installment due one month after purchase. The Truth in Lending Act required the dealer to disclose the true annual interest rate of 12 percent.

QUESTIONS

1. Should East Coast Insulation Supply Company lease or borrow? Ignore taxes.
2. What is the effective interest rate implied in the lease?
3. Did the Pontiac dealer disclose the "true" rate of interest?

Exhibit 20-1
LEASE AGREEMENT

Lease No. _____

Stock No. _____

Delivery Date _____

THIS LEASE AGREEMENT made and entered into this_____day of
_____, 19____, by and between_____
_____, of_____, State of_____,
hereinafter referred to as the Lessor; and_____
_____, of_____, State of_____,
hereinafter referred to as the Lessee;

WHEREAS, Lessee desires to lease a motor vehicle from the Lessor, it is
mutually agreed between the parties, as follows:

WITNESSETH

1. **Vehicle Leased:** The Lessor hereby leases to the Lessee, the following
described vehicle with special equipment and accessories as set forth:

YR.	MODEL	MAKE TRADE NAME	NO. OF CYL.	MODEL NUMBER	BODY STYLE	VEHICLE IDENTIFICATION NUMBER
1970	Catalina	Pontiac	8	25692	4 Dr. Sed.	X526690210802

EQUIPMENT _____

2. **Lease Term, Charges, Etc.:** The vehicle shall be leased for the term set
forth in 2a, below, and subject to the provisions and conditions set forth in 2b,
through 2n:

TERM	MONTHLY RENT		SALES TAX	TOTAL MONTHLY RENT	LICENSE FEES	SECURITY DEPOSIT
24 Mo.	$114.00	—0—	$6.25	$120.25	$9.00	$200.00
a	b	c	d	e	f	g

INITIAL PAYMENT	PRORATA 1ST MONTH TOTAL RENT UNTIL DUE DATE	TOTAL AMOUNT DUE BY DELIVERY
—0—	$120.25	$329.25
h	i initial	j initial

\

MONTHLY DUE DATE EACH MONTH	DATE TERM ENDS	VALUE AT END OF TERM	MONTHLY PREMATURE TERMINATION FACTOR
1st	*Mar. 31, 1972*	*$2,000.00*	*$96.20*
k	l	m	n

3. Security Deposit: Lessee shall deposit with Lessor the sum set forth at 2g, above, as security for the performance by the Lessee of the terms and conditions of this lease agreement. If the Lessee shall have fully complied with all the terms, covenants, and conditions hereof required of the Lessee, the deposit shall be refunded upon termination of the lease agreement. Should Lessee fail to comply with any of such terms, covenants, and conditions, such deposit may be applied by Lessor toward payment of any part or all of the costs and expenses, including Attorney's fees, incurred by the Lessor because of such default. The making of such deposit shall not be considered as payment of rent nor in any manner release Lessee from obligations to pay rent or from performing any of the other obligations herein assumed by Lessee and is forfeited and not refundable upon default.

4. Maintenance, Licensing, Taxes and Other Expenses: Lessor shall, at Lessee's expense, as provided for in 2f, above, obtain the original registration and license for the current year as required by law. Lessee agrees to pay all expenses incurred in connection with the use and operation of the vehicle, including but not limited to State Vehicle Inspection Laws, maintenance and repair expenses (including installation of any mandatory device or equipment now or hereafter required by law), gasoline, lubrication, washing, polishing, storage, parking, tolls, and all other expenses incident to the use and operation of the vehicle, and also including personal property taxes, excise, use, sales, or other taxes or fees of any nature assessed or imposed by any governmental body or agency by reason of the acquisition, disposition, lease, possession, use, operation, or maintenance of the vehicle, or based on any rentals derived therefrom; and Lessee agrees to save harmless from all liability therefor, and to promptly reimburse Lessor upon demand for any of such items paid or advanced by Lessor on behalf of Lessee.

5. Termination: (a) Premature Termination: Lessee may terminate this lease Agreement with respect to any vehicle at any time after *Twelve (12)* months from the date of delivery, and prior to the end of the lease term, by giving Lessor thirty (30) days' notice in writing, provided that Lessee shall bear any loss or receive any gain which results from final disposition of the vehicle, as noted below, or the Lessee may purchase the vehicle for the "Value at End of Term," as set forth in 2m, above, plus the following: The product of the "Monthly Premature Termination Factor," 2n, above, multiplied by the number of months from the "Date Term Ends," 2l, above, plus fifteen (15) percent of such product plus any annual license fees and taxes due on the vehicle.

(b) Termination at end of term: This Lease Agreement will terminate on the "Date Term Ends," 2l, above, provided the Lessee shall purchase for cash, on or before such date, the vehicle for the "Value at End of Term," 2m, above, plus any annual license fees and taxes due on the vehicle, or, the Lessee shall deliver said vehicle on the date the term ends to Lessor, as set forth in Paragraph 17, and Lessee then bears any loss or receives any gain which results from final disposition of the vehicle, as noted below.

(c) Disposition of Vehicle: In the event the Lessee does not elect to purchase the vehicle, Lessee will surrender the vehicle, in accordance with Paragraph 17, below, on or before the "Date Term Ends," 21, above. Upon such
return, Lessee and Lessor, or their agents, shall inspect the returned vehicle and
provide a jointly signed report on the condition of the vehicle. Lessor and Lessee
will attempt to agree upon its then value; if Lessor and Lessee cannot so agree
within two days after the return of the vehicle then Lessor shall obtain three
bonafide bids for the cash purchase of the vehicle, and Lessee may name one of
the three parties to bid. Should the agreed value (or the highest bid) be more
than the termination value computed in 5a, or 5b, above, then such excess, less
$25.00, shall be paid to Lessee; if such agreed value or bid be less than the
termination value, Lessee will pay the difference to Lessor, plus sum of $25.00
(unless Lessee enters into a new Lease Agreement with Lessor with respect to a
different vehicle, in which event such $25.00 payment shall be waived).

(d) This Lease Agreement shall terminate and Lessee's obligation shall cease,
only upon such sale by Lessor and the payment by Lessee of any such sums due
upon such sale or purchase, as set forth herein.

6. Delivery of Vehicle: Lessor shall use all reasonable diligence to deliver
the vehicle to Lessee, but Lessor shall not be liable to Lessee for any loss or
damage resulting from any failure or delay in obtaining the vehicle or making
delivery thereof; nor shall such delay void this Lease Agreement or give Lessee
any right to rescind the same; however, if delivery shall go beyond 60 days from
the estimated date of delivery, as set forth hereafter, the Lease Agreement shall
be null and void. In the event that delivery of this vehicle shall be on a date
other than the date of this Lease Agreement, then the verification of delivery, as
set forth at the end of this Lease Agreement, shall be executed and made a part
hereof and the Vehicle Identification Number and items set forth in Paragraph
2i, 2j, and 2l, shall be inserted as of that date and shall be initiated and become a
part of this Lease Agreement.

9. Risk of Loss: Lessee shall bear all risks of damage to or loss of the
vehicle. All replacements, repairs, or substitution or parts or equipment shall be
at the cost and expense of the Lessee and shall become accessions of the vehicle.
The rent otherwise due hereunder shall not be prorated or abated while the
vehicle is being serviced or repaired.

12. Insurance: Lessee at Lessee's expense agrees to provide insurance with
insurers satisfactory to Lessor, naming Lessor as an additional insured and
Lessor's assignee as loss payee, providing minimum coverages, as follows: (1)
Public liability: $100,000.00, individual bodily injury; and $300,000.00, total
bodily injury per accident; and $25,000.00, property damage per accident; (2)
Physical damage: actual cash value comprehensive, and $100.00, deductible
collision. Lessee is absolutely forbidden to operate or to permit the operation of
the vehicle at any time when said insurance is not in full force and effect, and at
any such time Lessee shall be deemed to be a nonpermissive user of the vehicle
and this Lease Agreement shall be in default. Lessee shall furnish to Lessor certificates of insurance, or other evidence of insurance satisfactory to the Lessor,
naming Lessor as an additional insured and showing the coverages required
herein. Said certificate(s) shall provide that such insurance may not be cancelled without ten (10) days' written notice to Lessor in advance.

13. Default: Time is of the essence of this Lease Agreement. If the Lessee
shall default in the payment or performance of any of its obligations or under-

takings hereunder, or if Lessee shall be named a debtor in any proceeding in bankruptcy or under any other law for the relief of debtors, or if Lessee shall make any assignment for the benefit of creditors, or if Lessee shall attempt to transfer its interests therein, or if there should be an involuntary transfer hereof by operation of law, or if any policy or policies of insurance agreed to be paid for by the Lessee shall not be so paid or if any other payments required hereunder to be paid by Lessee, shall not be paid, then, in any such events, this Lease Agreement shall be in default, and thereupon Lessor may demand that the vehicle be surrendered and delivered to the Lessor, and Lessor may take possession of the vehicle wherever the same may be found, with or without process of law, and for that purpose may enter upon any premises of the Lessee. Upon default, and Lessor's election to terminate this Lease Agreement, neither Lessee and any deficiency shall be due from Lessee or any surplus paid to Lessee, in the manner provided in said Paragraph, except that there shall be deducted all costs, including Attorney's fees, incurred by Lessor in the enforcement of its rights nor any successor to Lessee's interest shall have any further right, title or interest in and to the vehicle, or the possession or use thereof, and Lessor shall be entitled to retain all rents, and other sums including but not limited to the Security Deposit, if any, paid by the Lessee hereunder with respect to the vehicle as liquidated damages. Lessor may then proceed to dispose of the vehicle in the same manner as is provided in Paragraph 5c, above, with respect to a Premature Termination of the Lease Agreement, as is provided in Paragraph 5a, above, hereunder and any surplus or deficiency thereafter resulting shall be paid to or by Lessee. The rights and remedies of the Lessor hereunder are not to be deemed exclusive, but shall be cumulative and in addition to all other rights and remedies provided by law.

17. Surrender of Vehicle: Upon termination of the Lease Agreement term, the Lessee shall surrender the motor vehicle in the same condition as when received, less reasonable wear and tear, and free from collision or upset damage, to the Lessor at the Lessor's principal place of business.

Portions of lease agreement are reproduced here for instructional purposes only by permission of Richard W. Schanz and Alf Bostrom, Salt Lake City, Utah.

21

Principles
of
Accounting

At the beginning of this book accounting was defined as an art. It was noted that the determination of profits was not a precise process, but an art requiring expert estimates and practical judgments. In spite of these limitations, we have seen that accounting is structured with a great deal of logic and order. This structuring is accomplished by employing what are often referred to as the "principles of accounting." These principles, or concepts, are broad rules upon which accounting practice is based; they tend to serve as a unifying force.

Although it is evident that accounting is based upon some deeply rooted principles, no universally acceptable list of them has ever been compiled. Even in this area one finds wide disagreement among accountants as to just what constitutes a principle. Several years ago, the American Institute of Certified Public Accountants commissioned a research study to compile an inventory of generally accepted accounting principles for business enterprises. This study was not an attempt to discover new or improved principles, but to list those that were currently accepted practice. The nature of these accounting principles is seen in the following statement taken from inventory.

> Accountants are generally agreed that accounting principles cannot be derived from or proven by the laws of nature. They are rather in the category of conventions or rules developed by man from experience to fulfill the essential and useful needs and purposes in establishing reliable financial and operating information control for business entities. In this respect they are similar to principles of commercial law and other social disciplines.
>
> There is general agreement, also, among accounting teachers and practitioners that there are a number of concepts which underlie or permeate accepted accounting principles. . . .
>
> Concepts, as well as principles, are derived from experience in the conduct of business and the meeting of its accountabilities within our society whose objectives include: (a) the exercise of government power in a manner responsive to the will of the people, and (b) the maintenance of an economic system based upon individual incentives and opportunities for employment and investment in competitive business enterprises.[1]

ACCOUNTING PRINCIPLES

Although some writers distinguish between accounting principles and concepts, no such distinction will be made in this text. These terms will be treated as synonymous. The discussion that follows will center around the ten concepts listed in the inventory:

1. A society and government structure honoring private property rights
2. Specific business entities
3. Going concerns
4. Consistency between periods for the same entity
5. Monetary expression in accounts
6. Diversity in accounting among independent entities
7. Conservatism
8. Dependability of data through internal control
9. Materiality
10. Timeliness in financial reporting requiring estimates[2]

---

[1]Paul Grady, *Inventory of Generally Accepted Accounting Principles for Business Enterprises, Accounting Research Study No. 7* (New York: American Institute of Certified Public Accountants, 1963), pp. 23-24.

[2]Ibid., p. 24.

Property Rights

The accounting and reporting techniques followed in the "free world" are based upon a society and government structure that honor private property rights. Accordingly, the accounting and reporting procedures which we employ are designed to account for a business which has been set up to make a profit. The free enterprise system, in which individual citizens have the right to invest, is a necessary condition. This does not mean that we cannot account for a nonprofit enterprise or a governmental unit. It simply means that we cannot use the same principles, or concepts, since the "rules" are different, and, therefore, the accounting techniques must also differ.

Business Entity

It was noted in chapter 2 that accountants are primarily concerned with economic entities rather than with legal entities. Each business unit is considered as a separate entity, regardless of its legal form. The transactions of the owners are kept separate from those of the business so that the financial statements reflect only the transactions of the respective economic entities. Where corporations are interrelated through stock ownership, the accountants generally prepare consolidated statements to reflect the economic reality of the combined entity.

Going Concern

Our accounting methods and reporting techniques are based upon the assumption that the business will continue to operate indefinitely. Where this assumption is not valid, we must abandon conventional accounting techniques. For example, a balance sheet would not adequately disclose the financial position of a firm facing bankruptcy in the near future. In this instance the accountant would depart from conventional practice, which assumes a going concern, and prepare a special statement (a statement of affairs) that has application to this instance. Many of the rules which underlie figures in the balance sheet simply are not valid unless the firm is going to continue in business.

Monetary Measure

In order to account properly for a business enterprise we must have some common unit of measure. In our economy money serves not only as the medium of exchange, but also as the basis of accountability. Business transactions are all recorded and summarized in dollar terms. We record the acquisition of assets, for example, in terms of historical costs measured by the goods or services that change hands in the transaction. These assets are then carried on the books at unamortized cost, with no real consideration being given to current values.[3]

This technique of recording transactions in historical terms implies a stable unit of measure. This constant dollar assumption is, in fact, not valid in our economy. We read almost daily of inflation and the changing value of our dollar. In spite of this fact, accountants continue to record transactions in terms of historical costs. A departure from this concept, the use of price level indexes, is discussed later in the chapter. However, the practice may not be regarded as generally accepted.

Consistency

While the accountant may choose from a variety of methods, he must be consistent in their application between accounting periods for the same entity. For example, it would not be proper to use straight-line depreciation in one period and the sum-of-the-years'-digits method in the following period. Nor would it be appropriate to calculate inventory values by last-in, first-out (LIFO) one period and then switch to first-in, first-out (FIFO) the next. Where changes in procedures such as these are deemed advisable, the effect of such changes on the financial statements must be disclosed.

The committee on auditing procedures of the American Institute of Certified Public Accountants states:

> The objective of the consistency standard is: (1) to give assurance that the comparability of financial statements as between periods has not been materially affected by changes in the accounting principles employed or in the method of their application; or (2) if comparability has been materially affected by such changes, to require a statement of the nature of the changes in their effects on the financial statements.[4]

Diversity of Methods

Accountants have generally continued to support the position that no one method can properly be employed in all instances. While there is rather wide agreement that consistency within the individual firm is desir-

[3]Current assets are carried at the *lower* of cost or market (replacement price) which in most cases is cost. Fixed assets may be written *down* where the decline appears to be major and permanent. Otherwise they are carried at cost less the accumulated depreciation.

[4]*Statements on Auditing Procedures Number 33* (New York: American Institute of Certified Public Accountants), p. 42.

able, it is usually held that diversity among enterprises is necessary. A manufacturing firm, for example, may select straight-line depreciation for its building because each period receives equal benefit from the structure. For the purpose of housing the manufacturing operation, an old building serves just as well as a new one. The owner of an apartment house, on the other hand, may select declining balance depreciation as best. He could point to the fact that rates and occupancy will be higher when the apartment is new than will be the case when it is old. The early periods of the building's life will enjoy greater revenue than the later periods and, therefore, should receive a greater depreciation charge. It is apparent that an accounting technique (in this case the depreciation method) that is appropriate for one concern may be grossly inadequate for another. This fact has caused accountants to support the principle of diversity of methods among independent entities.

The wide diversity of accounting methods has caused much criticism of the accounting profession. Critics have made attempts to narrow the choice of methods in hopes of enhancing the comparability between statements of independent concerns. In spite of these attacks, the concept of diversity continues to be generally accepted in practice. The controversy between diversity and comparability is discussed later in this chapter.

Conservatism

We have noted throughout this book that the accounting process requires the exercise of careful judgments and countless estimates. The accountant attempts, of course, to make the necessary estimates with as much precision as circumstances will permit. The concept of conservatism simply states that it is better to guess low than to guess high. It is safer to make a mistake in judgment which will understate profits than it is to run the risk of overstatement. The concept of conservatism states that

> Sales, revenues, and income are not to be anticipated. Recognition ordinarily requires consummation of sale and delivery, and
> All known liabilities or losses should be recorded regardless of whether the definite amounts are determinable.[5]

Sound Control

The importance of sound internal control was discussed in chapter 14. The accuracy and reliability of the accounting data and the reports prepared therefrom are directly related to the effectiveness of the company's

---

[5]Grady, op. cit., p. 36.

internal control. The Committee on Auditing Procedure has stated that a satisfactory system must include:

1. A plan or organization which provides appropriate segregation of functional responsibilities,
2. A system of authorization and record procedures adequate to provide reasonable accounting control over assets, liabilities, revenues and expenses,
3. Sound practices to be followed in performance of duties and functions of each of the organizational departments, and
4. A degree of quality of personnel commensurate with responsibility.[6]

Materiality

The concept of materiality enables the accountant to disregard almost any principle or rule of conduct where the results are not material in amount. For example, the accountant may follow the tax method of recording the exchange of fixed assets, provided there is not a significant difference between what is actually recorded and what would be recorded if the theory method were followed.

On the other hand, the accountant has an obligation to disclose all material facts, whether they have actually given rise to an accounting transaction or not. Purchase commitments, lease obligations, and pending lawsuits are examples of items that often have not given rise to an accounting transaction on the balance sheet, but may be of such significance that their disclosure is required.

The question of just what constitutes a material item has been left to the judgment of the individual accountant. The following definition may serve as a general guide.

> A statement, fact, or item is material, if giving full consideration to the surrounding circumstances, as they exist at the time, it is of such a nature that its disclosure, or the method of treating it, would be likely to influence or to "make a difference" in the judgment and conduct of a reasonable person. The same tests apply to such words as significant, consequential, or important.[7]

Timeliness

In order to be useful, any report must be timely. It does little good to note that the gate is open hours after the lambs have fled. Nor is it sufficient

---

[6]Ibid., p. 37.
[7]Ibid., p. 40.

to wait until the business is dissolved to provide the owners with an accounting of how well they did. It would be easy to measure profit if we could wait until all assets were realized and all liabilities were liquidated. In such a case, we could accurately measure profit right down to the very last cent.

Investors, managers, creditors, and government agencies, including the Internal Revenue Service, are not content to wait for prolonged periods for such reports. They need to know how the business is doing before it is too late to do something about it. Progress reports are needed at regular time intervals to serve as a basis for decisions. This need for timely reporting has forced accountants to divide the life of the business into arbitrary segments known as accounting periods. Since many transactions do not fit neatly into these periods, estimates and arbitrary allocations are necessary. Profits and other key data are, of necessity, estimated.

A PROFESSION UNDER FIRE

Recent years have seen the public accounting profession hammered by criticism. CPAs have been charged with certifying misleading financial statements and, in general, failing to protect the public from distortions and fraud. In 1967, the eight largest public accounting firms had more than fifty major lawsuits pending against them.[8] One of these firms, Peat, Marwick, Mitchell, and Company, had twenty-eight suits asking total damages in excess of $20 million filed against it in just a two-year period.[9] As these lawsuits have continued to mount, insurance companies have boosted by 30 percent or more the rates of liability insurance for accounting firms.[10] Some companies, alarmed at the trend in lawsuits, have stopped issuing such policies altogether.

The Role of the CPA

What lies behind this barrage of public criticism and legal action? A number of factors seem to be important. First of all, the public at large does not seem to understand the nature of accounting nor the role of the certified public accountant. We have noted here that, at best, accounting is not an exact science, but instead an art requiring countless estimates. No accountant, no matter how honest or diligent he may be, can determine a company's precise income or exact financial position. The CPA is *not* a

---

[8]"What Are Earnings? The Growing Credibility Gap," *Forbes*, May 15, 1967, p. 28.
[9]*Wall Street Journal*, Nov. 15, 1966, p. 1.
[10]Ibid.

public protector against all wrong and evil that might appear in the business world. The primary purpose of a typical audit is *not* to disclose fraud. The auditor's opinion does *not* constitute a warranty that the financial statements are accurate. And yet, the critics of the profession would have the CPA accomplish all these feats.

The role of the CPA might be likened to that of a medical doctor. In fact, the CPA might be designated the doctor of the business world. His job is to examine a business and appraise its general health. If it appears to be sick, the CPA is expected to prescribe a cure, if one has been discovered. If the business appears to be in good health, he may outline some rules to help keep it that way. In any case, the CPA invites the patient back for his regular checkup.

A person can die of a heart attack having just received a clean bill of health from his doctor. That does not mean the doctor has failed to do his duty nor that he lacks adequate professional skills. It would be foolish to sue the doctor under the pretense that his findings guaranteed that the patient was in perfect health and that he would live for a given period of time. No doctor, regardless of his dedication or training, can give such a guarantee. Likewise, the CPA cannot guarantee the health of a business no matter how hard he may try. Why then cannot the public accept the true role of the CPA and accept his reports for what they are? The solution to this dilemma will probably come partially from educating the public.

The "Whale's Mouth"

A second reason for the intense criticism levied against the public accounting profession stems from the wide diversity of accounting practices. One CPA stated that the profession currently has latitude "as wide as a whale's mouth" in deciding how to treat certain items.[11] The seriousness of this problem was highlighted in a recent case study where two different bookkeeping methods were used to arrive at a firm's earnings per share.[12] Both methods employed generally accepted accounting practices, but the first always followed the more conservative practices and the second the more liberal practices. Method A reported earnings per share of $1.99, while method B reported earnings per share of $3.14 for the same company and the same time period. The difference was entirely attributed to variations in accounting practices, such as methods of recording depreciation and inventories, and treatment of research and development costs and investment credits, regarded by the profession as acceptable.

---

[11]Ibid.
[12]"What Are Earnings?" *Forbes*, p. 28.

Most accountants agree that some action needs to be taken to narrow the wide range of acceptable practices. Just how this should be done and who should initiate the action is not clear. Should we wait for a natural evolution to come through practicing accountants? Should professional organizations such as the American Institute of Certified Public Accountants be given more power to enforce their rules and lead the way? Should agencies of the federal government such as the Securities and Exchange Commission and the Internal Revenue Service adopt regulations with which the profession should be forced to comply? Should an accounting court of appeals be established where a judge, after a hearing for all interested parties and on the basis of public record and pertinent facts, could rule on what is and is not acceptable?[13] The answer to these questions is not yet clear, but it appears that some combination of government and professional regulation that will narrow the range of acceptable accounting practices will be forthcoming.

Some Evolving Concepts

A third factor which has subjected the accounting profession to attack is the fact that some techniques appear to be obsolete and grossly inadequate. Two such practices which have been severely criticized will be discussed here: *accounting for price level changes* and *accounting for long-term leases*.

The Price Level Problem. We have already noted that accepted accounting practices at the present time require accounting in terms of historical costs with no recognition of price level changes. Yet, it is a recognized fact that the general purchasing power of the dollar has declined steadily during the last several decades as the economy has experienced varying degrees of inflation. This failure to recognize the declining value of the dollar has caused a gross misstatement of the earnings and the financial position of most American firms. Accountants have treated dollars with a very different purchasing power as being identical, and have let each of these dollars have equal weight in the determination of the firm's profits.

The nature of the problem may be more easily illustrated by taking a nonbusiness situation. Suppose that a person is contemplating buying a new car. He has narrowed the field down to two competing models and has decided to select the one which gets the best gas mileage rate. The two cars are given an economy run by the respective manufacturers. Car

---

[13]One of the largest public accounting firms, Arthur Andersen and Company, has proposed that such a court be established and has actually hired legal counsel to draft a bill creating a United States Court of Accounting Appeals as an independent agency in the executive branch of the federal government. See *Establishing Accounting Principles—A Crisis in Decision Making* (Chicago: Arthur Andersen and Co., 1965).

A reports a mileage rate of 17.3 miles per gallon, having used 130 gallons of gasoline to travel 2,249 miles, while car B reports 15.7 miles per gallon, having used 150 gallons of gasoline to travel 2,355 miles. Based on these performance reports, the customer buys car A. Later he is disappointed with the mileage rate and upon investigation learns that car A was tested in Canada, where one gallon equals five quarts (the imperial gallon), while car B was tested in the United States, where one gallon equals four quarts. The comparison of mileage rates was not valid because the expression "gallon" was used to signify two different measures.

The problem could easily have been solved had the customer known all the facts. The mileage of car A could have been expressed in terms of U.S. gallons as follows:

    1 U. S. gallon = 4 U. S. quarts
    1 imperial gallon = 5 U. S. quarts
    Let x = the number of U. S. gallons
    Then: 4/5x = the number of imperial gallons
    Given: 130 imperial gallons
    Then: .8x = 130 gallons
            x = 162.5 gallons
    U. S. miles traveled = 2,249 miles
    U. S. gallons used   = 162.5
    Average miles per gallon = 13.8 (2,249 miles ÷ 162.5 gallons)

When the mileage rate is placed on a common basis (stated in terms of U. S. gallons), car A reports 13.8 miles per gallon compared with 15.7 for car B.

We have similar problems every day in the business world, where important decisions are based upon faulty comparisons. Investments are made, loans granted, taxes assessed, wage increases demanded, dividends expected—all based upon earnings reports which overstate performance in real terms. Many companies report increases in profits that would disappear or even turn to decreases if their financial statements were adjusted to reflect the change in buying power that has taken place.

The Use of Price Indexes.   It has been suggested by some that financial statements could be made more meaningful by adjusting the various figures with a price level index. This would be done in a manner similar to the mileage adjustment just illustrated. If we are given the true buying power in terms of a price index, it is a relatively easy task to express the dollars in comparable terms. For example, if we know that the buying power in year one is twice that of year two, i.e., the same amount of money will buy twice as much in terms of goods or services in year one as in year two, then we can make proper adjustment. If sales in year one were stated as $150,000 and in year two as $200,000 (an apparent increase), the figures could be adjusted as follows:

Index in year one = 100
Then index in year two = 50 (one half that of year one)
$150,000 × 100/100 = $150,000 sales in year one
$200,000 × 50/100 = $100,000 sales in year two (restated in terms
    of year one dollars)

In this instance, sales actually *decreased* in terms of units sold, whereas the initial sales figures reported would have led us to believe that they had increased.

The Problems of Price Level Indexes. While the principle of price level indexes is easily understood, the application is difficult. The first problem faced is selecting the appropriate index. Probably the best-known price level indexes are the Consumer Price Index and the Wholesale Price Index. Both of these are compiled and published by the Labor Statistics Bureau of the U. S. Department of Labor.

All price level indexes, however, are averages and do not purport to measure the specific price changes in a given product or business. While the general buying power in our economy has obviously declined, it has not declined uniformly for all products. A dollar today will actually buy more kilowatt hours of electricity than it would twenty years ago.[14] That same dollar will buy much less medical service than it would twenty years ago.

Construction of an adequate price level index is not easy. Those constructing such indexes are constantly faced with the problem of deciding how much of a given price increase represents mere inflation and what portion actually represents improved quality. Although a given automobile price may have doubled in the last twenty years, it is not fair to say that the dollar will only buy half as much. There are a number of major improvements present in the current automobile which were not available in a model twenty years ago. For example, electric windshield wipers, four headlights, side rear-view mirror, seat belts, backup lights, and collapsible steering column are standard equipment today, whereas many of these were not even available as extras some years ago.

The perplexing problem then, is to find a price level index which will accurately convert the figures in the financial statements of a specific company. Since each product would require the construction of a separate index, the task seems hopeless. The question then is whether, if we apply a general index to a specific case, the financial statement will be made more meaningful or will become even more distorted.

A research study, commissioned by the American Institute of Certified Public Accountants on the problem of reporting the financial effects of

---

[14]As reported by the Utah Power and Light Company in local advertising.

price level changes, was published in 1963. The following highlights summarize the conclusions made.[15]

1. The annotated bibliography of actual cases where price-level adjustments have been carried out (see Appendix E, Accounting Research Study Number 6) together with the volume of literature on the subject give clear evidence of the widespread concern of businessmen and accountants with the need for changes in the financial reporting to reflect the effects of inflation and deflation.

2. The examples quoted from financial statements around the world are sufficient to demonstrate that recognition of price-level changes in financial statements is practical and not misleading or dangerous to investors.

3. The study of the index-number problem indicates that at least one index of the general price level is available in the United States and is reliable enough for use in financial statements.

4. The effects of price-level changes should be disclosed as a supplement to the conventional statements. This disclosure may take the form of physically separate statements, or of parallel columns in a combined statement, or of detailed supporting schedules (including charts and graphs), or some combination of these.

5. In the supplementary data, all elements of the financial statement (e.g., balance sheet, income statement, analysis of retained earnings) should be restated by means of a single index of the general price level as of the balance-sheet date so that all financial data will be expressed in terms of dollars of the same purchasing power.

6. Restatement by means of a single index of the general price level is not a means of introducing replacement costs into the financial statements. To introduce replacement costs requires the use of current market prices, or appraisals, or a series of highly specific indexes, one for each account or group of accounts in the financial statements. For the sake of simplicity and precision in analysis, this study assumes that replacement costs are *not* to be introduced into the financial statements. With or without replacement costs, the measurement and disclosure of the effects of changes in the purchasing power of the dollar (as measured by an index of the movement in *all* prices) is still desirable.

7. Gains or losses do not arise from recognizing the effect of a changing price level on the nonmonetary items (principally the inventories, the fixed assets, and the equity of the common shareholders). The recognition of the effect of a changing price level on these items is merely a restatement of acquisition cost or of owners' equity in terms of the purchasing power of the dollar at the balance-sheet date.

---

[15]The conclusions reached in any of these research studies have not been approved, disapproved, or otherwise acted upon by the Accounting Principles Board, the only agency of the American Institute of Certified Public Accountants having authority to make or approve public pronouncements on accounting.

8. Gains or losses do arise from recognizing the effect of a changing price level on the monetary items (principally the cash balance and the contracts to receive or pay money). The recognition of the effect of a changing price level on these items results in a gain or loss from inflation which should be separately disclosed.
9. This study neither expresses nor implies any recommendations on questions of social policy (e.g.: Who is injured by inflation or deflation? Who benefits from it? Who should pay for it? How can it be controlled?) or on the impact on rate regulation in the case of public utilities or on the tax definition of income. The study is centered on the proposition that the major accounting issue created by a changing price level is the accuracy of the *measurements* of the results of operations and of financial position, and that more accurate measures will be beneficial to all who use or are influenced by financial statements.
10. Because so many of the goods and services currently available resulted from wartime (World War II) and postwar technology, the precision of comparisons of current price levels with those prevailing in periods prior to World War II are unreliable. For this reason, a 1945 cut-off date is proposed in preference to using prewar or even wartime index numbers for the adjustment of the applicable data in financial statements.[16]

Price Level Adjustments Illustrated. Two income statements for the Brahms Box Company, both prepared by conventional accounting techniques, are presented in Figure 21-1.

Figure 21-1

BRAHMS BOX COMPANY
Income Statement
For the Year Ended December 31

	19X8		19X9	
Sales		$250,000		$270,000
Less: Cost of goods sold:				
Beginning inventory	$ 20,000		$ 25,000	
Purchases	160,000		170,000	
Goods available	$180,000		$195,000	
Less: Ending inventory	25,000	155,000	30,000	165,000
Gross margin		$ 95,000		$105,000
Expenses:				
Building depreciation	$ 10,000		$ 10,000	
Equipment depreciation ...	5,000		5,000	
Other expenses	40,000	55,000	48,000	63,000
Net profit		$ 40,000		$ 42,000

[16]*Reporting the Financial Effects of Price-Level Changes*, Accounting Research Study No. 6 (New York: American Institute of Certified Public Accountants, 1963), pp. xi and xii.

Based upon these statements, it would appear that the company's profit position has improved. In 19X9, the company reported an increase in profits of 5 percent over those of the preceding year. Because of changes in the purchasing power of the dollar, however, these statements present a misleading picture. To illustrate, let us assume that the following price level indexes are applicable:

DECEMBER 31	INDEX
19X0	100
19X5	150
19X7	160
19X8	180
19X9	200

Utilizing the above data, modified income statements can be prepared that give recognition to the declining value of the dollar. The modified statements would appear as shown in Figure 21-2.

Figure 21-2

Income Statement in Constant Dollars
For the Year Ended December 31

	19X8		19X9	
Sales		$294,125a		$284,202b
Less: Cost of goods sold:				
Beginning inventory	$ 25,000c		$ 27,778d	
Purchases	188,240f		178,942g	
Goods available	$213,240		$206,720	
Ending inventory	27,778d	185,462	30,000e	176,720
Gross margin		$108,663		$107,482
Expenses:				
Building depreciation	$ 20,000h		$ 20,000h	
Equipment depreciation	6,667i		6,667i	
Other expenses	47,060j	73,727	50,525k	77,192
Net profit		$ 34,936		$ 30,290

[a]Sales year 19X8 at average price level index of 170
($250,000 × 200/170 = $294,125)

[b]Sales year 19X9 at average price level index of 190
($270,000 × 200/190 = $284,202)

[c]Inventory at Dec. 31, 19X7, at price index of 160
($20,000 × 200/160 = $25,000)

[d]Inventory at Dec. 31, 19X8, at price level index of 180
($25,000 × 200/180 = $27,778)

[e]Inventory at Dec. 31, 19X9, at price level index of 200
($30,000 × 200/200 = $30,000)

These modified statements indicate that actual sales volume, as well as profits, have declined during the period. This fact was concealed in the conventional statements which were prepared under the assumption that the value of the dollar had not changed.

Accounting for Long-term Leases. Accountants have traditionally relegated long-term commitments of various types to footnote disclosure. It has been argued that these obligations should be excluded from the accounting records and the body of the reports because they have not yet given rise to an accounting transaction.

The footnote treatment has generally been regarded as adequate except in the case of long-term leases. A number of critics, both inside and outside the profession, have noted that many long-term leases are really nothing but a form of borrowing. Such persons have argued that these financial leases should be recorded in the books of account and reported in the body of the financial statements. Some of the financial implications of the long-term leasing were discussed in chapter 20.

Capitalization has generally been suggested as the best method for disclosing long-term lease commitments by those who regard current practices as inadequate. Capitalization is accomplished by discounting the rentals payable during the term of the lease to their present value at the effective rate of interest implied in the lease.

Capitalization Illustrated. The capitalization procedure may be illustrated by referring to an actual case.[17] A plant was built by the XYZ Company to its specifications at a cost of $5,600,000. The building had an estimated useful life of forty years. Upon completion, the building was sold at cost to an insurance company under a sale-and-lease-back agreement. The lease had an original noncancellable term of twenty years, during which it

---

[17]Taken from A. Tom Nelson, *The Impact of Leases on Financial Analysis* (East Lansing, Mich.: Bureau of Business and Economics Research, 1963), p. 40.

---

[f]Purchases year 19X8 at average price level index of 170
($160,000 × 200/170 = $188,240)

[g]Purchases year 19X9 at average price level index of 190
($170,000 × 200/190 = $178,942)

[h]Building purchased Dec. 31, 19X0, at price level index of 100
($10,000 × 200/100 = $20,000)

[i]Machinery purchased Jan. 1, 19X6, at price level index of 150
($5,000 × 200/150 = $6,667)

[j]Other expenses year 19X8 at average price level index of 170
($40,000 × 200/170 = $47,060)

[k]Other expenses year 19X9 at average price level index of 190
($48,000 × 200/190 = $50,525)

called for annual rentals of $420,000. The XYZ Company had options to renew the lease for an additional forty years at the following reduced rentals: first five-year renewal at $196,000 per year; second five-year renewal at $168,000 per year; next six renewals of five years each at $112,000 per year.

The capitalization value of the lease rentals (which will always equal the cost or cash price of the asset at the beginning of the lease term) is placed on the books by the following entry:

Rights to Use of Leased Property.	5,600,000	
Rental Obligation under Long-term Leases. .		5,600,000

The account Rights to Use of Leased Property should be shown on the balance sheet as a fixed asset, and the balance in that account should be amortized over the term of the lease, just as other fixed assets would be depreciated. The periodic entry required to accomplish the amortization is as follows:

Rent Expense, Leased Property	140,000	
Right to Use of Leased Property		140,000

The account Rental Obligations under Long-term Leases would be shown on the balance sheet as a liability. The portion payable within a year would be listed under the "current" caption, and the remainder would be carried as a "long-term" liability. The lease liability account would be adjusted at the end of the year and the periodic interest recorded by the following entry:

Rental Obligations under Long-term Leases.	105,858	
Interest Charges	314,142	
Accrued Rent Payable		420,000

The liability established in the above entry would be liquidated at the time the rentals are paid. Each rental payment would thus include an element of principal and an element of interest. The entry to record the periodic rental payment is as follows:

Accrued Rent Payable	420,000	
Cash in Bank		420,000

The journal entries that would be required over the entire forty-year period, based upon the capitalization technique just described, are summarized in Figure 21-3. Note that the lease transaction has been separated into its operational and financial elements. The cost of the leased asset is spread over its expected useful life (forty years) in some systematic manner. The straight-line method of amortization has been used here, but this has no bearing on the theory presented. Any acceptable method of amortization could have been used with equal application. The significant

Figure 21-3

JOURNAL ENTRIES REQUIRED UNDER CAPITALIZED XYZ COMPANY LEASE FOR FORTY-YEAR TERM

END OF YEAR	RENT (DEPR.) EXP.	LEASE ASSET	INTEREST CHGS.	LEASE LIABILITY	CASH	REMAINING BALANCE IN LEASE LIABILITY ACCOUNT
0		$5,600,000		<$5,600,000>		$5,600,000
1	$140,000	<140,000>	$314,142	105,858	<$420,000>	5,494,142
2	140,000	<140,000>	308,204	111,796	<420,000>	5,382,346
3	140,000	<140,000>	301,932	118,068	<420,000>	5,264,278
4	140,000	<140,000>	295,309	124,691	<420,000>	5,139,587
5	140,000	<140,000>	288,314	131,686	<420,000>	5,007,901
6	140,000	<140,000>	280,927	139,073	<420,000>	4,868,828
7	140,000	<140,000>	273,125	146,875	<420,000>	4,721,953
8	140,000	<140,000>	264,886	155,114	<420,000>	4,566,839
9	140,000	<140,000>	256,185	163,815	<420,000>	4,403,024
10	140,000	<140,000>	246,995	173,005	<420,000>	4,230,019
11	140,000	<140,000>	237,290	182,710	<420,000>	4,047,309
12	140,000	<140,000>	227,041	192,959	<420,000>	3,854,350
13	140,000	<140,000>	216,217	203,783	<420,000>	3,650,567
14	140,000	<140,000>	204,785	215,215	<420,000>	3,435,352
15	140,000	<140,000>	192,712	227,288	<420,000>	3,208,064
16	140,000	<140,000>	179,962	240,038	<420,000>	2,968,026
17	140,000	<140,000>	166,497	253,503	<420,000>	2,714,523
18	140,000	<140,000>	152,276	267,724	<420,000>	2,446,799
19	140,000	<140,000>	137,257	282,743	<420,000>	2,164,056
20	140,000	<140,000>	121,397	298,603	<420,000>	1,865,453

Figure 21-3 (continued)

END OF YEAR	RENT (DEPR.) EXP.	LEASE ASSET	INTEREST CHGS.	LEASE LIABILITY	CASH	REMAINING BALANCE IN LEASE LIABILITY ACCOUNT
21	140,000	<140,000>	104,646	91,354	<196,000>	1,774,099
22	140,000	<140,000>	99,521	96,479	<196,000>	1,677,620
23	140,000	<140,000>	94,109	101,891	<196,000>	1,575,729
24	140,000	<140,000>	88,393	107,607	<196,000>	1,468,122
25	140,000	<140,000>	82,357	113,643	<196,000>	1,354,479
26	140,000	<140,000>	75,982	92,038	<168,000>	1,262,441
27	140,000	<140,000>	70,819	97,181	<168,000>	1,165,260
28	140,000	<140,000>	65,367	102,633	<168,000>	1,062,627
29	140,000	<140,000>	59,610	108,390	<168,000>	954,237
30	140,000	<140,000>	53,530	114,470	<168,000>	839,767
31	140,000	<140,000>	47,108	64,892	<112,000>	774,875
32	140,000	<140,000>	43,468	68,532	<112,000>	706,343
33	140,000	<140,000>	39,624	72,376	<112,000>	633,967
34	140,000	<140,000>	35,563	76,437	<112,000>	557,530
35	140,000	<140,000>	31,276	80,724	<112,000>	476,806
36	140,000	<140,000>	26,747	85,253	<112,000>	391,553
37	140,000	<140,000>	21,965	90,035	<112,000>	301,518
38	140,000	<140,000>	16,914	95,086	<112,000>	206,432
39	140,000	<140,000>	11,580	100,420	<112,000>	106,012
40	140,000	<140,000>	5,947	106,053	<112,000>	-41

SOURCE: A. Tom Nelson, *The Impact of Leases on Financial Analysis* (East Lansing, Mich.: Bureau of Business and Economic Research, 1963), pp. 42-43. Reprinted by permission.

NOTE: This illustration assumes straight-line amortization of the lease asset; credits shown in brackets < >.

point is that the amortization of the asset has no relation to the method of financing employed.

The lease rentals have been applied first to interest and then to principal, in accordance with the United States rule. Interest charges were computed by multiplying the implicit rate of interest (5.61 percent) by the declining balance of the lease liability.

Position of AICPA. The widespread use of the lease as a means of obtaining the use of property caused the Accounting Research Division of the American Institute of Certified Public Accountants (AICPA) to undertake a research study on the reporting of leases in financial statements. The results of this study were published in May 1962 as Accounting Research Study Number 4.[18] The basic conclusion of this study was that current lease-reporting practices were inadequate and that financial leases should be capitalized as illustrated in the previous paragraphs. However, in September 1964, the Accounting Principles Board issued Opinion Number 5, which disagreed with the conclusions reached in the research study and took a position supporting the footnote method of disclosure.[19] Inasmuch as the Accounting Principles Board is the official spokesman of the AICPA in such matters, the footnote practice continues to be regarded as acceptable reporting. It would appear that Opinion Number 5 was a step backward in our attempt to make financial statements more meaningful.

SUMMARY

Accounting is not an exact science, but an art requiring the exercise of careful judgment and the use of many estimates. It is, nevertheless, based upon some notions or conventions that have received rather wide acceptance by practicing accountants. These rules of conduct are often referred to as generally accepted principles or concepts of accounting. The ten such concepts listed in the American Institute of Certified Public Accountants *Inventory of Generally Accepted Accounting Principles for Business Enterprises* were discussed in this chapter. These concepts serve as the basis of accounting for all enterprises engaged in conducting business for a profit.

The public accounting profession has been subject to much abuse and criticism in recent years. This has been caused by several factors. First, the public at large has not understood the function of the certified public

[18]John H. Myers, *Reporting of Leases in Financial Statements,* Accounting Research Study No. 4 (New York: American Institute of Certified Public Accountants, 1962).

[19]"Reporting of Leases in Financial Statements of Leasee," *Opinions of the Accounting Principles Board No. 5* (New York: American Institute of Certified Public Accountants, 1964).

accountant, nor the limitations under which he works. Second, there is such a wide diversity in what is regarded as acceptable accounting practice that comparability of financial statements has been weakened. Third, some of the techniques followed by accountants appear to be obsolete in the rapidly changing business world. Two notable instances where current practices appear to be inadequate were discussed in this chapter: the failure of accountants to recognize price level changes in the accounts, and their failure to recognize the financial lease as a form of debt. These and other deficiencies which appear in current practice will likely be corrected as accounting techniques evolve to meet the needs of a dynamic business world.

QUESTIONS

1. In what way are accounting principles different from those found in science? Do these principles have equal application in nonprofit and profit-making enterprises?
2. It might be said that accountants are more concerned with economic entities than with legal entities. Comment.
3. What is the principle of consistency? Does this principle mean that all companies within an industry must follow the same accounting procedures?
4. What is meant by the statement that accountants are conservative? How does this principle apply to the recognition of losses, revenues, and gains? How does it apply to liabilities?
5. What should a satisfactory system of internal control include? Does the principle of internal control extend beyond the record-keeping functions of a business? Explain.
6. Would a conventional balance sheet and income statement present fairly the financial position and operating results of a firm that is being liquidated? Explain.
7. What are some arguments in support of the principle of diversity in accounting methods? What is the great disadvantage of having many methods for treating a particular item?
8. Why are many estimates, skilled judgments, and arbitrary allocations necessary in accounting?
9. Does the opinion of a certified public accountant guarantee that the financial statements are correct? Explain the reason for the great increase in lawsuits against public accounting firms in recent years.
10. Why do changes in the level of prices pose an especially difficult task for accountants? What are some of the problems associated with showing price level changes in the financial statements?
11. Is it generally accepted accounting practice to reflect price level changes in published financial statements? Do you agree with current accounting practice? Why or why not?
12. Some people have been highly critical of the wide range of acceptable accounting practices. Do you feel that accounting practices should be more uniform? Explain your position.

13. What is the current practice for disclosing leases in financial statements? Present arguments for and against this method of disclosure.

PROBLEMS

Problem 21-1

The Logan Asphalt Company has need of a new bit paver. The required model would cost Logan $37,077 in cash, but it can acquire an identical model under a financial lease agreement with the manufacturer. In this event, Logan would lease the machine for its estimated ten-year life at an annual rental of $5,200 per year, the rents being payable at the beginning of each year. Logan would have an option to buy the machine at the end of the lease at an estimated salvage value of $5,000. The management of Logan Asphalt Company recognizes that this type of lease is just a form of borrowing; it therefore desires to record the asset and liability on the books and account for the lease as though it had purchased the machine outright and borrowed the necessary funds. The lease rentals fall due on January 3 of each year, and the Logan Asphalt Company closes on a calendar-year basis. Straight-line depreciation is used on all equipment.

Required:
- a. Calculate the effective interest rate on the lease.
- b. Prepare all entries required during the first three years of the asset's life, assuming that the company capitalizes the lease.

Problem 21-2

In each of the following cases indicated what you regard as the best accounting treatment and discuss the accounting principles involved.

- a. A company which purchases $100,000 worth of new equipment each year acquired ten new pencil sharpeners at a cost of $6.95 each. The pencil sharpeners are expected to have a five-year useful life, after which they will have no salvage value.
- b. The Johnstown City Hospital had revenues of $2,573,000 last year and expenses of $3,194,500 for the same period. Some of the local citizens question the ability of the hospital administrators, inasmuch as this is the fifth consecutive year the hospital has operated at a net loss.
- c. Kermit Wood operates a small flower shop. The local bank recently adopted a policy of no service charges for customers who maintain a $300 minimum balance. Kermit decided to combine his personal and business checking accounts to take advantage of this no-service-charge policy. During the year, deposits total $35,212; personal checks written, $6,990; business checks written, $21,119.
- d. Big Bull Barns is in the fertilizer business. He is a recent graduate of business college and has been taught that a firm should always attempt to maximize profit. Therefore, the firm alternates between FIFO and LIFO inventory, according to which method will maximize profit for the particular year.

e. A company which has just been declared bankrupt in court asks you to prepare a conventional income statement and balance sheet to present to the court.

Problem 21-3

James Logan has operated the shoe department of the Bagley Department Store for the past five years on a leased-department basis. Mr. Logan pays a monthly rental of $500 plus 2 percent of gross sales. The rent covers all space and equipment used in the shoe department, plus all utilities except telephone. Mr. Logan purchases his own merchandise, establishes his own selling prices, and pays his own employees. The shoe department has enjoyed a continual rise in both sales and profits, as shown by the following summary statements:

	19X1	19X2	19X3	19X4	19X5
Sales	$800ª	$850	$910	$930	$950
Cost of goods sold	482	520	600	615	625
Gross margins	$318	$330	$310	$315	$325
Operating expenseᵇ	190	196	170	172	179
Net profit	$128	$134	$140	$143	$146

ªAll figures represent thousands of dollars.
ᵇSalesmen's commissions, telephone expense, rent expenses.

Mr. Logan is concerned because the above statements have been prepared in accordance with generally accepted accounting principles and, therefore, do not reflect changes in price levels. He wishes some supplementary statements that will recognize the price level changes. The following price level indexes are obtained as of December 31:

YEAR	PRICE INDEX
19X0	94
19X1	100
19X2	108
19X3	116
19X4	126
19X5	130

Required:

Prepare supplementary income statements (restated in terms of current dollars) for each of the five years, and comment on the value of such statements.

Problem 21-4

The public accounting profession has been subjected to much criticism and ridicule in recent years, as indicated by the following statement:

Perhaps the classic case in which the auditors were talked into stretching accounting methods was the Ethyl Corporation sale of nearly five years ago. The implications of this case still worry thoughtful accountants.

Late in 1962 the tiny Albemarle Paper Manufacturing Company had put together a fancy financial deal to acquire far-larger Ethyl from its two joint owners, General Motors and Standard Oil of New Jersey. The deal was virtually the same for both giant sellers: Each owned 50 percent of Ethyl's shares, each had held them for 38 years, each would net about $40 million on the sale. But when Jersey and GM stockholders opened their annual reports a few months later, the deal could not have looked more different.

GM recorded the proceeds as *income* for the year, even before a penny of operating expenses was deducted. All the way down its income statement, to the net earnings figure at the bottom, the subtotals were inflated. Jersey went to the other extreme. It never showed the Ethyl profit on its earnings statement at all, not even under "nonrecurring income" below the net income figure. Instead, it buried its profit on Ethyl back in the "statement of stockholders' equity," a section of an annual report few people bother to read.

The contrast was spectacular. Here were the two largest industrial corporations in the world, with over two million stockholders and most of the financial community looking on. Yet, each came up with a radically different treatment of earnings from the identical transaction. What's more, the treatments had been duly certified by two of the nation's most respected accounting firms, Haskins & Sells for GM and Price Waterhouse for Jersey.[20]

Required:

Was one firm right and one firm wrong in the above case? What is the basic accounting principle involved in this controversy? Discuss both sides of the controversy, supporting first the position of Haskins & Sells and General Motors and then the position of Price Waterhouse and Standard Oil of New Jersey.

Problem 21-5

The conventional income statement of U-Do-It Laundry is shown below:

U-DO-IT LAUNDRY

Income Statement
For the Year Ended December 31, 19X6

Washing revenue		$47,200
Drying revenue		21,950
Total revenue		$69,150
Expenses:		
Building depreciation	$ 6,300	
Equipment depreciation	20,625	
Gas and power	13,920	
Other	8,000	48,845
Net income		$20,305

[20]"What are Earnings?" *Forbes*, p. 34.

The building was acquired December 31, 19X1, at a cost of $252,000. On January 2, 19X2, the company spent $99,000 on new washing machines and on December 20, 19X4, it spent another $66,000 on new washing machines. All machines are depreciated over an eight-year period with no consideration being given to salvage. The price index at December 31 for each of the last six years is as follows:

YEAR	PRICE INDEX
19X1	100
19X2	112
19X3	121
19X4	130
19X5	135
19X6	140

Required:

Prepare a supplementary income statement in terms of current dollars.

Problem 21-6

The Grow Company purchased land with an appraised value of $10,000 and a building with an appraised value of $80,000 for a lump-sum "bargain" price of $72,000. In the transaction, Grow Company agreed to pay the 6 percent real estate commission, as well as survey and title-search fees amounting to $1,500. Prior to moving into the building, the company's name was painted on the front door at a cost of $25. When Grow Company had occupied the building for about six months, the community experienced a combination wind and rain storm which covered the windows with mud. All windows in the building were washed at a contract price of $1,119. Other maintenance costs for the first year amounted to $17,335.

Required:

Indicate how each of the above costs should be treated, and cite the accounting principles involved.

Problem 21-7

You have been assigned to examine the vouchers of a lumber company which cuts approximately 40,000,000 board feet of logs per year and has sales of approximately $2,800,000. The senior auditor cautioned you to be alert for errors in distribution caused by the inexperience of the bookkeeper in charge of recording company purchases. During the course of your examination, you find the following payments and distributions thereof:

1. Purchase of new band saw blades for the sawmill: $14,567. Charged to Sawmill Supplies Expense.
2. Purchase of two-ton truck: $3,500. Charged to fixed asset, Autos and Trucks account.
3. Cost of firebrick used to reline the boiler chamber: $8,000. Charged to Steam Plant and Power Expense.
4. Travel expense for Mr. and Mrs. R. L. Jones, manager and his wife: $1,000 (no detail). Charged to Travel Expense.

5. Purchase of electric stove for sales manager's personal residence: $350. Charged to Miscellaneous Sales Expense.
6. Payment of an adjusted sales invoice which had originally given the wrong price: $110. Charged to Freight Adjustments.
7. Purchase of a used crane to lift logs from the pond: $1,500. Charged to Pond Expense, Repairs.
8. Purchase of new conveyor chain for a newly constructed dry kiln: $2,500. Charged to Dry Kiln Repairs.
9. Purchase of new conveyor chain to replace worn-out chain on the log deck: $2,500. Charged to Sawmill Repairs.

Required:
a. State and explain the general considerations governing whether an item should be charged to fixed assets or to expense.
b. Comment briefly on the propriety of each distribution (account to which charged), emphasizing the governing considerations or principles involved. Do not rewrite the statements made, but key your answer to the number of the statement.

AICPA Adapted

Problem 21-8
There has been a good deal of criticism of the traditional "historical" cost records and the data which they reflect, especially during times of inflation or deflation. To facilitate the interpretation of accounting reports as normally prepared, many accountants have suggested utilizing the recorded cost data in the preparation of the conventional financial statements and as a supplementary technique, converting these statements into dollars having a uniform purchasing power through the application of price indexes to the recorded dollar amounts. There has been considerable difference of opinion among these accountants as to whether to use a "general" price index (such as the Wholesale Price Index or the Consumer Price Index), or a more "specific" price index that would be more applicable to the industry involved or to the particular items being converted (for instance, a construction index for the conversion of plant and equipment items, or a special price index constructed for a specific industry).

Give arguments in favor of and against each of these two types of indexes.

AICPA Adapted

Case 21
CONTINENTAL CORN COMPANY

Continental Corn Company has been in business for fifteen years, operating in the midwestern section of the U. S. During that period, Continental Corn has grown from a one-man business to a reasonably sized operation. This past year gross sales amounted to nearly $3 million, compared to only $50 thousand the first year. The owners have decided to float a new stock issue to provide the funds necessary to expand operations to the West Coast. The president and chief stockholder, Mr. Claire Whipple, has been informed that the Securities and Exchange Commission will require audited financial statements before approving the new stock issue. He is advised that since the auditor's report will be included in the prospectus, it is important that the company be given a "clean" report. A business associate and fellow golfer gave Mr. Whipple the following auditor's opinion, which he said accompanied his firm's last annual report:

CERTIFICATION OF FINANCIAL STATEMENTS

Anderson and Smith
Certified Public Accountants   February 10, 1971

Hornet Corporation, Its Directors and Stockholders:

We have examined the Consolidated Balance Sheet of Hornet Corporation and consolidated subsidiaries as of December 31, 1970, and 1969, and the related Statements of Consolidated Income, Consolidated Net Income Retained for Use in the Business, Consolidated Capital Surplus, and Consolidated Source and Application of Funds for the years then ended. Our examination was made in accordance with generally accepted auditing standards, and accordingly included such tests of the accounting records and such other auditing procedures as we considered necessary in the circumstances.

In our opinion, the accompanying Consolidated Balance Sheet and related Statements of Consolidated Income, Consolidated Net Income Retained for Use in the Business, Consolidated Capital Surplus, and Consolidated Source and Application of Funds present fairly the financial position of the companies at December 31, 1970, and 1969, and the results of their operations and the source and application of their funds for the years then ended, in conformity with generally accepted accounting principles consistently applied.

Anderson and Smith

Mr. Whipple contacts you, a partner of Anderson and Smith, CPAs, and explains his problem: "Karl Moore recommended your firm to help us with some 'red tape' required by the SEC. We've been in business for fifteen years, have a capable accountant, and have never really felt the need for an audit. Karl says your firm has spent a lot of time with SEC filings and that you know how to doctor up the books to get by those guys. It's getting so you can't even turn around anymore without some government official asking you why. Anyway, can you fix us up with one of those Good Housekeeping Seals of Approval?"

After considerable discussion in which you try to clarify the role of the independent CPA, you agree to accept the assignment. The financial statements prepared by the company's accountant are shown in Exhibits 21-1 and 21-2. During the course of your examination you note the following:

1. The Land account consists of a five-acre tract, purchased five years ago at a cost of $75,000, on which the existing office building is located, and a ten-acre tract, purchased last year at a cost of $125,000. The ten-acre tract is being held for possible future expansion and is not currently in use.

2. The marketable securities are all carried at cost and consist of the following:

	COST	CURRENT MARKET
Newton Fig Company	$10,000	$18,000
Gregory Building Supply	50,000	49,000
General Book Company	25,000	22,000

The Gregory Building Supply Stock is being held as a long-term investment, and the other securities are short-term investments.

3. The administrative expense account has been charged with five pencil sharpeners, purchased January 10 at a cost of $6.95 each. Experience has shown that this type of equipment generally lasts ten years, after which it typically has no salvage value.

4. The Mortgage Payable account balance includes a $20,000 installment payment due in six months.

5. It has been the company policy to pay the rent on the president's personal residence. This amounted to $4,800 this past year, and the entire amount was charged to rent expense.

6. Harvey Slack owes Mr. Whipple $50,000 on a personal gambling note. Mr. Whipple has been kind enough to permit the company to list this on its balance sheet to help present a strong financial position.

7. The inventory has generally been valued in past years at FIFO, except in those years when prices increased substantially. The inventory at the beginning of the current year was $410,000 when valued at FIFO, or $300,000 when valued at LIFO. The ending inventory had a value of $350,000 when priced at LIFO and $455,000 when priced at FIFO.

QUESTIONS

1. What would be required before Continental Corn Company could be given a "clean" audit report?

2. Do you agree with the financial statements prepared by the company? What changes would you make, if any?

3. Has the company followed generally accepted accounting principles? List any principles which you feel have been violated and cite an example of each.

Exhibit 21-1

CONTINENTAL CORN COMPANY

Income Statement
December 31, 1970

Revenue:

Sales		$2,752,000
Interest earned		13,000
Gain on sale of capital asset		65,000
Total revenue		$2,830,000
Cost of goods sold:		
Inventory, January 1, 1970	$ 410,000	
Purchases	1,750,000	
Goods available	$2,160,000	
Inventory, December 31, 1970	315,000	1,845,000
Gross margin		$ 985,000
Expenses:		
Sales returns	$ 28,000	
Sales discounts	25,000	
Rent expense	20,000	
Administrative salaries	140,000	
Depreciation expense	200,000	
Sales salaries	125,000	
Income taxes	198,000	
Other expenses	22,000	758,000
Net profit		$ 227,000

Exhibit 21-2

CONTINENTAL CORN COMPANY
Balance Sheet
For the Year Ended December 31, 1970

Current Assets:

Cash	$ 141,000
Accounts receivable	720,000
Note receivable	50,000
Inventories	455,000
Marketable securities	85,000
	$1,451,000

Fixed Assets:

Equipment	$1,500,000
Land	200,000
Building	2,000,000
	$3,700,000

Other Assets:

Treasury stock	$ 102,000
Prepaid expenses	23,000
	$ 125,000
Total assets	$5,276,000

Current Liabilities:

Accounts payable	$ 827,000
Notes payable	200,000
Taxes payable	198,000
	$1,225,000

Long-term Liabilities:

Twenty-year mortgage payable	$ 200,000
Bonds payable, 1992	1,000,000
	$1,200,000

Reserves:

Allowance for depreciation, building	$ 352,000
Allowance for depreciation, equipment	400,000
Reserve (Retained earnings appropriated for plant expansion)	500,000
Reserve for doubtful accounts	8,000
	$1,260,000

Stockholders' Equity:

Capital stock	$ 55,000
Retained earnings	1,536,000
Total stockholders' equity	$1,591,000
Total liabilities and stockholders' equity	$5,276,000

Appendix

Table A

AMOUNT OF ONE DOLLAR

n	½%	1%	1½%	2%	2½%	3%	3½%	4%	5%	6%	7%	8%	9%	10%	15%	20%	25%
1	1.005	1.010	1.015	1.020	1.025	1.030	1.035	1.040	1.050	1.060	1.070	1.080	1.090	1.100	1.150	1.200	1.250
2	1.010	1.020	1.030	1.040	1.050	1.060	1.071	1.081	1.102	1.123	1.144	1.166	1.188	1.210	1.322	1.440	1.562
3	1.015	1.030	1.045	1.061	1.076	1.092	1.108	1.124	1.157	1.191	1.225	1.259	1.295	1.331	1.520	1.728	1.953
4	1.020	1.040	1.061	1.082	1.103	1.125	1.147	1.169	1.215	1.262	1.310	1.360	1.411	1.464	1.749	2.073	2.441
5	1.025	1.051	1.077	1.104	1.131	1.159	1.187	1.216	1.276	1.338	1.402	1.469	1.538	1.610	2.011	2.488	3.051
6	1.030	1.061	1.093	1.126	1.159	1.194	1.229	1.265	1.340	1.418	1.500	1.586	1.677	1.771	2.313	2.985	3.814
7	1.035	1.072	1.109	1.148	1.188	1.229	1.272	1.315	1.407	1.503	1.605	1.713	1.828	1.948	2.660	3.583	4.768
8	1.040	1.082	1.126	1.171	1.218	1.266	1.316	1.368	1.477	1.593	1.718	1.850	1.992	2.143	3.059	4.299	5.960
9	1.045	1.093	1.143	1.195	1.248	1.304	1.362	1.423	1.551	1.689	1.838	1.999	2.171	2.357	3.517	5.159	7.450
10	1.051	1.104	1.160	1.218	1.280	1.343	1.410	1.480	1.628	1.790	1.967	2.158	2.367	2.593	4.045	6.191	9.313
11	1.056	1.115	1.177	1.243	1.312	1.384	1.459	1.539	1.710	1.898	2.104	2.331	2.580	2.853	4.652	7.430	11.641
12	1.061	1.126	1.195	1.268	1.344	1.425	1.511	1.601	1.795	2.012	2.252	2.518	2.812	3.138	5.350	8.916	14.551
13	1.066	1.138	1.213	1.293	1.378	1.468	1.563	1.665	1.885	2.132	2.409	2.719	3.065	3.452	6.152	10.699	18.189
14	1.072	1.149	1.231	1.319	1.412	1.512	1.618	1.731	1.979	2.260	2.578	2.937	3.341	3.797	7.075	12.839	22.737
15	1.077	1.160	1.250	1.345	1.448	1.557	1.675	1.800	2.078	2.396	2.759	3.172	3.642	4.177	8.137	15.407	28.421
16	1.083	1.172	1.268	1.372	1.484	1.604	1.733	1.872	2.182	2.540	2.952	3.425	3.970	4.594	9.357	18.488	35.527
17	1.088	1.184	1.288	1.400	1.521	1.652	1.794	1.947	2.292	2.692	3.158	3.700	4.327	5.054	10.761	22.186	44.408
18	1.093	1.196	1.307	1.428	1.559	1.702	1.857	2.025	2.406	2.854	3.379	3.996	4.717	5.559	12.375	26.623	55.511
19	1.099	1.208	1.326	1.456	1.598	1.753	1.922	2.106	2.526	3.025	3.616	4.315	5.141	6.115	14.231	31.947	69.388
20	1.104	1.220	1.346	1.485	1.638	1.806	1.989	2.191	2.653	3.207	3.869	4.660	5.604	6.727	16.366	38.337	86.736
21	1.110	1.232	1.367	1.515	1.679	1.860	2.059	2.278	2.785	3.399	4.140	5.033	6.108	7.400	18.821	46.005	108.420
22	1.115	1.244	1.387	1.545	1.721	1.916	2.131	2.369	2.925	3.603	4.430	5.436	6.658	8.140	21.644	55.206	135.525
23	1.121	1.257	1.408	1.576	1.764	1.973	2.206	2.464	3.071	3.819	4.740	5.871	7.257	8.954	24.891	66.247	169.406
24	1.127	1.269	1.429	1.608	1.809	2.032	2.283	2.563	3.225	4.048	5.072	6.341	7.911	9.849	28.625	79.496	211.758
25	1.132	1.282	1.450	1.640	1.853	2.093	2.363	2.665	3.386	4.291	5.427	6.848	8.623	10.834	32.918	95.396	264.697
26	1.138	1.295	1.472	1.673	1.900	2.156	2.445	2.772	3.555	4.549	5.807	7.396	9.399	11.918	37.856	114.475	330.872
27	1.144	1.308	1.494	1.706	1.947	2.221	2.531	2.883	3.733	4.822	6.213	7.988	10.245	13.109	43.535	137.370	413.590
28	1.149	1.321	1.517	1.741	1.996	2.287	2.620	2.998	3.920	5.111	6.648	8.627	11.167	14.420	50.065	164.844	516.987
29	1.155	1.334	1.539	1.775	2.046	2.356	2.711	3.118	4.116	5.418	7.114	9.317	12.172	15.863	57.575	197.813	646.234
30	1.161	1.347	1.563	1.811	2.097	2.427	2.806	3.243	4.321	5.743	7.612	10.062	13.267	17.449	66.211	237.376	807.793
31	1.167	1.361	1.586	1.847	2.150	2.500	2.905	3.373	4.538	6.088	8.145	10.867	14.461	19.194	76.143	284.851	1009.741
32	1.173	1.374	1.610	1.884	2.203	2.575	3.006	3.508	4.764	6.453	8.715	11.737	15.763	21.113	87.565	341.821	1262.177
33	1.178	1.388	1.634	1.922	2.258	2.652	3.111	3.648	5.003	6.840	9.325	12.676	17.182	23.225	100.699	410.186	1577.721
34	1.184	1.402	1.658	1.960	2.315	2.731	3.220	3.794	5.253	7.251	9.978	13.690	18.728	25.547	115.804	492.223	1972.152
35	1.190	1.416	1.683	1.999	2.373	2.813	3.333	3.946	5.516	7.686	10.676	14.785	20.413	28.102	133.175	590.668	2465.190

Table A (continued)

n	½%	1%	1½%	2%	2½%	3%	3½%	4%	5%	6%	7%	8%	9%	10%	15%	20%	25%
36	1.196	1.430	1.709	2.039	2.432	2.898	3.450	4.103	5.791	8.147	11.423	15.968	22.251	30.912	153.151	708.801	3081.487
37	1.202	1.445	1.734	2.080	2.493	2.985	3.571	4.268	6.081	8.636	12.223	17.245	24.253	34.003	176.124	850.562	3851.859
38	1.208	1.459	1.760	2.122	2.555	3.074	3.696	4.438	6.385	9.154	13.079	18.625	26.436	37.404	202.543	1020.674	4814.824
39	1.214	1.474	1.787	2.164	2.619	3.167	3.825	4.616	6.704	9.703	13.994	20.115	28.815	41.144	232.924	1224.809	6018.531
40	1.220	1.488	1.814	2.208	2.685	3.262	3.959	4.801	7.039	10.285	14.974	21.724	31.409	45.259	267.863	1469.771	7523.163
41	1.226	1.503	1.841	2.252	2.752	3.359	4.097	4.993	7.391	10.902	16.022	23.462	34.236	49.785	308.043	1763.725	9403.954
42	1.233	1.518	1.868	2.297	2.820	3.460	4.241	5.192	7.761	11.557	17.144	25.339	37.317	54.763	354.249	2116.471	11754.943
43	1.239	1.533	1.896	2.343	2.891	3.564	4.389	5.400	8.149	12.250	18.344	27.366	40.676	60.240	407.386	2539.765	14693.679
44	1.245	1.549	1.925	2.390	2.963	3.671	4.543	5.616	8.557	12.985	19.628	29.555	44.336	66.264	468.495	3047.718	18367.099
45	1.251	1.564	1.954	2.437	3.037	3.781	4.702	5.841	8.985	13.764	21.002	31.920	48.327	72.890	538.769	3657.261	22958.874
46	1.257	1.580	1.983	2.486	3.113	3.895	4.866	6.074	9.434	14.590	22.472	34.474	52.676	80.179	619.584	4388.714	28698.592
47	1.264	1.596	2.013	2.536	3.191	4.011	5.037	6.317	9.905	15.465	24.045	37.232	57.417	88.197	712.522	5266.457	35873.240
48	1.270	1.612	2.043	2.587	3.271	4.132	5.213	6.570	10.401	16.393	25.728	40.210	62.585	97.017	819.400	6319.748	44841.550
49	1.276	1.628	2.074	2.638	3.353	4.256	5.396	6.833	10.921	17.377	27.529	43.427	68.217	106.718	942.310	7583.698	56051.938
50	1.283	1.644	2.105	2.691	3.437	4.383	5.584	7.106	11.467	18.420	29.457	46.901	74.357	117.390	1083.657	9100.438	70064.923
51	1.289	1.661	2.136	2.745	3.523	4.515	5.780	7.390	12.040	19.525	31.519	50.653	81.049	129.129	1246.206	10920.525	87581.154
52	1.296	1.677	2.168	2.800	3.611	4.650	5.982	7.686	12.642	20.696	33.725	54.706	88.344	142.042	1433.136	13104.630	109476.442
53	1.302	1.694	2.201	2.856	3.701	4.790	6.192	7.994	13.274	21.938	36.086	59.082	96.295	156.247	1648.107	15725.557	136645.553
54	1.309	1.711	2.234	2.913	3.793	4.934	6.408	8.313	13.938	23.255	38.612	63.809	104.961	171.871	1895.323	18870.668	171056.941
55	1.315	1.728	2.267	2.971	3.888	5.082	6.633	8.646	14.635	24.650	41.315	68.913	114.408	189.059	2179.622	22644.802	213821.176
56	1.322	1.745	2.301	3.031	3.985	5.234	6.865	8.992	15.367	26.129	44.207	74.426	124.705	207.965	2506.565	27173.762	267276.471
57	1.328	1.763	2.336	3.091	4.085	5.391	7.105	9.351	16.135	27.697	47.301	80.381	135.928	228.761	2882.550	32608.515	334095.588
58	1.335	1.780	2.371	3.153	4.187	5.553	7.354	9.725	16.942	29.358	50.612	86.811	148.162	251.637	3314.932	39130.218	417619.485
59	1.342	1.798	2.407	3.216	4.292	5.720	7.611	10.115	17.789	31.120	54.155	93.756	161.496	276.801	3812.172	46956.261	522024.357
60	1.348	1.816	2.443	3.281	4.399	5.891	7.878	10.519	18.679	32.987	57.946	101.257	176.031	304.481	4383.998	56347.514	652530.446
70	1.417	2.006	2.835	3.999	5.632	7.917	11.112	15.571	30.426	59.075	113.989	218.606	416.730	789.746			
80	1.490	2.216	3.290	4.875	7.209	10.640	15.675	23.049	49.561	105.795	224.234	471.954	986.551	2048.400			
90	1.566	2.448	3.818	5.943	9.228	14.300	22.112	34.119	80.730	189.464	441.102	1018.915	2335.526	5313.022			
100	1.646	2.704	4.432	7.244	11.813	19.218	31.191	50.504	131.501	339.302	867.716	2199.761	5529.040	13780.612			

Table B

AMOUNT OF AN ORDINARY ANNUITY
(Amount of One Dollar Deposited Annually for n Years)

n	½%	1%	1½%	2%	2½%	3%	3½%	4%	5%	6%
1	1.000	1.000	1.000	1.000	1.000	1.000	1.000	1.000	1.000	1.000
2	2.005	2.010	2.015	2.020	2.025	2.030	2.035	2.040	2.050	2.060
3	3.015	3.030	3.045	3.060	3.075	3.090	3.106	3.121	3.152	3.183
4	4.030	4.060	4.090	4.121	4.152	4.183	4.214	4.246	4.310	4.374
5	5.050	5.101	5.152	5.204	5.256	5.309	5.362	5.416	5.525	5.637
6	6.075	6.152	6.229	6.308	6.387	6.468	6.550	6.632	6.801	6.975
7	7.105	7.213	7.322	7.434	7.547	7.662	7.779	7.898	8.142	8.393
8	8.141	8.285	8.432	8.582	8.736	8.892	9.051	9.214	9.549	9.897
9	9.182	9.368	9.559	9.754	9.954	10.159	10.368	10.582	11.026	11.491
10	10.228	10.462	10.702	10.949	11.203	11.463	11.731	12.006	12.577	13.180
11	11.279	11.566	11.863	12.168	12.483	12.807	13.141	13.486	14.206	14.971
12	12.335	12.682	13.041	13.412	13.795	14.192	14.601	15.025	15.917	16.869
13	13.397	13.809	14.236	14.680	15.140	15.617	16.113	16.626	17.712	18.882
14	14.464	14.947	15.450	15.973	16.518	17.086	17.676	18.291	19.598	21.015
15	15.536	16.096	16.682	17.293	17.931	18.598	19.295	20.623	21.578	23.275
16	16.614	17.257	17.932	18.639	19.380	20.156	20.971	21.824	23.657	25.672
17	17.697	18.430	19.201	20.012	20.864	21.761	22.705	23.697	25.810	28.212
18	18.785	19.614	20.489	21.412	22.386	23.414	24.499	25.645	28.132	30.905
19	19.879	20.810	21.796	22.840	23.946	25.116	26.357	27.671	30.539	33.759
20	20.979	22.019	23.123	24.297	25.544	26.870	28.279	29.778	33.065	36.785
21	22.084	23.239	24.470	25.783	27.183	28.676	30.269	31.969	35.719	39.992
22	23.194	24.471	25.837	27.298	28.862	30.536	32.328	34.247	38.505	43.392
23	24.310	25.716	27.225	28.844	30.584	32.452	34.460	36.617	41.430	46.995
24	25.431	26.973	28.633	30.421	32.349	34.426	36.666	39.083	44.501	50.815
25	26.559	28.243	30.063	32.030	34.157	36.459	38.949	41.645	47.727	54.864
26	27.691	29.525	31.513	33.670	36.011	38.553	41.313	44.311	51.113	59.156
27	28.830	30.820	32.986	35.344	37.912	40.709	43.759	47.084	54.669	63.705
28	29.974	32.129	34.481	37.051	39.859	42.930	46.290	49.967	58.402	68.528
29	31.124	33.450	35.998	38.792	41.856	45.218	48.910	52.966	62.322	73.639
30	32.280	34.784	37.538	40.568	43.902	47.575	51.622	56.084	66.438	79.058
31	33.441	36.132	39.101	42.379	46.000	50.002	54.429	59.328	70.760	84.801
32	34.608	37.494	40.688	44.227	48.150	52.502	57.334	62.701	75.298	90.889
33	35.781	38.869	42.298	46.111	50.354	55.077	60.341	66.209	80.063	97.343
34	36.960	40.257	43.933	48.033	52.612	57.730	63.453	69.857	85.066	104.183
35	38.145	41.660	45.592	49.994	54.928	60.462	66.674	73.652	90.320	111.434
36	39.336	43.076	47.275	51.994	57.301	63.275	70.007	77.598	95.836	119.120
37	40.532	44.507	48.985	54.034	59.733	66.174	73.457	81.702	101.628	127.268
38	41.735	45.952	50.719	56.114	62.227	69.159	77.028	85.970	107.709	135.904
39	42.944	47.412	52.480	58.237	64.782	72.234	80.724	90.409	114.095	145.058
40	44.158	48.886	54.267	60.401	67.402	75.401	84.550	95.025	120.799	154.761
41	45.379	50.375	56.081	62.610	70.087	78.663	88.509	99.826	127.839	165.047
42	46.606	51.878	57.923	64.862	72.839	82.023	92.607	104.819	135.231	175.950
43	47.839	53.397	59.791	67.159	75.660	85.483	96.848	110.012	142.993	187.507
44	49.078	54.931	61.688	69.502	78.552	89.048	101.238	115.412	151.143	199.758
45	50.324	56.481	63.614	71.892	81.516	92.719	105.781	121.029	159.700	212.743
46	51.575	58.045	65.568	74.330	84.554	96.501	110.484	126.870	168.685	226.508
47	52.833	59.626	67.551	76.817	87.667	100.396	115.350	132.945	178.119	241.098
48	54.097	61.222	69.565	79.353	90.859	104.408	120.388	139.263	188.025	256.564
49	55.368	62.834	71.608	81.940	94.131	108.540	125.001	145.833	198.426	272.958
50	56.645	64.463	73.682	84.579	97.484	112.796	130.997	152.667	209.347	290.335
51	57.928	66.107	75.788	87.270	100.921	117.180	136.582	159.773	220.815	308.756
52	59.218	67.768	77.924	90.016	104.444	121.696	142.363	167.164	232.856	328.281
53	60.514	69.446	80.093	92.816	108.055	126.347	148.345	174.851	245.498	348.978
54	61.816	71.141	82.295	95.673	111.756	131.137	154.538	182.845	258.773	370.917
55	63.125	72.852	84.529	98.586	115.550	136.071	160.946	191.159	272.712	394.172
56	64.441	74.580	86.797	101.558	119.439	141.153	167.580	199.805	287.348	418.822
57	65.763	76.326	89.099	104.589	123.425	146.388	174.445	208.797	302.715	444.951
58	67.092	78.090	91.435	107.681	127.511	151.780	181.550	218.149	318.851	472.648
59	68.427	79.870	93.807	110.834	131.699	157.333	188.905	227.875	335.794	502.007
60	69.770	81.669	96.214	114.051	135.991	163.053	196.516	237.990	353.583	533.128
70	83.566	100.676	122.363	149.977	185.284	230.594	288.937	364.290	588.528	967.932
80	98.067	121.671	152.710	193.771	248.382	321.363	419.306	551.244	971.228	1746.599
90	113.310	144.863	187.929	247.156	329.154	443.348	603.205	827.983	1594.607	3141.075
100	129.333	170.481	228.803	312.232	432.548	607.287	862.611	1237.623	2610.025	5638.368

Table B (continued)

n	7%	8%	9%	10%	15%	20%	25%
1	1.000	1.000	1.000	1.000	1.000	1.000	1.000
2	2.070	2.080	2.090	2.100	2.150	2.200	2.250
3	3.214	3.246	3.278	3.310	3.472	3.640	3.812
4	4.439	4.506	4.573	4.641	4.993	5.368	5.765
5	5.750	5.866	5.984	6.105	6.742	7.441	8.207
6	7.153	7.335	7.523	7.715	8.753	9.929	11.258
7	8.654	8.922	9.200	9.487	11.066	12.915	15.073
8	10.259	10.636	11.028	11.435	13.726	16.499	19.841
9	11.977	12.487	13.021	13.579	16.785	20.798	25.802
10	13.816	14.486	15.192	15.937	20.303	25.958	33.252
11	15.783	16.645	17.560	18.531	24.349	32.150	42.566
12	17.888	18.977	20.140	21.384	29.001	39.580	54.207
13	20.140	21.495	22.953	24.522	34.351	48.496	68.759
14	22.550	24.214	26.019	27.974	40.504	59.195	86.949
15	25.129	27.152	29.360	31.772	47.580	72.035	109.686
16	27.888	30.324	33.003	35.949	55.717	87.442	138.108
17	30.840	33.750	36.973	40.544	65.075	105.930	173.635
18	33.999	37.450	41.301	45.599	75.836	128.116	218.044
19	37.378	41.446	46.018	51.159	88.211	154.739	273.555
20	40.995	45.761	51.160	57.274	102.443	186.687	342.944
21	44.865	50.442	56.764	64.002	118.810	225.025	429.680
22	49.005	55.456	62.873	71.402	137.631	271.030	538.101
23	53.436	60.893	69.531	79.543	159.276	326.236	673.626
24	58.176	66.764	76.789	88.497	184.167	392.484	843.032
25	63.249	73.105	84.700	98.347	212.793	471.981	1054.791
26	68.676	79.954	93.323	109.181	245.711	567.377	1319.488
27	74.483	87.350	102.723	121.099	283.568	681.852	1650.361
28	80.697	95.338	112.968	134.209	327.104	819.223	2063.951
29	87.346	103.965	124.135	148.630	377.169	984.067	2580.939
30	94.460	113.283	136.307	164.494	434.745	1181.881	3227.174
31	102.073	123.345	149.575	181.943	500.956	1419.257	4034.967
32	110.218	134.213	164.036	201.137	577.100	1704.109	5044.709
33	118.933	145.950	179.800	222.251	664.665	2045.931	6306.887
34	128.258	158.626	196.982	245.476	765.365	2456.117	7884.609
35	138.236	172.316	215.710	271.024	881.170	2948.341	9856.761
36	148.913	187.102	236.124	299.126	1014.345	3539.009	12321.951
37	160.337	203.070	258.375	330.039	1167.497	4247.811	15403.439
38	172.561	220.315	282.629	364.043	1343.622	5098.373	19255.299
39	185.640	238.941	309.066	401.447	1546.165	6119.048	24070.124
40	199.635	259.056	337.882	442.592	1779.090	7343.857	30088.655
41	214.609	280.781	369.291	487.851	2046.953	8813.629	37611.819
42	230.632	304.243	403.528	537.636	2354.996	10577.355	47015.774
43	247.776	329.538	440.845	592.400	2709.246	12693.826	58770.717
44	266.120	356.949	481.521	652.640	3116.633	15233.591	73464.396
45	285.749	386.505	525.858	718.904	3585.128	18281.309	91831.496
46	306.751	418.426	574.186	791.795	4123.897	21938.571	114790.370
47	329.224	452.900	626.862	871.974	4743.482	26327.286	143488.962
48	353.270	490.132	684.280	960.172	5456.004	31593.743	179362.203
49	378.998	530.342	746.865	1057.189	6275.405	37913.492	224203.754
50	406.528	573.770	815.083	1163.908	7217.716	45497.190	280255.692
51	435.985	620.671	889.441	1281.299	8301.373	54597.628	350320.616
52	467.504	671.325	970.490	1410.429	9547.579	65518.154	437901.770
53	501.230	726.031	1058.834	1552.472	10980.716	78622.785	547378.212
54	537.316	785.114	1155.130	1708.719	12628.824	94348.342	684223.765
55	575.928	848.923	1260.091	1880.591	14524.147	113219.011	855280.707
56	617.243	917.837	1374.500	2069.650	16703.770	135863.813	1069101.884
57	661.450	992.264	1499.205	2277.615	19210.335	163037.576	1336378.355
58	708.752	1072.645	1635.133	2506.377	22092.885	195646.091	1670473.943
59	759.364	1159.456	1783.295	2758.014	25407.818	234776.309	2088093.429
60	813.520	1253.213	1944.792	3034.816	29219.991	281732.571	2610117.787
70	1614.134	2720.080	4619.223	7887.469			
80	3189.062	5886.935	10950.574	20474.002			
90	6287.185	12723.038	25939.184	53120.226			
100	12381.661	27484.515	61422.675	137796.123			

Table C

PRESENT VALUE OF ONE DOLLAR

n	1%	2%	3%	4%	5%	6%	8%	10%	12%	14%	15%	16%	18%	20%	22%	24%	25%	30%	35%	40%	45%	50%
1	0.990	0.980	0.970	0.962	0.952	0.943	0.926	0.909	0.893	0.877	0.870	0.862	0.847	0.833	0.820	0.806	0.800	0.769	0.741	0.714	0.690	0.667
2	0.980	0.961	0.942	0.925	0.907	0.890	0.857	0.826	0.797	0.769	0.756	0.743	0.718	0.694	0.672	0.650	0.640	0.592	0.549	0.510	0.476	0.444
3	0.971	0.942	0.915	0.889	0.863	0.840	0.794	0.751	0.712	0.675	0.658	0.641	0.609	0.579	0.551	0.524	0.512	0.455	0.406	0.364	0.328	0.296
4	0.961	0.924	0.888	0.855	0.822	0.792	0.735	0.683	0.636	0.592	0.572	0.552	0.516	0.482	0.451	0.423	0.410	0.350	0.301	0.260	0.226	0.198
5	0.951	0.906	0.862	0.822	0.783	0.747	0.681	0.621	0.567	0.519	0.497	0.476	0.437	0.402	0.370	0.341	0.328	0.269	0.223	0.186	0.156	0.132
6	0.942	0.888	0.837	0.790	0.746	0.705	0.630	0.564	0.507	0.456	0.432	0.410	0.370	0.335	0.303	0.275	0.262	0.207	0.165	0.133	0.108	0.088
7	0.933	0.871	0.813	0.760	0.710	0.665	0.583	0.513	0.452	0.400	0.376	0.354	0.314	0.279	0.249	0.222	0.210	0.159	0.122	0.095	0.074	0.059
8	0.923	0.853	0.789	0.731	0.676	0.627	0.540	0.467	0.404	0.351	0.327	0.305	0.266	0.233	0.204	0.179	0.168	0.123	0.091	0.068	0.051	0.039
9	0.914	0.837	0.766	0.703	0.644	0.592	0.500	0.424	0.361	0.308	0.284	0.263	0.225	0.194	0.167	0.144	0.134	0.094	0.067	0.048	0.035	0.026
10	0.905	0.820	0.744	0.676	0.613	0.558	0.463	0.386	0.322	0.270	0.247	0.227	0.191	0.162	0.137	0.116	0.107	0.073	0.050	0.035	0.024	0.017
11	0.896	0.804	0.722	0.650	0.584	0.527	0.429	0.350	0.287	0.237	0.215	0.195	0.162	0.135	0.112	0.094	0.086	0.056	0.037	0.025	0.017	0.012
12	0.887	0.788	0.701	0.625	0.556	0.497	0.397	0.319	0.257	0.208	0.187	0.168	0.137	0.112	0.092	0.076	0.069	0.043	0.027	0.018	0.012	0.008
13	0.879	0.773	0.680	0.601	0.530	0.469	0.368	0.290	0.229	0.182	0.163	0.145	0.116	0.093	0.075	0.061	0.055	0.033	0.020	0.013	0.008	0.005
14	0.870	0.758	0.661	0.577	0.505	0.442	0.340	0.263	0.205	0.160	0.141	0.125	0.099	0.078	0.062	0.049	0.044	0.025	0.015	0.009	0.006	0.003
15	0.861	0.743	0.641	0.555	0.481	0.417	0.315	0.239	0.183	0.140	0.123	0.108	0.084	0.065	0.051	0.040	0.035	0.020	0.011	0.006	0.004	0.002
16	0.853	0.728	0.623	0.534	0.458	0.394	0.292	0.218	0.163	0.123	0.107	0.093	0.071	0.054	0.042	0.032	0.028	0.015	0.008	0.005	0.003	0.002
17	0.844	0.714	0.605	0.513	0.436	0.371	0.270	0.198	0.146	0.108	0.093	0.080	0.060	0.045	0.034	0.026	0.023	0.012	0.006	0.003	0.002	0.001
18	0.836	0.700	0.587	0.494	0.415	0.350	0.250	0.180	0.130	0.095	0.081	0.069	0.051	0.038	0.028	0.021	0.018	0.009	0.005	0.002	0.001	0.001
19	0.828	0.686	0.570	0.475	0.395	0.331	0.232	0.164	0.116	0.083	0.070	0.060	0.043	0.031	0.023	0.017	0.014	0.007	0.003	0.002	0.001	
20	0.820	0.673	0.553	0.456	0.376	0.312	0.215	0.149	0.104	0.073	0.061	0.051	0.037	0.026	0.019	0.014	0.012	0.005	0.002	0.001	0.001	
21	0.811	0.660	0.537	0.439	0.358	0.294	0.199	0.135	0.093	0.064	0.053	0.044	0.031	0.022	0.015	0.011	0.009	0.004	0.002	0.001		
22	0.803	0.647	0.521	0.422	0.341	0.278	0.184	0.123	0.083	0.056	0.046	0.038	0.026	0.018	0.013	0.009	0.007	0.003	0.001	0.001		
23	0.795	0.634	0.506	0.406	0.325	0.262	0.170	0.112	0.074	0.049	0.040	0.033	0.022	0.015	0.010	0.007	0.006	0.002	0.001			
24	0.788	0.622	0.491	0.390	0.310	0.247	0.158	0.102	0.066	0.043	0.035	0.028	0.019	0.013	0.008	0.006	0.005	0.002	0.001			
25	0.780	0.610	0.477	0.375	0.295	0.233	0.146	0.092	0.059	0.038	0.030	0.024	0.016	0.010	0.007	0.005	0.004	0.001				
26	0.772	0.598	0.463	0.361	0.281	0.220	0.135	0.084	0.053	0.033	0.026	0.021	0.014	0.009	0.006	0.004	0.003	0.001				
27	0.764	0.586	0.450	0.347	0.267	0.207	0.125	0.076	0.047	0.029	0.023	0.018	0.011	0.007	0.005	0.003	0.002	0.001				
28	0.757	0.574	0.437	0.333	0.255	0.196	0.116	0.069	0.042	0.026	0.020	0.016	0.010	0.006	0.004	0.002	0.002	0.001				
29	0.749	0.563	0.424	0.321	0.242	0.185	0.107	0.063	0.037	0.022	0.017	0.014	0.008	0.005	0.003	0.002	0.002					
30	0.742	0.552	0.411	0.308	0.231	0.174	0.099	0.057	0.033	0.020	0.015	0.012	0.007	0.004	0.003	0.002	0.001					
40	0.672	0.453	0.306	0.208	0.142	0.097	0.046	0.022	0.011	0.005	0.004	0.003	0.001	0.001								
50	0.608	0.372	0.228	0.141	0.087	0.054	0.021	0.009	0.003	0.001	0.001	0.001										

Table D

PRESENT VALUE OF AN ORDINARY ANNUITY

(Present Value of One Dollar Received Annually for n Years)

n	1%	2%	3%	4%	5%	6%	8%	10%	12%	14%	15%	16%	18%	20%	22%	24%	25%	30%	35%	40%	45%	50%
1	0.990	0.980	0.970	0.962	0.952	0.943	0.926	0.909	0.893	0.877	0.870	0.862	0.847	0.833	0.820	0.806	0.800	0.769	0.741	0.714	0.690	0.667
2	1.970	1.942	1.913	1.886	1.859	1.833	1.783	1.736	1.690	1.647	1.626	1.605	1.566	1.528	1.492	1.457	1.440	1.361	1.289	1.224	1.165	1.111
3	2.941	2.884	2.828	2.775	2.723	2.673	2.577	2.487	2.402	2.322	2.283	2.246	2.174	2.106	2.042	1.981	1.952	1.816	1.696	1.589	1.493	1.407
4	3.902	3.808	3.717	3.630	3.545	3.465	3.312	3.170	3.037	2.914	2.855	2.798	2.690	2.589	2.494	2.404	2.362	2.166	1.997	1.849	1.720	1.605
5	4.853	4.713	4.579	4.452	4.329	4.212	3.993	3.791	3.605	3.433	3.352	3.274	3.127	2.991	2.864	2.745	2.689	2.436	2.220	2.035	1.876	1.737
6	5.795	5.601	5.417	5.242	5.075	4.917	4.623	4.355	4.111	3.889	3.784	3.685	3.498	3.326	3.167	3.020	2.951	2.643	2.385	2.168	1.983	1.824
7	6.728	6.472	6.230	6.002	5.786	5.582	5.206	4.868	4.564	4.288	4.160	4.039	3.812	3.605	3.416	3.242	3.161	2.802	2.508	2.263	2.057	1.883
8	7.652	7.325	7.019	6.733	6.463	6.210	5.747	5.335	4.968	4.639	4.487	4.344	4.078	3.837	3.619	3.421	3.329	2.925	2.598	2.331	2.108	1.922
9	8.566	8.162	7.786	7.435	7.107	6.802	6.247	5.759	5.328	4.946	4.772	4.607	4.303	4.031	3.786	3.566	3.463	3.019	2.665	2.379	2.144	1.948
10	9.471	8.983	8.530	8.111	7.721	7.360	6.710	6.145	5.650	5.216	5.019	4.833	4.494	4.192	3.923	3.682	3.571	3.092	2.715	2.414	2.168	1.965
11	10.368	9.787	9.252	8.760	8.306	7.887	7.139	6.495	5.937	5.453	5.234	5.029	4.656	4.327	4.035	3.776	3.656	3.147	2.752	2.438	2.185	1.977
12	11.255	10.575	9.954	9.385	8.863	8.384	7.536	6.814	6.194	5.660	5.421	5.197	4.793	4.439	4.127	3.851	3.725	3.190	2.779	2.456	2.196	1.985
13	12.134	11.343	10.634	9.986	9.393	8.853	7.904	7.103	6.424	5.842	5.583	5.342	4.910	4.533	4.203	3.912	3.780	3.223	2.799	2.468	2.204	1.990
14	13.004	12.106	11.296	10.563	9.899	9.295	8.244	7.367	6.628	6.002	5.724	5.468	5.008	4.611	4.265	3.962	3.824	3.249	2.814	2.477	2.210	1.993
15	13.865	12.849	11.937	11.118	10.379	9.712	8.559	7.606	6.811	6.142	5.847	5.575	5.092	4.675	4.315	4.001	3.859	3.268	2.825	2.484	2.214	1.995
16	14.718	13.578	12.561	11.652	10.838	10.106	8.851	7.824	6.974	6.265	5.954	5.669	5.162	4.730	4.357	4.033	3.887	3.283	2.834	2.489	2.216	1.997
17	15.562	14.292	13.166	12.166	11.274	10.477	9.122	8.022	7.120	6.373	6.047	5.749	5.222	4.775	4.391	4.059	3.910	3.295	2.840	2.492	2.218	1.998
18	16.398	14.992	13.753	12.659	11.689	10.828	9.372	8.201	7.250	6.467	6.128	5.818	5.273	4.812	4.419	4.080	3.928	3.304	2.844	2.494	2.219	1.999
19	17.226	15.678	14.323	13.134	12.085	11.158	9.604	8.365	7.366	6.550	6.198	5.877	5.316	4.844	4.442	4.097	3.942	3.311	2.848	2.496	2.220	1.999
20	18.046	16.351	14.877	13.590	12.462	11.470	9.818	8.514	7.469	6.623	6.259	5.929	5.353	4.870	4.460	4.110	3.954	3.316	2.850	2.497	2.221	1.999
21	18.857	17.011	15.415	14.029	12.821	11.764	10.017	8.649	7.562	6.687	6.312	5.973	5.384	4.891	4.476	4.121	3.963	3.320	2.852	2.498	2.221	2.000
22	19.660	17.658	15.936	14.451	13.163	12.042	10.201	8.772	7.645	6.743	6.359	6.011	5.410	4.909	4.488	4.130	3.970	3.323	2.853	2.498	2.222	2.000
23	20.456	18.292	16.443	14.857	13.488	12.303	10.371	8.883	7.718	6.792	6.399	6.044	5.432	4.925	4.499	4.137	3.976	3.325	2.854	2.499	2.222	2.000
24	21.243	18.914	16.935	15.247	13.798	12.550	10.529	8.985	7.784	6.835	6.434	6.073	5.451	4.937	4.507	4.143	3.981	3.327	2.855	2.499	2.222	2.000
25	22.023	19.523	17.413	15.622	14.094	12.783	10.675	9.077	7.843	6.873	6.464	6.097	5.467	4.948	4.514	4.147	3.985	3.329	2.856	2.499	2.222	2.000
26	22.795	20.121	17.876	15.982	14.375	13.003	10.810	9.161	7.896	6.906	6.491	6.118	5.480	4.956	4.520	4.151	3.988	3.330	2.856	2.500	2.222	2.000
27	23.560	20.707	18.327	16.330	14.643	13.211	10.935	9.237	7.943	6.935	6.514	6.136	5.492	4.964	4.524	4.154	3.990	3.331	2.856	2.500	2.222	2.000
28	24.316	21.281	18.764	16.663	14.898	13.406	11.051	9.307	7.984	6.961	6.534	6.152	5.502	4.970	4.528	4.157	3.992	3.331	2.857	2.500	2.222	2.000
29	25.066	21.844	19.188	16.984	15.141	13.591	11.158	9.370	8.022	6.983	6.551	6.166	5.510	4.975	4.531	4.159	3.994	3.332	2.857	2.500	2.222	2.000
30	25.808	22.396	19.600	17.292	15.372	13.765	11.258	9.427	8.055	7.003	6.566	6.177	5.517	4.979	4.534	4.160	3.995	3.332	2.857	2.500	2.222	2.000
40	32.835	27.355	23.114	19.793	17.159	15.046	11.925	9.779	8.244	7.105	6.642	6.234	5.548	4.997	4.544	4.166	3.999	3.333	2.857	2.500	2.222	2.000
50	39.196	31.424	25.729	21.482	18.255	15.762	12.234	9.915	8.304	7.133	6.661	6.246	5.554	4.999	4.545	4.167	4.000	3.333	2.857	2.500	2.222	2.000

484

Index